SPORT FACILITY OPERATIONS MANAGEMENT

Anybody working in sport management will be involved in the operation of a sport facility at some point in their career. It is a core professional competency at the heart of successful sport business. *Sport Facility Operations Management* is a comprehensive and engaging textbook that introduces cutting-edge concepts in facilities and operations management, including practical guidance from professional facility managers.

Now in a fully revised and updated second edition – which introduces new chapters on capital investment and operational decision making – the book covers all fundamental aspects of sport facility operations management from a global perspective, including:

- ownership structures and financing options;
- planning, design, and construction processes;
- organizational and human resource management;
- financial and operations management;
- legal concerns;
- marketing management and event planning;
- risk assessment and security planning;
- benchmarking and performance management.

Each chapter contains newly updated real-world case studies and discussion questions, innovative 'Technology Now!' features, and step-by-step guidance through every element of successful sport facilities and operations management, while an expanded companion website offers lecture slides, a sample course syllabus, a bank of multiple-choice and essay questions, glossary flashcards, links to further reading, and appendices with relevant supplemental documentation.

With a clear structure running from planning through to the application of core management disciplines, *Sport Facility Operations Management* is essential reading for any sport management course.

Eric C. Schwarz is a Senior Lecturer of Sport Management in the College of Sport and Exercise Science at Victoria University, Melbourne, Australia, where he is also an associate of the Institute of Sport, Exercise and Active Living (ISEAL). He has been a professor of sport business management in the United States and Australia for the past 15 years after a career in college athletics and recreation. Eric has published numerous articles on sport marketing and experiential learning in peer-reviewed journals; and is also the lead author of *Advanced Theory and Practice in Sport Marketing* – the second edition published by Routledge in 2012. He has also presented on various topics in sport business management around the world including the United States, Canada, Europe, Australia, China, and New Zealand. Eric also served as President and Executive Director of the Sport Marketing Association from 2010–2013. He currently resides in Melbourne, Australia.

Stacey A. Hall is the Associate Director of the National Center for Spectator Sports Safety and Security (NCS[4]) and an Associate Professor of Sport Management at the University of Southern Mississippi (USM), USA. She has been published in leading international sport management, homeland security, and emergency management journals; and was the lead author on the textbook *Security Management for Sports and Special Events*. She has been referred to as one of the nation's leading experts in sport security, including having been the principal investigator on numerous external grant awards and several service projects in collaboration with the US Department of Homeland Security. A competitive soccer player, she was team captain for the Northern Ireland International Soccer Team. She now resides in Hattiesburg, Mississippi.

Simon Shibli is Professor of Sport Management at Sheffield Hallam University, UK, and has been the Director of the Sport Industry Research Centre (SIRC) since 2004. He is a qualified accountant with the Chartered Institute of Management Accountants (CIMA). After a career as a facility manager in the arts and entertainments industry, Simon returned to academic life as a lecturer specializing in finance and he wrote his first book *Leisure Manager's Guide to Budgeting and Budgetary Control* in 1994. He has subsequently developed a research career and has peer reviewed publications in numerous peer reviewed journals, notably *Managing Leisure: An International Journal*. Simon lives in Sheffield, England.

SPORT FACILITY OPERATIONS MANAGEMENT

A GLOBAL PERSPECTIVE

SECOND EDITION

ERIC C. SCHWARZ, STACEY A. HALL AND SIMON SHIBLI

Routledge
Taylor & Francis Group

LONDON AND NEW YORK

First published 2009
by Elsevier

This edition published 2015
by Routledge

2 Park Square, Milton Park, Abingdon, Oxon OX14 4RN
and by Routledge

711 Third Avenue, New York, NY 10017

Routledge is an imprint of the Taylor & Francis Group, an informa business

British Library Cataloguing-in-Publication Data
A catalogue record for this book is available from the British Library

Library of Congress Cataloging in Publication Data
A catalog record has been requested for this book

ISBN: 978-1-138-83103-2 (hbk)
ISBN: 978-1-138-83105-6 (pbk)
ISBN: 978-1-315-73681-5 (ebk)

Typeset in Melior
by GreenGate Publishing Services, Tonbridge, Kent

MIX
Paper from
responsible sources
FSC
www.fsc.org   FSC® C013056

Printed and bound in Great Britain by
TJ International Ltd, Padstow, Cornwall

CONTENTS

FIGURES

TABLES

PREFACE

Sport facilities of all shapes and sizes are an integral part of the global sport business management landscape. As such, it is inevitable that students who enter into the field of sport management will interact with the management and operations of a sport facility at some point during their career. This book is being published with the sport management educator and student in mind, specifically aimed at those sport management programs that require a facility management unit as a part of their curriculum.

The majority of sport facility management books in the market today focus on the basic theoretical framework of sport facility management, but fail to relate many of the concepts to the traditional operations management units taught in business management. In addition, there is limited relevant practical professional experience infused through those books. Finally, there is a lack of identification, interpretation, and recognition of the individual differences in managing and operating facilities across the globe.

The second edition of *Sport Facility Operations Management: A Global Perspective* goes further to address these limitations by bringing an update to the most comprehensive and significant sport facility management textbook in the marketplace today that addresses this important area of sport management from a global perspective. This continues to be crucial in textbooks within this field of study as the sport industry is truly global, hence the education of readers in this field must reflect this global awareness.

This book brings together three authors with significant experience teaching sport business management in the United States, Europe, and Australia; conducting research related to sport facility management and operations around the globe; and having practical experience in sport facility operations management. With this background, the purpose of the textbook is to provide a theoretical and applied foundation for sport facility operations management, and is supplemented both in the text and in the online appendices with practical applications via case study scenarios, real-world excerpts, and functional documentation that can be utilized by the sport facility operations manager. In addition, each author has infused research and experiences from sport facilities around the world (North America; Europe; Middle East/Asia; Australia and New Zealand) to ensure that a global perspective for the textbook is achieved.

The initial chapter of the book serves to provide an overview of sport facility operations management, including a basic review of those topics commonly covered in an introductory sport facility operations management course. The remainder of this text will provide the reader with a framework understanding of sport facility operations management from a global perspective by: (1) connecting the behind-the-scene concepts that must be understood before even entering into management and operations of sport facilities; (2) implementing management and operations in sport facilities and the ancillary and support issues inherent to sport facility operations management; (3) and providing methods for measuring and evaluating the performance of operations and management for sport facilities that aid in the successful implementation of activities that meet the needs, wants, and desires of users.

PART I – PRE-MANAGEMENT AND PRE-OPERATIONS ISSUES

Ownership structures

The reader will be presented with the various business ownership and governance structures for sport facilities across the globe. Sport facility owners must first understand the legal authority under which the sport facility can operate as a business, i.e. sole proprietorship, partnership, or form of corporation. At the same time, sport facility owners must determine how they want to structure their sport business – either as a public entity, non-profit business, or a commercial enterprise; and also whether the governance structure will be as a public entity, a private entity, a public-private partnership, or under a voluntary structure. In addition to these structures, the reader will be presented with models of organizational effectiveness that can assist in efficiently managing the ownership structure.

Financing

The reader will gain an appreciation of the intricacies of financing sport facilities as related to various business issues, the costs of ownership, life-cycle costing, cost-effectiveness/efficiency, and the principles of economic impact analysis. The comprehension of these issues will then allow the reader to recognize and understand the different sources of financing to be used for sport facilities, including public sector funding, private sources of revenue, public-private partnerships, and the influence of the voluntary sector.

xi

Preface

Capital investment appraisal

The reader will be made aware of how the decisions to build new facilities, upgrade existing facilities, or invest in new equipment have a significant effect on the future financial wellbeing of an organization. Through the use of a variety of techniques known as capital investment appraisal, readers will gain an appreciation of the principles and applications of the concepts, a practical overview of what the techniques are, how to use them in practice, and how they can help managers make informed decisions. Methods to be presented include the traditional methods such as the payback method and accounting rate of return; as well as modern methods that take into account the time value of money, namely discounted cash flows and the internal rate of return.

Planning, design, and construction processes

The reader will learn about the various stages of the planning, design, and construction processes, including preliminary planning; the development of design; actual construction; and preparation for training and management of facilities. By understanding these issues in advance, the reader will have a stronger conceptual underpinning of the management framework applied to sport facilities, and be able to more clearly connect that knowledge with the implementation processes inherent to management and operations of sport facilities.

PART II – IMPLEMENTATION OF MANAGEMENT AND OPERATIONS

Organizational management

The reader will learn how to distinguish, identify, and classify the important concepts of organization management as related to individual and group behavior in sport facilities. These will include the principles of motivation, stress management and wellbeing, leadership, use of power and authority, politics, conflict management, decision making, and problem solving. The reader will then be able to connect these concepts with various leadership and organizational management concepts that affect international and global sport facility operations, including determinants of organizational culture and change, and the effects of cultural diversity and global organization behavior.

Human resource management

The reader will be presented with an overview of the increased growth, interest, and complexity of human resource management in sport facilities, with significant emphasis on managerial competencies, the strategic importance of human resource management, and the implications of legislative, governance, and ethical issues in terms of employees, volunteers, and customers of sport facilities. This will be accomplished by providing the reader with foundational concepts regarding the individual differences in people and their interactions in groups, which in turn will lead to an explanation of how to effectively manage those groups strategically through the integration of strategic human resource management and performance management processes.

Financial management

The reader will be presented with numerous financial functions that a sport facility manager must understand. This includes an overview of why financial skills are an integral part of the sport facility manager's overall portfolio of management of skills, how finance is the 'language' of business, the importance of being fluent in financial language both in terms of understanding it and being able to communicate in it, and the need for sport facility managers to continuously develop and enhance their financial skills. There are two important financial questions to which all businesses need to be able to provide positive answers. These questions are stated and explained in full in this chapter.

Operational decision making

The reader will appreciate that to manage sport facilities efficiently and effectively, managers need to understand the concept of cost and how to apply it in real-world situations. This chapter is concerned with helping managers to understand the nature of cost and to use this knowledge to improve a sport facility's financial performance. Vital concepts such as cost behavior, breakeven analysis, and the margin of safety are explained and illustrated with practical examples with which sport facility managers can readily identify.

Operations management

The reader will gain an understanding of the various maintenance, control, and organizational activities that are required to produce products and services for consumers of the sport facility. This will include an explanation of how the operational structure integrates with the operation of the sport facility, the need for a comprehensive, structured approach that seeks to improve the quality of facility services, and the general sport facility operating procedures that need to be managed within governmental guidelines and budget parameters.

Legal concerns for owners and managers

The reader will be provided with an overview of the relationship between legal issues and sport facility operations. With it being impossible to make the reader a legal expert, and impractical to cover all the specific laws worldwide that affect sport facility operations management, the authors strive to articulate the effects of the legal environment on sport facilities by dispelling the myth that law and risk management in sport facilities are one and the same. Therefore, the reader will be provided with an overview of the major legal principles and standards related to the management and operations of sport facilities, and recommendations regarding the level of legal expertise a sport facility manager should have – including when they should defer to individuals with a higher level of proficiency in the law.

PART III – ANCILLARY ISSUES IN MANAGEMENT AND OPERATIONS

Marketing

The reader will gain an appreciation of the significant role sport marketing and communications play in sport facility operations management. The goal is for the reader to develop knowledge and skill in the marketing process as it relates to understanding the sport consumer, logistics, promotions, and public relations activities in sport facilities that focus on studying and understanding the consumer in terms of marketing a sport facility, developing marketing strategies for the sport facility, clarifying the needs and goals for a sport facility, and implementing sport marketing plans to support the management and operations of a sport facility.

Event planning

The reader will gain an understanding about the relationship between sport facility operations management and event planning. The concepts in this chapter will specifically focus on the role facility management plays in supporting event management through the sport-facility event-planning process; the role of the sport facility management personnel before, during, and after an event; and the evaluation processes integral to staging future events.

Risk assessment

The reader will recognize that sport facility managers must plan for all types of emergencies that may disrupt normal operations. In order to manage and mitigate potential incidents, sport facility managers need to possess a sound knowledge of risk management practices. Therefore, the reader will gain knowledge about risk management concepts including risk assessment, risk control strategies, and risk planning options.

Security planning

The reader will gain an appreciation of the ever-growing global security issues involved in protecting sport facilities from threats and risks. Security best practices,

XIV

Preface

systems, and planning options are provided to equip the 21st century sport facility manager with an all-hazard's approach to security planning.

PART IV – EFFECTIVENESS OF MANAGEMENT AND OPERATIONS

Performance management and benchmarking

This final chapter will bring together the various strands of performance management referred to throughout the book, providing the reader with an understanding that anything a sport facility manager does is measured. Therefore, sport facility managers need to be clear about what their priorities are and what measures they need to monitor in order to demonstrate individual, team, facility, and corporate effectiveness. The chapter will specifically discuss the concept of benchmarking, and how measuring performance helps sport facility managers achieve better results by enabling them to understand the drivers of performance and how to influence them. The chapter also outlines the technique of process benchmarking that a sport facility manager can utilize to integrate benchmarking and performance management within organizational culture. Furthermore the chapter addresses how process benchmarking provides the basis for a clear focus on business essentials, and offers courses of action for continuous improvement of any sport facility.

PEDAGOGICAL FEATURES

The second edition of *Sport Facility Operations Management – A Global Perspective* enhances learning with the following pedagogical devices:

- Each chapter opens with a chapter outline and a list of chapter objectives.
- Key terms are defined in the text when they first appear. They are also defined alphabetically on flashcards found on the website for the book.
- Each chapter has an updated case study embedded within the text to enhance critical thinking related to real-world concepts associated with the chapter material. Questions associated with each case study allow the learner to apply theoretical knowledge to the scenarios.
- Each chapter has an 'In the field' piece written by a professional currently employed in the field of sport facility operations management.
- Each chapter has a 'Technology now!' excerpt spotlighting relevant technology for readers to be aware of.
- A comprehensive review at the end of each chapter that summarizes the chapter objectives in terms of the pertinent information from the chapter.

CRITICAL THINKING

One of the most important skills for students to develop through their college and university years is critical thinking. This mental process of analyzing and evaluating information is used across all disciplines, and serves as a process for reflecting on the information provided, examining facts to understand reasoning, and forming conclusions and plans for action.

The authors of this book have provided a series of opportunities for students to enhance their critical-thinking skills while also verifying their understanding of the materials presented in this text. A test bank has been provided in the online supplements for each chapter, with ten multiple choice questions that provide students the opportunity to verify their comprehension of the chapter's main concepts. To supplement that verification, there are also four discussion questions. These questions, which can be used as essay topics or in-class discussion issues by instructors, are based on the information provided in the chapter, the research available in the specific aspect of sport facility operations management, and the education and experiences of the authors.

In addition, embedded within each chapter are three supplemental items to enhance critical thinking as related to real-world concepts associated with the text material. First is a case study to provide the reader with the maximum opportunity to analyze, evaluate, and ponder possible solutions to the specific situation. Questions associated with each case study will help the student focus their efforts on key theoretical aspects from the chapter, and apply that knowledge to deal with the specific scenario. Second is an 'In the field' entry written by a professional currently working in the field of sport facility operations management. This will allow the reader to understand current events in the field, how many of these professionals attained the position they are in today, and to receive advice from those professionals about the field. Finally, there is also a 'Technology now!' excerpt within each chapter highlighting relevant technologies that the reader should be aware of as they are actively used in the profession.

This text provides a unique opportunity for critical thinking and application in association with sport facility operations management. An online appendix has been provided with diagrams, schematics, manuals, and forms that will provide additional information for the reader about the role and responsibilities of sport facility managers and owners, as well as providing the readers with actual documentation they can modify for use when they enter the profession of sport facility operations management.

SUPPLEMENTS

The second edition of *Sport Facility Operations Management – A Global Perspective*, available in both traditional hardcopy and online e-book formats, provides the instructor with the following teaching aides:

- Updated case studies within each chapter with suggested discussion topics.
- NEW 'In the field' and 'Technology now!' excerpts to be used to further discussion about current real-world concepts.
- Website dedicated to this book including:
  - PowerPoint presentations for each chapter;
  - an electronic test bank with both multiple choice and essay questions;
  - online appendices with diagrams, schematics, manuals and forms;
  - flashcards for students to test their knowledge on terms and definitions;
  - sample master course syllabus with suggested class activities connected to chapters in the book.

ACKNOWLEDGEMENTS

DR. ERIC C. SCHWARZ

I would like to dedicate this book to my best friend and the love of my life Loan. As we journey through our new phase of life with our move to Australia, I continue to be blessed with having a wife who shows unconditional love and continues to support my work and my writing. You are the foundation for all of our success, as your calming influence and belief in my abilities gives me the strength to be the best person and professional that I can be. I love you with all of my heart and soul!!!

In addition, I would like to recognize the efforts and show my appreciation to my co-authors on this book, Stacey Hall and Simon Shibli. It was a pleasure working with both of you on this second edition. Your professionalism, academic integrity, and expertise are a staple throughout this book – and I believe this second edition is an even better version of this text that will be well received in academia. I look forward to continued collaborations with you.

And finally, to Max…

DR. STACEY A. HALL

I would like to thank my family in Northern Ireland for their unconditional love and support in both my professional and personal endeavors. I would also like to thank my friends and colleagues at Southern Miss for their support and guidance. Lastly, I thank Dr. Eric Schwarz for the opportunity to contribute to this book. Eric's leadership skills and professionalism made this project an enjoyable experience.

PROF. SIMON SHIBLI

My contribution to this book is dedicated to my wife Tracey, and our three children Alice, James, and Mary. Thanks too are due to my team at the Sport Industry Research Centre at Sheffield Hallam University for creating the time and space to do this sort of thing. Finally, I would like to acknowledge the efforts of Eric Schwarz to make this book a reality. There are not many academics who meet their own self-imposed deadlines to submit their work to publishers. With his exemplary project management skills, Eric has made sure not once but twice that we have nailed our deadlines.

Acknowledgements

ABOUT THE AUTHORS

DR. ERIC C. SCHWARZ

Dr. Schwarz is a Senior Lecturer of Sport Management in the College of Sport and Exercise Science, and an associate of the Institute of Sport, Exercise and Active Living (ISEAL) at Victoria University in Melbourne, Australia.

Previously, he spent nearly seven years as a Professor of Sport Business at Saint Leo University – including four years as Chair of the Department of Sport Business, International Tourism and Hospitality Management. He has been recognized by Saint Leo in 2010 with the Distinguished Publications Award, in 2011 with the School of Business Excellence in Teaching Award, and awarded tenure in 2014.

Prior to Saint Leo, he spent nine years at Daniel Webster College in New Hampshire, where he was an Associate Professor and Program Coordinator of Sport Management within the School of Business, Management, and Professional Studies. During the 2006–2007 academic year, he took a sabbatical leave to serve as Visiting Senior Lecturer and Researcher at the University of Ballarat in Australia.

Dr. Schwarz has presented on various topics in sport marketing and experiential learning around the world including in the United States, Canada, Europe, Australia, China, and New Zealand. He has been most active with the Sport Marketing Association (SMA), where he has been a regular presenter, with articles published in the conference book of papers. He served as the Conference Academic Committee Chair for the conference held in Cleveland, Ohio in October 2009 and New Orleans, Louisiana in 2010; served as President of the organization from 2010–2012; and was the Executive Director of the National Office from 2010–2013. In addition, he is a two-time recipient of the SMA Honorary Service Award (2009 and 2014).

Dr. Schwarz has published numerous articles in journals including the *International Journal of Sport Management and Marketing*, the *International Journal of Entrepreneurship and Small Business*, and the *Journal of Applied Marketing Theory*. In addition to the second edition of this book, Dr. Schwarz is the lead author of *Advanced Theory and Practice in Sport Marketing* – the second edition also published by Routledge in 2012.

Dr. Schwarz received a B.S. degree in Physical Education from Plymouth State University in 1991; a M.Ed. in Administration and Supervision from Salisbury University in 1992; and an Ed.D. in Sport Management from the United States Sports Academy in 1998.

Dr. Schwarz lives in Melbourne, Australia with his wife Loan and miniature schnauzer Max.

DR. STACEY A. HALL

Dr. Stacey Hall is the Associate Director of the National Center for Spectator Sports Safety and Security (NCS[4]) and an Associate Professor of Sport Management at The University of Southern Mississippi (USM). She has earned a Bachelor's degree in Management, a Master's in Business Administration, and Ph.D. in Sport Administration.

Dr. Hall's expertise is in the area of sport safety and security management. She has been published in leading international sport management, homeland security, and emergency management journals. She was the lead author on the textbook *Security Management for Sports and Special Events* published in 2012. Additionally, she has been invited to publish in national magazines such as *Athletic Management*, *Athletic Administration*, and *Security Magazine*. Dr. Hall has been referred to as one of the nation's leading experts in sport security with interviews in USA Today, ESPN the Magazine, CBS New York, and also appeared on a live national broadcast of ESPN Outside the Lines. Dr. Hall was one of 150 experts from across the globe invited to attend the first International Sport Security Conference in Doha, Qatar in 2011.

Dr. Hall has been the principal investigator on external grant awards in excess of $4m. Funded projects included awards from the US Department of Homeland Security to: develop risk management curriculum for sport security personnel at NCAA institutions; conduct risk assessments at college sport stadia; develop training programs for sport venue staff; and develop sport evacuation simulation software.

Dr. Hall has been involved in several service projects; including development of a risk assessment tool for US sport stadia in conjunction with the Department of Homeland Security and International Association of Venue Managers; development of a disaster mitigation plan post-Katrina for the Mississippi Regional Housing

Authority; and development of a sport safety and security system for a K-12 school district in Houston, TX.

Dr. Hall has completed threat/risk assessment training through the National Emergency Response and Rescue Training Center; terrorist bombing training through New Mexico Tech Energetic Materials and Testing Center; and special events contingency planning for public safety agencies training through the FEMA Emergency Management Institute.

Dr. Hall teaches undergraduate and graduate sport management courses in economics, law, finance, marketing, and security. She developed a graduate-level emphasis area in sport security management for the Master's program at Southern Miss.

A competitive soccer player, Dr. Hall was team captain for the Northern Ireland International Soccer Team. She retired in 2008. In 2013, she was inducted into the Southern Miss Sports Hall of Fame. Dr. Hall now resides in Hattiesburg, Mississippi.

PROF. SIMON SHIBLI

Simon Shibli is Professor of Sport Management at Sheffield Hallam University in the United Kingdom, and is the Director of the Sport Industry Research Centre (SIRC). He is a qualified accountant with the Chartered Institute of Management Accountants (CIMA). At the age of 12, Simon went to work at the Alton Towers theme park in North Staffordshire and has been hooked on the leisure industry ever since. He graduated from Loughborough University in 1985 after studying Physical Education, Sport Science, and Recreation Management. After leaving university Simon worked for seven years as a facility manager in the arts and entertainments industry. In 1992 Simon returned to academic life as a lecturer specializing in finance and he wrote his first book *Leisure Manager's Guide to Budgeting and Budgetary Control* in 1994. He has subsequently developed a research career and has peer reviewed publications in numerous peer reviewed journals notably *Managing Leisure: An International Journal*. Since 2004 Simon has been in charge of the Sport Industry Research Centre (SIRC) at Sheffield Hallam University. SIRC is an 18-strong team of hard working, talented and passionate individuals who successfully deliver whatever challenge is set for them year in and year out. Simon lives in Sheffield, England with his wife Tracey, three children Alice, James, and Mary, and a cat called Lotte.

CHAPTER 1

INTRODUCTION TO SPORT FACILITY OPERATIONS MANAGEMENT

CHAPTER OUTLINE

- What is sport facility operations management?
- Why sport facility operations management is important
- The discipline of sport facility operations management
- Chapter review

CHAPTER OBJECTIVES

The purpose of this prologue is to provide the reader with some initial background on the concept of sport facility operations management. First will be an explanation of the concepts of facility management and operations management in general terms, followed by how these concepts interact with each other in terms of sport facilities. This will be followed by a presentation of global scenarios where poor management and/or operations of a sport facility led to significant problems. This prologue will conclude with an explanation of how this book will help the reader learn to deal with the scenarios presented, and much more. This will be accomplished through a description of the discipline of sport facility operations management in terms of the various concepts that will be covered in this book.

WHAT IS SPORT FACILITY OPERATIONS MANAGEMENT?

In order to effectively understand sport facility operations management, it is important to consider each of the two main concepts – facility management and operations management. Facility management is an all-encompassing term referring to the maintenance and care of commercial and non-profit buildings, including but not limited to sport facilities, including heating, ventilation, and air conditioning (HVAC); electrical; plumbing; sound and lighting systems; cleaning, groundskeeping, and housekeeping; security; and general operations. The goal of facility management is to organize and supervise the safe and secure maintenance and operation of the facility in a financially and environmentally sound manner.

There are numerous associations that oversee the profession of facility management worldwide. These associations have further clarified the definition of facility management, and also provide guidance and education for those who are employed in the field. The world's largest and most widely recognized international association for professional facility managers is the International Facility Management Association (IFMA). According to their website (www.ifma.org), they support more than 24,000 members in 94 countries through 130 chapters and 17 councils. They define facility management as 'a profession that encompasses multiple disciplines to ensure functionality of the built environment by integrating people, place, process and technology'; and further clarify this definition as 'the practice of coordinating the physical workplace with the people and work of the organization; integrates the principles of business administration, architecture, and the behavioral and engineering sciences'. Other organizations include the British Institute of Facilities Management (BIFM – www.bifm.org.uk), the Facility Management Association of Australia (FMA Australia – www.fma.com.au), the Venue Managers Association Asia and Pacific (www.vma.org.au), the International Association for Sports and Leisure Facilities (www.iaks.info), and the International Association of Venue Managers (IAAM – www.iavm.org).

While facility management focuses on the overall maintenance and care of a building, operations management focuses on administrating the processes to produce and distribute the products and services offered through a facility. This would include the processes of production (tangible and intangible), inventory control, supply-chain management, purchasing, logistics, scheduling, staffing, and general services – with the goal of maintaining, controlling, and improving organizational activities. The operations management field also has numerous associations that support the profession. The largest is the Association for Operations Management (APICS – www.apics.org), whose mission is to build knowledge and skills in operations management professionals to enhance and validate abilities and accelerate careers. Other global organizations that support the profession of operations management include the European Operations Management Association (EurOMA

2

– www.euroma-online.org), the Production and Operations Management Society (POMS – www.poms.org), and the Institute of Operations Management (www.iom-net.org.uk).

WHY SPORT FACILITY OPERATIONS MANAGEMENT IS IMPORTANT

Every day, thousands of facilities around the globe host sport, recreation, and lei-sure activities with minimal or no problems. But when a problem occurs, or there is a lack of planning ahead for activities, the results can be harmful and damaging. This can range from damage to the facility or equipment to injuries to personnel, participants, and visitors – with the injuries ranging in severity from minor (cuts, bruises, sprains) to major (broken bones, torn ligaments, back and eye injuries) to catastrophic (loss of limb, paralysis, death). Sport facility operations management seeks to maintain and care for public, private, and non-profit facilities used for sport, recreation, and leisure to ensure safe and secure production and distribution of products and services to users.

The discipline of sport facilities operations management has many different components that need to be understood. However, before an explanation of these various sub-disciplines is provided, let us take a look at a number of real scenarios where poor facility operations and management have led to significant problems...

- In 1972, 11 Israeli athletes (along with one German police officer and five ter-rorists) were killed by the Palestinian terrorist group 'Black September' due to inadequate security at the Munich Olympic Games. Eight Palestinians, with bags of weapons, were able to scale the fence that surrounded the Olympic vil-lage, and then proceeded to enter the Israeli accommodation to take the athletes hostage.
- In 1985 at Valley Parade football stadium, the home of Bradford City, a flash fire broke out during a match with Lincoln City. The fire consumed one side of the stadium, killing 56 people and injuring over 250. The fire was believed to have been caused by either a match or cigarette that fell through a hole in the stands and into rubbish below. Even though the fire brigade was called, there was no way to keep the fire at bay as fire extinguishers had been removed from passageways to prevent vandalism.
- Also in 1985, Liverpool and Juventus were facing each other in the European Cup final at Heysel Stadium in Belgium. Before the match started, Liverpool supporters reacted to taunts from the Italian fans by charging through the lines of Belgian police. The Juventus fans could do nothing, but retreat as far as a wall, which collapsed under the pressure and onto their own fans below. In the ensuing panic 39 supporters died and over 600 were injured. Based on further

3

inquiries, as well as an evaluation of concerns voiced prior to the event, it was determined that 58,000 people being allowed into a stadium to watch the game at a stadium that was crumbling from disrepair and only could hold 50,000 contributed significantly to the disaster.

■ In 1988 in Kathmandu, Nepal, 80 soccer fans seeking cover during a violent hail storm at the national stadium were trampled to death in a stampede. The reason – the stadium doors were locked.

■ In 1989 at Hillsborough Stadium (the home of Sheffield Wednesday Football Club), there was a human crush that occurred during an FA semi-final match with Liverpool that resulted in the deaths of 96 people. This deadliest stadium-related disaster in British history (and one of the worst in international football history) could have been prevented, as the inquiry into the disaster (the Taylor Report) named the cause as failure of police and security control.

■ In 1993, during a quarter-final tennis match in Hamburg, Germany, a fan ran from the middle of the crowd to the edge of the court between games and stabbed Monica Seles between the shoulder blades. The individual (who was deemed to be 'psychologically abnormal' by the courts) was a fan of Seles' rival, Steffi Graf (whom was not Seles' opponent in this match). While her injuries were not life threatening, she did not return to professional tennis for over two years.

■ In 1996 at the Mateo Flores National Stadium in Guatemala City (seating capacity 45,800), Costa Rica and Guatemala were playing a World Cup qualifier. According to FIFA, the world soccer association, forgers apparently had sold fake tickets to the match, bringing far more people to the stadium than could fit (estimated at over 60,000). This, combined with gatecrashers (people without tickets), pushed into the bleachers through a concrete causeway, overwhelmed other fans below, and caused a mass of people to tumble down on top of one another. Ticket-takers were seen to also continue admitting fans even after bleachers were clearly filled to capacity.

■ Known as the Accra Sports Stadium disaster, in 2001 a match between two teams from the West African nation of Ghana was expected to have unrest and extra security was provided. The losing team's fans started throwing plastic seats and bottles onto the soccer pitch expressing their displeasure with the result. Police responded by shooting tear gas and plastic bullets into the crowd, creating a stampede of people which resulted in the deaths of 127 spectators. This was the worst stadium disaster in Africa to date.

■ In 2007 at the Australian Open tennis tournament a brawl between Serbian and Croat spectators erupted outside a merchandise tent when the two groups began trading insults. Punches, bottles, and beer cups were thrown as about 150 members of the two groups of rivals clashed. No injuries were reported, but 150 people were ejected from the event, and Tennis Australia announced the need to revise plans for handling these types of situations in the future.

4

- Multiple reports published between 2006 and 2009 have examined significant risks to players and spectators due to air poisoning from exhaust systems from zambonis because of lack of ventilation in ice arenas. Medical studies have shown the results can cause a significant increase in asthma and chronic coughs in hockey players that play in poorly ventilated arenas due to carbon monoxide and nitrogen dioxide poisoning.
  - Ventilation problems have also been related to 'sick pool syndrome' in aquatic centers/natatoriums due to the high humidity and the contaminants cause by chemicals and biologics.
- In 2009 at the Dallas Cowboys practice facility, a thunderstorm ripped the roof off the inflatable bubble and collapsed the infrastructure, injuring 12 people including the paralysis of one coach. The question of negligence on behalf of the Cowboys arose due to a number of factors, including (1) was this an adequate and safe facility to be holding practice in during the tornadic weather conditions; (2) was there substandard maintenance on the facility to withstand the winds from the storm; and (3) should the Cowboys have used Summit Structures LLC to build the facility when they had prior knowledge that a similar type of facility built for the Philadelphia Regional Port Authority collapsed under similar weather conditions (which are more regular in Texas).
- Also in 2009, Stan Kroenke and Kroenke Sport Enterprises, owners of the Pepsi Center in Denver, signed a contract with World Wrestling Entertainment (WWE) to hold their Monday Night Raw wrestling show that is televised worldwide on Memorial Day. At the same time, the Denver Nuggets of the NBA (also owned by Kroenke) made it to the semi-finals of the NBA playoffs, which resulted in Game 4 of the playoffs being scheduled the same day as the WWE event. The WWE, who had a legal and binding contract, were bumped from the facility for the Denver Nuggets – less than one week before the event.
- In the lead-up to the 2010 FIFA World Cup in South Africa, a 64-year-old person was crushed to death while in line to buy tickets in central Cape Town, There were riots across the country at other selling points – to the point of police in Pretoria needing to use pepper spray on people fighting to get into a FIFA ticket outlet. The cause of making fans irate in many cases was because the computer system serving many of those outlets crashed minutes after opening, and people were not able to buy the discounted tickets for matches.
- In 2012 in Port Said, Egypt, at least 74 people were killed and many dozens injured in a fight between the fans of two rival soccer clubs. Security measures at the stadium came into question as many fans used knives and other weapons in the fight. Fans were also easily able to storm the field after the match and attack players and fans alike, as well as set part of the stadium on fire.
- In 2013, two bombs exploded near the finish line of the Boston Marathon as runners were finishing the race. Three people were killed and more than 175 injured. Three other devices were found at other locations nearby.

5

So – how would you deal with each of these scenarios? Could they have been pre-vented? What would you have done differently? You probably cannot answer those questions right now, but the goal of this book is to provide you with a body of knowledge in sport facility operations management that can be transferred to any type of facility around the globe. As with any textbook, the theoretical foundations presented offer the reader the opportunity to conceptualize the practices within a subject, then take that knowledge and apply it in practical settings. While this book will not and cannot cover every individual unique aspect of sport facility operations management from the viewpoint of every type of facility – this would be impossible – it does provide a framework understanding that will allow an individual to enter a sport facility operations management situation, have a base understanding of what is happening, and conceptually understand how to start the process of managing the situation.

THE DISCIPLINE OF SPORT FACILITY OPERATIONS MANAGEMENT

The first section of the book seeks to provide the reader with an understanding of behind-the-scenes concepts that must be understood before even entering into management and operations of sport facilities. First is an explanation of the vari-ous business, ownership, and governance structures for sport facilities across the globe. It is equally important to understand the legal authority under which the sport facility can operate as a business, as well as the business, governance, and organizational effectiveness structures. Second is an analysis of the intricacies of financing sport facilities including the costs of conducting business, life-cycle costing, cost-effectiveness/efficiency, and the importance of economic impact analyzes. By understanding these financing concepts, sport facility operations managers can connect the financing options to the ownership and governance structures, and understand how the facility came into being. Furthermore, this information serves as a foundation for looking at the current and future trends that will affect the management and operation of sport facilities. The third concept focuses on how the decisions to build new facilities, upgrade existing facilities, or invest in new equipment have a significant effect on the future financial well-being of a sport organization. To help make these decisions on an informed basis is a variety of techniques known as capital investment appraisal. This will be examined through an analysis of traditional methods such as the payback method, and the accounting return on investment, as well as contemporary approaches based on the time value of money, such as discounted cash flows and the internal rate of return. The final area to be covered in this section is the planning, design, and construction processes for sport facilities. While not all individuals will be involved in these processes from the initial concept of a facility, it is inevitable

6

that sport facility management professionals will be involved with modification, refurbishment, and/or expansion of a facility sometime in their career. The goal is to provide background about preliminary planning, developing designs, construction processes, and preparation planning for training and management of sport facilities.

The second section of the book will focus on the implementation of management and operations in sport facilities, including organizational management, human resource management, financial management, operations management, and legal responsibilities. Organizational management involves the planning, organizing, leading, and coordinating functions within a business to create an environment that supports continuous improvement of personnel, the organization, and the customers. Human resource management is the logical and strategic supervision and managing of the most important asset within an organization – the employees. Without a quality group of individuals working for the facility, goals and objectives could not be met, tasks would not be completed, and customers would not be served. Understanding the various types of human resources and the generally accepted practices of human resource management is crucial to the success of sport facility operations management. Equally important is financial management, as concepts such as financial reporting, budgeting, and break even analysis are vital to the fiscal health of the sport facility, and hence the ability to continue business operations. In addition, operational decision making is crucial to success. To manage facilities efficiently and effectively managers need to understand the concept of cost and how to apply it in real-world situations, as well as how to understand the nature of cost and to use this knowledge to improve a sport facility's financial performance. All of these concepts above lead into actual operations management, which is the maintenance, control, and improvement of organizational activities that are required to produce products and services for consumers of the sport facility. In order to effectively manage operations, a sport facility manager must understand how the operational structure integrates with the operation of the sport facility in terms of total quality management and generating operating procedures to be utilized in various facility operations and services. In addition, general legal concerns for sport facility owners and managers will be covered, including the effects of the legal environment on sport facilities; general legal principles and standards inherent to sport facility operations management; and an explanation of the level of legal expertise an owner or manager needs.

The third section of the text will focus on ancillary issues in sport facility operations management, including marketing, event planning, risk planning, and security planning. In the marketing chapter, basic theories and principles of global sport marketing and communications will be covered to provide the reader with broad knowledge and skill in marketing process related to understanding the sport consumer, logistics, promotions, and public relations activities. As far as event planning, while without events a facility would have no purpose, it

7

is important to understand that the goals and operational procedures of facilities are often not the same as that of an event manager. Hence the intent is to articulate the role facility management plays in supporting event management through the sport facility event planning process pre-event, during the event and post-event. This includes the activation of a facility event marketing plan, actual event implementation, the level of involvement in managing events, preparing for unexpected circumstances, and the evaluation of events after they have taken place. As with almost any activity related to sport, recreation, or leisure, there is some element of risk. The next chapter will articulate the need to plan for all types of emergencies that may disrupt normal operations through knowledge about risk management practices and being able to identify potential facility threats, vulnerabilities, and security countermeasures. Security will be expanded upon in the final part of this section by introducing security best practices, systems, and planning options to equip the 21st century sport manager with an all-hazard's approach to facility security planning through the development of plans, policies, and protective measures.

The final section of the text focuses on benchmarking and performance management. Benchmarking is the process of measurement based on a specific set of standards of comparison. Performance management is a visionary process of setting goals and evaluating progress towards accomplishing those goals. Benchmarking and performance management are equally important concepts for facility managers to understand and implement. The data can explain the drivers of performance and how to influence them. It also provides a detailed process for reporting and evaluating performance. As a result, integrating these processes as part of organizational culture will provide the basis for a clear focus on the business essentials for the facility, and a direction for continuous improvement in connection with all the concepts covered in this text.

CHAPTER REVIEW

Facility management is an all-encompassing term referring to the maintenance and care of commercial and non-profit buildings, with the goal of organizing and supervising the safe and secure maintenance and operation of a facility in a financially and environmentally sound manner. Operations management focuses on administrating the processes to produce and distribute the products and services offered through a facility, with the goal of maintaining, controlling, and improving organizational activities. Therefore, sport facility operations management seeks to maintain and care for public, private, and non-profit facilities used for sport, recreation, and leisure to ensure safe and secure production and distribution of products and services to users. For a sport facility owner or manager to be successful, there must be an understanding about the various components of sport facility operations

8

management including (1) pre-management and pre-operations issues (ownership structures, financing, capital investment appraisal, and planning/design/construction); (2) the implementation of management and operations (organizational management, human resource management, financial management, operational decision making, operations management, and legal concerns); (3) ancillary issues in management and operations (marketing, event planning, risk assessment, and security planning); and (4) measuring effectiveness of management and operations (benchmarking and performance management).

BIBLIOGRAPHY

APICS (2014). *About APICS*. Retrieved March 11, 2014 from: www.apics.org/About

Big D Disaster (2009). *Sports Illustrated, 110*(19), 30.

Bodden, V. (2014). *The Boston Marathon bombings.* North Mankato, MN: ABDO Publishing.

Darby, P. (2012). *Accra sports stadium disaster.* In Nauright, J. and Parrish, C. (Eds.), *Sports around the world: History, culture, and practice* (pp. 80–81). Santa Barbara: ABC-Clio Inc.

Evans, R. (1996). Bogus tickets blamed for overflow crowd. *Amusement Business, 108*(44), 15.

From the archives: June 1985. (2003). *World Soccer, 43*(9), 82.

Raub, A. (2012). Soccer in the Middle East: an introduction. *Soccer and Society, 13*(5–6), 619–638.

Savage assault. (1993). *Sports Illustrated, 78*(18), 18–21. Retrieved from Research Library Core database.

Taylor, I. (1987). Putting the boot into a working-class sport: British soccer after Bradford and Brussels. *Sociology of Sport Journal, 4*(2), 171–191.

Webster, M. (2007). Ethnic rivalry mars first day of Aussie Open: [Echosport Edition]. *Northern Echo*, January 16, p. 19.

What is the international facility management association? (2014). Retrieved March 11, 2014 from: www.ifma.org/about_ifma/index.cfm

Wolff, A., Cazeneuve, B., and Yaeger, D. (2002). When the terror began. *Sports Illustrated, 97*(8), 58–72.

World Wrestling Entertainment, Inc. (2009). WWE vs. NBA. *Entertainment Business Newsweekly*, 45.

IN THE FIELD ...

Interview with: Rick Nafe, Vice President of Operations, Tampa Bay Rays of Major League Baseball (MLB)

Please explain to the reader about your current position and what your responsibilities are.

My current position is Vice-President of Operations/Facilities. I am basically responsible for everything related to the building, grounds, the event bookings and operations of the building, as well as the support factors that enter into playing MLB at this facility. Under my direction are the following departments:

- Building maintenance and utilities;
- Building conversion;
- Security;
- Grounds and landscape maintenance;
- Baseball field maintenance;
- Event bookings for non-baseball events;
- Event management for all events;
- All aspects of the event-parking, ushers/ticket takers, security, and concession monitoring.

Tell us a little about your track from your university years to get to the position you are in now.

I majored and graduated in Mass Communications (Broadcasting) and Public Relations from Florida State University. Upon graduation, I worked for two years as Assistant Sports Director at WCTV-Channel 6 (the CBS affiliate in Tallahassee). I then ventured out of television and moved to Tampa to work at the MacDonald Training Center for three years as their Director of Community Affairs.

In 1980, I was named the Director of Operations for the Tampa Sports Authority and Stadium Director for Tampa Stadium. After 12 years running Tampa Stadium, Al Lopez Field, and the Yankee Training Complex, I became the Executive Director of the Tampa Sports Authority. During my five year tenure as the Executive Director, we brought the New York Yankees (MLB) operation to town and their Spring Training. We built Legends Field, which is now referred to as George Steinbrenner Field. We also financed and built the Ice Palace, now Amalie Arena, in downtown Tampa to house the (NHL's) Tampa Bay Lightning, as well as financed and built Raymond James Stadium for the (NFL's) Tampa Bay Buccaneers and University of South Florida.

What advice would you give to someone wanting to get into the field of sport facility operations management?

I speak to interns all the time and the message I try to leave them with is one of attitude and enthusiasm. I was one of 249 applicants for the Tampa Stadium Director's job with no prior stadium experience. I sold myself on the attitude of hard work and that nobody works for me ... they work with me. No job is beneath me. I attacked each challenge with enthusiasm no matter what the job was.

There are so many people ... after so few jobs ... you must set yourself apart from the pack.

TECHNOLOGY NOW!

AwareManager is one of the foremost sport facility operations software being used by some of the most recognized facilities in the world including the homes of the Boston Red Sox of Major League Baseball (Fenway Park), the New York Giants and New York Jets of the National Football League (MetLife Stadium), and Arsenal Football Club of the Barclays Premier League (Emirates Stadium in London). The goal of AwareManager is to optimize operations within sport facility management with the most current mobile, database, and business intelligence solutions.

The platform is used for the following functions:

- Catalogues all assets within the sport facility with the ability to include comprehensive information about equipment, infrastructure, and fixed assets.
- Scheduling of sport facility areas, staffing, and associated event activities.
- Organizes sport facility communication with stakeholders ranging from requests, space allocation, and responses – including report status information throughout the process.
- Tracks all parts of the maintenance functions for a sport facility ranging from immediate issues that arise from events to longer-term issues with structures and equipment.
- Inventories all parts of the purchasing and supply chain management functions related to the sport facility.
- Maintains records for legal issues and risk management including incident tracking, risk ledgers, and contract governance.

11

The purpose of this type of software for sport facility operations management is to optimize operations so that all stakeholders will meet their goals and objectives, and ultimately succeed as a business. Utilizing a quality platform such as AwareManager can help a sport facility enhance their brand, meet the needs of clients, deliver quality guest experiences, become more effective and efficient in operations through a transparent process, streamline workflow and operations, minimize risk throughout the event planning and implementation process – all of which results in increased revenue generation.

Source: AwareManager (2014). Retrieved November 17, 2014 from: www. awaremanager.com

PART I

PRE-MANAGEMENT AND PRE-OPERATIONAL ISSUES

CHAPTER 2

OWNERSHIP STRUCTURES

CHAPTER OUTLINE

- General business structures for sport facilities
  - Sole proprietorships
  - Partnerships
    - General partnerships
    - Limited partnerships
- Corporations
  - Types of corporations
- Sport facility ownership and governance structures
  - Public
  - Private
  - Non-profit/voluntary governance
  - Trusts
- Models of organizational effectiveness
- Chapter review

CHAPTER OBJECTIVES

This chapter will cover the various business, ownership, and governance structures for sport facilities across the globe. Sport facility owners must first understand the legal authority under which the sport facility can operate as a business, including as a sole proprietorship, a partnership, or under any number of forms of corporations. At the same time, the sport facility owners must determine how they want to structure their sport business. Sport business organizations are generally structured in three ways: public, non-profit, or commercial. While these categories are general and independent in definition, many sport business organizations can operate under multiple structures. As a result, the ownership must also make choices regarding the governance of the structure, which may be as a public entity, a private entity, a public–private partnership, or under a voluntary structure. Each of these structures will be examined to provide the reader with a holistic understanding of the various configurations of sport facility ownership. In addition, models of organizational effectiveness will be presented to assist sport facility managers to efficiently manage the ownership structure. Models to be covered will include the goals model, the system resource model, the process model, and the multiple constituency model. The chapter will conclude with an explanation that in order to maximize effectiveness and efficiency, ownership and sport facilities managers must use a contingency approach in all they do, because there is no best model – only an optimum solution for a specific set of circumstances.

GENERAL BUSINESS STRUCTURES FOR SPORT FACILITIES

As with any type of business, a sport facility must operate under a specific legal business structure to be a viable business. Understanding these various business structures, and the operational framework that each allow, is crucial to the operations and management of a sport facility from a legal and functional standpoint. The three main categories of business structures are sole proprietorships, partnerships, and corporations. While these main structures are generic in nature, partnerships and corporations have numerous sub-structures that need to be considered for the maximum effectiveness and efficiency in managing the sport facility business.

Sole proprietorships

The most basic form of business ownership is a sole proprietorship. A sport facility under this form of ownership has only one individual who owns the facility, and hence that individual is responsible for the overall administration of the sport facility. In addition, the sole proprietor is accountable for all business operations, including the management of all assets, and having personal responsibility for all debt and liabilities incurred by the sport facility. This includes the tax liability, which is incurred by the owner as part of their personal income tax. Sole proprietors will often pass their business down to their heirs, as in the case of most family-owned sport facilities.

In addition to having complete control over the decision making and management processes of the sport facility, there are a number of additional advantages of a sole proprietorship. There are relatively minimal legal costs and few formal business requirements to create a sole proprietorship, and should the owner choose to sell the sport facility, they can do so without consultation from others. Sole proprietorship businesses can usually open their doors fairly easily; however, it is important to recognize the unique licensing, legal, and zoning regulations that are present in different jurisdictions. A further advantage of sole proprietorships, and arguably a disadvantage for other ownership types, is the degree of scrutiny that outside bodies can have on the financial performance of a sole proprietor. In practice, the financial affairs of a sole proprietor are confidential between him or her and the tax authorities. As you will discover later in the chapter, one of the prices to be paid for the more complex types of business entity is the requirement for a higher level of scrutiny over an entity's financial affairs.

There are some disadvantages to sole proprietorship for sport facilities over and above the personal liability of the sport facility from business operations. First, the owner is personally liable for the actions of their employees – hence any acts of negligence or other illegal conduct related to the sport facility will become the legal responsibility of the sole proprietor. Second, since investors and venture capitalists usually will not invest in sole proprietorships it is difficult for businesses of this type to raise additional funding (or capital) for expansion and development. Most sole proprietors rely on profits, bank loans, and personal assets to finance their sport facility initially, which has the effect of limiting the funding that can be sourced to support a business. In the future, if and when the business grows, the sole proprietor may choose to take on partners or incorporate to secure additional funding, but obviously that would change the entire structure of the business.

Sole proprietorships come in all sizes. Many sole proprietorships are small 'mom-and pop' type businesses such as a hot dog vendor, golf course owners, fitness and recreation clubs, or local retail shop owners. However, a sole proprietorship can be a large business with thousands of employees. From a sport team perspective, one example is Jeffrey Vinik, who is the sole owner of the National Hockey League's Tampa Bay Lightning and the Arena Football League's Tampa Bay Storm. The key is not the size of the business; it is that there is one owner.

Partnerships

A partnership is an ownership structure where more than one individual shares the overall administration and business operations of the sport facility. There are a number of partnership structures utilized for sport facilities including general partnerships and limited partnerships.

General partnerships

The most basic form of partnership is a general partnership, where two or more partners are responsible for all business operations and management responsibilities for a sport facility. The structure is similar to that of a sole proprietorship in that there is personal responsibility for all debt and liabilities incurred by the sport facility including tax liability, but where it differs is that the liabilities are shared by the partners based on the percentage of ownership each partner has in the sport facility. In addition to the shared financial commitment and the relative ease of creation, a partnership allows for a stronger top management structure, as multiple owners bring multiple strengths to the business, and often one partner's strength is another partner's weakness. This allows for more effective and efficient management of the sport facility, a stronger business plan, and the potential for acquiring additional resources and investors.

However, if the partners have different personalities, especially as it comes to how each view the management and administration of the sport facility, problems can occur. This is especially true if the goals and vision of the partners differs, and consensus cannot be reached. This can become even more contentious if there is a majority partner who tries to drive the business because of their majority ownership in the sport facility. Another disadvantage of a partnership, which is the same as a sole proprietorship, is that the partners are personally liable for the negligence or illegal conduct of their employees when acting as an agent of the sport facility. This disadvantage is elaborated in a partnership because each partner is liable for all decisions made and actions taken by the other partner(s), including any debts they incur in the name of the partnership. As a result of these disadvantages, general partnerships should have agreements that are drawn up by lawyers, mutually agreed upon and signed, and include provisions for the dissolution of the partnership. Reasons for dissolution may include death or disability of one or more of the partners, if a partner wishes to sell their share of the sport facility, or a partner chooses to cease involvement in the business.

Limited partnerships

Limited partnerships are different from general partnerships specifically in the way the roles and responsibilities are undertaken by the partners. Also known as a limited liability partnership (LLP), the limited partner provides financial backing, but does not take an active role in the day-to-day operation and management of the sport facility (this responsibility reverts solely to the general partner(s) in the limited partnership). This is an attractive financial investment for an individual who does not have the expertise or time to run the sport facility. The limited partner(s) still have a say in major decisions that affect the sport facility and take on the financial risk of the sport facility, although they do not take on the liability risk because they are not involved with the management or day-to-day operations. However, this does not include protection from personal negligence related to a limited partner's actions related to the sport facility, or that of an employee acting under the direct supervision of a limited partner. Many sport marketing agencies are LLPs, as well as numerous professional sports teams including the Boston Red Sox and Minnesota Twins of Major League Baseball.

18

Corporations

A corporation is a business structure created under the laws and regulations of governmental authority made up of a group of individuals who obtain a charter authorizing them as a legal body where the powers, rights, authority, and liabilities of the entity are distinct from the individuals making up the group. The individuals in charge of the corporation are normally referred to as shareholders, and the corporation acts as a legally recognized entity in its own right – eligible to enter into contracts, obtain assets, be responsible for liabilities, and conduct the day-to-day management and business operations.

The process of incorporation or company formation is a very complex process that may vary from jurisdiction to jurisdiction, and based on the type of corporation chosen for the business – such as a C-Corporation, a close corporation, an S-Corporation, a limited liability corporation, a publicly traded corporation, or a non-profit corporation. Generally, there is a three-step process to incorporate. First is to determine a name for the corporation and verify with the appropriate jurisdiction that the company name is available for incorporation. The name must be unique and cannot create deception in its similarity to another incorporate business. The second step is to file all the necessary documentation as required by the specific incorporation. This documentation is usually referred to as the Articles of Incorporation, but can also be called a Certificate of Incorporation, a Corporate Charter, or Articles of Association. These articles of incorporation include the name of the corporation, names and contact information of the directors of the corporation, information about membership (if applicable), where the registered office and/or principal location are, the purpose of the corporation, the limitations of the corporation, the activities of the corporation, and how the corporation would be dissolved. The final step is to pay any fees charged by the jurisdiction. This may include governmental fees, franchise taxes, and business initiation fees. In addition, if there is any legal representation assisting in the incorporation of the business, fees incurred would also need to be paid.

There are numerous advantages to setting up a sport facility as a corporation. The major reason is because of the limited liability that is provided to owners, the personal assets of owners are not at risk for the debts or liabilities of the corporation. This is extended to tax liabilities since the corporation is a separate legal entity – the corporation pays the taxes, not the owners. Corporations are also generally considered to be attractive investments; therefore it is often easier to attract investors to improve the corporation. From an employee standpoint, there are a few interesting advantages. For general employees, there are opportunities for profit sharing and stock ownership – a benefit that often attracts higher-quality employees. For owner-employees, many of the general expenses incurred by the individual, including insurance, are often able to be reimbursed through the corporation, or used as a tax deduction at the end of the year. From a structural standpoint, the management structure is usually very clear and ordered, and the organization will have perpetual existence until all of the shareholders either dissolve the corporation or merge with another.

There are also disadvantages to incorporating a sport facility, not the least of which is the cost to file the articles of incorporation, pre-pay taxes, file governmental documentation, and pay for legal fees. Paperwork is very extensive, including corporate reports, tax filings, banking and accounting records, minutes of corporate actions and shareholder meetings, and documents related to any licenses and certifications. In addition, the formalities required to run a corporation are significant, hence why many meetings use Robert's Rules of Order or the Democratic Rules of Order; and why there is a need for such a strict organizational structure. In addition, the dissolution of a corporation is very time consuming and complex, as a result of the processes related to liquidating assets, organizing payments to creditors, and distributing remaining cash value to shareholders.

Types of corporations

There are a variety of legal structures a corporation can take for sport facilities, including C-Corporations, close corporations, S-Corporations, limited liability corporations, publicly traded corporations, or non-profit corporations. The general structure discussed in the previous section on corporations is indicative of the most common structure – a C-Corporation. A C-Corporation is for for-profit, incorporated sport facilities, and provides a structure that allows for an unlimited number of owners, shareholders, and shares of stock. Another type of corporation – a close corporation – is a similar structure to a C-Corporation; however it is designed for sport facilities that have a corporate structure with as few as one owner (a sole proprietor that chooses to use a corporation structure) to a maximum of usually no more than 50 owners/shareholders.

The other types of corporations have some unique characteristics that may be beneficial to various sport facility owners. For example, while the S-Corporation is formed in a similar manner to C-Corporations and close corporations, its tax structure is very different because taxes are paid similarly to a sole proprietorship or partnership – where the income from the S-Corporation is passed on to the shareholders, and they pay the taxes on the profit (or take the deduction in case of a loss) rather than the corporation. The advantage to this type of corporation for the owners of the sport facility is that they can act as a sole proprietor or partnership with all the tax and liability benefits of a corporation, and it also allows the owners to seek investors as a corporate structure – which is often more attractive. On the negative side, there are significant regulations on S-Corporations, including limits on the number of shareholders, and the close scrutiny by governmental agencies regarding compensation of shareholders who are also employees of the sport facility. S- Corporations are relatively expensive to set up in comparison to sole proprietorships and partnerships, and have unique governmental regulations that vary from jurisdiction to jurisdiction. In addition, to avoid any legal

20

problems, the owners need to be diligent to keep personal financial records and corporate financial records separate.

Similar to a limited liability partnership (LLP), a limited liability corporation (LLC) has characteristics of both a partnership and a corporation. Over the past decade, this has become the single most popular form of ownership for sport-related business entities not only because of its hybrid structure, but as a result of the status of the individuals who act as the owners. A LLC is formed by members of the organization, not shareholders. In the case of a sport facility, they create an operating agreement to run the facility without the strict guidelines and organizational structures of a corporation. This includes not having to write annual reports, run structured meetings, and deal with shareholder issues. By not having to operate under these strict formalities, the ownership can focus on the operation of the facility, have more flexibility in the management of the facility (including developing and implementing contracts, assigning human and physical resources, and allocating income), and meeting the needs of their clients. In addition, the LLC provides the same personal liability protection as any other corporation.

Publicly traded (or publicly-owned) corporations have a number of meanings based on the part of the world. In general the concept of a public corporation refers to a business entity that has registered securities such as stocks and/or bonds that can be sold to the general population through stock offerings. Public corporations have also been referred to as government-owned corporations because of the public ownership of the assets and because the benefits provided by the business entity are for the interest of the public. This latter reference is most commonly used globally in terms of sport facilities. The benefits of being a publicly-owned/government-owned corporation center on the ability to have better access to capital through the sales of stocks and/or bonds, and a higher level of support as a result of governmental backing. However, this type of corporation requires total public disclosure of all financial and operational actions.

A final corporation that is prevalent in sport business, but not as widely seen in the ownership structure of sport facilities (however it is prevalent in many of the events and companies that use sport facilities) is the non-profit corporation. A non-profit corporation is a business whose purpose is not to make a profit, but rather to offer services that are beneficial to the general public. Most non-profit corporations are tax exempt because of their nature as a public benefit business. Examples of sport facilities that may be categorized under non-profit status include those related to religious, charitable, and educational purposes. Many facilities that have the purpose of fostering international sports events are often categorized as non-profit, such as those hosting the Olympics. In addition, facilities that are owned and operated by civic leagues and recreational clubs are often classified under non-profit corporation status. These types of corporations are kept under close scrutiny by the government as a result of the benefits they receive.

SPORT FACILITY OWNERSHIP AND GOVERNANCE STRUCTURES

In looking at the general business structures for sport facilities as discussed previously, we can generalize the types of sport business facility ownership into three basic categories. Public sport facilities are usually operated under governmental or quasi-governmental ownership either through federal, regional, or local jurisdictions. Non-profit sport facilities are those managed by volunteer executives and hired paid staff to carry out day-to-day operations, with the ultimate goal not based on profit but for public benefit. The main goal of commercial sport facilities is to make a profit.

While the three sport facility ownership structures are generic in nature, the methods employed to govern these structures can vary. For sport facilities, there are four main governance structures that are prevalent globally – public governance, private governance, non-profit/voluntary governance, and governance via trusts. It is important to remember that these governance structures can be applied individually, or can also be applied in combination with each other, such as public–private governance.

Public

Public governance of sport facilities is usually conducted as a responsibility of an elected public body for a governmental jurisdiction, and usually assigned as the main responsibility of an appointed governmental official. The main reason for a publicly-owned facility is often related to the importance of offering high-quality facilities for the use of the population based on their needs. When it comes to larger facilities for the purpose of holding large events and/or having a professional team, municipalities believe that these sport facilities are important engines of economic development – especially in urban areas. These officials believe that the sport facilities contribute new spending and jobs in the municipality, hence providing justification for public subsidies for the construction and maintenance of these sports facilities.

In this type of governance, the facility manager usually reports directly to these government officials, and must work within the operational efficiency constraints, regulations, and procedures evident in bureaucratic management. This often has a direct effect on many of the operational functions of a sport facility manager, including purchasing processes (which often must go through a tedious bidding and approval process), contract approvals (which must go through the various levels of legislative bureaucracy), and human resource management (hiring, promotion, and firing – which all must go through governmental approval and clearance procedures). There are also challenges when the governmental officials/bodies who are overseeing the public facilities are politicians who truly do not understand the managerial processes of a sport facility. As a result of this, many publicly governed

22

sport facilities have commissioned independent boards to oversee the facilities – made up of individuals who understand facility management, but still report back to the governmental agencies. Another viable option is noted below.

PRIVATE MANAGEMENT OF PUBLIC FACILITIES

In many cases, public bodies have chosen to outsource the management of municipal sport stadiums, arenas, and recreational facilities by hiring private management groups to manage the day-to-day operations of the sport facility, and provide reports back to the governmental agency. Two of the major companies in the world who offer this type of service to sport facilities are SMG and Global Spectrum.

SMG (www.smgworld.com) is one of the largest companies in the world focused on venue management, marketing, and development. It manages convention centers, exhibition halls and trade centers, arenas, stadiums, performing arts centers, theaters, and specialized-use venues, and has partnerships and relationships with both municipal and private clients. SMG has global reach in sport arena and stadium management – just a few examples of prominent sport facilities include in the United States the NRG Stadium, Arena, and Astrodome in Houston; the Mercedes-Benz Superdome in New Orleans; and the Chesapeake Energy Arena in Oklahoma City; and in Europe König Pilsener Arena in Germany; the Odyssey Arena in Northern Ireland; and Wroclaw Stadium in Poland. SMG is also in the process of expanding its operations into Latin America through its offices in Puerto Rico.

Global Spectrum (www.global-spectrum.com), a subsidiary of Comcast Spectacor, provides management, marketing, operations, and event booking services for public assembly facilities, including arenas, convention and exhibition centers, stadiums, theaters and performing arts centers, ice facilities, fairgrounds, amphitheaters, and entertainment and retail districts. In addition to providing full scope-of-services for existing facilities that decide to privatize, Global Spectrum also provides pre-opening design and construction consulting services for the development phase of facilities under construction. The global reach of this company is growing – some examples of current facilities around the world managed by Global Spectrum include the United States (Wells Fargo Center in Philadelphia, and the University of Phoenix Stadium in Arizona); Canada (Budweiser Gardens in London, Ontario; and Abbotsford Centre in British Columbia); Asia (Singapore Sports Hub Arena, National Stadium, and Indoor Stadium); and Du Forum in Abu Dhabi, UAE. The company is also expanding into Europe and Brazil.

Sources

Global Spectrum. (2014). *Company Background*. Retrieved March 28, 2014 from: www.global-spectrum.com/region/en/who-we-are.aspx

SMG. (2014). *About SMG*. Retrieved March 28, 2014 from: smgworld.com/company-history

Suggested discussion topics

1   What are the advantages and disadvantages to outsourcing the management of public sport facilities?
2   Other than SMG and Global Spectrum, identify two other private management companies for sport facilities. Compare and contrast the mission and service offerings – how are each of those companies similar to and different from SMG and Global Spectrum?

Private

The fastest growing structure for governing sport facilities of all types is private governance. As public funding dries up because of changes in the economy, the determination that other municipal projects are more needed, and the lack of human resources to appropriately manage and oversee sport facilities, private enterprises have evolved to meet the needs of communities. These privately-managed sport facilities run as an independent business under any number of ownership structures include sole proprietorships, partnerships, or corporations – and can be either commercial or non-profit. The owners have the ability to exercise their own power and authority over the entire governance structure of the sport facility, including development of the mission and vision, determining who the users of the facility are, and are the regulatory power for anything that happens within the sport facility.

Non-profit/voluntary governance

Non-profit and voluntary governance organizations are an integral part of the sport business landscape, especially as related to sport facilities that are part of educational, charitable, and religious sport entities. Involvement of individuals in the day-to-day operations of these sport facilities are usually voluntary in nature, although there may be some compensated employees within the organization. However, the governance of the sport facility is usually voluntary. The main responsibilities as related to voluntary governance involve the ability to work within the external environments to secure resources from market operations, governmental subsidies, or from reciprocity (volunteering, donations) while pursuing the goals and objectives set forth for the sport facility. Organizations under a voluntary governance structure usually work under a constitution and a set of bylaws. The constitution is a document that outlines the purpose, structure, and limits of an organization. The bylaws are the rules adopted to define and direct the internal structure, policies, and procedures of the sport facility.

Trusts

The importance of managers being aware of the jurisdiction in which they are working is well illustrated by the case of the United Kingdom where the use of sport and leisure 'trusts' is an increasingly common trend. The term 'trust' does not really have a legal definition and tends to be used as a catch-all description for organizations that are specifically set up to run local authority leisure services independently, and for public good rather than financial gain. The essence of what a trust is can be appreciated from the three-stage diagram presented in Figure 2.1.

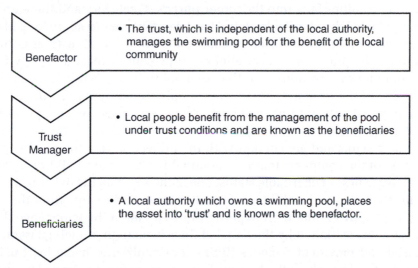

Benefactor
- The trust, which is independent of the local authority, manages the swimming pool for the benefit of the local community

Trust Manager
- Local people benefit from the management of the pool under trust conditions and are known as the beneficiaries

Beneficiaries
- A local authority which owns a swimming pool, places the asset into 'trust' and is known as the benefactor.

Figure 2.1 Three elements of a trust

There are three types of trust that local authorities can consider using: (1) a company limited by guarantee with or without charitable status; (2) an industrial and provident society (IPS) with or without charitable status; and (3) public interest companies (PICs).

A company limited by guarantee is a legally recognized business entity in its own right – the same as any other limited company. However, unlike conventional limited companies where the owners' liability is limited to the extent of their investment in the business, in a company limited by guarantee there is no individual investment and the liability of the owners is limited to a guarantee of a fixed amount in the event of the company failing. In practice, the amount that directors of companies limited by guarantee are asked to contribute in the event of failure is a nominal amount should it be called for. In order to achieve limited-by-guarantee status a company needs to have objectives that are for the public good, such as the provision of recreational or cultural opportunities for the community. A further distinguishing feature of a company limited by guarantee is that surpluses or profits are not allowed to be distributed to the directors or trustees. This does not mean that it is not permitted for companies of this type to make profits; rather those who control the company are not permitted to benefit financially from its trading performance. Indeed it may be essential for companies limited by guarantee to make profits in order to maintain their facilities and to reinvest in the business. For many facility providers in the UK, achieving the status of company limited by guarantee is but a stepping stone to achieving charitable status. Charitable status provides desirable tax advantages for organizations whose objectives include: the relief of poverty, the advancement of education, the advancement of religion; or other purposes deemed beneficial to the community. The provision of sports facilities and sporting opportunities falls into the 'other purposes' category and there are plenty of precedents whereby charitable status has been awarded to sports organizations. The major financial benefits of charitable status are exemption from corporation tax on the profits plus mandatory relief of 80 percent of local authority business rates (a form of local taxation) with the potential to increase this to 100 percent at the discretion of the local authority. Thus simply from rate relief alone, registered charities have a significant financial competitive advantage over suppliers that are not registered charities. Some companies that are limited by guarantee do not pursue charitable status and are content with the protection that their status provides the directors of the company, that is, a nominal limit on their liability in the event of failure. Regardless of charitable status, one of the key benefits of being a company limited by guarantee is the ability to attract competent directors from the community who are happy to offer their expertise for free safe in the knowledge that their liability for debts is limited by the value of their (usually nominal) guarantee.

Industrial and provident societies (IPS) are recognized as being legal entities in their own right and have broadly the same benefits as companies limited by guarantee. To achieve IPS status in the context of sport, applicants are required to demonstrate that they are providing benefits for the community and not just the membership. The key features of an industrial and provident society are that it will have:

- a written set of rules which govern its activities;
- a recognized separate legal identity;
- the right to own property;
- the right to enter into contracts;
- additional legal requirements made of it such as company law;
- limited liability (i.e. the liability of the management committee is usually limited to a nominal amount); and
- a profit making ability, which is put back into the organization.

Pre-management and pre-operational issues

Greenwich Leisure Limited (GLL) is an innovative example of a staff led 'Leisure Trust', which uses the industrial and provident society format. GLL manages more than 65 public leisure centers in Greater London. Not only is the legal format of the business an ideal way to run the trust, it also benefits from economies of scale in terms of procurement whereby it can negotiate bulk discounts on energy costs and other supplies. Like companies limited by guarantee it is also possible for industrial and provident societies to qualify for charitable status and hence benefit from mandatory rate relief.

A public interest company (PIC) is a relatively new legal format for delivering public services, and exists to deliver a specific public benefit such as providing equitable sporting opportunities for the community. This benefit cannot be changed without direct agreement from the appropriate publicly accountable body, protecting the public's interest in the services provided, and distinguishing PICs from commercial companies and the not-for-profit sector. PICs are independent bodies. The government cannot manage them directly nor interfere with management processes and day-to-day decisions. PICs can only be held accountable for their results and standards of delivery by government. This makes PICs different from public sector organizations and allows them to be entrepreneurial and responsive to the needs of users.

The intricacies of what type of business format to adopt is best left to those with current legal skills and experience to provide advice to managers expertly. However, as a manager you should have a working knowledge of the available options and should be conversant with the advice that lawyers give you. It is therefore worthwhile knowing the strengths and weaknesses of various formats so that decisions are made using the best available information.

In sum, the strengths of 'trust' status are:

- Trusts operate as 'social enterprises' which provides them with the ability to run as a business, whilst working towards the community's needs and a local authority's strategic direction.
- There is a proven record of trusts improving the performance of their partners through the achievement of social targets and the setting of clear strategic goals.
- Evidence gathered over a long period suggests that trusts reduce the cost of a service to the local authority which in turn reduces an authority's financial risk. Trusts do not pay tax on profits, they qualify for rate relief and tend to find it easier to fund raise for both revenue and capital projects than local authorities.
- Local authorities retain some control over trusts by agreeing shared targets to ensure that sport facilities are managed to optimize the achievement of an authority's objectives. In practice, this is achieved through partnership working and service level agreements.
- Local authorities can retain influence on the board of a trust via the nomination of trustees who will protect the authority's interests.

- Sports facilities can be operated with greater financial and management autonomy, enabling them to respond to market changes dynamically and hence remain competitive.
- Trustees have the ability to develop business and financial plans over sustainable periods of time, creating the ability to plan for the future.
- Previous evidence suggests the trusts improve the opportunity for community involvement in service delivery.
- Trusts have the ability to deliver a wide spectrum of varying leisure facilities, as long as the activities can be considered to be 'charitable activity'. Examples include running sport facilities ('other purposes beneficial to the community') and arts facilities ('advancing education').
- The Trust option creates a perceived 'middle ground' towards outsourcing public services and does not necessarily involve such a fundamental shift in political ideology as contracting facilities and services out to the private sector.
- The board of trustees, if appointed successfully, should add expert financial, business, and marketing experience with no additional cost to the service as these are voluntary posts.

In contrast, the weaknesses of 'trust' status are:

- There is a widely held view that establishing a trust is resource intensive both in terms of financial outlay and the time required to see the process through from inception to completion.
- By placing a facility or service into trust there is an inevitable loss of integration with other local authority services. For example, in the case of an emergency the authority would not be able to convert a trust-managed sports hall into a temporary shelter for homeless people as easily as it could if the facility was managed in-house.
- The success or failure of a trust hinges crucially on the ability to recruit a suitable board of trustees, with the requisite skills, experience, and knowledge to provide strategic direction and leadership. There is the danger that in deprived areas particularly, appropriate community leadership will not emerge and under these conditions trust status can be more of a hindrance than a help.
- In the early stages of running a trust it may be difficult to attract financing owing to the company's unproven trading record. As discussed in Chapter 8 (Finance) potential trading partners like to vet the accounts of companies they do business with. If a trust does not have a financial track record, and is unable to provide copies of its last three years' worth of audited accounts, some firms may be reluctant to trade or will set punitive trading conditions such as payment in advance.
- Facilities often receive hidden subsidies from local authorities such as help with central administration and maintenance costs. These should be planned

for so that there is no duplication of effort or that in reality the trust is more expensive to run than under the in-house model.

■ If a trust fails financially there is potentially a large financial risk that may need to be borne by the authority. This type of situation can be seen as local authorities bearing much of the risk but not benefiting from the rewards. However, evidence to date indicates that in the last 20 years there have been very few trusts that have failed.

The essential points emerging from the information presented on the types of ownership structure in this chapter are twofold. First, there are numerous types of legal format available to the sport facility manager. The reality is that in the early part of your career this type of activity will have been taken care of and you will work in a predetermined ownership structure over which you have no strategic control. As your career develops and you take on a more strategic role, which could involve deciding the ownership model and legal identity of a facility, you will be required to explore and advise on various options accordingly. Second, issues around ownership structures and legal identity are complex. Whilst you should be conversant with the issues, it is also important to realize the limitations of your knowledge. Some things are best left to specialists and the sign of a good manager is one who knows when to ask for help.

MODELS OF ORGANIZATIONAL EFFECTIVENESS

To be able to appropriately govern a sport facility, a manager must have a clear understanding of organizational effectiveness. Organizational effectiveness is the concept of how successful a business is in achieving the outcomes set forth in the planning processes. Measuring organizational effectiveness is central to the evaluation of what a sport facility delivers from programmatic, operational, and managerial perspectives. It is an integral process to proving to investors and donors that the money being provided is being used to accomplish the goals of the organization, to evaluating the communication processes and ethical actions of the business, and serves as a foundational process for determining strategic growth.

For a sport facility to be effective and achieve its goals and objectives, the ownership and the governance structures must be able to successfully respond to changes in its environment. Changes in the environment may be internal to the sport facility organization/management/operation, or external (examples include customers' needs, the economy, politics, legal issues, and the media). At the same time, there is a need for an organization to understand the attributes of flexibility in correlation to control. Flexibility allows faster change, whereas control allows a firmer grasp on current operations. How these two concerns work in congruency in both the internal and external environments is a significant measure of organizational effectiveness.

Numerous models have been developed to help sport facilities measure organizational effectiveness based on the varying levels of environmental and organizational attributes. Table 2.1 chart articulates the major models of organizational effectiveness that are utilized in sport facilities globally.

Table 2.1 Models of organizational effectiveness

Model	Description

Goal (or rational goal)	▪ Where the achievement of specific organizational goals determines effectiveness:
	  – Establish the general goal.
	  – Discover objectives for accomplishment.
	  – Define activities for each objective.
	  – Measure level of success.
	▪ Designed to enhance strategic planning by linking program goals and resource allocation levels.
	▪ Is output-based and in measureable terms – not always good because all effectiveness is not output-based.

Process (or internal process)	▪ Focuses on the effectiveness of the internal transformation process. ▪ Emphasis on control and the internal focus, and stresses the roles of information management, communication, stability, and control.
Systems resources	▪ Where effectiveness is determined in terms of the ability to attract and secure valuable resources, such as operating capital, physical resources, and quality human resources.
Multiple constituency	▪ Where effectiveness is not internally judged, but is based on the judgment of its constituents. – In the case of a sport facility, it may include spectators, promoters, resident teams, and vendors. ▪ Often used as a viable alternative to the goal and systems approaches.
Strategic constituencies	▪ Effectiveness is determined by the extent to which the organization satisfies all of its strategic constituencies. ▪ For a sport facility, it would include spectators, vendors, home teams, the media, sponsors, etc.
Open system	▪ Effectiveness is measured as a result of the degree that an organization acquires inputs from its environment and has outputs accepted by its environment.

Competing values	▪ Effectiveness that is measured based on the interaction between four sets of competing values:
	  – internal focus and integration
	  – external focus and differentiation
	  – flexibility and discretion
	  – control and stability.

High-performing system	▪ Effectiveness as a measurement that compares itself to other similar organizations (to be covered in more detail in Chapter 16 on benchmarking).

Model	Description
Human relations	■ Effectiveness is measured based on the development of the organization's personnel. ■ Places emphasis on flexibility and internal focus. ■ Stresses cohesion, morale, and human resources as development criteria for effectiveness.
Legitimacy	■ Effectiveness measured by acting lawfully and ethically in the eyes of the internal and external environment.
Fault-driven	■ Effectiveness seeks to eliminate traces of ineffectiveness in its internal functioning through the design of backup plans to be reliable even if some components fail.

On a final note, sport facility managers and owners need to acknowledge a contingency approach to organizational effectiveness, as there is no best model. There are numerous variables that influence organizational effectiveness, including changes in the organizational structure, the implementation of new technologies, opportunities and threats in the environment that affect the sport facility, and the people using the sport facility (both customers and human resources) – to name a few. As a result, owners and managers of sport facilities must take a situational approach to organizational effectiveness to attain an optimum solution for a specific set of circumstances that arise.

CHAPTER REVIEW

A sport facility must operate under a specific legal business structure to be a viable business. Understanding these various business structures and the operational framework each allows is crucial to the operations and management of a sport facility from a legal and functional standpoint. The three main categories of business structures are sole proprietorships, partnerships, and corporations. The most basic form of business ownership is a sole proprietorship, where only one individual owns the facility and is responsible for the overall administration and liabilities of the sport facility. A partnership is where more than one individual shares the overall administration and business operations of the sport facility. There are a number of partnership structures utilized for sport facilities including general partnerships and limited partnerships. General partners are directly involved with the day-to-day operations of the facility and have full liability, whereas limited partners have financial liability but not operational liability or responsibility. Corporations are business structure created under the laws and regulations of governmental authority made up of a group of individuals who obtain a charter authorizing them as a legal body where the powers, rights, authority, and liabilities of the entity are distinct from the individuals making up the group. There are various corporate structures for sport facilities including a C-Corporation, a close corporation, an S-Corporation, a limited liability corporation, a publicly traded corporation, or a non-profit corporation.

Sport facility ownership usually falls under one of three governance structures. Public sport facilities are usually operated under governmental or quasi-governmental ownership either through federal, regional, or local jurisdictions. Non-profit sport facilities are those managed by volunteer executives and hire paid staff to carry out day-to-day operations, with the ultimate goal not based on profit but for public benefit. Commercial sport facilities' main goal is to make a profit. A unique governance structure is governance by trust, where a benefactor places an asset (such as a sport facility) into a trust that is managed by an assigned party (trust manager) to ensure the customers (beneficiaries) benefit from the services of the sport facility. These trusts can be either as a charitable organization, a non-profit without charitable status, or a public interest company.

To appropriately govern a sport facility, a manager must have a clear understanding of the concept of organizational effectiveness, which is the concept of how successful a business is in achieving the outcomes set forth in the planning processes. While there are multiple models of organizational effectiveness, it is important to recognize and acknowledge the need for a contingency approach to governing a sport facility, as there is no best model – only an optimum solution for a specific set of circumstances.

BIBLIOGRAPHY

Ackerman, A. M. (1994). Privatization of public-assembly-facility management. *Cornell Hotel and Restaurant Administration Quarterly, 35*(2), 72.

Anand, A., Milne, F., and Purda, L. (2006). *Voluntary adoption of corporate governance mechanisms.* Retrieved March 28, 2014 from: http://law.bepress.com/expresso/eps/1277

Baker, K. and Branch, K. (2002). *Concepts underlying organizational effectiveness: Trends in the organization and management science literature.* Retrieved February 16, 2014 from: www.au.af.mil/au/awc/awcgate/doe/benchmark/ch01.pdf

Bushardt, S. C., Debnath, S. C., and Fowler, A. F. (1990). A contingency approach to organizational effectiveness through structural adaptation. *American Business Review, 8*(1), 16–24.

Coates, D. and Humphreys, B. R. (2003). Professional sport facilities, franchises and urban economic development. *Public Finance and Management, 3*(3), 335–357.

Ferkins, L., Shilbury, D., and McDonald, G. (2009). Board involvement in strategy: Advancing the governance of sport organizations. *Journal of Sport Management, 23*(3), 245–277.

Greenwich Leisure Limited (2009). *London's most successful social enterprise.* Retrieved May 11, 2009 from: www.gll.org

Lindqvist, K. (2012). Effects of public sector reforms on the management of cultural organizations in Europe. *International Studies of Management and Organization, 42*(2), 9–28.

Martinez-Tur, V., Piero, J. M., and Ramos, J. (2001). Linking service structural complexity to customer satisfaction: The moderating role of type of ownership. *International Journal of Service Industry Management, 12*(3/4), 295–306.

McNamee, M. J. and Fleming, S. (2007). Ethics audits and corporate governance: The case of public sector sports organizations. *Journal of Business Ethics, 73*(4), 425–437.

Misener, K. and Doherty, A. (2009). A case study of organizational capacity in nonprofit community sport. *Journal of Sport Management, 23*(4), 457–482.

Moorhouse, A. (2014). Look to sport for the answers. *Director, 67*(9), 36.

Moosa, I. and Li, L. (2013). The frequency and severity of operational losses: A cross-country comparison. *Applied Economics Letters, 20*(2), 167–172.

Papadimitriou, D. (2007). Conceptualizing effectiveness in a non-profit organizational environment: An exploratory study. *The International Journal of Public Sector Management, 20*(7), 571–587.

Parkhouse, B. L. (2005). *The management of sport: Its foundation and application* (4th ed.). New York: McGraw-Hill Higher Education.

Potoski, M. and Prakash, A. (2005). Green clubs and voluntary governance: ISO 14001 and firms' regulatory compliance. *American Journal of Political Science, 49*(2), 235–248.

Rosentraub, M. S. (2009). *Sport facilities, a new arena in Edmonton, and the opportunities for development and a city's image: Lessons from successful experiences.* Retrieved February 25, 2014 from: www.edmonton.ca/city_government/documents/PDF/RosentraubReport. pdf

Rosentraub, M. S. and Swindell, D. (2009). Of devils and details: Bargaining for successful public/private partnerships between cities and sports teams. *Public Administration Quarterly, 33*(1), 118–148.

Russo, F. E., Esckilsen, L. A., and Stewart, R. J. (2009). *Public assembly facility management: Principles and practices* (2nd ed.). Coppell, TX: International Association of Assembly Managers.

Steinberg, G. M., Singer, R. N., and Murphey, M. (2000). The benefits to sport achievement when a multiple goal orientation is emphasized. *Journal of Sport Behavior, 23*(4), 407–422

Torkildsen, G. (2011). *Leisure and recreation management* (6th ed.). London: Routledge.

Trendberth, L. (ed.) (2003). *Managing the business of sport.* New Zealand: Dunmore Press Ltd.

Unison (2006). *Leisure Trusts Briefing 148 December 2006: Charitable trusts delivering public leisure and cultural services.* Retrieved June 8, 2011 from: www.unison-scotland.org.uk/ briefings/leisuretrusts.html

Watt, D. C. (2003). *Sports management and administration* (2nd ed.). London: Routledge.

Wicker, P. and Breuer, C. (2013). Understanding the importance of organizational resources to explain organizational problems: Evidence from nonprofit sport clubs in Germany. *Voluntas: International Journal of Voluntary and Nonprofit Organizations, 24*(2), 461–484.

Yeh, C., Hoye, R., and Taylor, T. (2011). Board roles and strategic orientation among Taiwanese nonprofit sport organisations. *Managing Leisure, 16*(4), 287–301.

IN THE FIELD ...

Interview with Mike Tatoian, Executive Vice President and Chief Operating Officer, Dover Motorsports Inc.

Please explain to the reader about your current position and what your responsibilities are.

I am the Executive Vice President and Chief Operating Officer of Dover Motorsports, Inc. (NYSE: DVD). The organization includes Dover International Speedway (capacity 113,000) and Nashville SuperSpeedway (capacity 35,000).

I joined the organization in January 2007 as Executive Vice President, where I am responsible for all facets of the organization, which are primarily focused around NASCAR race weekends, Firefly Music Festival, and other special events held at the facility.

Dover, Delaware takes on a carnival-like atmosphere as the most popular names in NASCAR's premiere series come to Dover International Speedway, affectionately known as the 'Monster Mile'. The venue plays host to the largest sporting events in the Mid-Atlantic region and is known as the fastest one-mile oval in the world.

Held on the speedway's property since 2012, Firefly Music Festival is a four day music festival attracting 80,000 fans per day, and in three years has become the fastest growing, most successful music festival of all time according to Rolling Stone magazine.

Tell us a little about your track from your university years to get to the position you are in now.

As a senior level sports and entertainment executive, I have over 25 years of experience in professional sports/entertainment management, where I have successfully managed over $750 million in sports teams, facilities, and properties.

The first opportunity I had to get into sports management was back in the mid-80s working for the Tulsa Drillers 'AA' minor league baseball team. After I graduated from the University of Northern Iowa with a Public Relations/Marketing degree, I moved to Tulsa, Oklahoma on a whim, to take the position of Telemarketing Sales Representative for the Drillers. The current vernacular we hear today that describes the positon is Event Experience Specialist, Ticket Sales Executive, Inside Sales Representative, Group Sales Executive, or Corporate Account Executive ... call it what you want but the bottom line is today and back then the position requires the employee to MAKE PHONE CALLS.

My co-workers and I used phone books, recipe cards, and pencils for our notes. No CRM, no software, no training, no Big Data, no nothing, just 'smile and dial' with four or five of us jammed in a small space sharing a couple of tables and folding chairs. While it was not a glamorous job, it was very exciting for me to be a part of a professional sports team with the responsibilities of selling fans the experience of attending a minor league baseball game. It was then I realized that I wanted to make a career in the sport industry. It was a terrific experience and opportunity that I very much still appreciate today.

In a brief three-year period, I then became an Administrative Assistant. This position was basically do what needs to be done and is where I developed the acronym that we all need a WIT (whatever it takes) attitude in sport management. This was followed by becoming Director of Stadium Operations (aka Groundskeeper) for the Drillers and shortly after that I moved in the position of Director of Media Relations for the team.

I was then fortunate to be afforded the opportunity to move to my hometown of Bettendorf, Iowa to take another minor league baseball position as the Assistant General Manager of the Quad City Angels (class 'A' affiliate of the then California Angels) and then quickly moved into the GM position of that team shortly thereafter. After a few years there, I launched a brand new team in Fort Wayne, IN (Fort Wayne Wizards, class 'A' affiliate of the Minnesota Twins).

It was at that point that I entered into a more corporate/ownership position when I became Chief Operating Officer of United Sports Ventures. Over the next seven years as COO, I was involved with building, owning, managing, or operating teams all over the country: minor league baseball teams at all levels, minor league hockey teams as well as arena football league teams. For me it was a terrific experience learning the fundamentals of municipal financing, politics, building teams from the ground up, learning new sports, assembling business plans, meeting new people, and putting to test time management skills and balancing priorities.

As our ownership group successfully sold the teams under the United Sports Ventures umbrella, I decided to launch Victory Sports Group (VSG), which ostensibly was the same type of sport management and ownership company. During this time, I fortunately mirrored the same success with VSG, which subsequently led me to my current opportunity here in Dover, Delaware as the Chief Operating Officer of Dover Motorsports.

What advice would you give to someone wanting to get into the field of sport facility operations management?

There is a framed print hanging in my office that is a wide angle view of Dover International Speedway filled with fans during one of their race weekends.

When people come into my office, many times I will ask them to comment on the print. It is amazing to me the diverse perspectives they 'see' in the print.

A *sales team member* will note how well they were able to brand the track with corporate partners, a *board member* will comment on the gross revenue that race must have generated, a *security staff* member noted how many people were carrying cooler bags, and the *safety director* noticed how many people were not wearing sunscreen ... all looking at the exact same print – each with a different perspective.

My point in asking the question is to recognize that a successful career in the field of sport facility/team management and operations requires a diverse understanding of the various components that all equally contribute to the success.

The focus of various departments such as sales, operations, safety, security, food and beverage, communications, which are inextricably linked to fans, sponsors and members of the media, combined with the pressure of meeting budget goals and objectives all need to be balanced, prioritized and understood to have a long successful career in sports management.

Just like an engine, there are so many parts that are critical to making it work correctly, so too is each element of managing a sport facility or entity. An effective promoter/operator has to have command of the financial impact of the decisions they are making. Each department has to understand and respect the importance of the other departments and in my opinion it is up to Senior Management to ensure it and to make sure to knit it all together.

TECHNOLOGY NOW!

One of the challenges owners and investors who want partial ownership of a company face is finding detailed information about a business that is accurate, in-depth, and functional. One such resource being used by owners and investors across the United Kingdom and Ireland is FAME, which stands for Financial Analysis Made Easy. FAME is a comprehensive business intelligence tool used by owners and investors alike when considering mergers, acquisitions, and investments in companies throughout the UK and Ireland. The tool, which includes information on over nine million active and dissolved companies, allows for researching of general company information, investigation of specific profiles of companies, and for analysis of the business intelligence.

FAME provided an abundance of information for owners and investors to use, including:

- financial information on companies – with up to a decade of financial history in many cases;
- financial strength indicators;
- organizational structure information, including key executive personnel and their contact info;
- ownership, shareholders and subsidiary information;
- original tax filings information;
- any filings against the company;
- stock data for companies that are publically traded; and
- industry research, company news, and any merger/acquisition reports.

The tool provides easy access to all of this information, and much more, in a quick, easy-to-use electronic format. The user-friendly tool allows the user to query on hundreds of criteria including trends, financial analysis, news, market research, tax filings, corporate structures and changes, and to monitor competition. The tool also allows for comparative analyses of companies, can create graphical representations of data, and can even be set to monitor a specific company so the user can receive alerts when new information is posted in the system.

As a day-to-day practical tool FAME can be very useful in providing insight into people and businesses you might deal with. If the person who rings you up to hire your stadium seems too good to be true, use FAME to check them out.

- What is the financial track record of their company?
- What is their liquidity rating like and can they pay their bills?
- Have any of the directors ever been disqualified?
- Is your contact really a mouse with a lion's roar?

FAME is a highly recognized and respected business intelligence tool – winning the Business Intelligence Publisher of the Year Award for the UK at the Acquisition International M&A (Mergers and Acquisitions) Awards; and the UK M&A Solutions Provider of the Year (Business Intelligence) Awards at the ACQ5 Global Awards.

FAME is an excellent tool for owners and investors alike to use to gather significant business intelligence; learn more about leads, prospects, and potential investors; and can enhance the information available with a company's customer relationship management (CRM) system.

Source: Bureau Van Duk (2014). *FAME: Detailed information on UK and Irish companies.* Retrieved November 15, 2014 from: https://fame.bvdinfo.com/version-2014108/Home.serv?product=fameneo

CHAPTER 3

FINANCING SPORT FACILITIES

CHAPTER OBJECTIVES

This chapter will delve into the intricacies of financing sport facilities. Recurring themes in financing will be discussed, including business issues, the costs of ownership, life-cycle costing, cost-effectiveness/efficiency, and the principles of economic impact analysis. The recurring issues have a direct effect on the source of financing to be used for sport facilities, such as public sector funding, private sources of revenue, public–private partnerships, and the influence of the voluntary sector. As significant economic change has taken place early in the 21st century, the effects on sport facility investment are significant; hence the chapter will conclude with a look at the current and future trends that will affect the management and operation of sport facilities.

FINANCING CONCEPTS

Financing is defined as the act of obtaining or providing money or capital for the purchase of a business enterprise. For a sport facility, many of these financing issues are related to the types of financing available and the significant changes that have occurred in sport facility investment in the 21st century. However, prior to delving into those topics, it is important to understand recurring themes that are central to the understanding of basis financing themes. In addition to basic business issues related to financing sport facilities, other concepts to be understood include the costs of ownership/life-cycle costing and the principles of economic impact analysis.

Business issues

Developing new sport facilities is a risky process that invariably requires complex financial arrangements. These two points are interrelated. First, it is unlikely that any organization from any sector will have the spare cash available to develop and build a sport facility from the outset of a project. It is therefore current practice that the financing of sport facilities tends to be made with financial contributions from a variety of sources. For example, Wembley Stadium in England opened in 2007 with an estimated cost of £757m ($1.157 billion). The stadium was funded by the Football Association (FA), distributions from the National Lottery, the London Development Agency, and a series of commercial banks. As you will discover in Chapter 8 when we look at finance more closely, it is essential for businesses to make a profit and to be able to service their debts. In 2012, Wembley National Stadium Ltd had long-term debts of £385m ($625.4m) and paid £42.6m ($69.2m) in interest to service those debts. Second, because of the risks involved and the scale of developing sports facilities, developers seek to share the risk involved in a project with partners. These are drawn from those who wish to risk their money on taking a stake in a business by buying the right to share in future profits (equity financing); and those who are prepared to loan money for the development in return for a fixed rate of interest and the knowledge that in the event of business failure they will get their money back (debt financing). The bigger the project, the more complex the web of relationships underpinning it is. When public sector money is involved there is also the scope for controversy as perhaps best demonstrated by adverse publicity surrounding the $450m US public sector subsidies provided by the New York authorities for Yankee Stadium and the £120m ($194.9m) provided by the National Lottery for Wembley Stadium.

When borrowed money (or debt) is used to finance a development the stance of those borrowing the money is the belief that they can make sufficient profit to be able to service interest costs and still make a profit. For the providers of loans, the stance taken is that the interest being paid on the loans justifies the risk of lending to the developer. In practice the two parties' fates are inextricably linked – for everyone to get a fair return on their investment the development has to succeed.

The complex nature of sport facility development helps to provide further insight into the role and responsibilities of the sport facility manager. At the most basic level it is important that day-to-day operations are profitable and sustainable. There is little point in using public subsidies and other people's money to develop a facility for sport only for further money to be required to underwrite operating losses. One of the first rules of business is that you need to make a profit if your business is to have a long-term future. In the case of public sector facilities, for which there may be legitimate grounds to subsidize operating costs, managers must operate within the subsidy levels that have been allocated to them. The importance of appropriate financial performance can also be appreciated by looking at the bigger picture. If as a manager you do not deliver, then you place at risk the livelihoods of your staff, your suppliers, and other stakeholders. Equally, by performing well you pave the conditions for growth, re-investment, higher salaries, more staff, and so on. Whilst this is a weighty responsibility in its own right, things do not stop at sound financial performance. Sport facilities are investments that have the potential to grow in value. Most property tends to increase in value over time and sport facilities are no different. One method by which investors can profit from their initial investment in a sport facility is by selling it for a higher price than the facility cost to develop in the first place. Some of the key factors that determine how much a business is worth are:

■ how well the business is performing financially;
■ the condition of the land, buildings, fixtures, and local infrastructure; and
■ the opportunity for future development in the locality.

Thus a further set of responsibilities for the sport facility manager is the importance of ensuring that the asset is well maintained and kept in a suitable condition such that it is attractive to potential purchasers or indeed new investors. Finally, the managers of sport facilities should be aware of the wider context in which they operate. When a facility is built, it supports jobs in the construction industry, and when the facility is operational numerous other people may be directly or indirectly dependent on the facility for some or all of their income. With this responsibility comes the importance of being a good corporate citizen, not only looking after your own interests but also those of the wider community. A good facility manager will operate at all three levels and look after the interests of the business, the facility, and the wider community. You should now realize that effective sport facility management is much more than taking care of day-to-day operations.

The costs of ownership and life-cycle costing

Considerations around financing sport facilities are not confined to how much a building will cost to construct in the first instance. In our own lives we know that buying a car is simply the start of an expensive relationship with an asset which

40

will require further expense in terms of tax, insurance, fuel servicing, parking, and valeting. A second hand luxury car might cost the same as a new small car but we all know that the costs of owning the former will be much greater than the latter. The same type of commonsense thinking is applicable to sport facilities. For both buildings and equipment due consideration must be given to what are known as 'life-cycle costs', which are defined by the Chartered Institute of Management Accountants as:

> the maintenance of physical asset cost records over the entire asset lives, so that decisions concerning the acquisition, use, or disposal of the assets can be made in a way that achieves the optimum asset usage at the lowest cost to the entity.
>
> (CIMA, 2005)

The importance of being aware of life-cycle costing can be appreciated by the finding that as much as 90 percent of the lifetime costs attributable to an asset are determined by decisions made in the early part of the asset's life. For example, in the case of a swimming pool the purchase costs of an ozone treatment plant for water cleansing compared with a chlorine based plant might make the ozone option seem prohibitive on price. However, when the full lifetime costs of each option are evaluated to account for costs such as energy usage, chemical costs, and plant maintenance, it may well be the case that the more expensive option to buy actually works out to less expensive to own and operate in the longer term than the cheaper option. It is important to avoid 'buy now pay later' situations as cheaper items may have higher running costs and a lower disposal value. Managers of sport facilities are routinely required to make long-term judgments about the optimal solution for a given set of circumstances. For example, is it more cost effective to purchase gym equipment outright and to take responsibility for maintaining and replacing it, or is a better option to lease the equipment whereby maintenance is part of the service level agreement? By using the principles of lifetime costing, these decisions can be made on the evidence of the best information available and in the best interests of the business.

The evidence that life-cycle costing for an asset is based on can be complicated as indicated in the range of considerations listed below.

- Purchase costs (how much does an asset cost to purchase?)
- Running costs (what are the operational costs of using an asset, such as the hourly costs of running air conditioning in a sport arena?)
- Maintenance costs (how much does it cost to retain an asset in a fit-for-purpose condition?)
- Training costs (how much will it cost to train staff in the use of a new box office system?)

■ Decommissioning and disposal costs (how much will it cost to wind down an asset and to dispose of it bearing in mind operational and environmental issues?).

In reality it is difficult to forecast what might happen in the future and life-cycle costing decisions are based on people's attitude towards risk and financial issues such as how quickly they want their money back. Nonetheless, the importance of making good decisions can be appreciated by examining the case of health and fitness clubs that are part of a chain. If proper life-cycle costing is carried out to inform an organization's business model, then when the model is rolled out to multiple sites the benefits will be reaped at every site. Conversely, if you get it wrong at one site and roll out a flawed business model, then the error will be compounded in every site affected. An alternative way of looking at life-cycle costing is to call it 'cost effectiveness' which is defined as an assessment, before a decision, of the available options, which are assumed to deliver the same outcomes, in terms of their relative costs.

Thus whether we are talking about the construction materials for a sports hall; the type of plant to use to cleanse the water in a swimming pool; or the purchase or leasing of fitness equipment; we should always be mindful of the importance of cost effectiveness and the impact our decisions now will have on costs in the future.

The principles of economic impact analysis

The justification for financing many sport facilities is often based on arguments made about the economic benefits that the development will have on the local community. Indeed it is precisely this argument that developers present to public bodies in order to lever funding or other financially advantageous concessions for proposed projects. In recent years there has been no higher profile example of economic impact arguments being used to justify investment in sport facilities than the London 2012 Olympic and Paralympic Games. London 2012 was staged during a time of global recession with a degree of severity that had previously been unseen since the Great Depression of the 1930s. There is a proven logic for governments to spend their way out of financial trouble during recessions and the expenditure of around £9.2 billion ($14.9 billion) on sport facilities and supporting infrastructure can be looked upon as a financial lifeline contributing to bringing the economy out of recession rather than an expensive luxury.

Given the claimed benefits of investing in sport facilities, what is meant by economic impact and what are the benefits that it brings? A simple definition of economic impact is 'the net economic change in a host community that is directly attributable to a facility or an event'. There are two points of note arising from this definition. First, the word 'net' means that it is important to take into account both positive and negative aspects of economic impact. Thus the opening of a new health club might create 30 new jobs, but it also might lead to the closure of a rival facility with the loss of say 20 existing jobs. The 'net' economic impact in this case would be 10 new jobs. Second, the words 'directly attributable' mean that the facility or event must cause the economic impact to occur. If people attending a conference in a city decide to attend a game of baseball as part of their visit, the economic impact is actually attributable to the conference and not the game of baseball. That is to say, the visitors were in the area for a primary reason (the conference) and the baseball just happened to be on at the same time and was secondary to the main purpose of the visit. There is something of a culture in the sport industry for people to exaggerate the economic impact of facilities and events in order to make them look more attractive for public funding.

For sport facilities there are five key areas in which positive economic benefits can be delivered as discussed below.

- Construction: during the construction phase of a facility jobs will be supported or created in the building industry. In the UK, it is widely accepted by economists that every £100,000 ($153,000) of construction costs will support or create one job in the industry. It is therefore no surprise that in 2009 some 4,500 construction workers were employed on the Olympic Park site in London. There can also be positive economic benefits in the construction supply change with increased demand for building materials and the fixtures and fittings needed to equip a new building.
- Employment: when a facility opens it will need staff to operate it and this leads to increased employment opportunities for the local community. Working in sport is a customer focused occupation and people can acquire useful customer care and operations management experience that is transferable to many other occupations.
- Supply chain: sport facilities need supplies such as food and drink to be sold to customers as well as services such as utilities. Those businesses which service new sports facilities will see an increase in the demand for their products as the ripples of economic impact spread wider.
- Local income: the presence of more money in the local community from the spending of employees, the increased demand in the supply chain, and increased tax revenues means that the community as a whole will enjoy increased prosperity that can be linked to the opening of a new sport facility.
- Events: some new sport facilities change the local infrastructure and enable activities that were previously not possible to occur. For example, if a new stadium is built to host an NFL franchise there will be a guaranteed eight regular season home matches per year. The stadium will therefore have to be put to other uses such as staging concerts, conferences, and exhibitions. Without the stadium these would not have been possible and the spending from out-of-town visitors at these events can provide a welcome additional revenue stream to the local community.

The manner in which potential economic impacts are quantified is by the use of specially commissioned 'economic impact studies'. These studies attempt to model the future economic impacts of a sport facility or to measure the actual economic impact of a facility or an event. They are as much art as science and radically different figures can be derived for the same development by consultants depending on who they are working for and the assumptions they use to drive their models. It is therefore important that economic impact studies are carried out independently and make full use of all of the data available. Furthermore, there should be a transparent audit trail of how the economic impact has been derived and what the key drivers of it are. A manager should have an awareness of the economic impact of the sport facility on the local community. Where appropriate managers should also develop the skills necessary to exploit this knowledge for the benefit of an organization.

SOURCES OF FINANCING FOR SPORT FACILITIES

Financing of sport facilities comes in three basic forms – public financing, private funding, and public–private partnerships. All three have had a significant effect on financing sport facilities throughout modern history. Public financing involves the collection of taxes from those who receive benefits from the provision of public goods by the government, and then uses those tax revenues to produce and distribute the public goods to the beneficiaries. Private financing is providing funding for capital investments by non-governmental individuals and/or businesses to provide products and services to the public under the management and operation of the private entity, and the public usually has to pay a fee to utilize the products and services. Public–private partnerships are agreements between government and the private sector regarding the provision of public services or infrastructure – the public municipality transfers the burden of capital expenditures and risks of cost overruns to the private entity, but maintains a partnership in the offering of products and services to the public.

Public sector funding

As with any type of governmental funding, the appropriations have to come from some type of taxation. Public funding of sport facilities comes from both hard taxes and soft taxes. Hard taxes are assessments that are applied to the entire population, where soft taxes are assessments applied to specific product users, or to non-residents of a municipality.

Examples of hard taxes include the following:

- real estate tax
- property tax
- income tax

- general sales tax
- road tax
- utility tax.

Soft taxes include the following examples:

- tourist development tax
- lodging or hotel/motel tax
- restaurant or food service tax
- automobile rental and taxi/limousine/livery service tax
- sin tax (liquor, tobacco)
- players tax
- team tax
- business license/permit tax
- lottery and gaming tax.

Bonds are interest-bearing certificates that are issued by either a jurisdiction or a business that are a binding promise to repay the initial investment of money (called the principal) and an agreed-upon level of interest at a specified date in the future. Quality bonds are usually issued by businesses and/or jurisdictions with a good repayment history, and are bought by investors seeking the most favorable interest rates or tax benefits. Bonds have similar characteristics to long-term loans, as they are effectively contracts where a borrower makes payments on certain dates over a defined period of time in exchange for receiving repayment of the principal with interest at a date in the future. The advantages of investing in bonds include that they are relatively inexpensive – especially for those organizations that have a long history and a good credit rating – the bond market is fairly strong and established, and interest on bonds is tax deductible. Disadvantages of bonds include interest is a fixed amount that must always be paid – regardless of earning revenue/making a profit – and the principal that was loaned must be paid on the maturity date – again regardless of earning revenue/making a profit. In addition, if a bond is secured with collateral, a jurisdiction or company cannot sell the collateral asset without bond-holder approval, and bondholders have the upper hand in collecting their principal and interest if a jurisdiction or corporation goes into bankruptcy.

There are various types of bonds, but most fall under two categories – taxable bonds and municipal bonds. Taxable bonds are usually issued by corporations, and do not offer the same tax-exempt benefits of a municipal bond. These types of bonds are rarely used in the financing of sport facilities. The two types of taxable bonds most often used to finance sport facilities are private-placement bonds and asset-backed securitizations. Private-placement bonds are long-term, fixed-interest certificates issued by a non-municipal organization developing a sport facility to venture capitalists and other private lenders of funds. These bonds are secured by the total revenues generated by the sport facility. Asset-backed securitizations are similar to private-placement bonds, however only the most financially viable revenue streams are bundled into the bond offering (example – naming right sponsorships or luxury suites might be part of the asset-backed security whereas concessions and parking revenues revert directly to the facility).

On the other hand, municipal bonds are widely used to finance sport facilities. Municipal bonds are issued by a governmental agency, and the interest is tax exempt. There are a variety of bond options available under this category, either guaranteed or non-guaranteed. The most often used guaranteed bonds (also known as full-faith or credit obligations) in financing sport facilities are general obligation bonds and certificate of obligation. General obligation bonds are bonds that are repaid with a portion of the general property tax – also known as an ad valorem tax – and are backed by the full faith and credit of the issuing body (in most cases the jurisdiction). Certificates of obligation are bonds that are secured by unlimited claims on tax revenues. These types of bonds usually have a low interest rate, and are easily obtained through governmental sources because the issuance does not require approval by vote of the population.

A variety of non-guaranteed bonds are utilized for the financing of sport facilities including revenue bonds, certificates of participation, tax increment financing, special authority bonds, straight governmental appropriations, and public grants. Revenue bonds are backed exclusively from the revenue that accrues from the sport facility or associated revenue sources. Certificates of participation (COP) involve a jurisdiction purchasing the sport facility and leasing parts of the facility back to the general public or associated agencies. The revenue from those lease payments is then utilized to pay off the capital expenses for the sport facility. Tax-increment financing (TIF) is utilized when there is an area identified as needing some type of renewal or redevelopment. The jurisdiction freezes the tax base in that area until the development or renewal takes place, and then taxes are raised to pay off the TIF. Special authority bonds are financed through public organizations that have jurisdictional power outside the normal constraints of the government. This is most often used when the general public is against financing sport facilities, but the local government wants the sport facility built. So the jurisdiction uses these agencies, including power authorities, turnpike/roadway authorities, water works authorities, and other public works departments, to fund sport facilities through raised fees. Straight governmental appropriations is the setting aside of public funding from a municipality's budget for a specific purpose – such as financing a sport facility. Public grants to finance sport facilities are awards of financial assistance from a municipality to carry out a project of support or stimulation for the good of the public. This financing does not have to be repaid since it is technically not categorized as governmental assistance or individual loans.

In addition to these public funding options, there are other types of public sector contributions including the purchase of donated land; the funding of site improvements, parking garages, or surrounding infrastructure; direct equity invest-ments; and the construction of related facilities. Regardless of the source of funding, there are always questions as to whether public financing is appropriate for the use of sport facilities. These questions center on uncertainty by the public about whether available alternative sources of private financing should supersede the use of public financing, and the contention that the economic returns accruing from public investments do not necessarily equate to the initial investment in the sport facility. However, there are alternate sources of spillover benefits that justify these public subsidies as documented in Table 3.1.

Private sources of revenue

A sport facility cannot be financed solely from public sources. Sport businesses need to create sources of revenue to enhance the financing efforts for a sport facility. When we look at the traditional forms of obtaining revenue in business, we typi-cally look at donations of cash, gifts, in-kind contributions, bequests, endowments, trusts, and revenues from fundraising efforts. In sport facilities, there are numerous additional sources of revenue that play a crucial role as economic generators for a sport facility. Table 3.2 depicts these various revenue sources.

Public–private partnerships

Many times, to effectively finance sport facilities, there is a need for a relation-ship between municipalities and private entrepreneurs. The public sector has the authority to implement project funding through the governing process, while the private sector has the ability to contribute financing and management expertise in the area of sport facilities. While there are advantages to combining the funding and revenue resources as discussed in the previous two sections, there are two major challenges to facilitating a successful public–private partnership.

The first challenge is for public and private entities to understand, respect, and acknowledge the differences between each other, especially as related to value sys-tems and customer expectations. Public sector organizations exist to meet the need and wants of their target population as related to social benefits and outcomes. Private business look to maximize financial return and/or return on investments (i.e. be able to pay off their investors), and hence target their efforts to those who can provide the greatest opportunity to earn revenue and make a profit. There is a need within these types of partnerships to ensure that social and financial considerations are included in the decision making process related to financing for a sport facility.

The second challenge is the concern that each element of the partnership only looks out for itself – hence unfairly competing against each other through the part-nership. It is usually the public agency that must address this issue, as many private entities serve to help the public sector satisfy the needs of their constituents in areas they cannot provide service for.

Table 3.1 Spillover benefits justifying public subsidies

Increased community visibility	A professional sport facility often results in a significant increase in the amount of media coverage for the municipality in which it is located. It also keeps the community's name in front of regional, national, and sometimes even international/global audiences.
Enhanced community image	Many municipalities engage in place marketing, which strives to sell the image of a place so as to make it more attractive to businesses, tourists, and inhabitants. The omnipresent popularity of sport in the media has persuaded many municipalities to realize that sport facilities may be useful vehicles to enhance their image.
Making a 'major league city'	There is a lot of public interest in the belief that a municipality cannot be considered a 'major league city' or 'first-tier city' without a 'major league' sports team. As such, it is near impossible to have a 'major league' sports team without a quality sport facility. In many municipalities, the facility is seen as being indicative of their character and as defining the external perceptions of the city.
Loss of a major sports team	If a municipality loses a sports franchise, it may create the impression that local businesses and governmental officials are not supportive of the community, that the community is declining, and that its residents lack civic pride. Hence, if a municipality does not provide quality sport facilities, they may create a worse image for themselves than if they never had the teams or facilities at all.
Stimulation of other development	Municipalities believe that the investment in sport facilities will stimulate additional development and hence contribute to expansion of a city's tax base. There are three types of development to be addressed when financing a sport facility: Proximate development is utilized to stimulate economic development as part of an integrated redevelopment plan around the sport facility. Complementary development comes from the need to support the proximate development around the sport facility, either as a result of the municipality's desire to host a hallmark or mega event, or to upgrade the level of service near the sport facility (restaurants, bars, retail stores, etc.). General development goes beyond proximate and complementary development into the increased availability of public services including roadways and public transportation.
Psychic income	Psychic income is the emotional and psychological benefit residents of a municipality perceive they receive, even though they do not physically attend events at the facility, and are not involved in organizing them. Sport facilities are a medium through which cities and their residents express their personality, enhance their status, and promote their quality of life to a regional, national, and even international/global audience. This is often measured using the contingent valuation method (CVM), which places currency values on goods/services not exchanged in the marketplace.

Table 3.2 Private sources of revenue

Naming rights and sponsorships	The entitlement to name a sport facility (or a part thereof) in exchange for financial considerations.
Lease agreements/building rentals	The amount of money earned by the facility for its use, either by tenants (usually sport teams but may include outside vendors who can fill spaces not used by the sport facility for sports), outside travelling events (examples include concerts, WWE, and monster truck shows), and local events (municipal gatherings, graduations, corporate gathering etc.).
Advertising rights	The percentage of revenue earned by the facility for signage and other advertisements within the sport facility.
Luxury suites and corporate/private boxes	Yearly leases of specialized seating typically located near the middle section of the sport facility that allows the best view of events. Usually has glass paneling that can open to the playing area; includes amenities such as a bar, TVs, Wi-Fi, private seats, and a bathroom; catered food service; and private parking and entrances to the facility.
Preferred/premium/club seating	A level below luxury boxes, but offers special amenities above and beyond general admission seating, including private restaurants, lounge areas, and merchandise stands. The main difference is that the seating is not enclosed as with the luxury box – it is open-air similar to general admissions – hence this specialty seating provides the elements of both.
Permanent/personal seat licenses (PSLs)	PSLs (known as debentures in Europe) are a fee paid to buy tickets for a specific seat within a specific sport facility. PSLs are usually limited to those buying season tickets.
Ticket sales	The percentage a sport facility gets back for every ticket sold for events within the facility. A higher percentage comes back for tickets sold through the box office.
Concessionaire exclusivity/restaurant rights	Organizations purchase the sole rights for all concessions within a sport facility.
Concessions revenue	The percentage of revenue that comes back to the sport facility for all food service and merchandising sold within the facility.
Parking fees	The amount a sport facility makes for allowing parking at the facility, whether it is the full parking price minus expenses when management is kept in-house, or the percentage of the fee when parking management is outsourced.
Ancillary entertainment revenue	Revenue earned from extras within the stadium such as amusement parks, halls of fame, museums, and facility tours.

There are numerous models that have been created to articulate the various public–private partnerships evident in sport facility financing. The models used most often utilized are documented in Table 3.3.

Table 3.3 Public–private partnership models

Public sector leasing	This is the most common form of public–private sport facility partnership, where private entities pay a lease fee in order to use the publically funded and managed sport facility.
Leaseback agreements (private sector leasing)	Where a municipal agency uses a sport facility it has leased from a private owner.
Public sector takeovers	The seizing of a struggling or failing private sports facility should help in the effort to keep an existing sport asset within the municipality because without it the sport/entertainment opportunity would cease to exist in the area.
Private sector takeovers	Where a private organization takes over responsibility for operation of a sport facility owned by the public sector because the municipality either does not have the expertise or finance to appropriately manage/operate the facility.
Private pump-priming	Where a private entity uses its assets to force a public entity to invest in a sport facility project.
Multiparty arrangements	Where multiple financial partners initiate a complex agreement to finance the sport facility. These are usually seen in large-scale public–private sport partnerships, and are most often organized by independent quasi-governmental bodies that facilitate collaborative exchange between the various public and private entities involved with the project.

HISTORY OF SPORT FACILITY FINANCING

Prior to understanding the specific sources of financing, it is important to understand the history of financing for sport facilities. Generally, the period before 1960 can be referred to as the Period of Antiquity for sport facilities. During this period, the government was the primary source of funding for sport facilities – although there were still privately financed stadiums and arenas (but very few). Most of these sport facilities were funded through the government through general obligation bonds, where the repayment of the bonds came from the general property tax.

During the 1960s (1960–1969), there was the start of a transformation as to how sport facilities were funded. This Period of Growth was where municipalities started building sport facilities that focused on multipurpose use and unique architectural designs – some of which became 'cookie-cutter' in nature; similar designs repeated in numerous cities. From a financing standpoint, the money was still flowing from public sector funding through the government, however with the increase in need for funding the government started offering bonds secured through a multitude of hard (on the entire population) and soft (on targeted parts of the population) taxes.

The 1970s through 1983 saw significant public subsidy offered to sport facilities. This Period of Revitalization in sport facilities focused on building sport facilities in conjunction with improving the infrastructure of cities. As a result of the multipurpose function of financing, municipalities extended their public subsidies through more revenue bonds borne from taxes, continued the issuance of general obligation bonds from the general property tax, and enhanced both with annual appropriations from the government.

The Period of Discontinuance hit between 1984 and 1986. This was a significant time of change in the way in which sport facilities of the future would be financed. There were significant questions regarding the logic of dumping significant amounts of money into sport facilities when there were bigger economic and financial issues that needed to be addressed with governmental appropriations. In the United States, two laws were passed that had a direct effect on sport facility financing. The Deficit Reduction Act of 1984 mandated that because of the need to lower the national deficit, public funding of projects such as sport facilities were to be given a lower priority. This was followed up two years later by the Tax Reform Act of 1986, which significantly reduced the availability of tax exempt bonds for building sport facilities. Many other countries around the world followed this lead, exacting similar laws and regulations reducing the amount of public subsidy available for sport facility financing.

As a result, there was a need for change, and hence the period from 1986 to around 1995 is referred to as a Period of Change in sport facility financing. During this time, there was a transition from fully public financing to public–private partnerships, and there was some growth taking place in privatized facilities. The public–private partnerships that were indicative of this period involved public entities providing land, investment capital through debt or equity financing, some operating knowledge, and the ability to take on some of the risk associated with sport facilities. In turn, private entities paid taxes that resulted from facility operations and corporate guarantees, and also ushered in the introduction of alternative sources of revenue through luxury suites, premium seating, personal seat licenses, concessionaire rights, and naming rights.

Since 1995, sport facility financing has taken another shift into the Period of Partnerships, where the shift has gone to funding being provided by both private and public entities, and has extended into the running of sport facility operations. Since this era requires private owners to cover a percentage of the bill before governmental agencies will chip in, private entities are building new 'fully-loaded' stadia and arenas with amenities including restaurants, fan experiences, and technology; and infrastructural designs such as retractable roofs and retractable fields of play. The price tags for these new facilities are increasing exponentially, with new facilities opening in New York and Dallas in 2009 exceeding US $1 billion, and naming rights deals to help pay the private entities part of the bill around US $20 million per year over average terms of 20–30 years.

FUTURE TRENDS IN SPORT FACILITY FINANCING

So now that multi-billion dollar stadiums have been built in Dallas, New York, and the latest in San Francisco with the opening of Levi's Stadium for the NFL's San Francisco 49ers in 2014, what is next? Will there be a return to multipurpose facilities that can be justified by public subsidy? Perhaps total privatization of stadia and arena, with municipalities showing their support as corporate sponsors? How about corporate ownership of sport facilities – taking it out of the hands of municipalities and team owners? Could changes in technology affect how we watch the sport experience in the stadium/arena, and how spectators are viewed in the stadium by participants? How about a reduction in need of specialized seating, concessions, amenities, etc. (except for those deemed necessary for the participants to play), as a result of breakthroughs in technology such as through virtual fans that dial in from home and virtually sit in the stadium?

THE FUTURE OF SPORT FACILITY FINANCING INVESTMENT

As the economy and public outcry create a reduction in public subsidy, there are concerns of where facility financing will come from. From a professional sport facility standpoint, if a municipality balked at providing funding for a new facility, the professional team would threaten to move and the municipality would eventually come up with the money. One example in 2007 was when the owners of the NHL's Pittsburgh Penguins threatened to sell the team, and secured a new facility agreement only a few hours before they were set to be sold and leave for Kansas City. However, there is a shift in this trend in recent times. In 2008, the NBA's Seattle Supersonics and the City of Seattle could not come up with a viable solution to replace the aging Key Arena – so the team picked up and moved to Oklahoma City. Another example is when the NHL's New York Islanders could not secure a partnership for a new facility to replace the aging Nassau Veterans Memorial Coliseum; they opted to move in 2014 from that facility and Nassau County on Long Island to the Borough of Brooklyn in New York City and the new Barclays Center.

For smaller recreational and community sport facilities, the amount of public money available to construct these facilities has reduced significantly, and has resulted in private building of these types of complexes. However, with the increase in the privatization of sport facilities, the question is whether this

52

will trickle up to the professional level – i.e. fully privatized facilities with no governmental interaction. While the trends show less public involvement (and hence more private involvement), there does not seem to be a time in the near future that public subsidy totally disappears from sport facilities. Municipalities need to show support in their communities for sport – since a large majority of the population has an interest in some aspect of sport, recreation, and/or leisure. Tax dollars need to support the interests of the public that pays those taxes – however it is becoming abundantly clear that there is a cap to the spending recommended.

On the private side, it is possible that we are nearing an economic and financial cap. The money is not endless, and with shifts in the economic and financial climate globally, the amount corporations are willing to spend on naming rights may be reaching a crescendo. They are discovering other sponsorable products that offer the potential of a great return on investment and return on objectives. Hence facilities are trying to meet this shift with offering sponsorships and advertising on everything from turnstiles to steps in the arena, so that they can get more money from more sponsors at a lower cost per sponsor.

Suggested discussion topics

1 In these trying economic times, how would you justify to a municipality (both the elected officials and the taxpayers) to enter into a public–private partnership for a recreation or community sport facility?
2 Identify ten sponsorable non-traditional inventories within a professional sport arena or stadium (no naming or traditional signage rights), and explain how you would utilize those areas for a greater return on the infrastructure's investment without turning the facility into a mass of advertisements that distracts from the events.

There are numerous projections we can make here, however only time will tell what will come down the road and how the changes will have a direct effect on the financing of sport facilities in the 21st century and beyond. However, there are two areas that are projected to have a direct effect on the future of sport facility financing: (1) the emergence of the voluntary sector as an additional niche in the financing of sport facilities; and (2) as a result of the globalization of sport, the effects of currency values as related to international/global investments will be significant.

The influence of the voluntary sector

In years to come it is our view that the voluntary sector will have an increasingly important role to play in the provision of sport facilities for communities. The voluntary sector already owns and controls many facilities such as clubs, pitches, and club houses. Rather than public authorities taking additional risk in trying to provide facilities themselves, there is some logic in the strategy of incentivizing the voluntary sector to open its facilities for the benefit of the wider community. An obvious example is the use of club facilities for after school clubs and as resources for young people to use during school holidays. It is widely accepted that sport and the voluntary sector can be used to help deliver wider government agendas such as health improvements, community cohesion, reductions in delinquency, and improvements in educational attainment. It is therefore more cost effective to offer clubs financial contributions than it is to provide new facilities from scratch. Not only does this approach make sound commercial sense, there are also strategic benefits as well. The voluntary sector is more dynamic than government and can react quickly to changes in the external environment as it is not constrained by bureaucracy. The voluntary sector is also able to get closer to the customer than public authorities. Furthermore, the voluntary sector is capable of operating at lower cost than public authorities and is more able to attract funding from charities and lotteries. Thus for these reasons it is a win-win situation for public and voluntary bodies to work together closely. In an era when public money for investment in sport facilities will be increasingly scarce, there will be a strong business and environmental case to make best use of that which already exists before new facilities can be justified. Consequently, at community level the voluntary sector is likely to have an increasingly important role to play in helping to provide new sport facilities and wider community access to existing sports facilities.

Effect of currency value on international/global investments

The notion that sport is a global business is well illustrated by the fact that many high profile sports facilities are funded by international investors as well as domestic investors. Much of the debt that has been raised to support the development of the aforementioned Wembley Stadium in London is owed to German banks. The United Kingdom uses Sterling as its currency whereas Germany uses the Euro. The net effect of this situation is that if the two currencies fluctuate against each other, then one party will be better off than expected and the other worse off. For example, in 2009 Sterling (UK currency) had fallen from £1 being worth around €1.40 to €1.10 (Euros) – a fall of just over 20 percent. As discussed earlier the owners of Wembley Stadium paid £42.6m in interest in 2012. An adverse currency fluctuation of 20% would add around £8.5m per year to the company's interest charges and could make the difference between the company being viable or being in financial trouble. There are very few sport facilities that could take a financial hit of £8.5m without it having an adverse effect on the business whether this be cutting costs or having to stage more events to recover the deficit. In real life it is unlikely that such a stark situation would ever materialize. As part of Wembley Stadium's efforts to manage its financial risks it will have negotiated sources of mitigation such as fixed exchange rates or exchange rates that float between two agreed fixed points but not beyond something that would impact too unfavorably on one party. More advanced sources of mitigation might include the use of currency hedge funds and options. Now is not the time to explain what these financial instruments are. However, their existence and application in the financing of sport facilities serves to illustrate further the broad range of skills and knowledge that sports facility managers may be required to call upon throughout their careers.

CHAPTER REVIEW

Financing is defined as the act of obtaining or providing money or capital for the purchase of a business enterprise. Developing new sport facilities is a risky process that invariably requires complex financial arrangements, as it is unlikely that any organization from any sector will have the spare cash available to develop and build a sport facility from the outset of a project. It is therefore current practice that the financing of sport facilities tends to be made with financial contributions from a variety of sources. When borrowed money (or debt) is used to finance a development the stance of those borrowing the money is the belief that they can make sufficient profit to be able to service interest costs and still make a profit. For the providers of loans, the stance taken is that the interest being paid on the loans justifies the risk of lending to the developer. In practice the two parties' fates are inextricably linked – for everyone to get a fair return on their investment the development has to succeed.

Considerations around financing sport facilities are not confined to how much a building costs to construct in the first instance. For both buildings and equipment due consideration must be given to what are known as 'life-cycle costs', which are defined as the maintenance of physical asset cost records over the entire asset lives, so that decisions concerning the acquisition, use, or disposal of the assets can be made in a way that achieves the optimum asset usage at the lowest cost to the entity. The importance of being aware of life-cycle costing can be appreciated by the finding that as much as 90 percent of the lifetime costs attributable to an asset are determined by decisions made in the early part of the asset's life. The evidence that life-cycle costing for an asset is based on can be complicated as indicated in the range of considerations including purchase costs, running costs, maintenance costs, training costs, and decommissioning and disposal costs.

The justification for financing many sport facilities is often based on arguments made about the economic benefits that the development will have on the local community. For sport facilities there are five key areas in which positive economic benefits can be delivered – construction, employment, supply chains, local income, and events. The manner in which potential economic impacts are quantified is by the use of specially commissioned economic impact studies, which attempt to model the future economic impacts of a sport facility or to measure the actual economic impact of a facility or an event.

Financing of sport facilities comes in three basic forms – public financing, private funding, and public–private partnerships. Public funding of sport facilities comes from hard taxes, soft taxes, and bonds. Private funding comes from revenue created by sport businesses to enhance the financing efforts for a sport facility. Many times, to effectively finance sport facilities, there is a need for there to be a relationship between municipalities and private entrepreneurs. The public sector has the authority to implement project funding through the governing process, while the private sector has the ability to contribute financing and management expertise in the area of sport facilities.

Historically, the financing for sport facilities before 1960 was referred to as the Period of Antiquity, where the government was the primary source of funding for sport facilities through general obligation bonds funded from the general property tax. The Period of Growth in the 1960s saw municipalities build sport facilities that focused on multipurpose use and unique architectural designs – funding through the government was still provided via general obligation bonds. However with the continued increase of funding needed to build sport facilities, governments started offering bonds secured through a multitude of hard and soft taxes. The 1970s and early 1980s saw significant public subsidy offered to sport facilities during the Period of Revitalization in sport facilities, which focused on building sport facilities in conjunction with improving the infrastructure of cities. The Period of Discontinuance hit between 1984 and 1986. This was a significant time of change in the way in which sport facilities would be financed, and there were questions regarding the logic of dumping significant amounts of money into sport facilities when there were bigger economic and financial issues that needed to be addressed with governmental appropriations. As a result, there was a need for change, and hence the period from 1986 to around 1995 is referred to as a Period of Change in sport facility financing. During this time, there was a transition from fully public financing to public–private partnerships, and there was some growth taking place in privatized facilities. Since 1995, sport facility financing has taken another shift into the Period of Partnerships, where the shift has gone to funding being provided by both private and public entities, and has extended into the running of sport facility operations.

So what does the future hold for sport facility financing? Only time will tell. But we can safely project that economic issues affecting both public and private entities will be at the center of the discussion. In addition, the emergence of the voluntary sector as an additional niche in the financing of sport facilities, and the effects of currency values as related to international/global investments seem to be significant concerns related to the financing of sport facilities in the future.

BIBLIOGRAPHY

Baade, R. A. (2003). Evaluating subsidies for professional sports in the United States and Europe: A public-sector primer. *Oxford Review of Economic Policy, 19*(4), 585–597.

Baade, R. A. and Matheson, V. A. (2006). Have public finance principles been shut out in financing new stadiums for the NFL? *Public Finance and Management, 6*(3), 284–305,307–320.

Bovaird, T. (2007). Beyond engagement and participation: User and community coproduction of public services. *Public Administration Review, 67*(5), 846–860.

Chartered Institute of Management Accountants (2005). *CIMA's Official Terminology* (2nd ed.). London: CIMA.

Crompton, J. L. and Howard, D. R. (2013). Costs: The rest of the economic impact story. *Journal of Sport Management, 27*(5), 379–392.

deMause, N. and Cagan, J. (2008). *Field of schemes: How the great stadium swindle turns public money into private profit* (rev. ed.). Lincoln, NE: Nebraska Press.

Fried, G., DeSchriver, T. D., and Mondello, M. (2013). *Sport finance* (3rd ed.). Champaign, IL: Human Kinetics.

Greenberg, M. J. (2004a). Sports facility financing and development trends in the United States. *Marquette Sports Law Review, 15*(1), 93–173.

Greenberg, M. J. (2004b). The stadium game. In S. R. Rosner and K. L. Shropshire (Eds.). *The business of sports* (pp. 113–126). Sudbury, MA: Jones and Bartlett Publishers.

Howard, D. R. and Crompton, J. L. (2014). *Financing sport* (3rd ed.). Morgantown, WV: Fitness Information Technology.

Miller, W. S. (1998). Sport facility issues, part one. The boom in stadium construction and financing new facilities. *For The Record (Marquette University Law School), 9*(4), 7.

Misener, K. and Doherty, A. (2009). A case study of organizational capacity in nonprofit community sport. *Journal of Sport Management, 23*(4), 457–482.

Parkhouse, B. L. (2005). *The management of sport: Its foundation and application* (4th ed.). New York: McGraw-Hill Higher Education.

Propheter, G. (2012). Are basketball arenas catalysts of economic development? *Journal of Urban Affairs, 34*(4), 441–459.

Rebeggiani, L. (2006). Public vs. private spending for sports facilities – The case of Germany 2006. *Public Finance and Management, 6*(3), 395–424,429–435.

Rosentraub, M. and Swindell, D. (2009). Of devils and details: Bargaining for successful public/private partnerships between cities and sports teams. *Public Administration Quarterly, 33*(1), 118–148.

Santo, C. A. and Mildner, G. C. S. (2010). *Sport and public policy: Social, political, and economic perspectives.* Champaign, IL: Human Kinetics.

Sawyer, T. H. (2006). Financing facilities 101. *Journal of Health, Physical Education, Recreation, and Dance, 77*(4), 23–28.

Sawyer, T. H. (2013). *Facilities planning for health, fitness, physical activity, recreation and sports: Concepts and applications* (13th ed.). Champaign, IL: Sagamore Publishing.

Wembley National Stadium Limited (2012). *Report and financial statements.* Retrieved March 30, 2014 from: www.wembleystadium.com/~/media/Files/WNSL/WembleyStadium/Documents/WNSL%20Accounts%20Glossy%20FINAL%20-%2031%20December%202012.ashx

Interview with Dev Pathik, Founder and Chief Executive Officer, The Sports Facilities Advisory and The Sports Facilities Management

Please explain to the reader about your current position and what your responsibilities are.

I am the Founder and CEO of The Sports Facilities Advisory (SFA) and The Sports Facilities Management (SFM). The Sports Facility Advisory (SFA) is a sport center planning consultant. SFM is a sport center management company. Both companies assess feasibility, master plan entire community programs, produce funding documents, structure public–private partnerships, oversee new facility openings, and we manage and advise many of today's most notable community sport and recreation centers. Since 2003, SFA | SFM have become the preeminent resource for public and private clients seeking to plan, fund, open, and optimize indoor and outdoor recreation venues. From sports tourism and tournament style venues to community recreation – we are making a difference in communities around the world. In 2013 and 2014 alone, SFA | SFM opened 1.5 million square feet of indoor facilities and nearly 800 acres of outdoor complexes! In 2015, SFA | SFM client facilities will host more than 15 million visits.

Tell us a little about your track from your university years to get to the position you are in now.

My path was not linear. I was an adventure athlete and became passionate about team performance and expedition leadership. I earned my BA in psychology from the University of Maryland College Park and assumed I would go on to earn a PhD.

I worked in a group home for kids with very difficult family backgrounds and I began using my outdoor skills and counseling training with our kids. It was powerful. We helped kids overcome fear and experience moments of triumph. I knew then that adventure sports would always be a part of my career.

During a semester break I went on an Outward Bound Dogsledding Expedition and it was transformational for me. It was a study in teamwork, leadership, process, and motivation. All taking place in a beautiful and extremely cold environment.

I was hooked. I completed Wilderness rescue and first responder training and applied with Outward Bound. It was a perfect fit and I ascended quickly to become a lead instructor and eventually was trained to lead corporate expeditions that are designed to improve the way leadership teams approach adversity and teamwork. It was highly effective and powerful work and it was a very good match for my skill set. I learned how to take a group of people, a block of time ranging from a day to a week, set goals that are difficult but attainable, and develop a culture and communication norms that allowed team members to bring the very best of themselves to the mission. I also learned how to craft the experience in a way that let others shine.

I use those lessons now on a daily basis in my role as the senior-most leader of our organizations.

When I left Outward Bound, I eventually opened a 10 acre corporate team development center in Florida. We led powerful training programs for large corporate groups. That business grew quickly and I eventually sold my interest to open a consulting firm that helped corporations, universities, and private owners open their own leadership and team development centers. I was a leader to leadership development professionals. I loved this because I was able to have an impact through others.

We assessed market opportunity, wrote business plans, and helped our clients develop powerful curriculum and programs. The results were fantastic. We taught a lot of people how to grow successful leadership development and teambuilding businesses.

I got into the sport industry by request. As part of our work I was engaged to help a sport facility with the development of a corporate teambuilding center. It became a nearly instant success and other sport facilities began to call. It was clear that the sport facility and recreation center industry needed proper business planning and fresh ways to approach the markets they served.

In 2003 I launched SFA by building the brand, developing our website, and attending a few conferences. We have now provided planning, funding, opening, and management services to a portfolio of more than $4 billion in planned and operational facilities around the world.

What I know how to do is to see a vision, not give up on that vision, and enjoy the incredible experience of winning as a team.

What advice would you give to someone wanting to get into the field of sport facility operations management?

Do what you love and learn to listen to your instinct about people. Avoid cheaters of any kind. And from a business perspective – understand the numbers. That means understanding every aspect of the budget. Read facility budgets and let them tell you the story of the operation. If you can read a budget and understand how it translates into the mission of the operation – you will be leaps and bounds ahead of other potential candidates.

TECHNOLOGY NOW!

With over 35 years of experience, IMPLAN began creating economic impact modelling data by using an approach that is automated via a software program. Cities looking to attract a professional sport team will often commission an economic impact study to provide the evidence that it is a good idea to build a new stadium for the incoming team. IMPLAN has provided data to help government agencies and businesses – including sport facilities of all shapes and sizes – conduct studies and make decisions.

IMPLAN, which stands for **Im**pact Analysis for **Plan**ning, was initially developed for the United States Department of Agriculture Forestry Service as an economic impact modeling system. Over the years, the company has evolved to provide the most complete and precise United States Economic data to create accurate economic impact analysis documentation. IMPLAN promotes its data as being trusted, transparent, flexible, bias-free, and cost-effective.

In addition to United States data, IMPLAN also offers Organization for Economic Cooperation and Development (OECD) data for multiple countries around the world, and has the ability to collect and customize data for countries it does not have data for.

The most valuable resource is that when a company or individual client purchases a dataset from IMPLAN, they get a complementary version of the IMPLAN software (version 3.0 at print of this book). The software provides the user to conduct economic impact studies as a variety of complexity levels, ranging from locations, economic statuses, and industry-specific analyzes. Users can also look back through the supply chains to analyze impact in terms of production, employment, and taxes.

In the UK, UK Sport and its public sector partners commissioned eventIMPACTS (www.eventIMPACTS.com) to provide a free-to-use event evaluation framework. Built into eventIMPACTS is an economic impact calculator which allows event managers to input the details about their event and then receive an estimate of the event's likely economic impact. EventIMPACTS is highly regarded and can be trusted to deliver a credible, 'at least' estimate, which can be supported by an audit trail of evidence and reasonable assumptions.

Source: IMPLAN Group LLC (2014). Retrieved November 11, 2014 from http://implan.com

CHAPTER 4

CAPITAL INVESTMENT APPRAISAL

CHAPTER OUTLINE

- ▓ The purpose of capital investment appraisal (CIA)
- ▓ Raw data
- ▓ Traditional methods of CIA
- ▓ Modern methods of CIA
- ▓ Chapter review

CHAPTER OBJECTIVES

By now you should be quite clear that businesses face the twin challenges of making profits (the selling price is higher than the cost) and being able to pay their liabilities as they fall due (the business is well set to continue trading). To survive in the long term a business must reconcile these two fundamental require-ments. Before a sport facility can make any profits it will typically have to invest in fixed assets. If we take the case of a gym or fitness center this will often be the cost of a building and the purchase of gym equipment such as cardiovascular exercise machines and resistance equipment such as weights and benches. This type of expenditure is called capital investment. There is risk attached to capital expenditure because there may be a considerable time lag between incurring the expenditure and receiving a return on it from paying customers.

What are the thought processes that go through someone's head when they decide to open a new gym or to build a new sport stadium? One of the thoughts that bring these ideas to fruition is that by taking a calculated risk, often with borrowed money, they can make sufficient profit to meet their expenses and have enough left over to make the decision worthwhile. The key words in the previous sentence are 'calculated risk' and in this chapter we will demonstrate the techniques that are routinely used to calculate risks and thus to evaluate whether or not to invest in a particular project or not. Being responsible for capital investment decision making takes managerial responsibility to a whole new level and requires managers to have an entirely new set of skills to help support the decision making process. More often than not entrepreneurs do not have the cash required to fund capital expenditure themselves. To raise the money required means presenting a convincing business case to a supportive bank or supportive friends and family. Either way the entrepreneur is taking a risk with other people's money and there is a pressure and responsibility to pay it back, often with interest, that is, additional cost for the privilege of borrowing the money in the first place.

If we are developing an existing sport facility, for example refurbishing a gym, we are taking responsibility for other people's livelihoods. If our grand idea to take a rundown gym and upgrade it into a premium health and fitness spa does not work, we may find ourselves putting people out of work. Finally, as entrepreneurs we are taking a risk with our own careers. Why try to run a business which pays the bank back and keeps your staff in a job when there is nothing in it for you? In this chapter we will examine the techniques that are used to frame capital investment choices and the techniques that are used to evaluate such choices. Before progressing it is worth testing whether or not you understand capital investment decisions intuitively. If a close friend who you trusted asked to borrow $1,000, what two questions would you ask before deciding whether or not to lend the money? For those who get the basic principles intuitively, the two questions will be 'when do I get my money back?' and 'how much interest will you pay me?' If these were your questions, well done, the rest of the chapter will come easily to you. If not, there is still hope but you will have to sharpen up your sense of business acumen.

THE USA'S MOST EXPENSIVE SPORTS STADIA

MetLife Stadium, Home to the New York Giants and the New York Jets
(US$1.6 billion)
Yankee Stadium, Home to the New York Yankees (US$1.5 billion)
AT&T Stadium, Home to the Dallas Cowboys (US$1.15 billion)

With all three of these stadiums costing over US$1 billion, there is clear evidence of the enormous financial scale and risk attached to the facility management side of professional team sports in the USA. Where does the money come from to pay for these stadia, and what kind of financial performance do they need to achieve to be viable propositions? Happily these are not questions that have to be answered as you embark upon a career in sport facility management. However, the magnitude of the investment in these facilities gives an insight into the level of responsibility required by those who are involved in the decision making process. Somewhere along the line there will have been the involvement of people with capital investment appraisal skills. These are the people who subject the business cases for these stadia to detailed financial scrutiny and who make the case to banks, investors, and local authorities for funding. In this chapter, we look at the various principles involved in evaluating investment decisions – but on a much smaller scale. Use them consistently throughout your career and get them right, and in time it could well be you working on the next billion dollars plus stadium.

Suggested discussion questions

1   Think of a sport facility that you have used recently as a participant in active sport, such as a gym or a swimming pool and answer the questions below:
   a   Where did the money come from to pay for the construction of the facility?
   b   How long do you think it takes for the investors to see a return on their funds?
   c   How would you feel about taking a risk on this type of investment?
   d   When you embark on your career do you see yourself as an employee working for someone else, or as an entrepreneur taking business risks and hiring employees?
2   During the regular season NFL teams are guaranteed eight home matches, yet there are 365 days in a year. What else do stadium owners do to ensure that sufficient activity takes place to justify the investment in their facilities?

THE PURPOSE OF CAPITAL INVESTMENT APPRAISAL

Because of the risks involved with capital expenditure, capital investment appraisal (CIA) techniques have evolved to inform and underpin the decision making process. When we borrow money to fund a new project we need to know that we can afford to pay back the loan (or principal) as well as any interest we have to pay to service the loan. We also need to make sure that we do not run out of money and can pay our liabilities as they fall due. In this regard, CIA is concerned with the total investment needs of a project. When a gym is being constructed it will need staff to market it and sell memberships even though the facility is not yet open. Therefore money will also be required to fund these day-to-day expenses as well as the purchase of fixed assets. Regardless of how good our business ideas might seem to us, there is no guarantee that funders will see things in the same way. The reality is that funding for capital investment will be limited in supply relative to the demand for it and therefore will be rationed. This means that in practice only the most advantageous loans for the banks will be made, where advantageous is a function of the likelihood of being paid and the amount of interest that can be charged. It is therefore vitally important that those people looking to make capital investment decisions do so on the basis of a sound business case. This then brings us to the purpose of capital investment appraisal which can be described as comparing the cost of a project now (the investment) with the expected benefits (returns) that will accrue in the future. The chances are that you are reading this book because you have made a decision to invest in your education now, with the expectation that your future lifetime earnings will compensate for the time you took out to go to university and the fees you incurred in so doing. In short the purpose of CIA can be summarized as follows:

■ to test the financial viability of a project; and
■ to rank different projects so that limited funding is allocated to the best project.

The techniques described in this chapter are decision support techniques and not decision making techniques. There will always be an element of judgment required and there will also be non-financial considerations to factor in. For example, there are many instances in the United States where local authorities will invest in the construction of a new stadium to attract a professional team franchise. The stadium might never recover the costs that were invested into it. However, the prestige of having a franchise in their city plus the economic impact a professional team might bring to the city overrides the basic financial viability considerations. In this chapter we will focus primarily on financial viability and acknowledge that at times other factors may make a seemingly unviable project at face value viable in terms of the bigger picture. As you will see, there is a variety of capital investment appraisal techniques and the answers derived from them may be conflicting. One technique might say a project is worthwhile and another might contradict this. The proactive manager will gather as much information from different sources in order make as informed decisions as possible.

RAW DATA

Capital investment appraisal involves creating a scenario around an investment decision and then modeling the subsequent impacts of the decision. There is a recognized technique for laying out CIA data. We will use the data below to conduct CIA on a project whereby an entrepreneur decides to invest $250,000 in launching a new gym. If we assume that the building is leased and the majority of the investment is made on gym equipment, to populate our CIA tools we need to know the following:

1 the amount of investment required ($250,000);
2 the duration of the project in years (assume 5);
3 the cash inflows arising from trading, in this case gym memberships and other sales;
4 the cash outflows linked to the project such as interest to the bank and staff wages; and
5 any residual value left in the investment after the project end (assume the gym equipment has a resale value after five years of $25,000).

For items 3 and 4 in the list above, managers are required to produce detailed business plans to model the cash inflows and outflows that will occur. As an example, in year one, the manager might assume that the facility will sell 1,000 memberships at $175 which will provide a year one revenue of $175,000. Similarly the costs of running the gym might be $50,000 in year one. Taking all of the assumptions into account we can set the data up in a form suitable for CIA analysis as shown in Table 4.1

In essence what Table 4.1 does is to structure the assumptions so that we can cover the initial investment, with future net cash flows in order to derive a project lifetime surplus. Students often ask the question 'where does this data come from?' In real life, the cost for the gym equipment will come from inviting suppliers of gym equipment to tender for the right to supply you. When you receive their tenders you select what is known as the MEAT tender (MEAT stands for most economically advantageous tender). This could be the cheapest tender or it could be the one which offers the greatest all round value for money when factoring in after sales

Table 4.1 CIA data for gym example

	Inflows ($)	Outflows($)	Net Cash Flow ($)
Year 0 (Investment)		250,000	−250,000
Year 1	175,000	50,000	125,000
Year 2	175,000	50,000	125,000
Year 3	125,000	60,000	65,000
Year 4	200,000	70,000	130,000
Year 5	200,000	85,000	115,000
Residual value	25,000		25,000

service and residual value. The project duration of five years might be determined by the duration of the lease you have on the building, the length of time the bank will loan you money for, or the life expectancy of the equipment. The inflows and outflows for each year are the summary figures that fall out of the business planning processes in response to questions such as:

- How many customers will we be able to get?
- How much will they be willing to pay?
- How much revenue will this generate?
- How much will it cost to pay the interest on the loan?
- How much will it cost to rent the premises?
- How much will staff cost each week?
- How much are the total outgoings each year?
- How much will I get from the sale of the equipment in five years' time?

These are difficult questions because in effect you are trying to predict the future. However, using research data, prior experience, and intuition it is possible to model scenarios that provide a sense of what an investment might achieve. This modeling of the future provides yet more evidence as to how important considerations such as breakeven analysis and margin of safety are in helping to provide a reality check for businesses. The important point of note is that techniques like CIA must be underpinned by high-quality data to power your assumptions otherwise you face the age old problem of 'garbage in equals garbage out'.

Simply by looking at the data in Table 4.1 we can see that in the most basic terms it delivers a project lifetime surplus after having paid off the initial loan. In principle this is a positive finding, but how does CIA enable us to make an effective diagnosis of the data?

TRADITIONAL METHODS OF CIA

If you said that one of the questions you would ask of a friend who wanted to borrow $1,000 from you was 'when will I get my money back?', then you have demonstrated an intuitive grasp of the most basic CIA technique, the 'Payback Method'. Because of its simplicity it is no surprise that the payback method is the most widely used technique in CIA. It is simply a measure of how quickly a project will repay its initial capital investment, in our case $250,000 spent on gym equipment. Because the future is uncertain and there can be no guarantee that there will be any financial return, the speed with which projects repay their initial outlay is crucially important. Using our data in Table 4.1 we can add an extra column to compute the cumulative net cash flow (Table 4.2).

What we can see in Table 4.2 is that after an initial investment of $250,000 there is a net cash inflow of $125,000 in years one and two. This is sufficient for

Table 4.2 The payback method

	Inflows ($)	Outflows($)	Net cash flow ($)	Cumulative ($)
Year 0 (Investment)		250,000	−250,000	−250,000
Year 1	175,000	50,000	125,000	−125,000
Year 2	175,000	50,000	125,000	0
Year 3	125,000	60,000	65,000	65,000
Year 4	200,000	70,000	130,000	195,000
Year 5	200,000	85,000	115,000	310,000
Residual value	25,000		25,000	335,000
Projected lifetime surplus			335,000	

the cumulative balance to be $0 at the end of year two and at this point the project has broken even. That is to say, we have paid off the loan after having also paid our operating costs (outflows) from the revenue generated by trading activities. Thus our gym investment project has a two year payback period. Is this good, bad, or average? Without having criteria against which to make a judgment it is impossible to say. However, many entrepreneurs and businesses will have their own thresholds against which they judge projects. So for a business that works on a three year payback period, a two year payback would be a good outcome; whereas for a business that preferred a two year payback period it would be average performance. Where the payback method is particularly helpful is in enabling managers to make informed decisions about two or more projects that are competing for the same investment. If you had two projects that both required $250,000 in initial investment and one paid back in two years and the other paid back in three years, then all other things being equal the two year payback project would be the preferred option. This is because the investor would get their money back quicker and therefore the level of risk is reduced relative to the three year payback period. If you had $1,000 to lend, would you lend it to the person who pays you back in two months, or the person who pays back in three months? Relying on the payback method in isolation could however cause you to make some inappropriate decisions which in turn could lead to expensive mistakes. Consider the case of a competing project that also required a $250,000 investment and had the data profile shown in Table 4.3.

Just like the data in Table 4.2, the project in Table 4.3 has a payback period of two years. Using the payback method in isolation would cause these two projects to be ranked equally. We can tell just by looking at the data that our project in Table 4.2 is far superior to the project in Table 4.3. This is because the project in Table 4.3 ends in year two and has no project lifetime surplus. The payback method has its strengths but it also has its weaknesses and should not be used for CIA on its own.

67

Table 4.3 Alternative project competing for a $250,000 investment

	Inflows ($)	Outflows($)	Net cash flow ($)	Cumulative ($)
Year 0 (Investment)		250,000	-250,000	-250,000
Year 1	175,000	50,000	125,000	-125,000
Year 2	175,000	50,000	125,000	0
Year 3	0	0	0	0
Year 4	0	0	0	0
Year 5	0	0	0	0
Residual value	0		0	0
Projected lifetime surplus			0	
Pays back by the end of Year 2				

- Strengths of the payback method
  - It is simple to use and to understand particularly for people in the decision making process with little or no background in finance.
  - Many businesses suffer from cash flow problems and to alleviate these they require a speedy return of investment. The payback method focuses people's attention on the time in which a project repays its investment.
  - Where investment is risky, which is quite often the case in sport, payback may be highly appropriate. This is because the forecasts of cash flows in the early years of a project are likely to be more accurate than those in later years. By concentrating on the short term, payback reduces the risks attached to forecasting. In our gym example, the equipment could become obsolete in three years or a new competitor could open up which would completely undermine a five year business plan. However, if we break even after two years then these problems are not so severe.
- Weaknesses of the payback method
  - Payback stops at the breakeven point and does not recognize the overall return on the investment. It is clear that Table 4.2 is a better investment than Table 4.3 just by looking at the data, but payback would rank them evenly.
  - Payback ignores what is known as the 'time value of money'. What would you rather have: $1,000 now or $1,000 in a year's time? If your answer is 'now', you intuitively understand the time value of money in that the certainty of money now is preferable to the risk of the same amount of money at some point in the future.

68

Despite its limitations, payback is the most widely used method of CIA and most investors will have criteria about how quickly they would like to have their money back. Payback is often used as an initial filter for projects whereby those that do not meet an investor's basic repayment period will be rejected without further consideration because they are perceived to have too much risk attached to them. To overcome the limitations of payback other methods have been devised which help to provide a more rounded view of an investment and thereby enable better decision making. The first of these that we consider is known as the accounting rate of return or ARR.

The ARR will be discussed further in Chapter 9 when analyzing the accounts of businesses. One of the most important measures is the 'return on capital employed' percentage, which tells you how much a business is generating relative to the resources that are tied up in running the business. To put this into perspective if we had $250,000 to invest it would be fairly easy to go to a local bank, put the money on deposit, and in a year's time achieve a return of something like 3 percent i.e. we could withdraw our $250,000 plus a further $7,500 (3 percent) simply for keeping our money in the bank so that it can lend it to others. Part of the thinking that entrepreneurs go through is to evaluate the return on their investment relative to what they could get from a safe investment such as putting money on deposit in a bank. If you put your money in a bank, you do not have to do anything else like fitting out a gym or hiring staff, and your investment is very safe as it is almost unheard of that banks default on deposits. Therefore, if your return for taking a significant financial risk is no better than putting your money in a bank, then why bother running a business? Furthermore, the chances are that most business people start off by borrowing money because they do not have enough of their own. So now they are faced with having to pay the interest costs attached to a loan as well as the loan itself and still make a worthwhile return. As a result questions such as 'what kind of return will my business give me?' and 'how does this compare with putting my money in a safe investment like a bank?' are very important.

If a weakness of payback is that it does not consider the full life of a project and stops at the point at which an investment breaks even, then ARR provides a different perspective by focusing on the overall profitability of a project which is shown in Tables 4.2 and 4.3 as the project lifetime surplus. It follows that the higher the rate of ARR, the more profitable a project is thought to be and therefore it is, at least on paper, more attractive to an investor. There are different methods of calculating ARR although they are variations on a basic theme. The basic point of note is that if you were using it to compare more than one project, you would use exactly the same formula for ARR on each of the different projects.

If we re-use our raw data from Table 4.1, it is possible to provide an illustration of how an ARR calculation is made in practice (Table 4.4).

Table 4.4 ARR data

	Inflows ($)	Outflows($)	Net cash flow ($)
Year 0 (Investment)		250,000	-250,000
Year 1	175,000	50,000	125,000
Year 2	175,000	50,000	125,000
Year 3	125,000	60,000	65,000
Year 4	200,000	70,000	130,000
Year 5	200,000	85,000	115,000
Residual value	25,000		25,000
Projected lifetime surplus			335,000

Calculation of ARR involves a four step process as outlined below.

1 **Calculate the average yearly surplus of the project (or, the return)**
   Project lifetime surplus/Duration of project in years
   $335,000 / 5 years = $67,000 per year.

2 **Calculate the net investment**
   Initial investment – Residual value
   $250,000 – $25,000 = $225,000

3 **Calculate the average investment**
   (Net investment/2) + residual value
   This calculation is concerned with identifying the average amount of capital invested during the project's life. The initial capital of $250,000 is not tied up for the life of the project as we already know from the payback method that it is actually paid back after two years. Thus a basic average of the investment tied up in the gym is the net investment divided by two. The residual value is added back to the basic average because it was a part of the investment that was genuinely tied up for the full five year duration of the project.
   ($225,000 / 2) + $25,000 = $137,500

4 **Calculate the annual rate of return (ARR)**
   Average yearly surplus (1 above)/Average investment (3 above)
   $67,000 per year / $137,500 average investment = 48.7%

With an annual rate of return of 48.7 percent the investment in the gym is much greater than could ever be achieved via a safe investment like a bank deposit account. The high return is the reward for taking a risk and being prepared to do the hard work to make a business idea a reality. Although the ARR looks at the full life of an investment, it does not address the issue of the time value of money. Clearly,

70

a four stage process to calculate ARR makes it mathematically more complex than payback and therefore less intuitive for untrained managers to grasp as a concept. This is because the end result of an ARR calculation is a percentage, and it is not possible to distinguish between the scales of the projects. For example in our gym example the gym owner is achieving a return of 48.7 percent from profits of $67,000 per year. A sport stadium might deliver profits of $6.7m per year which is equivalent to say a 10 percent return on investment. Unless we took the scale of a project into account, there is a danger that we favor a return of $67,000 per year over $6.7m per year because the former has a higher ARR. Furthermore, because of variations in the way in which the calculation of ARR can be made, it is a technique which is of only limited usefulness. Payback and ARR are said to be traditional methods of capital investment appraisal because they do not account for the time value of money. This weakness in both methods is addressed in the next section when we look at modern methods of CIA which overcome some of the drawbacks of payback and ARR.

MODERN METHODS OF CIA

Capital expenditure decisions involve committing resources to projects with no certain return (unlike bank deposits) for many years. The traditional CIA methods we have reviewed thus far, payback and accounting rate of return, use actual cash flows and do not take into account the time value of money. In our raw data the investment in the gym generates a net cash flow of $125,000 in both year one and year two. To understand the relevance of the time value of money, ask yourself the question 'what is better: $125,000 in a year's time or $125,000 in two years' time?' Most people will intuitively realize that $125,000 in a year's time is better than the same amount in two years' time because if we have the money sooner rather than later we can put it to work either in a safe investment like a bank or in some other business project. In reality when we are making capital expenditure decisions that involve cash flows that relate to years ahead in the future we need to take into account interest rates. Most adults will readily identify with the concept of interest rates because they affect how much we pay on our mortgages when buying a house, or how much we pay in interest on credit cards if we do not settle our accounts in full every month. The methods involved in allowing for the time value of money are compounding and discounting. It is discounting that is used in CIA but it helps to understand compounding first. Compounding or compound interest is concerned with calculating the future value of a sum of money today at a given rate of interest. The technique is called compounding because the value of the investment increases over time as interest is earned on top of interest (i.e. interest is compounded). This point is best illustrated with an example. If our gym owner had $250,000 to invest and put it on deposit for a year at 3 percent interest, at the end of the year the initial investment would have grown to $257,500 i.e. $250,000 + $7,500 (or 3 percent). If the investment was placed on deposit for a second year, the amount invested would now be $257,500 and 3 percent of this would be $7,725 giving a closing value at the end of year two of $265,225. The interest earned in year two is $225 more than in year one because the interest from year one has itself earned interest in year two. In contrast to compounding, discounting is concerned with converting money earned in the future to today's value, or as it is more commonly known, the 'present value'. If compounding is concerned with calculating the future value of money invested today, discounting is concerned with calculating the present value of receiving money in the future. If we bought goods with a discount we would be getting them for less than their face value. So too the promise of money in the future is worth less than money now, so we discount future cash flows to a present value. The relationship between discounting and compounding can be seen in Table 4.5.

Table 4.5 Compounding and discounting

PRESENT VALUE
(Day 1)

$250,000 $250,000

COMPOUNDS TO ↓   DISCOUNTS TO ↑

FUTURE VALUE
(After 2 Years at 3%)

$265,225 $265,225

After two years with interest rates of 3 percent, $250,000 is worth $265,225 and by the same logic $265,225 in two years' time is worth the same as $250,000 today, which is demonstrated long hand below.

Compounding
   $250,000 x 1.03 x 1.03 = $265,225
   or
   $250,000 x 1.0609 = $265,225 (note 1.0609 is derived from 1.03 x 1.03)

Discounting
   $265,225 ÷ 1.03 = $257,500 and
   $257,500 ÷ 1.03 = $250,000
   or
   $265,225 x 0.9425 = $250,000 (note 0.9425 is derived from 1 ÷ (1.03 x 1.03)

In practice we source compounding and discounting factors from pre-prepared tables or from spreadsheets. As an appendix to this chapter there is list of discount

72

factors from 0–25 years and from 0–25 percent interest. For a large scale project such as a sports stadium it is salutary to note that $1,000 in 20 years' time, assuming interest rates of 10 percent, is worth just $149 now, i.e. discount factor = 0.149. Take the time to look this factor up for yourself in the appendix. Find the row for 20 years and run your finger along the columns of interest rates until you come to the intersection between 20 years and 10 percent. You will see the factor is 0.149, which is the value we multiply cash received in 20 years' time by in order to convert it into today's value if interest rates were 10 percent.

The first method of CIA using discounting is called the net present value (NPV) where all future cash flows are discounted to today's value (the time at which we make the investment). The purpose of this exercise is to see whether or not the investment is viable when we allow for the fact that future cash flows are not worth as much as cash in the hand now. Using our $250,000 investment in a gym example and assuming interest rates of 10 percent we can model the NPV of the project as shown in Table 4.6.

Table 4.6 Net present value calculation assuming interest rates of 10%

	Inflows ($)	Outflows($)	Net cash flow ($)	Discount factor (10%)	Present value
Year 0 (Investment)		250,000	−250,000	1.000	−250,000
Year 1	175,000	50,000	125,000	0.909	113,625
Year 2	175,000	50,000	125,000	0.826	103,250
Year 3	125,000	60,000	65,000	0.751	48,815
Year 4	200,000	70,000	130,000	0.683	88,790
Year 5	200,000	85,000	115,000	0.621	71,415
Residual value	25,000		25,000	0.621	15,525
Projected lifetime surplus			335,000	Net present value = 191,420	

When we allow for the time value of money with interest rates of 10 percent, the gym investment has a net present value of $191,420 which, although positive, is considerably less than the project lifetime surplus of $335,000 calculated earlier which does not take into account the time value of money. However, so long as a project returns a positive NPV it means that the investment is worthwhile at the level of interest specified. Thus in our case if the gym owner could borrow $250,000 at an interest rate of 10 percent he or she could be confident that they could service the bank loan. The net present value method is useful for appraising single projects and also multiple projects that are competing for the same capital funds. Where there is competition for funds, technically the best option is the project with the highest NPV and this even includes investments which have different durations. The main problem with discounting is that for some people it is too complex a skill to master, particularly for those with limited or no financial training. For those who do understand the basic principles, the mechanics of producing a discounted cash flow forecast as in Table 4.6 are quite straightforward. What is more difficult is being able to choose meaningful interest rates and discount factors for some time in the future. As an example of how hard it can be to model future interest rates, do you know what the interest rate will be on your credit card in three years' time? There is also the added problem of the reliability of the assumptions upon which the calculations are based. It is quite easy to assume that a gym can recruit 1,000 members at $175 per year and thereby generate revenue of $175,000, but if this does not happen or if running costs are higher than expected then the apparent simplicity of CIA models is undermined by the quality of the data upon which they are based.

Uncertainty over interest rates and their discount rates gives rise to a second modern method of CIA, known as the internal rate of return (IRR). The IRR poses the simple question: at what rate of interest would the net present value of a particular project be equal to $0? If we cannot predict interest rates with any degree of accuracy, then the next best thing is to know the range of interest rates at which a project is still viable. In our gym example we know that with interest rates at 10 percent the investment is viable because there is a positive NPV, but at what rate of interest does the project in effect break even? This line of thinking is another form of sensitivity analysis which we will look at in the operational decision making chapter (Chapter 9). So in this case, how sensitive is the project to variations in interest rates? One straightforward method is simply to use trial and error, or what is also known as the iterative method. What this means is that you simply experiment with a range of interest rate values until you get as reasonably close to $0 as possible. So we know that at 10 percent the NPV is positive so it follows that the IRR will be higher than this. We also know that the accounting rate of return is 48.7 percent (see previous section of the chapter) and because this is based on the project lifetime surplus and is not discounted, then the IRR must be lower than this value. So in broad terms we are working on a range of between more than 10 percent and less than 48.7 percent. We could narrow this range down by experimenting with say 30 percent as shown in Table 4.7.

At 30 percent the NPV reduces to $32,860 which means that the project is still viable and therefore the IRR must be even higher than 30 percent. In practice, we can use a spreadsheet to experiment with different rates and there is even an IRR function built into Excel which will do the job automatically. If we went as high as 40 percent we would get a negative NPV (-$13,380) which now tells us that we are looking for a figure somewhere between 30 percent and 40 percent. It is possible to plot the various iterations of NPV on a graph and to work out the IRR by finding the point at which the line for NPV crosses the interest rate axis as shown in Figure 4.1.

In Figure 4.1 we can see that NPV is positive for all interest rates up to 35 percent and negative at 40 percent. The NPV line crosses the x axis at around 37 percent and we can confirm this using further iterations with the actual interest rate at which NPV = $0 being 36.8 percent as shown in Table 4.8.

74

Table 4.7 Iterative method to deriving IRR

	Inflows ($)	Outflows ($)	Net cash flow ($)	Discount factor (10%)	Present value
Year 0 (Investment)		250,000	−250,000	1.000	−250,000
Year 1	175,000	50,000	125,000	0.769	96,125
Year 2	175,000	50,000	125,000	0.592	74,000
Year 3	125,000	60,000	65,000	0.455	29,575
Year 4	200,000	70,000	130,000	0.350	45,500
Year 5	200,000	85,000	115,000	0.269	30,935
Residual value	25,000		25,000	0.269	6,725
Projected lifetime surplus			335,000	*Net present value* = 32,860

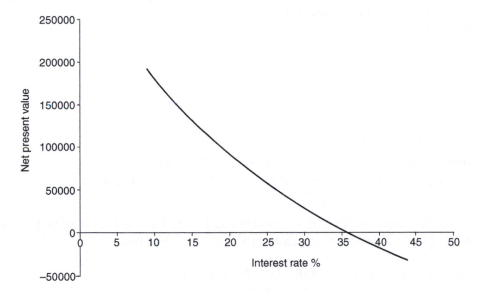

Figure 4.1 IRR represented graphically

Any project which has an IRR greater than the cost of the finance being borrowed to fund it is worth investing in. In our case, the gym owner has borrowed $250,000 to invest in equipping a gym at 10 percent and this rate of interest could increase to 36.8 percent before the NPV became negative. For the owner this is comforting news and enables him or her to worry about selling the targeted number of memberships rather than interest rates.

75

Table 4.8 The IRR = the point at which NPV = $0

	Inflows ($)	Outflows ($)	Net cash flow ($)	Discount factor (10%)	Present value
Year 0 (Investment)		250,000	-250,000	1.000	-250,000
Year 1	175,000	50,000	125,000	0.731	91,390
Year 2	175,000	50,000	125,000	0.535	66,817
Year 3	125,000	60,000	65,000	0.391	25,403
Year 4	200,000	70,000	130,000	0.286	37,145
Year 5	200,000	85,000	115,000	0.209	24,024
Residual value	25,000		25,000	0.209	5,223
Projected lifetime surplus			335,000	Net present value = 0	

The four CIA methods we have looked at in this chapter have limitations when used in isolation, but when they are pulled together it gives our gym owner some powerful information with which to support the decision to invest or not as shown in Table 4.9.

Table 4.9 Summary of CIA analysis $250,000 investment in a gym

Method	Score	Source of evidence
Payback	2 Years	Table 4.2
Accounting rate of return	48.7%	4 step process below Table 4.4
Net present value	+$191,420	Table 4.6
Internal rate of return	36.8%	Figure 4.1 and Table 4.8

Assuming the forecasts of income generated and costs incurred are correct, then we are looking at an investment which has the following features:

- Will be paid back in full at the end of two years.
- Has an accounting rate of return of 48.7 percent, which compares very favorably with return on capital employed calculations for conventional businesses.
- Has a positive net present value of $191,498 when interest rates are at 10 percent.
- Has an internal rate of return of 36.8 percent.

These are precisely the sort of details that lenders of finance wish to see when they are approached by entrepreneurs. Investors can get their money back quickly; the gym generates returns that are way in excess of safe investments such as bank deposits; and with an IRR the project is resilient to huge increases in interest rates. Anyone looking at a business proposal with this financial performance would be persuaded

76

that it is a good business proposition assuming the underlying assumptions were accurate. The argument is far more compelling than somebody walking in off the street and saying to an investor 'I am a health and fitness enthusiast and I think I can make some money running a gym, so please lend me $250,000'. What our examples demonstrate is that when making decisions about capital expenditure it pays to underpin the decision making process with as much supporting information as possible. By conducting the full range of capital investment appraisal techniques at your disposal rather than relying solely on say payback, you enable decisions to be made from a far more rounded perspective. Having gone through this process the gym owner can be in no doubt that the figures 'stack up' from an investment angle; the challenge is to deliver on the assumptions that underpin the business model.

Where the techniques become particularly powerful is in appraising proposed investments that are competing for the same money. If an investor has $250,000 to lend and there are three competing projects for the money, then CIA really comes into its own. This point can be appreciated by looking at a situation where there are three proposals for $250,000 from a tennis club, a sports retailer, and a swimming pool operator. The summary data for each project is shown in Table 4.10.

Table 4.10 CIA of three competing projects

	Tennis club	Sports retailer	Pool operator
Payback	2 years	3 years	4 years
ARR	25%	20%	17%
NPV @ 10%	+$69,730	+$62,190	+$58,400
IRR	22%	16%	13%

Faced with the data in Table 4.10 and only being able to fund one project, which one represents the best option for an investor? The tennis club repays its investment in two years and has a positive NPV which is also the highest NPV and the highest IRR. It is ranked highest on all of the CIA measures and would be the first to be funded. The sport retailer represents the second best option and the pool operator the third best option. There is always a surplus of demand for investment funds over the availability of the supply of such funds and thus it is a competitive process. What CIA has done in this instance is produce directly comparable measures for three different projects that enable them to be compared on a like-for-like basis in financial terms. The recommendation to support the investment in the tennis club is correct theoretically; it 'works' commercially; and it is the direct consequence of an objective process of evaluation. Used correctly, CIA is a powerful tool to help managers make decisions that involves taking calculated risks with large sums of money and which may have a significant impact on the future health of a business. Under these conditions managers need all of the help they can get, and being conversant in the principles of CIA is an important first step in getting that help.

CHAPTER REVIEW

The key point of note in this chapter is that when we make capital expenditure on fixed assets such as a stadium or equipment, there will be a time delay between us making the investment and it providing a return. There is therefore a degree of risk attached to capital expenditure because once your money has gone it is gone and whatever you have spent it on that has to generate a return for you. So in practice there are two sets of risks: first, the delay between spending your money and getting a return; and, second, whether or not the return received is sufficient to justify the investment in the first place. The purpose of capital investment appraisal can be summarized as being to test the financial viability of a project; and to rank different projects so that limited funding is allocated to the best project. What we are trying to do with CIA is to model the future and this is not certain. There is the risk that an investment may cost more than planned; there is the risk that the forecasts on which future income generation is based are too optimistic; and there is the risk that interest rates might change and damage the viability of a project. What CIA does is to provide a set of tools that enable us to evaluate the anticipated outcomes of capital expenditure and to enable us to then make a decision as to whether the likely returns outweigh the risks.

The simplest and most commonly used method is payback, which simply poses the question, 'how long does it take for the investment to be repaid?' It is an intuitive, easily understood method to which most people can relate. The key problem with the traditional measures of CIA such as payback and ARR is that they do not taken into account the time value of money, notably that projected future cash flows are not worth the same as the same amount of money today. Given a choice, most people would take $1,000 today rather than the same amount in a year's time, because they perceive (quite rightly) that $1,000 in a year's time is worth less than $1,000 now. The differential between money now and money in the future is called a discount and is determined by the prevailing rate of interest.

For long-term projects during periods of high interest rates, $1,000 now might be worth less than $150 in 20 years' time. To recognize this time value of money we use discount factors to produce the net present value and the internal rate of return. The net present value converts all future cash flows into their equivalent value today to test whether an investment is viable using this more demanding test relative to payback and ARR. Interest rates are rarely certain and will often fluctuate. Managers therefore need to know the range of interest rates within which an investment is viable. IRR identifies the interest rate at which the net present value is $0, or in effect, the breakeven point.

Where CIA is at its most powerful is when all of the techniques are used in combination to look at a single investment from a variety of perspectives or to rank different projects competing for the same funding. Getting involved in capital investment decisions represent some of the greatest responsibility and excitement

78

you will get in a career as a sport facility manager. The opportunity to work on capital projects is the domain of the few and they will inevitably have well-developed capital investment appraisal skills.

BIBLIOGRAPHY

Beech, J. and Chadwick, S. (Eds.) (2004). *The business of sport management*. Essex, UK: Prentice Hall Financial Times.

Emery, P. (2011). *The sports management toolkit*. Oxford, UK: Routledge.

Fried, G., DeSchriver, T., and Mondello, M. (2013). *Sport finance*. Illinois, USA: Human Kinetics.

Russell, D., Patel, A., and Wilkinson-Riddle, G. J. (2002). *Cost accounting: An essential guide*. London: Pearson Educational Ltd.

Tilley, C. and Whitehouse, J. (1992). *Finance and leisure*. London: ILAM/Longman.

Wilson, R. (2011) *Managing sport finance*. Oxford, UK: Routledge.

IN THE FIELD ...

Interview with Matt Whitaker, Business Manager, Hallamshire Tennis and Squash Club

Please explain to the reader about your current position and what your responsibilities are.

I am basically responsible for everything. I am in charge of the day-to-day operations of the Hallamshire Tennis and Squash Club, with the Board looking after Club policy. My role covers everything from organising work rotas, staff training, health and safety, human resource management, dealing with new suppliers, managing club refurbishments, preparing budgets, and so on. We have 25 employed members of staff, with another 15 self-employed tennis or squash coaches who work out of the Club.

Tell us a little about your track from your university years to get to the position you are in now.

I was fortunate that while studying Sport Science at Teesside University, the University funded me and three others to complete our tennis coaching qualifications. Shortly afterwards a new David Lloyd Racquets and Fitness Club opened nearby and I started working for them as a tennis coach. After five years I had progressed to Racquets Manager (more of an administration role) and then Sports Manager (totally off court), which included swimming programmes and the gym team.

Due to relocation, I moved to Canons Health & Fitness Club as Assistant General Manager, and then onto DC Leisure as a Contract Sales Manager looking after new membership sales in four new Leisure Clubs. When I saw the Business Manager role at the Hallamshire advertised, I thought it pulled together all the experience I had gained, and provided the opportunity to work in an iconic club.

What advice would you give to someone wanting to get into the field of sport facility operations management?

The advice I would give for anyone looking to work in this field would be to take on as many possible, diverse areas as possible. I have looked after physical training, beauty salons, hairdressers, spa treatments, cafe bars etc. ... not all of which are my area of expertise. You will never know when experience you have gained from years past will help you in the future.

TECHNOLOGY NOW!

The Hallamshire Tennis and Squash Club in the leafy suburbs of Sheffield, England is the club which boasts 2012 Wimbledon doubles tennis champion Jonny Marray and World Squash Champion Nick Matthew amongst its members. In addition to these elite performers, it also serves some 2,000 people in the local community who make use of the 12 tennis courts, 9 squash courts, gym, and social facilities. In 2013, the club was awarded a grant of £177,000 by Sport England, the lead sport development agency for England, as a contribution towards capital works that will help to reduce the club's environmental impact.

This grant funding will help the Club to complete a range of improvements and derive resulting benefits as shown in the table below.

Improvement	Benefits
Installation of a more efficient boiler system and radiators	Lower energy consumption, lower costs, and fewer carbon emissions
Replacement of six squash floors	Will enable removal of old inefficient heaters
Air conditioning to the gym	Better and more consistent customer experience
Replacement saunas for both the male and female changing rooms	Lower running costs

Improvement	Benefits
All lighting to squash courts and viewing areas to be replaced by LED lights	Better lighting, lower energy costs, and reduced bulb replacement costs
All lighting to tennis courts to be replaced by LED lights	Better lighting, lower energy costs, and reduced bulb replacement costs

The list of improvements and benefits will help to reduce the club's environmental impact by replacing old equipment with new more energy efficient alternatives. At the same time, there will also be improvements in the customer experience and a reduction in the club's future expenditure. This in turn will help the club to generate surpluses in the future and to keep costs down for the members. An intelligent approach to sport facility management such as this shows that capital investment is not solely confined to large scale projects like building AT&T stadium in Dallas. In addition to understanding the basics of capital investment appraisal the club's Business Manager Matt Whitaker also knows how to write a persuasive business case, as his application for the £177,000 grant was one of just 23 successful bids from a total of 350.

Source: Hallamshire Tennis and Squash Club (2014). Retrieved October 28, 2014 from: www.hallamshiretennis.co.uk

Years	0%	1%	2%	3%	4%	5%	6%	7%	8%	9%	10%	11%
						Discount rates						
0	1.000	1.000	1.000	1.000	1.000	1.000	1.000	1.000	1.000	1.000	1.000	1.000
1	1.000	0.990	0.980	0.971	0.962	0.952	0.943	0.935	0.926	0.917	0.909	0.901
2	1.000	0.980	0.961	0.943	0.925	0.907	0.890	0.873	0.857	0.842	0.826	0.812
3	1.000	0.971	0.942	0.915	0.889	0.764	0.840	0.816	0.794	0.772	0.751	0.731
4	1.000	0.961	0.924	0.888	0.855	0.823	0.792	0.763	0.735	0.708	0.683	0.659
5	1.000	0.951	0.906	0.863	0.822	0.784	0.747	0.713	0.681	0.650	0.621	0.593
6	1.000	0.942	0.888	0.837	0.790	0.746	0.705	0.666	0.630	0.596	0.564	0.535
7	1.000	0.933	0.871	0.813	0.760	0.711	0.665	0.623	0.583	0.547	0.513	0.482
8	1.000	0.923	0.853	0.789	0.731	0.677	0.627	0.582	0.540	0.502	0.467	0.434
9	1.000	0.914	0.837	0.766	0.703	0.645	0.592	0.544	0.500	0.460	0.424	0.391
10	1.000	0.905	0.820	0.744	0.676	0.614	0.558	0.508	0.463	0.422	0.386	0.352
11	1.000	0.896	0.804	0.722	0.650	0.585	0.527	0.475	0.429	0.388	0.350	0.317
12	1.000	0.887	0.788	0.701	0.625	0.557	0.497	0.444	0.397	0.356	0.319	0.286
13	1.000	0.879	0.773	0.681	0.601	0.530	0.469	0.415	0.368	0.326	0.290	0.258
14	1.000	0.870	0.758	0.661	0.577	0.505	0.442	0.388	0.340	0.299	0.263	0.232
15	1.000	0.861	0.743	0.642	0.555	0.481	0.417	0.362	0.315	0.275	0.239	0.209
16	1.000	0.853	0.728	0.623	0.534	0.458	0.394	0.339	0.292	0.252	0.218	0.188
17	1.000	0.844	0.714	0.605	0.513	0.436	0.371	0.317	0.270	0.231	0.198	0.170
18	1.000	0.836	0.700	0.587	0.494	0.416	0.350	0.296	0.250	0.212	0.180	0.153
19	1.000	0.828	0.686	0.570	0.475	0.396	0.331	0.277	0.232	0.194	0.164	0.138
20	1.000	0.820	0.673	0.554	0.456	0.377	0.312	0.258	0.215	0.178	0.149	0.124
21	1.000	0.811	0.660	0.538	0.439	0.359	0.294	0.242	0.199	0.164	0.135	0.112
22	1.000	0.803	0.647	0.522	0.422	0.342	0.278	0.226	0.184	0.150	0.123	0.101
23	1.000	0.795	0.634	0.507	0.406	0.326	0.262	0.211	0.170	0.138	0.112	0.091
24	1.000	0.788	0.622	0.492	0.390	0.310	0.247	0.197	0.158	0.126	0.102	0.082
25	1.000	0.780	0.610	0.478	0.375	0.295	0.233	0.184	0.146	0.116	0.092	0.074

						Discount rates							
12%	13%	14%	15%	16%	17%	18%	19%	20%	21%	22%	23%	24%	25%
1.000	1.000	1.000	1.000	1.000	1.000	1.000	1.000	1.000	1.000	1.000	1.000	1.000	1.000
0.893	0.885	0.877	0.870	0.862	0.855	0.847	0.840	0.833	0.826	0.820	0.813	0.806	0.800
0.797	0.783	0.769	0.756	0.743	0.731	0.718	0.706	0.694	0.683	0.672	0.661	0.650	0.640
0.712	0.693	0.675	0.658	0.641	0.624	0.609	0.593	0.579	0.564	0.551	0.537	0.524	0.512
0.636	0.613	0.592	0.572	0.552	0.534	0.516	0.499	0.482	0.467	0.451	0.437	0.423	0.410
0.567	0.543	0.519	0.497	0.476	0.456	0.437	0.419	0.402	0.386	0.370	0.355	0.341	0.328
0.507	0.480	0.456	0.432	0.410	0.390	0.370	0.352	0.335	0.319	0.303	0.289	0.275	0.210
0.452	0.425	0.400	0.376	0.354	0.333	0.314	0.296	0.279	0.263	0.249	0.235	0.222	0.210
0.404	0.376	0.351	0.327	0.305	0.285	0.266	0.249	0.233	0.218	0.204	0.191	0.179	0.168
0.361	0.333	0.308	0.284	0.263	0.243	0.225	0.209	0.194	0.180	0.167	0.155	0.144	0.134
0.322	0.295	0.270	0.247	0.227	0.208	0.191	0.176	0.162	0.149	0.137	0.126	0.116	0.107
0.287	0.261	0.237	0.215	0.195	0.178	0.162	0.148	0.135	0.123	0.112	3.103	0.094	0.086
0.257	0.231	0.208	0.187	0.168	0.152	0.137	0.124	0.112	0.102	0.092	0.083	0.076	0.069
0.229	0.204	0.182	0.163	0.145	0.130	0.116	0.104	0.093	0.084	0.075	0.068	0.061	0.055
0.205	0.181	0.160	0.141	0.125	0.111	0.099	0.088	0.078	0.069	0.062	0.055	0.049	0.044
0.183	0.160	0.140	0.123	0.108	0.095	0.084	0.074	0.065	0.057	0.051	0.045	0.040	0.035
0.163	0.141	0.123	0.107	0.093	0.081	0.071	0.062	0.054	0.047	0.042	0.036	0.032	0.028
0.146	0.125	1.108	0.093	0.080	0.069	0.060	0.052	0.045	0.039	0.034	0.030	0.026	0.023
0.130	0.111	0.095	0.081	0.069	0.059	0.051	0.044	0.038	0.032	0.028	0.024	0.021	0.018
0.116	0.098	0.083	0.070	0.060	0.051	0.043	0.037	0.031	0.027	0.023	0.020	0.017	0.014
0.104	0.087	0.073	0.061	0.051	0.043	0.037	0.031	0.026	0.022	0.019	0.016	0.014	0.012
0.093	0.077	0.064	0.053	0.044	0.037	0.031	0.026	0.022	0.018	0.015	0.013	0.011	0.009
0.083	0.068	0.056	0.046	0.038	0.032	0.026	0.022	0.018	0.015	0.013	0.011	0.009	0.007
0.074	0.060	0.049	0.040	0.033	0.027	0.022	0.018	0.015	0.012	0.010	0.009	0.007	0.006
0.066	0.053	0.043	0.035	0.028	0.023	0.019	0.015	0.013	0.010	0.008	0.007	0.006	0.005
0.059	0.047	0.038	0.030	0.024	0.020	0.016	0.013	0.010	0.009	0.007	0.006	0.005	0.004

CHAPTER 5

PLANNING, DESIGN, AND CONSTRUCTION PROCESSES

CHAPTER OBJECTIVES

The objectives for this chapter are to articulate the planning, design, and construction processes that are necessary prior to the management and operation of a sport facility. The four phases to be covered will be (1) preliminary planning; (2) development of design; (3) construction; and (4) preparation for training and management of facility. In the first section, the preliminary planning process will be explained in terms of how to create a program analysis for a sport facility, as well as how to conduct feasibility studies including project descriptions, scope and constraints of the project, identification of need for the facility, strategic significance, sport and economic impact, capital costs, revenue projects, and timelines. The second section will describe the basics of the design process, including space allocation, timetables, site selections, and cost estimates. The third section, about the construction process, will encompass the selection process for contractors, the creation process of detailed shop drawings, how to obtain building permits, what is involved with groundbreaking, and the actual construction process in terms of capital improvements, new construction, and technological innovations. Special attention will be given to the importance of the aging of the population, human rights and disability discrimination legislation, and diversity management related to universal design principles and the major dimensions of access (mobility, vision, hearing, cognitive and the sensitivities), as well as to the topics of 'greening' and sustainability of sport venues. The fourth and final section of the chapter will introduce the next section of the book regarding the implementation of management and operations in sport facilities, including organizational management, human resource management, financial management, operational decision making, operations management, and legal responsibilities.

PHASE 1 – PRELIMINARY PLANNING

In the previous chapters, the authors describe the various ownership structures, financing options, and capital investment appraisal methods for sport facilities. These three areas serve as a foundation for the preliminary planning process that eventually leads to the design, construction, and management of sport facilities.

Preliminary planning involves all of the initial tasks that need to be completed in preparation for a specific course of action. A sound preliminary planning process allows the sport facility manager to effectively and efficiently utilize resources to organize, implement, control, and make decisions. Through the preliminary planning process, timelines and standards are established, initial problems are addressed, and strategic, tactical, and operational goals are formalized – working within the philosophy and mission of the organization, and toward end results articulated in the vision.

With regard to sport facilities, there are generally six parts to the preliminary planning process: completing a program analysis, conducting feasibility studies, convening a planning committee, selecting an architect, developing a master plan, and creating a program statement.

Program analysis

A program analysis focuses on the need for the facility in terms of the programs that are either already established or are planned to be established. In order to conduct an appropriate program analysis, a sport facility manager must first have a clear understanding of the organizational PMV (philosophy, mission, and vision). The organizational philosophy focuses on what is important to the sport facility from a business values and beliefs standpoint. The organizational mission focuses on the reason for the sport facility and the guiding managerial principles. These guiding principles are articulated through the organizational goals – the tasks that need to be completed to achieve the mission – and the organizational objectives – the specific methods to be utilized to accomplish those tasks. These organizational goals and objectives are governed by the policies and procedures set forth by the organization – usually articulated through an operations manual, a human resources manual, and standard operating procedures in the industry. The organizational vision focuses on the future and where the sport facility and associated organizations ultimately want to be.

Feasibility studies

The program analysis is usually articulated through feasibility studies. A feasibility study is an examination of the likelihood that an idea or concept can be transformed into a business reality. Feasibility studies have a number of components including the project description and site selection; the scope and constraints of the project, a needs identification; the strategic significance of the project, the sport, economic, and societal impact; capital costs and revenue projections; and timelines. Table 5.1 defines each of these terms.

Most feasibility studies are conducted by hiring a consultant who specializes in this type of analysis. It is important that the sport facility planning committee be actively involved with the feasibility process – from the selection of the consultant through monitoring the progress of the consultant to receipt of the final report. Selecting the right consultant who connects to the project is crucial to the success of the feasibility study process, not only from a logistical standpoint, but as a result of the cost of a good in-depth study, choosing the wrong consultant can result in having to restart the process, which creates delays in the planning process and increases cost. It is also incumbent on the sport facility planning committee to not try to influence the consultant one way or the other; the best and most truthful feasibility studies are free from bias. However, while the sport facility planning committee should not try to influence the consultant, they definitely should monitor the progress of the study to ensure it is being conducted properly, provide relevant information regarding the needs for the sport facility, and receive and review periodic reports from the consultant to ensure efficient and effective use of time and to provide further clarity on the project.

86

Table 5.1 Feasibility study components

Component	Explanation
Project description	A general overview of the facility, including square footage, inclusions, and amenities.
Site selection	The location of the facility including attractiveness of location, acreage/hectare available, natural and environmental conditions (weather, soil, grading, wetlands, forestry, rocks/minerals), ease of access, community support.
Scope of the project	The processes that are required to define and control the work necessary to complete the project.
Constraints of the project	Specific restrictions that may have an adverse affect on the scope of the project and related actions.
Needs identification/assessment	The verification process as to whether the facility is essential. Includes identifying current and future trends, assessing similar facilities/competition, evaluating the relevant social indicators, and determining demand/usage potential.
Strategic significance	The potential of having a positive, long-term impact based on the vision of the organization.
Sport impact	How the facility will have a direct effect on the future development of sport in the locale.
Economic impact	How the facility will directly stimulate the total amount of expenditures in the area.
Societal impact	How the facility will directly affect the social fabric and wellbeing of the community.
Capital costs	The expenses incurred on land, buildings, construction, and equipment related to the management and operation of the facility.
Revenue projections	The forecasting of sales and other income sources to offset expenses and predict net profit or loss.
Timelines	The listing of specific benchmarks, deadlines, and schedules related to effective and efficient management and operation.

Planning committee

Once the feasibility study is completed and a decision to move forward is made, a planning committee is convened to move the project forward. The most difficult part of putting together a planning committee is to limit the size so work can be accomplished, but ensuring that all constituencies and key stakeholders are represented. Individuals who may have a role on a planning committee include the following:

- Initial investors/entrepreneurs in the facility (the individual who most likely conducted or commissioned the program analysis and feasibility study)
- Construction company
- Consultants/experts in the design and construction of sport facilities
- Bank representatives/financiers
- Accountants
- Elected community officials/administration
- At-large community representative(s)
- Representative(s) from organization(s) who plan to utilize the facility.

The purpose of the planning committee is to shape the design of the sport facility. Major responsibilities include advancing the development of the sport facility efficiently and systematically, establishing an information system about the sport facility, and standardizing the processes of facility use. The three initial responsibilities of the planning committee are selecting an architect, developing the master plan, and establishing the program statement.

Selecting an architect

The main responsibility of an architect is to help design a functional sport facility. The architect must have a full understanding of the purpose of the sport facility, be able to visualize the various uses of the sport facility, and foresee as many issues or problems with the design prior to construction. The communication process between the planning committee and the architect is crucial to the success of the sport facility – because if the architect does not understand the vision of the planning committee, the appropriate design cannot come to fruition.

In addition to drawing drafts and building scaled models, the architect can serve as a resource when updating site studies, securing zoning and planning approval, obtaining building permits, surveying land, groundbreaking, and any other pre-construction situations that may arise. To that end, there are three key places to look for architects. First would be through the construction company that has been selected. Often, as a result of relationships built during previous projects, the construction company can recommend an architect that would fit best for the project. Another way to find an architect would be to conduct research of similar facilities or projects and collect references about the architects used. A third method is to contact the governing body for architects in your area – in the United States it is the American Institute of Architects – to get a referral list.

The planning committee will publish a request for a proposal from architects, who will then submit their qualifications, references, examples of previous projects, and possibly even a first draft of the project. The planning committee would then review the applications, conduct reference checks and research previous projects, select their top choices, and bring the shortlisted architects in for a full interview process and presentation. The goal during this interview is to evaluate the knowledge of the architects, assess whether they understand the vision of the planning committee, and determine if personalities seem to fit together. The final determination should be made based on this interview process, the price of the bid, and the perceived quality of work expected to be produced by the successful architect.

Master plan development

After the architect is selected, the next step in the planning process is the development of the master plan. The development of a master plan allows the planning committee to take their vision for the sport facility and plot a path for making it a reality. The main purpose of the master plan is to break down the sport facility project into feasible segments based on numerous factors related to priorities, finances, and time. In addition, the master plan allows the planning committee to begin to contemplate the architectural design of the facility in terms of interior and exterior aesthetics – including look, feel, and appropriate fit within the landscape.

While drawings are often the end result of a master plan, the plan also seeks to answer the 'who, what, where, when, why, and how much' of the sport facility, including:

- site conditions and environmental/sustainability impact analyses;
- structural, architectural, mechanical, electrical, and plumbing factors;
- space requirements and mapping;
- financial issues;
- legal parameters;
- control and management considerations; and
- provisions for dealing with any potential errors and omissions.

In order to complete an effective master plan, there also need to be facility visits and trend analyses. Facility visits allow the planning committee to look at similar facilities to what they are designing. The function part of the visit involves a features analysis – where the planning committee evaluates the positive and negative aspects of the facilities they visit, and then use that information to incorporate the best functions into their design, while avoiding the pitfalls experienced by that facility. Trend analyses also need to be conducted to determine the changes in social, economic, political, or environmental patterns that may have an effect on the design and function of the sport facility.

Program statement

Once the master plan is completed, a program statement is developed to summarize the major components of the master plan. This program statement will ultimately be used to review the major components of the project, market the project to gain

89

financial and general support for the project, and serve as a framework document for the design and construction of the sport facility. Some of the inclusions within a program statement are:

■ project goals and objectives;
■ basic assumptions about the sport facility – supported through robust research;
■ current trends affecting the planning process;
■ a listing of the current and future programs to be a part of the facility;
■ initial specifications/features, space needs assessment, and space allocations;
■ facility usage plans – including auxiliary and service areas;
■ supplies needed – including items such as equipment, furniture, and other supplies; and
■ environmental and sustainability functions.

PHASE 2 – FACILITY DESIGN

Once the master plan and program statement have been developed and agreed upon, it is time to design the sport facility. The architect (in partnership with the planning committee) will create drawings and scaled models of the sport facility. As a part of this process, narratives will be written in support of space allotments and utilization plans, atmospheric conditions, environmental issues, and specification sheets – including the types of materials to be used in the construction of the facility.

Facility design basics

When designing a new facility, or modifying an existing one, space allocation and management is a crucial part of the process as it focuses on the planning, projection, allocation, evaluation, and use of space. The goals of effective space management are to ensure space is appropriately and fairly distributed based on the needs assessment, provides an avenue to establish standards for allocating space, affords the opportunity to determine needs that can be consolidated into the same space to help reduce other costs (utilities, maintenance, and operations), aids with the construction process by reducing the likelihood of errors and omissions, and allows the planning committee to conduct a final evaluation to determine any shortfalls in space inventories (especially prevalent in the area of storage).

The six step process that serves as the foundation for the sport facility space allocation and management process is shown in Figure 5.1.

The initial stage is the planning process, where current and future space requirements are addressed in terms of the needs assessment. Included in this planning is the amount and type of space needed; the configuration of the space including dimensions, square footage/meterage, volume, shape, and location; and space utilization in terms of specific activities, support functions, organizational control, and

90

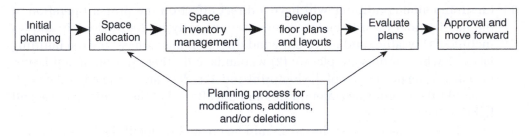

Figure 5.1 *Sport facility space allocation and management process*

required adjacencies. Next is the process of allocating space – which must be justified in terms of needs, the footprint of the facility, the organization of the facility in terms of similar requirements (e.g. bathrooms and locker rooms in adjacent zones due to similar plumbing needs), and the flow of the facility (ingress/egress/movement in/around facility). Third is space inventory management – which allows for keeping track of the types of sizes of space, an identification system for areas, an information database of key features required in specific spaces (utilities, heating, ventilation, air conditioning, and other special needs/uses), and a diary identifying the eventual uses for spaces. Once spaces are allocated, floor plans and layouts are developed so that the previous information can be transferred from a written form into a visual form. The plans are then evaluated by all pertinent parties with two results – either a return to the planning process for modifications, additions, or deletions from the plan, or approval to move forward.

During this process, there are a number of considerations that must be taken into account, both internal and external to the facility:

1   When spaces are allocated, errors are often made because the focus is only on the specialized spaces within the sport facility. Do not forget to spend equal time on shared spaces and flexible-use/multipurpose spaces to ensure those needs are met as well.
2   Storage space always seems to be the last item on the minds of designers/planners. Ensure that the appropriate storage spaces are designed into the building for equipment, maintenance, custodial, and electronics.
3   Security and management control of the sport facility is crucial to the ongoing safety and operation of space. Ensure your plans take into account appropriate ingress/egress (both general and emergency), sightlines and other observatory features for staff, and flow within the sport facility to ensure safe passage for users.
4   With regard to atmospherics, a sport facility manager must direct considerable attention to the way in which its atmosphere can promote the desired relationship with clientele, and the safe and enjoyable participation in specified activities. Atmospherics may include appropriate lighting, flooring, sound/noise levels, temperature, and the general ambiance of the sport facility.

91

5   Environmental conditions will have a direct effect on the proper operation of the facility, and need to be taken into account early in the process. Examples include: (1) weather and prevalent wind direction may affect how the building faces or where rooms are placed; (2) wetlands and other environmental issues may affect the placement of the footprint and ancillary areas related to the facility; and (3) surrounding communities and the affect that the facility's noise and lighting have on them.

6   Specification sheets (spec sheets) should be created to detail the types of materials to be used in the construction of the facility. This includes construction materials, paints and finishes; mechanical, electrical, plumbing, and other utility systems; doors, windows, floorings, ceilings, and wall coverings; appliances, fixtures, and electronics; and furniture and other pertinent equipment.

Timetables

Once these basics are confirmed, timetables are created to move the project forward in an effective and efficient manner. Timetables are usually created backwards from the projected opening date of the facility to the date the timetable is created. The timetable is designed not only to keep the progress of the construction within acceptable parameters, it provides a framework for the design and implementation of documents related to the management and operations of the sport facility – including the hiring and training of staff, publicity of the facility, and planning for the grand opening. A timetable is a living document – consulted, evaluated, and modified frequently. In general, the architect is responsible for the creation and management of the timetable – but the owners, planning committee, or the architect may 'fast track' certain parts of the project based on needs, environmental situations, or delays. While these 'fast tracks' may be more expensive initially, they are often needed to speed up the completion time of the facility to ensure other problems or issues do not occur.

Site selection

As described earlier in the chapter, the site selection is defined as the process of choosing a location for the facility – taking into account such considerations as the attractiveness of location, available acreage/hectare, natural and environmental conditions (weather, soil, grading, wetlands, forestry, rocks/minerals), ease of access, and community support. It is possible at this point in the process that a site has already been selected. If so, the planning committee will confirm if the site is appropriate for the facility designed, and determine if modifications are necessary. However, in some cases, planning committees will wait until this time to select a site based on the facility they have designed. In either scenario, an analysis of the site in terms of numerous factors needs to be conducted at this time, including:

92

- Access
  - Internal – movement within site
  - External
    - Ingress/egress
    - Roads and traffic generation/impact
    - Forms of public transportation available
- Utilities
  - Water
  - Electric
  - Sewers/cesspools
  - Telephone/cable/broadband
  - Oil/natural gas transmission
- Availability of space for adequate parking
- Environmental issues
  - Atmospherics
  - Climate
  - Nuisances (e.g. animals)
  - Natural features (topography, geology, hydrology, pedology)
- Community and political issues
  - Structural
  - Support
  - Easements
  - Zoning requirements
- Economic issues
  - Labor
  - Demographic trends
  - Taxes
  - Utility costs
  - Competition.

Cost estimate

There are multiple purposes for creating a cost estimate ranging from determining whether the planning committee can afford the facility they want to build to securing public and/or private financing.

The first part of the cost estimate is the building cost review. This major capital expenditure includes general construction costs for materials, personnel, and equipment; site works; fit out (the cost of the shell without adaptations for specific use – partitions, floors, ceilings, walls, mechanical, electrical, environmental); specific activity and ancillary area costs; car parking; contingencies; insurance; security; landscaping; and consultancy/project management fees. Another major cost is land acquisition. Fees over and above the purchase price include potential easements, appraisals, the purchase price, and attorney fees. Other possible fees may be related to zoning requirements, conveyancing, filing of deeds, stamp duties, banking/mortgage loans, and environmental issues. A final major cost is for support needs in the facility including furniture, equipment, communications, and supplies.

PHASE 3 – CONSTRUCTION

Once the design phase is completed, it is time to break ground and construct the sport facility (or in the case of an existing facility, start renovations). In order to initiate this process, a contractor needs to be chosen, detailed shop drawings need to be created, and groundbreaking and actual construction started – including securing necessary building permits. This section of the chapter takes you through this process.

Contractor selection process

The main responsibility of a contractor is as the main builder for the sport facility. While the overall responsibility of the project falls on the contractor, work is usually completed in coordination with subcontractors for specific tasks.

Many times a contractor will actually be a subcontractor to an architect. In many cases, this is the best scenario for a planning committee, as the contractor knows the work of the architect, and there is usually a more seamless transition through the construction process. While this may seem like the easiest and best route to take for the project, it is integral that the planning committee carry out due diligence and conduct a thorough bid process for the contractor.

As with the architect, the planning committee will publish a request for proposal from contractors, who will then submit their qualifications, references, and examples of previous projects. The planning committee reviews the applications, conducts reference checks, researches previous projects, selects their top choices, and brings the contractors in for a full interview process. The architect should be a part of the interview process to help in evaluating the knowledge of the contractor, assessing if the contractor understands the vision of the planning committee, and determining if the architect and contractor can effectively work together. The final determination should be made based on this interview process, the price of the bid, and the perceived quality of work expected to be produced by the contractor. Once the contractor is selected, contracts are negotiated and the construction process is put into action.

Creation of detailed shop drawings

One of the first responsibilities of the contractor is to create a detailed set of shop drawings from the architect's renderings. The architect needs to work closely with the contractor during this phase to ensure that all essential parts of the facility are included. The shop drawings will address all aspects of the facility including appearance, performance aspects, and governing principles. Also noted on the shop drawings are any modifications, additions, or deletions that have been made based on the recommendations of the architect and/or contractor. This information is extremely detailed to ensure that there is total clarity and completeness about the project, and so the planning committee can get a full visual of what the project will eventually look like. One of the issues a planning committee must look out for with regard to these changes is that they need to ensure that the changes do not represent a compromise that gives up essential aspects that are important as addressed in the original needs assessment. In addition, the planning committee needs to be open-minded to concepts brought forth at this stage, because this is the final chance to make any significant changes before ground is broken on the project. This is very important because any changes made once construction has started often will result in delays to the overall project and increased costs.

Groundbreaking and actual construction

In preparation for groundbreaking, the contractor will secure all building permits. Usually this process involves filing for a building notice with the municipality, having the site approved by the municipality (which may also involve town meetings for the community to speak on the project), plans and detailed shop drawings are evaluated and approved, zoning issues are addressed, and finally the application will be accepted and the permits issued.

The groundbreaking is an exciting time for all involved because it brings all the hard work through the planning and design process from concept to reality. As such, it is appropriate at this time to celebrate, and hence a groundbreaking ceremony should be scheduled. The first step is to select a date for the groundbreaking – one that can bring together the best audience. This audience usually will include owners, municipality officials, chamber members, and the community. Early afternoons during the week (Monday–Friday) have shown to be the best time for a groundbreaking – and also are a great time to entice the media to cover the event. Also, it is important to make sure that your groundbreaking does not conflict with other activities in the area, as you would like to maximize attendance, and that you plan for inclement weather in your planning process.

Invitations should be sent to all pertinent individuals who were integral to reaching the groundbreaking stage. This should include planning committee members, architects, contractors, business associates (bankers, consultants, project managers), local businesses near your construction site, volunteer associations in the area, community leaders, elected officials, and the media.

A master of ceremonies, or emcee, should be chosen for the event to welcome guests and introduce dignitaries. In addition, choose appropriate guest speakers for the groundbreaking – give those individuals enough advanced notice about their participation, and how long they will speak (two to three minutes is the standard).

Groundbreaking ceremonies should be between 20–30 minutes. Activities in addition to speeches that may be included during the groundbreaking would include having a plot of dirt with ceremonial shovels to enact the first dig on the site involving all pertinent dignitaries, tours of the site, exhibits of the shop drawings, music and/or entertainment, raffles, and refreshments. It is also important to have literature about the facility available to hand to all that attend.

After the groundbreaking, there are two important steps. First is to contact all pertinent media with a summary of the groundbreaking and pictures from the event. Second is to send out thank you notes to all speakers, sponsors, and other dignitaries.

Once the hoopla from the groundbreaking has died off, the construction process has started. During this phase of the project, it is important that there is open communication between designated planning committee members, owners, architects, and contractors. Depending on the scope of the project, it can take anywhere from 4–18 months to fully construct a sport facility.

'THE REVITALIZATION OF MONTOUR JUNCTION': A COUNTY'S VISION FOR A NEW ATHLETIC COMPLEX

In July 2008, administrators from Allegheny County in Pennsylvania, USA (www.county.allegheny.pa.us) announced the donation of 78 acres of land from the Sports Legacy Foundation to develop a world-class athletic complex. The donated property, located within the second most populated county in Pennsylvania, was formerly owned and operated by the Pittsburgh and Lake Erie Railroad. The land has been under environmental clean-up for years and ownership of the property will officially be transferred to Allegheny County Department of Parks once the environmental work is completed. The Sports Legacy Foundation stipulated that the land must be transformed into a facility offering nontraditional playing fields including rugby, soccer, and lacrosse.

'This is an incredible opportunity to transform a vacant brownfield into a world-class recreational facility,' Allegheny County Executive Dan Onorato said, adding that the project, which has been estimated to cost about $10 million to $15 million, will be funded through a number of public–private collaborations.

While still in the initial planning phase, there are three key criteria regarding the development of the facility. First, the facility will remain County owned and will ONLY be used for non-traditional sports (e.g. rugby, soccer, lacrosse). Second, the facility will have at least one 'stadium' to achieve the goal of being a 'world-class' recreational facility. Finally, the facility will contain a large, open green area for at least 10 athletic fields. Refer to Figure 5.2 for a visual perspective of the donated land.

Figure 5.2 Land donated to Allegheny County by the Sports Legacy Foundation

Other key aspects regarding the donated land

■ The property, although level in terrain, is irregular in shape. In addition to this planning and design challenge, the surrounding area has several physical barriers including the Ohio River to the north, a major four-lane route that runs through the greater Pittsburgh area to the south and residential areas to the south and east of the land.

■ The residential areas immediately surrounding the land can be described as blue collar industrial suburbs with a rich history in the railroad and steel mill industry.

■ The head of Montour Trail, a multi-use non-motorized recreational trail near Pittsburgh, PA that will ultimately extend 46 miles is only one-fifth of a mile to the south of the donated land. The trail is currently used for bicycling, walking, running, cross-country skiing, nature appreciation, and in some designated areas, horseback riding. It has been proposed to provide a mile-long extension of the trail within the property.

- A stocked trout stream, Montour Run, bisects the donated property. It has been proposed to allow trout fishing access once the facility is completed.

Other key aspects regarding Allegheny County

- The County currently has nine parks that encircle the City of Pittsburgh and encompass 12,000 acres. They provide recreational and leisure activities to more than 11 million visitors annually.
- The landscape can be characterized as rolling hills punctuated by several scenic river valleys. Despite a history of industrial growth, much of the area still contains forests and farming communities.
- All four seasons are experienced with average temperatures ranging anywhere from 18 degree Fahrenheit lows in January to 83 degree Fahrenheit highs in July. It is not uncommon for temperatures to be more extreme than these averages.
- The population in 2008 was approximately 1.2 million with a median income of $46,402 and mean age of 40 years old. In 2013, the population has not increased significantly (1.23 million); however the median income has risen to $50,664 and the mean age to 41 years old.

Note: case originally developed by Dr. Laura L. Miller, Assistant Professor; and Dr. Brian Wood, Assistant Professor – California University of Pennsylvania. Published with permission.

Sources

Post Gazette.com (2008). *County unveils plan for sports complex: Foundation donates 78-acre parcel in west suburbs.* Retrieved July 22, 2014 from: www.post-gazette.com/pg/08191/895693-57.stm

United States Census Bureau (2014). *State and Country QuickFacts: Allegheny County, Pennsylvania.* Retrieved July 22, 2014 from: http://quickfacts.census.gov/qfd/states/42/42003.html

Suggested discussion topics

1 Research and summarize one facility complex that could be used as a template/model for Montour Junction Sport Complex. What are the strengths and weaknesses of the researched facility? What amenities/characteristics are desirable or not desirable from this facility? Lastly, what main considerations need to be taken into account when planning and operating the proposed facility such as ADA compliance and accessibility specifications?

2   Considering the proposed development of ten playing fields within the new athletic complex, what issues or obstacles do you foresee relating to:
    a   the positioning, orientation and placement of the fields
    b   the type(s) of playing surfaces (natural grass vs. synthetic) chosen for the fields
    c   lighting of the fields
    d   parking?
As of the end of 2014, the complex still has not been built. Review recent newspaper articles and other publications to gain an understanding as to why 6+ years after the donation of the land the facility has yet to be built.

PHASE 4 – PREPARATION FOR TRAINING AND MANAGEMENT OF FACILITY

Throughout the construction process, and especially when construction is nearing completion, the focus turns to the management and operation of the sport facility. Included in this process is preparing the facility management infrastructure, attracting events to be staged in the facility, and then preparing an event management infrastructure.

The following chapters in this textbook will take you through a series of concepts that will aid in the preparation for training and management of sport facilities. Each of these areas is crucial to the understanding of global sport facility operations management, and will serve as a framework for realizing the scope of responsibilities involved in the implementation of management and operations.

- Organizational management (Chapter 6) – the processes involved in understanding human and organizational behavior, as well as leadership and governance methodologies used to improve organizational performance and effectiveness within the sport facility.
- Human resource management (Chapter 7) – the practices and procedures focused on managing sport facility personnel.
- Financial management (Chapter 8) – the basic fiscal and economic skills that are an important part of the sport facility manager's overall portfolio of management skills.
- Operational decision making (Chapter 9) – the efficient and effective management of facility-related costs and the knowledge necessary to improve the financial performance of a facility.
- Operations management (Chapter 10) – the general functions that are integral to the production of quality programming and services within a sport facility.

99

- Legal concerns (Chapter 11) – the general principles related to negligence law, contract law, and governmental law that affect the management and operation of sport facilities.
- Ancillary issues in sport facility operations management (Chapters 12–15) includes the relationship of sport marketing, event planning, risk assessment, and security planning to sport facility operations management.
- Effectiveness of management and operations (Chapter 16) focuses on the importance of benchmarking and performance management to the efficient and effective operation and management of sport facilities.

CHAPTER REVIEW

The purpose of this chapter was to introduce the planning, design, and construction processes – all of which are integral to the management and operation of a sport facility. The first process is the preliminary planning process, which encompasses the program analysis, a feasibility study, convening of a planning committee, selecting an architect, and development of the master plan and program statement. The program analysis focuses on the need for the sport facility in terms of the programs that are either already established or are planned to be established. The feasibility study serves to determine the likelihood that the facility concept can be transformed into a reality through the creation and evaluation of program descriptions; conducting project scope/constraint, site, needs, and impact analyses; and forecasting strategic significance, cost and revenue projections, and timelines. The planning committee is convened and represents all key constituencies and stakeholders in the project, and will shape the design of the sport facility. A key member that will be added to the committee through a bid, interview, and selection process is the architect, who will be the key individual to design a functional facility. Eventually, the development of the master plan and program statement will serve as the blueprint to take the vision for the sport facility and make it a reality.

The second phase is the actual design of the sport facility. Facility basics involve implementing a space management plan, which involves ensuring space is appropriately and fairly distributed, establishes standards for allocating space (including consolidation to reduce costs), reducing the likelihood of errors and omissions, and conducting final evaluations to determine any shortfalls in space inventories. As a part of this phase, timetables are created, sites are selected, and costs are estimated.

Phase three is the actual construction process. The initial step in this process is to select a contractor through a bid, interview, and selection process. Many times, the contractor may actually be a subcontractor of the architect to have a more seamless transition from planning and design to construction. Once the contractor is selected, detailed shop drawings are created that address all aspects of the sport facility including appearance, performance aspects, governing principles, modifications, additions, and deletions. Once these plans are finalized, ground-breaking is scheduled and construction is started.

The final phase is the preparation for training and management of the sport facility. Although much of the focus is on the actual construction process, which can take anywhere from 4–18 months to fully construct a sport facility, it is important that plans are implemented in preparation for the opening of the sport facility. Organizational structure must be created, human resource and operations manuals designed and implemented, financial plans evaluated and finalized, operational decision making and management processes developed and implemented, and legal issues and responsibilities taken into account. Furthermore, projections need to be made related to how the management and operational structure will look once implemented, and a procedure for evaluating efficiency and effectiveness needs to be established. These concepts are the framework for the rest of this textbook.

BIBLIOGRAPHY

Coots, D. G., Roper, K. O., and Payant, R. P. (2009). *The facility management handbook* (3rd ed.). New York: Amacom Books.

Geraint, J., Sheard, R., and Vickery, B. (2013). *Stadia: The populous design and development guide* (5th ed.). London: Routledge.

Goldman, A. J. (2006). Optimal facility-location. *Journal of Research of the National Institute of Standards and Technology, 111*(2), 97–101.

Hou, X. (2007). Fundamental research on development management of sports facility in Beijing universities. *Journal of Shenyang Institute of Physical Education, 26*(4), 36–38.

Hypes, M. G. (2006). Planning and designing facilities. *Journal of Physical Education, Recreation, and Dance, 77*(4), 18–22.

Koger, D. (2001). Expanding sports facilities. *American School and University, 73*(11), 48.

Ming, L., Yang, Z., Jianping, Z., Zhenzhong, H., and Jiulin, L. (2009). Integration of four-dimensional computer-aided design modeling and three-dimensional animation of operations simulation for visualizing construction of the main stadium for the Beijing 2008 Olympic games. *Canadian Journal of Civil Engineering, 36*(3), 473–479.

Naoum, S. (2001). *People and organizational management in construction.* London: Thomas Telford.

National Intramural-Recreational Sport Association (2008). *Space planning guidelines for campus recreational sport facilities: Planning, design, and construction guidelines.* Champaign, IL: Human Kinetics.

National Intramural-Recreational Sport Association (2009). *Campus recreational sports facilities: Planning, design, and construction guidelines.* Champaign, IL: Human Kinetics.

Newell, K. (2004). If you rebuilt it, they will come: Renovating your athletic facility is a win-win situation. *Coach and Athletic Director, 73*(6), 64–70.

Pate, D. W., Moffitt, E., and Fugett, D. (1993). Current trends in use, design, construction, and funding of sport facilities. *Sport Marketing Quarterly, 2*(4), 9–14.

Sangree, D. J. (2012). Perform market analysis with a feasibility study for indoor waterpark resorts and outdoor waterparks. *Appraisal Journal, 80*(2), 149–156.

Sawyer, T. H. (2009). *Facility planning for health, fitness, physical activity, recreation and sports: Concepts and Applications* (12th ed.). Champaign, IL: Sagamore Publishing.

Spoor, D. L. and Cox, S. (1998). Athletic facilities: Planning, designing, and operating today's physical-education centers. *American School and University, 70*(10), 3.

Stice, S. and Stice, W. (2007). A good design is no accident. *Athletic Administration, 33*(3), 18–19.

Stimac, J. (2000). Put 'awe appeal' into your community center: Crucial elements in planning for and designing a facility that will 'wow' your community. *Parks and Recreation, 35*(8), 96–102.

Thompkins, J. A., White, J. A., Bozer, Y. A., and Tanchoco, J. M. A. (2010). *Facilities planning* (4th ed.). Hoboken, NJ: John Wiley and Sons.

Torkildsen, G. (2010) *Leisure and recreation management* (6th ed.). London: Routledge.

Veal, A. J. (2010) *Leisure, sport and tourism: Politics, policy and planning.* Wallingford, Oxon, UK: CABI Publishing.

Westerbeek, H., Smith, A., Turner, P., Emery, P., Green, C., and van Leeuwen, L. (2006). *Managing sport facilities and major events.* London: Routledge.

IN THE FIELD …

Interview with Mickey Farrell, Senior Vice President of Stadium Operations, Tampa Sports Authority

Please explain to the reader about your current position and what your responsibilities are.

My current position is Senior Vice President of Stadium Operations. I am responsible for the general administration, management, coordination, and supervision of the day-to-day activities and long-term planning for Raymond James Stadium. A strong emphasis is placed on booking, contract management, event production, emergency planning, plant operations, custodial, maintenance, parking, grounds and related contractual services.

I am responsible for the overall planning, organizing, controlling, monitoring, event, and facility operations. These tasks ensure the maintenance and improvement of the overall safety, appearance and integrity of the facility, grounds, building structure and building systems to provide a superior experience to the tenants.

Tell us a little about your track from your university years to get to the position you are in now.

I graduated with a Bachelor's degree in Business Management from the University of Tampa. I then received my Master's degree in Sports Management from St. Thomas University. I did a semester long internship in the athletic department at the University of Tampa focusing in event management. I was fortunate to be hired by the University of Tampa following my internship. I

102

spent one year as an Event Coordinator prior to being promoted to Facilities Manager. I spent one year as a Facilities Manager and then was hired by the Tampa Sports Authority as the Assistant Director of Operations for Tampa Stadium. I spent five years as the Assistant Director and then became the Director of Operations in 1991. My duties continued to expand when the Authority built and moved into Raymond James Stadium in 1998. I became the Senior Vice President of Stadium Operations in 2012. During my time with the Authority we built George Steinbrenner Field, the Amalie Arena, and Raymond James Stadium. In addition, we have hosted three Super Bowls and will host the College Football Championship game in 2017.

What advice would you give to someone wanting to get into the field of sport facility operations management?

Classwork and grades are important as they show perseverance and help with the knowledge needed to draw upon in the field. Most definitely, get as much experience in the field as you can while you are attending school. It is very important to build your resume. Competition is fierce for entry level positions and what a person has done sets that person apart from other applicants. In addition, there are three things you should be looking for as you search for an internship:

- Sport facilities need to have a good reputation. You will be learning from the staff working at the sport facility and they will display standards and traits that you want to acquire.
- You should be able to continue building your network. There should be opportunities to be involved in meetings and other ways you can interact with others doing business with your host facility.
- Potential for a full time position with the sport facility or other entities doing business with the sport facility at the end of the internship.

During your internship your work ethic is crucial. You need to be punctual, energetic, and always looking to make yourself invaluable to your host facility. Be eager to learn by asking questions and giving input when opportunities arise. To be successful in any sports management career, adrenaline is a must – be tireless!

TECHNOLOGY NOW!

Regardless of the size of scope of the sport facility – from Olympics and World Cup venues to secondary school fields and private fitness facilities – there is a demand for quality and impressive building design to provide quality experiences for spectators. In order to create such designs, the latest computer aided design (CAD) software is needed to shape the vision of these sport facilities into a visual reality – both two dimensional (2D) and three dimensional (3D).

Major sport entities ranging from internationally renowned facility design firm Populous to national governing bodies such as Sport England have utilized AutoCAD software from Autodesk, Inc. For over three decades, Autodesk has provided software solutions to help sport facility designers, engineers, and architects imagine, design, and create the best sport facilities in the world.

A primary architectural tool used is AutoCAD Architecture software, the architecture-specific version of the software. This program provides architectural drafting tools that allows the user to map out the entire facility such as specific spaces (including walls, doors, and windows) and size of spaces (both linear and spatial – including elevations and sectioning). It also provides the ability to create and edit drawings throughout the design process, streamlining the information exchange process between those involved with the project. This ability to share and edit designs within the software allows for faster project review cycles between members of the project team and hence shortens decision times – resulting in shorter planning and design timelines and faster movement to the construction phase of the sport facility.

Another program being used by sport facility designers is Autodesk 3ds Max Design software. This takes the visualization of the project off a flat piece of paper and gives it more life in a three-dimensional view. This in turn allows for more detailed modeling, animation, and renderings that can address issues which cannot be duplicated on a two-dimensional scale such as daylight access and walkthrough animations.

The use of the Autodesk software is not just a planning and design software, it also plays a crucial role in the construction process. Sport facility contractors are adopting the use of building information modeling (BIM) as part of their construction philosophy. BIM involved creating a digital representation of the features of a sport facility, which is then translated into scheduling and coordination efforts during the construction process to know what people and materials are needed when and where.

Source: Autodesk, Inc. (2014). Retrieved October 16, 2014 from www.autodesk.com

PART II

IMPLEMENTATION OF MANAGEMENT AND OPERATIONS

CHAPTER 6

ORGANIZATIONAL MANAGEMENT

CHAPTER OUTLINE

■ Introduction to organizational management
■ Individual behavior in the workforce
  ■ Motivation
  ■ Stress management and wellbeing
■ Group behavior and teamwork
  ■ Leadership
    ■ Contingency theories of leadership
    ■ Transformational and charismatic leadership
    ■ Dysfunctional aspects of leadership
  ■ The influence of power and politics
  ■ Managing conflict
  ■ Decision making and problem solving
  ■ Issues with communication
■ Organizational culture and change
  ■ Cultural diversity and global organizational behavior
  ■ Organizational healing
■ Chapter review

CHAPTER OBJECTIVES

Organizational behavior is the study of human behavior in the work environment. Understanding the dynamics of organizational behavior is of great significance to a sport facility manager as it helps to explain employee behavior and performance.

107

In today's sport facilities, where organizations are competing in a global environment, managers must be capable of working effectively in diverse teams with diverse skills and abilities. This in turn improves employee performance, thereby enhancing organizational effectiveness and satisfying key stakeholders. However, the key to ensuring an optimal level of positive organization behavior is through quality organizational management of the sport facility.

The purpose of this chapter is to articulate the important concepts of organization management as related to individual and group behavior in sport facilities, including a description of the principles of motivation, stress management and wellbeing, leadership, use of power and authority, politics, conflict management, decision making, and problem solving. This chapter will also cover various leadership and organizational management concepts that affect international and global sport facility operations, including determinants of organizational culture and change, and the effects of cultural diversity and global organization behavior.

INTRODUCTION TO ORGANIZATIONAL MANAGEMENT

The job of a sport facility manager is best described in terms of management functions and roles. The four major functions of management are planning, organizing, leading, and coordinating (or controlling). Planning involves selecting and prioritizing goals and objectives and the methods to be used to achieve desired results. There are various types of planning, for example, strategic planning, business planning, project planning, and staff planning. Organizing is simply identifying resources and allocating those selected resources to meet specific goals and objectives established during the planning stage. Sport facility managers may organize their staff, teams, and events, or sponsoring agencies. Leading entails providing direction for the sport organization and its staff, and influencing staff to follow the desired direction. Coordinating or controlling activities include monitoring resources and processes to achieve goals and objectives in an efficient manner.

Management roles can be divided into three categories – interpersonal roles, informational roles, and decision making roles. Interpersonal roles are social in nature and include serving as a figurehead or 'face' of the sport organization. Informational roles include disseminating pertinent information to staff members and acting as a spokesperson to external constituencies. The sport facility manager also assumes a decision making role which includes initiating change, resolving disputes, and conducting negotiations with internal and external entities.

INDIVIDUAL BEHAVIOR IN THE WORKFORCE

Individual worker differences are based on personal characteristics. Workers may differ regarding demographic factors such as gender, age, socioeconomic background, education level, race and ethnicity. Additionally, the presence of various levels of abilities and skills has a relationship to job performance. It is the sport facility manager's job to align a person's abilities and skills to the appropriate job requirements. Job analysis is a common technique used to help a manager match the individual to a specific job. Job analysis involves identifying tasks and behaviors associated with the position, and the responsibilities, education, and training required to successfully perform the job's requirements. Personality characteristics play a major role in job success or failure. Many successful managers are extroverted or outgoing and are social, assertive, and active. Emotional stability also affects job performance. Positive emotional traits include being calm, enthusiastic, courteous, and friendly which is a necessity when dealing with facility patrons. The sport facility manager must be dependable and responsible, organized, and an effective planner.

Perceptions on the job are significant. Employees who perceive their job to be challenging and interesting have high job satisfaction and motivation, which results in better performance. Attitudes are also determinants of job behavior. An attitude is a mental state of readiness that is learned and organized through experience. Sport facility managers are sometimes required to change the attitude of workers to enhance job performance. To change a worker's attitude three factors must be considered: trust in the facility manager, the message being communicated, and the situation itself. If the manager is not trustworthy it is highly unlikely that the employee will change his or her attitude. Likewise, if the message being communicated is not convincing it will not be accepted. The facility manager must gain the respect of his or her staff to successfully initiate change in job behavior and performance.

The values and beliefs of employees influence job performance. In an ideal situation, the values of employees match the values of the job and organization thereby leading to higher job performance. Typical values sought by organizations include respect, uncompromising integrity, trust, credibility, and desire for continuous improvement. Personal ethics (individual beliefs on what constitutes right and wrong, or good and bad) is another key factor for understanding individuals in organizations. The ethical behavior of organization members can have an impact on the public's perception.

Motivation

Two foundational theories of motivation are Maslow's Hierarchy of Needs and Herzberg's Two Factor Theory. Maslow's Hierarchy of Needs model emphasizes five levels of individual needs, starting with basic physiological needs at the bottom and self actualization needs at the top (see Figure 6.1). Lower order needs

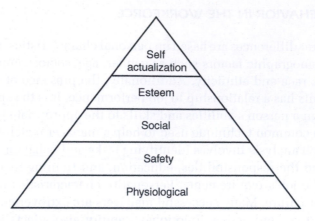

Figure 6.1 Maslow's Hierarchy of Needs

such as food, security, and human contact must be satisfied first before progressing to the higher order needs that are concerned with personal development. Physiological needs are the first order of needs and include basic bodily needs, i.e. water, food, rest, and sleep. Once physiological needs are satisfied the individual is concerned with their safety needs or obtaining a secure environment. Thirdly, social needs are addressed and this constitutes belonging to a group or affiliation with people. Once social needs are met, esteem needs are addressed with concern for self-respect, prestige, recognition, and appreciation. Lastly, at the pinnacle of the pyramid, self-actualization needs are satisfied through self-fulfillment and reaching one's fullest potential.

Herzberg's Two Factor Theory proposes two different sets of job factors: motivators (motivate and satisfy workers that relate to higher order needs) and hygiene factors (prevent dissatisfaction and relate to lower order needs). Motivator factors are intrinsic and include the work itself, responsibility, recognition, achievement, and job advancement. Hygiene factors are extrinsic and may include pay, status, job security, coworkers, or quality of management. The presence of motivators can help energize a work staff, and the absence of hygiene factors can cause dissatisfaction. This theory helped managers realize that job design was critical to make the job itself more intrinsically satisfying.

Enhancing motivation by job design is possible through job enrichment. Job enrichment refers to adding variety, responsibility, and managerial decision making to make the job more rewarding. Job enrichment can be achieved by providing direct feedback, new learning opportunities, control over scheduling, unique experience, control over resources, and personal accountability. Direct feedback provides immediate evaluation of the employee's work so necessary changes can be made. An enriched job provides employees the opportunity to acquire new knowledge through job-related experiences or professional training. Employees also prefer to schedule their own workload and working hours. A

Implementation of management and operations

job can provide unique experiences or qualities that are rewarding and uncommon in other positions, e.g. a sport facility manager may get the chance to meet famous athletes. Another source of job enrichment is having control of resources, such as finances and labor. Finally, personal accountability for job results is essential, meaning the employee accepts credit for a job well done and accepts the consequences of a poor job performance. To ensure the success of job enrichment, managers must know if their employees need or want more responsibility and personal accountability.

Stress management and wellbeing

Managers should be concerned with work-related stress as it affects productivity levels. Prolonged exposure to work stress may result in work exhaustion (burnout). Burnout is a pattern of emotional, physical, and mental exhaustion in response to job-related stressors. Sources of job-related stressors include: (1) work overload (long hours and less free time), (2) lack of control over one's work schedule, (3) lack of reward for one's contribution (lack of pay and no recognition), (4) breakdown of a work community (lack of connections among people), and (5) lack of fair treatment.

Individual consequences of stress include psychological, emotional, and behavioral reactions. Psychological symptoms include increased heart rate, blood pressure, or perspiration. Emotional symptoms may include anxiety, frustration, low self esteem, depression, poor concentration, or mental blocks. Behavioral effects may be accident proneness, impulsive behavior, or alcohol abuse. Work-related stress has financial implications on the organization because of reductions in operational effectiveness. There is also a cost associated with mental and physical health problems related to stress, such as medical bills, absenteeism, workplace accidents, or turnover.

Individual approaches to stress management fall into three categories: control, symptom management, and escape. Control simply means being in control of one's work life, such as practicing good work habits and time management, i.e. establishing daily priorities and minimizing procrastination. Physical exercise can manage symptoms of work-related stress. Exercise combats stress by releasing endorphins in the body that act like antidepressants. Escaping from the stressor is another stress management technique; however, eliminating the stressor is the most effective method (i.e. hiring additional event staff if the facility team is understaffed).

The sport organization can address employee stress management by providing an employee assistance (support) program (EAP) and/or establishing a wellness program. Employee assistance programs are designed to deal with both work- and non-work-related stress, such as emotional difficulties or substance abuse. It is also important for employees to stay in good physical and mental shape. An organization sponsored wellness and fitness program can educate workers on maintaining a healthy lifestyle. These types of programs can offer medical examinations and stress management seminars. Some organizations have supported on-site massages and 'nap time' during the workday.

GROUP BEHAVIOR AND TEAMWORK

Two commonly formed types of groups are formal groups and informal groups. Formal groups include command, task, and team groups. Command groups are specified in organizational charts and include employees reporting to a supervisor or manager. A task group is formed to complete a particular task or project, for example, a task force is assigned to develop a sport facility risk management plan. Teams are comprised of a group of people who work closely together and share a common vision or goal.

Informal groups include interest groups and friendship groups. Interest groups are formed to achieve a mutual objective among the group, not related to objectives of the organization. For example, certain interest groups may form to present a unified front to management for more pay or benefits. Friendship groups form because employees have something in common, such as age, ethnic background, or even similar sporting interests. Groups form for several reasons. Group members have social needs (enjoy interacting with others), esteem needs (belonging to a high status or prestige group), group goals (similar objectives), and economic benefits (when the productivity level of a group affects individual wages).

Leadership

Leadership is the process of influencing followers (employees) to attain organizational goals. Leaders provide direction, generate trust, take risks, and reinforce the belief that success will be attained. Leadership traits and personal characteristics have been researched since the early 1900s. Specific traits and characteristics of effective leaders include self confidence, trustworthiness, emotional intelligence, desire for power and achievement, and a sense of humor. A self-confident leader has the potential to instill confidence among his or her staff. Trustworthiness is critical to leadership effectiveness and is exhibited through behavioral consistency (being reliable and predictable) and integrity (telling the truth and keeping promises). Having a passion for the work and the people is an important aspect of emotional intelligence in order to inspire others about their work duties. Furthermore, a strong power motive encourages the leader to influence others, and the need for achievement propels a sense of urgency to act efficiently.

Studies conducted at The Ohio State University and University of Michigan originated much of the theory underlying leadership styles. The Ohio State researchers concluded that employees conceptualized their leaders' behavior on two leadership dimensions – consideration and initiating structure. Consideration is concerned with the degree to which a leader creates an environment of warmth, friendliness, trust, and support through leader behaviors such as being friendly, being concerned about the personal welfare of employees, and informing staff of new developments. Initiating structure describes the degree to which the leader establishes structure for staff members through activities such as assigning specific tasks, establishing procedures and protocols, scheduling workloads, and clarifying expectations. The Ohio Studies found that employee turnover was lowest and job satisfaction highest under leaders rating high in consideration.

The University of Michigan researchers studied the differences in employee-centered and production (job)-centered leaders. Employee-centered leaders focus on employees by delegating decision making and creating a supportive work environment. They are concerned with employees' personal advancement, growth, and achievement. Production-centered leaders focus on completing tasks and closely supervise employees to ensure work is completed using stated procedures. They use coercion, rewards, and positional power to influence behavior and performance. It has been reported that most productive work teams had leaders who spend time planning, are employee-centered, and not engaged in close supervision of employees.

Contingency theories of leadership

These behavioral theories of leadership led to researchers attempting to identify which leadership style would produce the best results. The contingency theory of leadership explains that the most effective style of leadership is dependent on factors relating to employees' and the work environment itself. The two contingency theories of leadership that we will discuss are the Path-Goal Theory of Leadership and the Situational Leadership Model.

The Path-Goal contingency theory focuses on how leaders influence employee perceptions of work goals, self development goals, and paths to goal attainment. The model explains what effects different types of leader behavior will have on employee morale (satisfaction) and productivity (performance). The four primary types of leader behavior are directive leadership, supportive leadership, participative leadership, and achievement-oriented leadership. Directive leadership involves setting standards and communicating expectations to workers. Supportive leadership emphasizes concern for the wellbeing of the workers and developing mutually satisfying relationships by treating workers as equals. Participative leadership involves consulting with workers to solicit suggestions and including them in the decision making process. The achievement-oriented leader sets challenging goals, expects high performance levels, and expects workers to assume responsibility.

Contingency variables considered in this theory are personal characteristics of workers and environmental pressures and demands that the worker must cope with to accomplish goals and satisfaction. Personal characteristics include a person's locus of control, experience, ability level and skill level. Environmental factors are not within the control of the worker and may include work tasks, authority system of the organization, or the work group itself. Any of these variables can motivate or constrain the worker.

Individuals with a highly perceived level of ability to perform task demands would not be suitable for a directive style of leadership. Additionally, individuals with an internal locus of control (believe rewards are contingent on their efforts) are more satisfied with a participative style of leadership. Individuals with an external locus of control (believe rewards are beyond their control) are more satisfied with a directive leadership style. Table 6.1 highlights the leadership style most appropriate in a given situation.

Table 6.1 Path-goal leadership styles and contingency relationships

Leadership style	Situation
Directive	Positively affects morale (satisfaction) and productivity (performance) on workers completing ambiguous and complex tasks with little or no experience in doing the tasks, and no formalized procedures to help them accomplish their tasks. However, this style of leadership will negatively affect satisfaction of workers completing clearly defined tasks.
Supportive	Positively affects the satisfaction and efforts of workers completing stressful, tedious, and frustrating tasks. This style of leadership enhances the intrinsic value of tasks, increases workers' self-confidence, and lowers anxiety so tasks can be successfully completed.
Participative	Positively affects satisfaction and effort when work tasks are unstructured. This style of leadership increases workers' understanding of the relationship between their efforts and goal attainment. It helps workers select their own goals resulting in increased motivation as they have control over their own work.
Achievement-oriented	Positively affects satisfaction and productivity when tasks are ambiguous and non-repetitive. This style of leadership will cause workers to strive for higher standards of performance and have more self-confidence in their ability.

Source: DuBrin (2002); Slack and Parent (2006).

Paul Hersey and Kenneth Blanchard developed the Situational Leadership Model (SLM) to assist leaders in selecting their leadership styles based on the readiness of employees. The SLM is based on two types of leader behavior: task behavior (similar to initiating structure) and relationship behavior (similar to consideration). The situational variable between the task and relationship behavior and leadership effectiveness is the worker's maturity level (or readiness). Readiness is defined as the ability and willingness or confidence of the worker to accomplish a specific task. Two dimensions measure worker readiness – job maturity (technical ability) and physiological maturity (level of self confidence and self respect). Hersey and Blanchard developed four styles of leadership for managers to utilize depending on the readiness level of the employee:

1 Telling: the leader defines roles and tells employees what, where, how and when to perform specific tasks.
2 Selling: the leader provides employees with instructions and is supportive.
3 Participating: the leader and employees share in the decision making process to complete a quality job.
4 Delegating: the leader provides little instruction, direction, or personal support to employees.

The key point to situational leadership is as the employee's readiness level increases, the leader should focus more on relationship behavior and less on task-oriented behavior. As an individual matures (becomes more skilled) they need less direction, although they may still need some motivation and encouragement. When an employee becomes self sufficient, a minimum of task and relationship behavior is needed. Suppose that a sport facility manager determines that his or her new employee has low self-confidence and is insecure about performing job duties. The sport facility manager would exercise a 'telling' style of leadership to provide specific instructions and closely monitor performance. However, as the employee grows personally and professionally in their job role, the leadership style may be adapted to meet their current needs. With employees who are considered self sufficient or provide an area of expertise, the sport facility manager would exercise a delegating style of leadership.

Transformational and charismatic leadership

Leaders are continuously forced to make changes in their organizations to address the evolving and highly competitive global nature of the business world. Transformational leaders are capable of influencing major changes in the organization's objectives, strategies, culture, or philosophy. Transformational leaders go beyond the routine transactional leader who is concerned with only exchanges between the leader and employee to achieve a set of goals. The transformational leader can develop new visions for the organization and inspire followers to attain these new visions. Transformational leaders exhibit several key characteristics. They have the ability to clearly communicate a positive vision of the future. They support and encourage staff development and treat employees as individuals. They provide encouragement and recognition to employees and empower their staff by fostering trust and involvement in decisions. Furthermore, they encourage innovative thinking, lead by example, and exude charisma to inspire staff to be highly competent.

Charisma is a major contributing factor to transformational leadership. Charismatic leaders possess several key characteristics. Charismatic leaders provide vision to the organization that extends beyond organizational goals. They are effective communicators and formulate achievable dreams and vision for the future. Inspiring trust is also critical in order to get followers to share their vision, and make sacrifices upfront with the potential for future success. Charismatic leaders are also very energetic, action-oriented, and serve as a model for getting tasks completed on time. Additionally, they are able to manage their impression well through physical appearance.

Dysfunctional aspects of leadership

Effective leadership is an extremely important asset to the sport organization. However, it can also be its worst liability. We have previously discussed the characteristics of successful leadership and the required traits and behaviors; it is now critical to highlight the dysfunctional patterns in leadership which may result in bad leadership and subsequently a dysfunctional organization. The Plochg Business Psychology Consulting Group highlighted dysfunctional leadership symptoms and common reasons leaders fail:

- Conflict avoidance: some managers need to be liked; therefore, they are unable or unwilling to make difficult decisions in case it threatens their acceptance.
- Micromanagement: managers may become so detail-oriented that they cannot let go of control. A lack of trust in the capabilities of others has a negative effect on performance and ruins morale.
- Manic executives: are possessed with boundless energy and push themselves and others to the limit. They are so hyperactive they do not know what they are doing wrong.
- Inaccessibility of leadership: some managers have no time for others, are unapproachable, or may hide behind assistants and closed door policies.
- Game players: can only talk and think about themselves; and lose attention when others talk. They refuse to let subordinates shine and use and abuse them rather than helping them grow and develop. Game players experience high turnover among their employees.
- No 360 degrees feedback: there is limited or no leadership performance feedback.
- Personal agendas: some managers recruit and award promotions based on internal politics, e.g. hiring friends to guarantee personal loyalty at the expense of more qualified candidates.
- Inefficient use of resources: budgets are allocated based on favoritism rather than business needs.

Implementation of management and operations

THE FAILURE-TOLERANT LEADER

Thomas Watson, Sr. of IBM once said, 'The fastest way to succeed is to double your failure rate'.

Executives who help employees overcome their fear of failure create a culture of intelligent risk taking that leads to innovation. These individuals are referred to as failure-tolerant leaders and are visible in all industries … business, politics, sports, and science. They are able to help employees understand that failure is not the opposite of success, but rather its complement.

Some common threads among failure-tolerant leaders include the ability to: reduce social and bureaucratic barriers between themselves and their followers, engage at a personal level with followers, avoid giving praise or criticism (preferring an analytical approach), openly admit their own mistakes, and try to eliminate the destructive competitiveness inherent in most organizations. *Moving beyond success and failure* – management has a responsibility to assess failures. Some are excusable errors; others may be a result of poor supervision or quality control. Distinguishing between excusable and inexcusable failures allows managers to build a nonpunitive environment for mistake making while encouraging thoughtfully pursued projects. Success should be approached in the same manner as all successes are not created equally. How much was due to good fortune or hard work of the employee? Did it help the organization reach its goals? Will it effectively serve our customers? Some managers may find it difficult to treat success and failure the same; however, if embraced, it may produce some innovative results and ideas for future projects.

Get engaged – according to NFL coaching great, Don Shula, 'I did not get consumed by losses and I did not get overwhelmed by successes'. Failure-tolerant leaders do the same in all fields; they focus on increasing the organization's intellectual capital through experience, knowledge, and creativity of the workforce. They are able to do this by taking a genuine interest in their employee's projects by expressing support and asking pertinent questions. Managers strive to be collaborative and not controlling. Engaged conversations create a failure-tolerant work environment that invites innovation. Listening is more critical to the process than talking.

Do not praise, analyze – managers should analyze the work process rather than praise or penalize. This involves asking questions, giving feedback, and showing interest. This can be time-consuming and also may threaten the manager's authority, as the more involved they get with employees the harder it becomes to reprimand when necessary. The challenge is to get closely involved with the employees' work without presuming to be friends.

Earn empathy – managers can create a risk-friendly environment by sharing some of their own mistakes or failures. This demonstrates self-confidence, forges closer ties with employees, and earns empathy. Leaders who own their errors present themselves as human and whom others can identify with.

Collaborate to innovate – creating a culture of failure-tolerance requires abandoning traditional ideas about personal competition. Competition drives the desire to win and not to solve problems and move projects forward. Employees who feel their work is judged on conventional concepts of success and failure, and who feel like they are competing with coworkers, will want to protect information rather than share it. For example, prizes for performance undermine teamwork and place competition above collaboration. Failure-tolerant leaders want to tap the imaginations of employees who are not competitive but have invaluable ideas.

Give the green light – failure-tolerant leaders emphasize that a good idea is a good idea regardless of whom it comes from. Some managers encourage suggestions via email that can be vetted appropriately, also, conducting meetings that utilize the 'barn raising' model in which members listen to each person's idea, then add their thoughts to potentially build the idea into a valuable contribution. The atmosphere of exploration ensures all members a sense of comfort as their ideas will receive the same treatment. Another method known as 'community of practice' is when a small group of employees meet regularly to discuss common interests.

Failure-tolerant leaders convey clear messages to their followers that constructive mistakes are acceptable, and worthwhile in some cases. Employees are given the green light to explore, not to be worried about success or failure, but thinking in terms of learning and experience.

Source: R. Farson and R. Keyes (2002). The failure-tolerant leader. *Harvard Business Review*, *80*(8), 64–71.

Discussion questions

1   As a leader, how would you break down barriers in the workplace to encourage a failure-tolerant environment – reducing competition and encouraging collaboration?
2   Identify two leaders in an industry of your choice. Describe their characteristics and strategies to encourage a risk-taking workforce.
3   What methods would you employ to increase employee engagement?

The influence of power and politics

Power is the ability to influence decisions and control resources and is obtained in a variety of ways. Interpersonal sources of power are legitimate, reward, coercive, expert, and referent. Legitimate power refers to the individual's ability to influence others based on his or her position within the organization. The position gives the individual the right to influence or command others. Reward power is the individual's ability to reward an employee for compliance and is normally used as a follow-up to legitimate power. Coercive power is the power to punish and employees tend to comply out of fear, i.e. fear of being blocked for a promotion. Expert power is exerted when the individual possesses a special expertise that is highly valued. The more difficult it is to replace the expert, the more power they possess. Referent power is based on an individual's personality or behavioral style. A person's charisma is an indication of their referent power to influence others. Structural power involves resources, decision making, and information power. Power may stem from access to resources such as money, labor, or technology. Additionally, the extent to which individuals can affect decision making and their accessibility to pertinent information affects power levels.

Organizational politics is the use of informal strategies and tactics to gain power. Political tactics involve developing power contacts and establishing alliances. Power contacts can help support proposals and recommendations for promotion. Controlling vital information and keeping informed of organizational developments is another key factor. Also, being courteous, pleasant, and using sincere flattery can influence people.

Managing conflict

Intergroup conflict can be either functional or dysfunctional. Functional conflict enhances the organization's performance. Employee disagreements may occur on the correct method to achieve project goals but this type of conflict leads to innovative solutions. Dysfunctional conflict hinders the organization's performance as employees waste time disagreeing and placing personal interests above the interests of the organization. Three main causes of group conflict are work interdependence, goal differences, and perceptual differences. Work interdependence occurs when organizational groups depend on one another to complete tasks. Depending on the level of interdependence, the conflict level potential ranges from low to high. When organizational groups have mutually exclusive goals problems may arise. Perceptual differences in what constitutes importance and priorities can also cause group conflict.

The need to exercise conflict management is inevitable in any organization. There are five different styles to handle conflict resolution; these include competitive, accommodative, sharing, collaborative, and avoidant. A competitive (dominating) style is one in which the person wants to win at the expense of another's concerns. Accommodative (appeasement) style is more concerned with taking care of another's concerns before one's own concerns. Sharing (compromise) style is in the middle between competitive and accommodative. This style results in moderate or incomplete satisfaction for both parties involved. Collaborative (integration) is concerned with a win-win situation for both parties; therefore both parties are fully satisfied with the outcome. Avoidant (neglect) style is when the person is indifferent to the concerns of either party and may withdraw from the conflict.

The most common method of managing conflict is the use of formal authority. The manager has the ultimate power to resolve disputes. Conflict avoidance is commonly used by ignoring the conflict; however, this is considered a short-term solution. Another way to manage conflict is to remove the interdependence between groups to complete tasks, or merge groups together to reduce conflict. Confrontation and negotiation requires a level of maturity for groups to sit down and acknowledge the conflict and search for a solution. When conflicts are drawn out, a third party may be used to resolve the issue. Finally, job rotation is a method utilized to prevent or manage conflict. Through this practice the individual is exposed to job roles and responsibilities within other units. They acquire an understanding of situations and needs in other units and are able to relay information about their home unit.

Decision making and problem solving

Managers make decisions on a daily basis. Decisions are either programmed or nonprogrammed. Programmed decisions are repetitive and routine, and are made on the basis of policies and past experiences. An example of a programmed decision for a facility manager is whether to increase the number of crowd management staff as the number of spectators increase. Nonprogrammed decisions are new and unique, and have no pre-established guidelines to aid decision making. An example of a nonprogrammed decision for a facility manager is whether to relocate a sport facility to a new site. Managers make decisions under three types of conditions: certainty, risk, and uncertainty. A decision made under a condition of certainty means the manager is aware of all the alternatives and the costs and benefits of each alternative. Sometimes decisions are made under conditions of risk. Managers may know the alternatives but are not exactly sure of all the benefits or costs associated with their options. Finally, a decision made under a condition of uncertainty is when the manager knows very little about the alternatives or their potential outcomes.

An individual's propensity for risk may influence decisions. Managers with high aversion to risk establish different objectives and alternatives than a manager with a low risk aversion. After a decision is made, managers may experience cognitive dissonance (or post-decision anxiety). There may be a conflict between what the decision maker knows and believes and the decision made, thereby resulting in second thoughts or doubts. The manager may also experience an escalation of commitment or increasing commitment to a previous decision when it would be better to withdraw (i.e. turn a poor decision into a good decision). The decision-making process involves several key elements:

- Establish specific goals, objectives, and measureable results.
- Identify and define the problem.
- Establish priorities.
- Consider causes of the problem identified.
- Develop alternative solutions.
- Evaluate alternative solutions.
- Select best solution.
- Implement.
- Follow-up.

In most organizations decisions are made through some sort of group (e.g. teams, task forces). Nonprogrammed decisions normally require pooled talent as a greater amount of knowledge helps reach the best solution. Specific techniques used by managers to gain the input of a group include brainstorming, idea quotas (i.e. management requires two ideas per month from workers), forming heterogeneous groups (diverse groups may bring various viewpoints), offering financial incentives (paying employees for useful suggestions), and designing a creative space within the building (creating the opportunity for physical interaction facilitates the flow of ideas).

Issues with communication

Considering all the processes of group behavior and teamwork – including leadership, power, politics, conflict management, decision making, and problem solving – one component is crucial ... communication. Communication, as a process for exchanging information between individuals, becomes a crucial component to organizational management across any business, but especially in sport facility operations management. However, there are common communication mistakes sport facility operations managers make as noted in Table 6.2.

ORGANIZATIONAL CULTURE AND CHANGE

Organizational culture is a system of shared values, beliefs, assumptions, and understandings that influence worker behavior. A strong (thick) organizational culture is characterized by employees sharing the same core values. A weak (thin) organizational culture is one in which employees do not possess common values. Organizational culture has the potential to affect organizational effectiveness. Managers can create an appropriate organizational culture by setting a vision and getting employees excited about the fundamental purpose of the organization. Secondly, they can help develop the culture by taking action, for example, the

Table 6.2 Seven communication mistakes managers make

---

1. *Making controversial announcements without doing groundwork first*

Prior to announcing a controversial decision to a large group, make sure to prep people one-on-one beforehand to learn who will object and why. Large-scale decisions can initiate rumors, anxiety, and resistance. Decisions about change, such as reorganization, budget cuts, or changing mission/goals creates the most uncertainty and anxiety. Make sure you convey concern and empathy.

2. *Lying*

Understanding that certain topics must remain confidential, you should be careful how you keep secrets. If people know you lied, you will lose their trust forever. Rather than lie, responses could be 'I'm not free to comment' or 'I can't answer that fully now'.

3. *Ignoring the realities of power*

The more power one has the less likely for them to hear about problems until late. Problems are usually filtered and softened as they ascend the organizational hierarchy. Conversely, messages are magnified as they descend the organizational hierarchy. Put an end to rumors by using plain and simple language and end meetings by reviewing your reactions and next steps.

4. *Underestimating your audience's intelligence*

Do not attempt to gloss over issues because 'people won't understand'. Employees deserve to know the rationale behind changes that affect them (even if you need to explain it to them).

5. *Confusing process with outcome*

It is easy to confuse process with outcome in goal-setting, compensation, and evaluation. For example, you promise your employees a 5% raise, but the board caps raises at 3%. You negotiate a 4% raise with the board; however, your employees are not happy. You promised them an outcome!

6. *Using inappropriate forms of communication*

Email is great for conveying information but should not be used for emotional issues as they are too easy to misconstrue. Phone calls and face-to-face meetings are inefficient for disseminating information, but great for discussing issues. You can respond directly to the listener's reaction and use your tone of voice and facial expressions to control the message. Furthermore, some people are listeners and some are readers. If you talk to a reader or write to a listener, your message may be wasted. Ask employees how they prefer to receive information.

7. *Ignoring acts of omission*

What you don't say may be sending a message as loud as what you do say. If you don't express appreciation, folks may feel unappreciated; if you don't explain the rationale behind decisions, folks may feel you don't trust them; and if you don't communicate the organizational vision then folks won't know how to help it get there.

Source: Robbins (2009).

NFL's partnership with United Way promotes to all NFL stakeholders their goal of assisting youth development and giving back to the community. Once a culture is created it must be maintained (or changed if it is not working). Ways to manage an organization's culture include: (1) what leaders pay attention to, measure, and control through comments or rewards, (2) their reaction to critical incidents and how they handle organizational crises (such as firing an employee for unethical conduct), (3) deliberate role modeling, teaching, and coaching by leaders as they set an example for the rest of the organization, (4) linking behavior to rewards and punishments, and (5) criteria for recruitment, selection, promotion, and retirement.

If the current culture is not appropriate then the manager is faced with the task of changing the culture. First, the manager must gain support for this change. Methods to gain support for change include education and communication. This allows for discussion and negotiation of aspects involved in the change process. Participation and involvement of employees provides an opportunity to have a say in the change that affects them, this also helps increase compliance. Financial benefits of the change should be openly communicated. An increase in salary could be an advantage. The change process should not be too overwhelming at first. Avoid change overload and try to make small changes over a period of time instead of sweeping changes overnight.

Cultural diversity and global organizational behavior

Cultural diversity in the workforce is important in today's global economy. To value diversity one must value a wide range of cultural and individual differences. A truly diverse organization is one where all employees, regardless of cultural backgrounds, achieve their full potential. Diverse organizations have a competitive advantage potential and offer benefits in various ways. A multicultural workforce enhances the ability to reach a multicultural client base and this marketing advantage leads to increased sales and profits. Effectively managing a diverse workgroup can prevent turnover and absenteeism. Furthermore, it reduces the likelihood of discrimination lawsuits, thereby reducing costs. Organizations with a history of employing and effectively managing a diverse workforce have an advantage in recruiting top talent from minority groups. Workforce heterogeneity also offers the organization a creativity advantage. Diverse groups are more likely to develop creative solutions to problems. To understand how to work well with diverse groups one must first examine different cultural values (see Table 6.3).

Culture also impacts management and leadership style in an organization. Research conducted by Geert Hofstede revealed national stereotypes of management styles. German managers are technical experts who assign tasks and solve problems and are primarily authoritarian. Japanese managers tend to rely on group consensus for decision making. French managers of major corporations are considered part of an elite class and exhibit superior and authoritarian characteristics. Dutch managers believe in quality and group problem solving and do not expect to impress employees with their status. Chinese managers maintain a low profile and major decisions in Chinese organizations are made by one dominant person who is often over the age of 65.

Table 6.3 Cross-cultural values

Individualism vs. collectivism

Individualistic cultures are made up of people who are concerned for their own interests first. They tend to be more concerned with their own careers than the good of the organization (e.g. United States, Canada, United Kingdom, and Australia). Collectivism is a feeling that the group or organization receives priority over individual interests (e.g. Japan, Mexico, Greece, and Hong Kong).

High power distance vs. low power distance

Power distance is the extent employees accept the idea that members of the organizations have different levels of power. In a high-power distance culture, employees willingly comply because they have a positive orientation towards authority (e.g. France, Spain, Japan, Mexico, and Brazil). In a low-power distance culture, employees only accept directions when they feel the superior is correct. They do not willingly recognize a power hierarchy (e.g. United States, Ireland, Germany, and Israel).

High uncertainly avoidance vs. low uncertainty avoidance

High uncertainty avoidance cultures contain a majority of people who do not tolerate risk and want predictable and certain futures (e.g. Japan, Italy, Argentina, and Israel). Low uncertainty avoidance cultures contain people who are willing to take risk and accept the unknown (e.g. United States, Canada, Australia, and Singapore).

Materialism vs. concern for others

Materialism refers to the acquisition of money and material objects and a de-emphasis on the caring for others (e.g. Japan, Austria, and Italy). A concern for others means building personal relationships and having a concern for the welfare of all (ex. Scandinavian countries).

Long-term orientation vs. short-term orientation

Employees from a long-term orientation culture believe in planning for the long term and not demanding immediate returns on investments (e.g. Pacific Rim Countries). Short-term orientation cultures demand immediate results and have a propensity not to save (e.g. United States and Canada).

Formality vs. informality

Cultures high on formality respect traditions, rituals, and ceremonies (e.g. Latin American countries). Informality cultures have a casual attitude toward tradition, social rules, and rank (United States, Canada, and Scandinavian countries).

Urgent time orientation vs. casual time orientation

Some cultures perceive time as a scare resource and are impatient; they tend to have an urgent time orientation (e.g. United States). Other cultures tend to view time as an unlimited resource and are more patient and have a casual time orientation (e.g. Asians and Middle Easterners).

Source: DuBrin (2002, pp. 282–285).

124

Organizational healing

Considering all these different methodologies in leadership and the inherent changes in the political and power structure, conflicts as a result of change are inevitable. This is especially true if there is a perception that the removal of previous management/ leadership was unwarranted, or new tactics are implemented regarding the processes of decision making and problem solving. All of these – and more – are common during a shift in organizational structure and changes within the organization. And while these organizational modifications may be necessary to help with the survival of the organization – i.e. keep the doors of the business open – many of the employees and management structure may not agree with, understand, or believe in the changes. These issues, if not dealt with, can erode the organization from the inside out.

Organizational healing is defined as the efforts related to repairing the social aspects of the organization, including issues related to continuity, vision, and broken self-concepts that are needed if an organization is to operate in a strong, fit, and well manner after an actual or other perceived negative situation. This is not the process of surviving a negative situation – it is dealing with the after-effects of the negative situation. While in general this is a group-oriented process that looks at all parts of the organization as one interacting unit, actions and beliefs of individuals still need to be taken into account.

One of the best methods to implement a process of organizational healing in a sport facility is to stop all operations, close the doors, and focus solely on healing. This may be accomplished through in-service programs, retreats, team building activities, and any activities that open the lines of communication across the organization. This should not be a judging process – rather a time to discuss, reflect, explain, and create an atmosphere of understanding and openness. The overall goals of this process are:

- To reinforce the importance of each individual and an integral part of the overall organization.
- To create and maintain a process of open communication and connection.
- To enhance and strengthen the organizational culture.
- To develop new organizational bonding methods that create new unity, sense of stability, and believe in the organization.

CHAPTER REVIEW

Organizational behavior is the study of human behavior in the work environment. A key difference between managers and leaders – managers preserve order and consistency, whereas leaders deal with change in a rapidly changing competitive environment. Four types of leader behavior are directive leadership, supportive leadership, participative leadership, and achievement-oriented leadership. Hersey and Blanchard (2012) developed four styles of leadership for managers to use depending on the maturity level of the follower: Telling, Selling, Participating, and Delegating. Transformational leaders influence major changes in the attitudes and assumptions of staff members and are capable of building commitment for major changes in the organization's objectives and strategies. Charismatic leaders exude several key characteristics, these include: their ability to establish an organizational vision (or lofty goal), are masterful communicators, inspire trust, are energetic, and are adept at impression management. Dysfunctional leadership symptoms may include: conflict avoidance, micromanagement, inefficient use of resources, and no 360 degree feedback.

Organizational culture is a system of shared values, beliefs, assumptions, and understandings that influence worker behavior. Diverse organizations have a competitive advantage potential and offer benefits in various ways, e.g. marketing advantage over a multicultural client base, lower turnover and absenteeism, reduces likelihood of discrimination lawsuits, advantages in recruiting top talent from minority groups, and possess a creativity advantage. To understand how to work well with diverse groups one must first examine different cultural values.

BIBLIOGRAPHY

Argyle, M. (1990). *Bodily communication* (2nd ed.). Madison, CT: International Universities Press.

Avolio, B. J., Waldman, D. A., and McDaniel, M. A. (1990). Age and work performance in nonmanagerial jobs: the effects of experience and occupational type. *Academy of Management Journal, 33*(2), 407–422.

Bennis, W. (1997). *Organizing genius: The secrets of creative collaboration.* Boston: Addison-Wesley.

Careless, S. A., Wearing, A. J., and Mann, L. (2000). A short measure of transformational leadership. *Journal of Business and Psychology, 14*(3), 389–405.

Chelladurai, P. (2006). *Human resource management in sport and recreation* (2nd ed.). Champaign, IL: Human Kinetics.

Conger, J. A. and Kanungo, R. N. (1998). *Charismatic leadership in organizations.* Thousand Oaks, CA: Sage.

Covell, D. and Walker, S. (2013). *Managing sport organizations: Responsibility for performance* (2nd ed.). New York: Routledge.

Cunningham, J. B. and Eberie, T. (1990). A guide to job enrichment and redesign. *Personnel, 67*(2), 56–61.

DuBrin, A. J. (2002). *The winning edge: How to motivate, influence, and manage your company's human resources.* Cincinnati, OH: South-Western College Publishing.

Filley, A. C., House, R. J., and Kerr, S. (1976). *Managerial process and organizational behavior* (2nd ed.). Glenview, IL: Scott Foresman.

Gardner, W. L. and Avolio, B. J. (1998). The charismatic relationship. *Academy of Management Review, 2*(1), 32–58.

Griffin, R. W. (1991). Effects of work redesign on employee perceptions, attitudes, and behaviors: A long term investigation. *Academy of Management Journal, 34*(2), 425–435.

Griffin, R. W. and Moorhead, G. (2014). *Organizational behavior* (11th ed.). Boston: Houghton Mifflin.

Hater, J. J. and Bass, B. M. (1988). Superiors' evaluations and subordinates' perceptions of transformational and transactional leadership. *Journal of Applied Psychology, 73*(4), 695–702.

Hequet, M. (1994). Giving good feedback. *Training, 31*(9), 72–76.

Hersey, P. and Blanchard, K. H. (2012). *Management of organizational behavior: utilizing human resources* (10th ed.). Englewood Cliffs, NJ: Prentice Hall.

Herzberg, F. (1974). The wise old Turk. *Harvard Business Review, 52(5),* 70–81.

Hofstede, G. (1980). *Culture's consequences: International differences in work-related values.* Beverly Hills, CA: Sage.

House, R. J. (1971). A path-goal theory of leadership effectiveness. *Administrative Science Quarterly, 16*(3), 321–329.

House, R. J. and Mitchell, T. R. (1974). Path-goal theory of leadership. *Journal of Contemporary Business, 3*, 81–97.

Ivancevich, J. M. and Matteson, M. T. (2013). *Organizational behavior and management* (10th ed.). New York: McGraw-Hill.

Kass, S. (1999). Employees perceive women as better managers than men, finds five year study. *APA Monitor, 30*(8), 6.

Kirmeyer, S. L. and Dougherty, T. W. (1988). Work load, tension, and coping: Moderating effects of supervisor support. *Personnel Psychology, 41*(1), 125–139.

Kotter, J. P. (1990). What leaders really do? *Harvard Business Review, 68*(3), 103–111.

Laabs, J. (1998). Satisfy them with more than money. *Workforce, 77*(11), 40–43.

Lewin, K. (1935). *A dynamic theory of personality.* New York: McGraw-Hill.

Maslach, C. and Leiter, M.P. (1997). *The truth about burnout: How organizations cause personal stress and what to do about it.* San Francisco: Jossey-Bass.

Miner, J. B. (1988). *Organizational behavior: Performance and productivity.* New York: Random House.

Moore, J. E. (2000). Why is this happening? A casual attribution approach to work exhaustion consequences. *Academy of Management Review, 25*(2), 335–349.

Plochg Business Psychology Consulting (2009). *Dysfunctional patterns in leadership.* Retrieved August 3, 2009 from: http://businesspsychologistconsulting.com

Powell, G. N. (1990). One more time: do female and male managers differ? *Academy of Management Executive 4*(3), 68–75.

S. Robbins (2009). Seven communication mistakes managers make. *Harvard Business Review.* Retrieved August 3, 2009 from http://blogs.hbr.org/2009/03/seven-communication-mistakes-m/

Schein, E. H. (2010). *Organizational culture and leadership* (4th ed.). San Francisco: Jossey-Bass.

Slack, T. and Parent, M. M. (2006). *Understanding sport organizations: The application of organization theory* (2nd ed.). Champaign, IL: Human Kinetics.

Thomas, K. W. (1979). Organizational conflict. In S. Kerr (Ed.) *Organizational behavior* (pp. 151–185). Columbus, OH: Grid Publishing.

Tichy, N. M. and Devanna, M. A. (1990). *The transformational leader.* New York: Wiley.

Trevino, L. K. and Nelson, K. A. (2006). *Managing business ethics: Straight talk about how to do it right* (4th ed.). New York: Wiley.

Wilson, J. Q. (1993). *The moral sense.* New York: The Free Press.

Yones, M. (2005). Dysfunctional leadership & dysfunctional organizations. *International Institute of Management Executive Journal.* Retrieved August 3, 2009 from: www.iim-edu.org/publications/executivejournal/dysfunctional-leadership-dysfunctional-organizations-paper/index.htm

Yukl, G. A. (2002). *Leadership in organizations* (5th ed.). Upper Saddle River, NJ: Prentice Hall.

IN THE FIELD ...

Pat Williams, keynote speaker at the NCS[4] Annual Conference – Orlando, July 2013

Pat Williams is a motivational speaker and sport executive, currently serving as a senior vice president of the NBA's Orlando Magic. Williams began his career as a minor league baseball player, and later joined the front office of his team. In the late 1960s he moved into basketball, with his biggest achievements being the 1983 title of the Philadelphia 76ers and being a partner in the creation of the Orlando Magic in 1987. In 1996, Williams was named one of the 50 most influential people in NBA history.

Seven ingredients of leadership

1   Vision: seeing before others. This keeps you focused and fueled, creating the passion and energy needed to get results. This helps you cross the finish line. Leadership is always about results.
2   Communicating the vision: believe in communication within the ranks of your organization. Your associates are key assets. Motivate them and make them care. Do it in a way that they understand – simplify things. This needs to be done verbally – leadership gravitates to those that can speak in front of people and they are usually great storytellers.
3   People skills: great leaders love people. Care about your people. Show an interest and empathy when needed. Be visible and available to people. Know them and what matters to them, listen carefully, and empower people. Express your appreciation for others out loud.
4   Character: good leadership involves strategy and character – honesty, integrity, and humility. Tell the truth no matter what, be consistent, and show humility with resolve.
5   Competence: be good at what you do. Leaders are born and made (developed). Leadership is about problem solving, teaching, and team-building. All leaders must be readers and lifelong learners.
6   Boldness: leaders must make decisions. Do not sit back and wait for things to happen. You must be proactive and make decisions when necessary – be bold.
7   Serving heart: it is not about the leader, it is about the members of the organization. You are there to serve them. You want to help them achieve their goals and reach their potential.

Source: personal notes from conference attendance – Dr. Stacey Hall, Associate Professor of Sport Management, The University of Southern Mississippi.

Implementation of management and operations

TECHNOLOGY NOW!

Communication technologies have fueled idea sharing. In many organizations today, management has encouraged bottom-up decision making. For example, some companies claim that most worthwhile innovations have come from employees via email. Although email is only the beginning, most communication technologies extend beyond this medium into various kinds of real-time and asynchronous electronic connections, such as chat rooms and news groups, conferencing systems, technologies for surveys, voting, and joint document preparation; distance education; remote control of computers for demonstrations or group graphic designs.

Electronic communications are ideal for involving creative people who might be shunned or perceived as marginal in organizations that rely too heavily on face-to-face idea exchange. The asynchronous nature of today's communication technologies gives employees the opportunity to edit and dig deeper into what they really want to say, the typical pressures of face-to-face meetings – of having to speak up and be aggressive with ideas – are reduced. Additionally, the use of electronic communications means that an employee's age, gender, ethnicity, physical appearance, and personality quirks no longer determine how suggestions are received. The result is that companies are better able to retain unconventional, creative employees who may be bad at office politics but good at generating fresh ideas.

Source: R. Farson and R. Keyes (2002). The failure-tolerant leader. *Harvard Business Review, 80*(8), 64–71.

CHAPTER 7

HUMAN RESOURCE MANAGEMENT

HUMAN RESOURCES IN SPORT FACILITIES

While the infrastructure of a sport facility is certainly important, without people working in and using the facility the infrastructure is useless. Hence it is safe to say that the most important resource for a sport facility is the human resource. Human resource management is the function within an organization that is responsible for the recruitment, training, and retention of personnel, but goes much more in depth in an effort to strategically move the organization forward toward a vision.

However, prior to analyzing these human resource practices, it is important to recognize who the major human resources are in a sport facility. For the purpose of this section, we will break down these human resources into three categories – professional staff, volunteers, and clients.

Professional staff

Professional staff are the employees of a sport organization who are hired to perform specific jobs/tasks in exchange for some form of remuneration. Within sport facilities, there are usually four levels of professional staff – executive, administrative, supervisory, and general.

The executive level has the most power and authority. It is made up of senior or top managers within the sport facility whom are usually responsible for the majority of the management and operations of the overall sport facility. Typical titles of professional staff at the executive level include presidents, chief executive officers (CEO), vice presidents of various operations, and general managers.

Administrative level professional staff, also known as middle managers, are accountable for the day-to-day operations of specific departments or operations within a sport facility. These staff members have a unique position within the organization since they connect both the upper and lower levels of management within the sport facility. Therefore, they must balance leadership of lower professional staff with managing the tasks set forth by upper management. In sport facilities, these individuals are usually directors or coordinators of various departments such as marketing, facility operations, business operations, sport programs, and food and beverage services.

Supervisory level professional staff are responsible for the day-to-day operations within a specific unit in a department. These assistant or associate level managers are responsible to ensure that the specific tasks within their unit are completed based on the directives from their middle manager, and are the connection between the specialists working in each unit. For example, within the department of sport programs, there may be assistant directors for boys/men's programs, girls/women's programs, kids' programs, and camps/clinics. These managers have little authority in the grand scheme of the overall sport facility, but are the ultimate authority general staff answer to.

General staff are the specialists within individual units who complete the tasks as assigned by the management structure within a sport facility. These professional staff are specialists in their area of employment – such as coaches, custodial staff, front office staff, security, and officials.

It is important to remember that the professional staff at the top levels are mostly responsible for the conceptual management of a sport facility, the general staff are in charge of conducting the technical aspect of running a sport facility, and the middle managers are accountable for the highest levels of interpersonal skills by ensuring concepts are communicated to general staff while at the same time technical issues are articulated to upper management. Regardless of the level of professional staff, ultimately each is responsible for ensuring that the planning, organizing, and controlling of the sport facility is appropriately administered through proper direction and adequate staffing.

Volunteers

However, one of the challenges in sport facilities, especially as related to many of the events that take place in them, is the cost of staffing those events appropriately. Sport facility managers need to ensure that all internal and external laws and regulations are followed, especially as related to the number of staff members that need to be present in various areas to ensure the safe and enjoyable experience of guests.

However, the costs to staff the required number of people would cripple most events – especially at the hallmark (Super Bowl, World Cups, etc.) and regional (marathons, triathlons, bike tours, etc.) levels. In addition, organizations without a large budget (especially non-profits such as Special Olympics) could not even dream of holding events. This would be devastating to sport facilities, because if there are no events, then there is no need for a facility. This has led to the significant growth of another major human resource that work in a sport facility – volunteers.

A volunteer is a non-employee who willingly becomes involved with an organization or event for no compensation to assist with a need that could not otherwise be offered. This definition is generic in nature, as there is truly no universally agreed upon description. This is because it depends on the viewpoint – those who volunteer look at volunteerism as giving time, effort, and expertise to an organization with a need for either socially responsible or altruist reasons; those who take on volunteers look to accomplish the goals and mission of the organization by securing individuals who have expertise to meet the need without having to put them on the payroll.

GLOBAL VOLUNTEERISM

Sports, no matter what the event, always are in need for volunteers, and hence sport facility professional staff members must recognize their importance. Volunteers are imperative to the success or failure of an event, and hence to the positive or negative image of a sport facility. Sport facilities that hold events ranging from the small local recreation basketball tournament to the Olympics need volunteers to succeed. These organizations usually will consider any volunteers they can get their hands on, regardless of their professional background.

As the volunteer concept has many definitions globally, a sampling of the volunteer concept from around the world is shown below.

Volunteering Australia

In Australia, Volunteering Australia is the national body that is charged with overseeing and advancing volunteerism across the country. With a mission 'to lead, strengthen, promote and celebrate volunteering in Australia', and a vision of 'strong, connected communities through volunteering', they seek to offer opportunities that are 'collaborative, accessible, inclusive, innovative, flexible, proactive, transparent, and accountable' (Volunteering Australia, 2014).

Through their strategic focus areas of research and policy; sector development; positioning and profiling of volunteering; governance and sustainability;

and advocacy, they seek to create formal volunteering as an activity which takes place through not-for-profit organizations or projects and is undertaken (1) to be of benefit to the community and the volunteer; (2) of the volunteer's own free will and without coercion; (3) for no financial payment; and (4) in designated volunteer positions only.

In general, Volunteering Australia promotes that volunteering

- provides benefits to the community and the volunteer;
- is unpaid;
- is always a matter of choice;
- should not be compulsorily undertaken to receive pensions or government allowances;
- can be a legitimate way in which citizens can participate in the activities of their community;
- should be a vehicle for individuals or groups to address human, environmental, and social needs;
- is an activity usually performed in the not-for-profit sector only;
- is never a substitute for paid work;
- does not replace paid workers nor constitute a threat to the job security of paid workers;
- respects the rights, dignity and culture of others;
- promotes human rights and equality.

Volunteer Canada

According to the 2010 Canada Survey on Giving, Volunteering and Participating, '13.3 million Canadians contribute 2.1 billion hours, which is the equivalent of 1.1 million full time jobs!' (Volunteer Canada, 2014). With a mission of 'providing leadership in strengthening citizen engagement and serving as a catalyst for voluntary action', and a vision of 'involved Canadians … resilient communities … a vibrant Canada', Volunteer Canada seeks to drive volunteerism throughout all communities via non-profit organizations, public-sector agencies, private business, and individuals within the population (Volunteer Canada, 2014).

The Canadian Code for Volunteer Involvement gives values for volunteer involvement, which are core statements on the importance and value of volunteer involvement in voluntary organizations and Canadian society. They include:

- Volunteer involvement is vital to a just and democratic society, as it fosters civic responsibility, participation and interaction.

- Volunteer involvement strengthens communities, as it promotes change and development by identifying and responding to community needs.
- Volunteer involvement mutually benefits both the volunteer and the organization, as it increases the capacity of organizations to accomplish their goals, and provides volunteers with opportunities to develop and contribute.
- Volunteer involvement is based on relationships, as it creates opportunities for voluntary organizations to accomplish their goals by engaging and involving volunteers, and it allows volunteers an opportunity to grow and give back to the community in meaningful ways through voluntary organizations.

The code also provides guiding principles for volunteer involvement, which detail the exchange between voluntary organizations and volunteers. These include:

- Volunteers have rights – hence voluntary organizations must recognize that volunteers are a vital human resource and will commit to the appropriate infrastructure to support volunteers. This includes ensuring effective volunteer involvement, and providing a safe and supportive environment for volunteers.
- Volunteers have responsibilities – therefore must make a commitment and are accountable to the organization. This includes volunteers acting responsibly and with integrity and respect for beneficiaries and community.

Volunteering England

In 2013, Volunteering England merged with the National Council for Voluntary Organisations (NCVO) to create the largest volunteering body in the United Kingdom. The NCVO has over 11,000 members focused on strengthening volunteerism and civil society ranging from small community organizations to large multinational charities. With a mission of 'helping voluntary organisations and volunteers make the biggest difference they can', and a vision of creating 'a society where we can all make a difference to the causes that we believe in', the NCVO seeks through research, innovation, collaboration, inclusiveness, and integrity to meet the needs of the civil society in the United Kingdom (National Council for Voluntary Organizations, 2014).

Their overarching goal is to bring ideas and people together, develop better networks and structures, and initiate projects to support volunteering in a wide range of fields, such as health, social care, sport, and employer-supported volunteering.

Sources

National Council for Voluntary Organisations (2014). *About us*. Retrieved November 18, 2014 from: www.ncvo.org.uk/about-us

Volunteer Canada (2014). *About us*. Retrieved November 18, 2014 from: http://volunteer.ca/content/about-us

Volunteering Australia (2014). *About us*. Retrieved November 18, 2014 from: www.volunteeringaustralia.org/about-us

Suggested discussion topics

1   Cultural differences will have a direct effect on volunteerism. However, over the last decade volunteerism has been growing in Brazil. Research how this increase in volunteerism was utilized and managed in conjunction with the hosting of the 2014 FIFA World Cup; and what the evaluation of the volunteer process showed for changes and implementation for the 2016 Summer Olympic and Paralympic Games.
2   What concerns should organizations and volunteers have from a legal and risk management standpoint? How would you address these concerns as a sport facility manager, and as a volunteer?

Customers and clients

Customers and clients are a unique human resource for sport facilities because of the service orientation involved. These individuals are often participants and/or have some involvement with sport events that take place in sport facilities. Sport in general is in the position of producing services and consuming services simultaneously. Therefore, the customer or client of a sport facility provide both inputs and outputs – and hence must be considered a human resource.

Similar to the volunteer, the customer/client as a human resource does provide the opportunity for a sport facility to offer a service through the events it hosts, while at the same time lowering the expense of paid staff by having customers and clients help staff the events. Examples might include scorekeepers and secondary officials for games, completing registration and waiver forms on behalf of the facility, as greeters to give directions to other guests and customers to the sport facility, and as extra security to help control crowds.

Individual differences in human resources

Regardless of the type of human resources, it is important to recognize the individual differences between people. Individual differences are usually affected by factors including personality, motivation, attitudes, and perceptions.

136

Personality is defined as the unique and personal psychological characteristics of an individual which reflects how they respond to their social environment. An individual's personality reflects their individual differences. While personality can change, it is generally permanent and consistent. Sport facility managers must be able to manage human resources in terms of their self-concept and their stage in the life cycle. Self-concept goes beyond self-image; it includes recognizing who the human resource wants to be (ideal self), how the human resource believes they are viewed by others (perceived self), and how the human resource interacts with their reference group (reference group self). As far as the stage in the life cycle, sport facility managers must recognize that human resources are different as they transition through life, which in turn modifies their individual attitudes, values, and identities.

Motivation is the influence that initiates the drive to satisfy wants and needs. For human resources in sport facilities, this may be achieved through motives such as accomplishment, fun, improvement of skill, health and fitness, or the desire for affiliation. Motives are emotional or psychological needs that act to stimulate an action. Emotional motives involve the selection of goals according to individual or subjective criteria. Rational motives entail selecting goals based on objective criteria. In general, motives will never fully satisfy needs, because new needs develop as a result of the satisfaction of old needs. Therefore, to motivate human resources, sport facility managers need to focus on three specific needs: power, affiliation, and achievement. Power is where the human resource wants to have control over their environment. Affiliation is the most basic concept of social interaction, and some human resources need interaction with other human beings and to be in an atmosphere of connectedness and belonging. Achievement involves the need for personal accomplishment through being self-fulfilled or having high self-esteem and/or prestige.

An attitude is a state of mind or behavioral predisposition that is consistently favorable or unfavorable with respect to a product or situation. Attitudes are formed in many different ways, but most often they are formed either from personality factors or are learned from environmental influences. Sport facility managers are constantly trying to influence the attitudes of their human resources. Some of the strategies employed include changing the basic motivational function of the human resource, associating their involvement as a human resource with a respected group or sport event; and working out conflicts between two attitudes, preferably moving from negative to positive.

Perceptions involve gaining an understanding of the individual values, attitudes, needs, and expectations of an individual by scanning, gathering, assessing, and interpreting those insights. For human resources, perception involves the process of interpreting the world around them (in this case the sport facility) through sensations, images, and affections. Sensations are the most basic element of perception as they are the immediate and direct responses from the sensory organs. Images are the pictures that are formed in the mind to differentiate what is perceived. Affections are the actual emotions emitted as a result of the perception. The perceptions of human resources can easily be transmitted to other human resources, customers, clients, and the general public, hence it is important for the sport facility manager to ensure that the sport facility is perceived in a positive light as often as possible.

HUMAN RESOURCE PRACTICES IN SPORT FACILITIES

As stated earlier in the chapter, human resource management is the function within an organization that is responsible for the recruitment, training, and retention of personnel, but goes much more in depth in an effort to strategically move the organization forward toward a vision. With this in mind, the sport facility manager has a number of responsibilities inherent in this area. These include developing the values and principles for leading and managing people in the sport facility, defining the strategies to be utilized, developing the policies to guide all human resources, and implementing procedures and methods to apply those policies – thus creating a human resource management structure for the sport facility.

This section of the book will cover the major human resource management practices for sport facilities. First will be an explanation of managing human resources for sport facilities, followed by an analysis of the various functions innate to strategic human resource management. This information will then be applied to the two most important concepts in human resource management as related to sport facilities – employment of personnel and performance management.

Managing human resources

The most important function within human resource management in sport facilities, and most likely in any organization, is to understand the best way to manage people. Management is the process of planning, organizing, directing, and controlling tasks to accomplish goals, meet the mission of the organization, and work towards a vision. As such, human resource management focuses on planning, organizing, directing, and controlling people within the organization. In human resource management, employees/personnel are looked at as assets – just like a piece of equipment or the infrastructure of the sport facility. Human resources have significant costs to the sport facility in the forms of outlays of payroll, benefits, and other perks. They also have significant costs as their actions (or lack thereof) as service providers could lead to additional expenses or reductions of revenues.

This leads to two questions. First is 'should human resources simply be looked at as another asset for a sport facility?' After all, these are human beings, not inanimate objects, and their knowledge and skills are a unique benefit to a sport facility. The second question is 'do all people want to be managed?' This is a deeper question that looks into the individual differences of people. It is true that many people prefer to just be told what to do, and they will accomplish the tasks. However, there are those who believe they are an asset that brings great value to the sport facility, and have a desire to grow both personally and in concert with the organization. As a result, this brings forward two additional concepts to consider in the managing of human resources – human capital management and leadership of human resources.

Human capital management

Human capital management is defined as the administration of the most important asset within an organization – people. This is a slightly different concept than human resource management, where many times the people are looked at as costs to the organization. However, it seems that more and more sport organizations – especially as the service-based economy becomes more prevalent in the sport industry – are injecting human capital management concepts into their human resource practices. The reason is the realization that human resources are more than just a necessity as a support service to a sport facility. Human resources add value to the overall organization, because of their training, expertise, adaptability, commitment, and loyalty. Their individual training and expertise determine the skills and services available within the sport facility. Adaptability to change provides strategic flexibility for the sport facility. Commitment and loyalty of human resources – because of the ownership they feel in being an integral asset to the organization – often equates to the ability to maintain competitive advantage.

Leadership

As a result of this shift towards implementing human capital management philosophies into the human resource management process, the other issue to evaluate is how the concept of leadership became part of managing human resources. Leadership is a very different concept than management, but is often improperly used interchangeably. Leadership is the process of guiding and inspiring people. Leadership is not straightforward, as people have different preferences in the way they want to be led. Therefore, leaders will utilize different styles of leadership based on the situation at hand.

While there are numerous different models of leadership, generally there are three basic styles of leadership – autocratic, democratic, and laissez-faire. Autocratic leadership is more of a dictatorial style of leadership where the leader tells human resources what to do, and limits discussion about alternative courses of action. While this does not promote a sense of teamwork in the organization, it is an important style to utilize when time is limited, there is a lack of skill or knowledge amongst the human resources (as in the case with entry-level employees), or when new groups of people have not worked together in the past (as in the case of a group of new employees).

Democratic leadership is a participative style of leadership where human resources are involved with the decision making and problem solving processes related to the operation of the sport facility. This style of leadership recognizes the importance of teamwork, and takes into account the individual skills and knowledge of human resources. This style of leadership is effective when there is time to make decisions and the human resources are motivated to be involved. This style of leadership is highly ineffective when there is a high level of conflict within a human resource group.

Laissez-faire (the French word for 'hands-off') leadership is where the leader defers decision making and problem solving to human resources because of their extensive experience, skill, and knowledge about a given process. This is an especially powerful style of leadership with long-time employees who are familiar with the routines and services within a sport facility. It is also very powerful when there is good communication and cooperation between human resources within the sport facility.

Managers complete tasks – leaders influence people. So as we look at the evolution of human resource management, it is important to recognize the shift in looking at human resources as costs necessary to complete tasks within a sport facility. Human resources are assets to the sport facility, and they may work more effectively by being influenced and inspired rather than by being told what to do. As this shift becomes more prevalent across human resource practice, it will have a direct affect on the process of strategic human resource management.

Strategic human resource management

Strategic human resource management for sport facilities involves an integrative approach to creating human resource strategies that seeks to accomplish goals based on the desired outcomes for the sport facility. There are numerous elements to having a strategic outlook for human resources in a sport facility, including the strategic intentions of the ownership structure; the availability and allocation of resources to meet the opportunities and needs of the sport facility; to attain a competitive advantage over similar sport facilities; and the strategic capabilities of the overall organizational structure of the sport facility. In order to attain these strategic outcomes, sport facility managers must be able to efficiently plan, organize, and control knowledge.

Knowledge management

Knowledge management is the acquisition, sharing, and use of intelligence, understanding, and expertise within a sport organization to aid in the accomplishment of tasks, processes, and operations. This is a crucial part of human resource management in a sport facility as the knowledge of personnel, and the sharing of knowledge throughout the organization, allows the operation of the sport facility to be more efficient and effective.

Knowledge within a sport facility usually falls under four categories:

- Embedded knowledge – the information which is articulated within rules and regulations, and organizational policies and procedures.
- Embodied knowledge – the practical skills, understandings, and applications of concepts exhibited by employees and management.
- Embraced knowledge – the theoretical/conceptual/cognitive skills exhibited by employees and management.
- Encultured knowledge – the collective intelligence, values, and beliefs of the entire organization.

In order to most effectively manage knowledge, sport facility managers seek to utilize all existing intelligence in the best possible manner. In some cases, this may involve choosing specific individuals to work on tasks where their expertise lie – in other cases it may entail documenting and storing information for referral by others in the future. The goal is to ensure productivity in all processes and procedures on a continuous basis. However, it is important to recognize that all knowledge may not exist internal to the organization. This is why recognizing the importance of professional development to renew the knowledge of personnel, as well as to bring in outside knowledge when necessary to accomplish tasks that cannot be completed by those in the organization, is crucial to knowledge management. Those organizations that do not stay ahead of change or their competition are setting themselves up for reduced success.

While it is important to know how to acquire the knowledge necessary to successfully operate a sport facility, this is not enough. Knowledge is only useful if it can be transformed into useable outputs. This is where understanding the structural capital and business strategy of a sport facility is crucial to success. Structural capital is the understanding of the organizational structure and how information and knowledge moves horizontally and vertically through that structure to accomplish tasks that meet the needs and desires of customers. Business strategy involves understanding the management practices of top managers and ownership, and how the competencies and capabilities of personnel are most effectively managed to accomplish the mission and goals set forth by them to move the sport facility forward as a business.

Knowledge management is crucial to the success of human resource management. However, knowledge is only as good as the people who own that knowledge, and the organization is set up to effectively utilize those individuals. Hence, the way in which jobs are designed, personnel are selected, and employees are integrated into the organization is essential to quality human resource management.

Employment of personnel

Employment is the process of making a living through work or conducting business. Managers seek to employ the most knowledgeable individuals to efficiently and effectively run the operations of sport facilities, especially because of the intricate designs, skills, and knowledge necessary based on the wide variety of facilities. In order to most effectively hire the best and brightest, job tasks need to be analyzed and appropriate positions designed. This also requires quality recruiting and selecting of personnel, followed by the implementation of an orientation, training, and development program for new personnel.

Job analysis and design

Job analysis is the process of examining and evaluating the specific tasks to be completed within an organization and determining the best way to design a method for completing them in the most timely and relevant way. Usually, job analysis for a sport facility requires understanding the current organizational structure of the sport facility, the work activities that need to be accomplished, and the knowledge and informational content present within the organization. Once this information is compiled, tasks are grouped, positions are determined, job titles are assigned, and organizational charts are modified as necessary.

This is followed by the process of designing a job description. The main purpose of the job description is to articulate the job responsibilities of the position opening and the expected competencies of candidates for the position. The following are usual inclusions within a job description:

- Job title
- Commitment required
    - Usually articulated in hours per week
- Salary
    - Including rewards and incentives available over and above the salary
- Summary of the job
    - Duties and responsibilities
    - Authority and reporting structure
    - Performance standards
- Knowledge
    - Education requirements
    - Experience requirements
    - Skills and abilities desired (including qualifications)
- Contact information
- Application deadlines
- General information about the sport organization/facility
- Any required legal or governmental statements

- Equal employment opportunity statements
- Background/criminal checks (especially when working with children in sport facilities).

The job description is used to standardize the information about a specific task or group of tasks, including the essential duties of personnel working under that description. This is important in standardizing and balancing the work assignments between employees in the organization, and can be effectively used to stylize the training and quality assessment programs within a sport facility, as well as to assure compliance with industry standards and legal responsibilities. Another major use of job descriptions is in the creation of job announcements to recruit new personnel – as the job description provides parameters for managers to do quality searching for employees, can be used to formulate questions during the interviewing process, and provides the most important information to potential job candidates.

Recruiting and selecting personnel

Recruiting and selecting of personnel occurs for one of two reasons – a new position has been created, or an individual has left a position either because of termination, temporary leave, or job change. Regardless of the reason, the sport facility manager must engage in the recruitment and selection process, which involves submitting recruiting documents, engaging in the actual selection process, empowering a search committee, conducting interviews, carrying out reference checks, making the hiring decision, and documenting the entire process.

The recruitment and selection process starts by submitting recruiting documents, which usually included a request for hire memorandum explaining the need for the hire, and an updated position description. Once approved, a job posting is created to be published in newspapers, websites, and other job listing services.

As applications come in, a major task is to go through all the applications to select the most qualified candidates for the position. It is important to review the position description point by point to ensure your understanding of all requirements, and then develop a plan to most effectively identify and assess the candidates. As a part of the selection process, depending on the number of applicants, there may be multiple levels of assessment. For example, assume there is a pool of 100 applicants, and eight are deemed to be most qualified. Phone interviews may be the appropriate next step to further assess the candidates and determine the most appropriate candidates to bring in for face-to-face interviews.

Applicant pools may be only assessed by the direct supervisor who is conducting the hiring process, but it is recommended that applicant assessments be conducted by a search committee. A search committee is a group of individuals who evaluate, screen, and interview individuals seeking employment. This often is a mix of direct supervisors, potential coworkers, and outside of department employees, and can give additional perspectives into the selection process of employees for the sport facility.

143

Once the applicant pool is reduced to the final candidates, interviews take place. The purpose of an interview is to elicit information from an applicant to determine their ability to perform the job. Successful interviewers learn how to ask the right kind of questions, how to keep the applicant talking about relevant information, and how to listen – because much of what is learned about applicants in an interview is based on their past experience, and past performance is one of the best indicators of future performance.

When conducting interviews, there are two types of questions – non-directive and directive. Non-directive questions do not give the applicant any indication of the desired answer, are usually phrased in the news reporter's style of who, what, when, where and how, and often they begin with the words 'describe' or 'explain'. Examples of non-directive questions include:

- Describe your experiences working as a scheduling manager for sport facilities.
- Explain what you consider to be the most important responsibilities of a sport facility manager.
- Why does this position interest you?
- How has your background prepared you for this position?

It is also important to ask follow-up questions if the response is unclear or incomplete. Clarify and verify any piece of information by asking the candidate to explain their answer again or to elaborate on the given answer.

Directive questions are useful for drawing out specific information. In direct questioning, the interviewer asks, directs, or guides the applicant to specifics. Often, these questions result in a 'yes' or 'no' response. Examples of directive questions include:

- Do you have experience running a specific type of scheduling software?
- Are you still employed at your current job?
- Do you have certifications in pool and spa operations?

In addition to non-directive and directive questions, interviewers often develop special questions that are unique to the specific candidate either because of the education or experience, or as a result of a previous answer during the interview. One type of question format would be using self-evaluation – where the interviewee is asked to provide their perceptions and beliefs. Many times, this type of question focuses on asking about an applicant's likes and dislikes, or strengths and weaknesses.

Another type of question may be behavioral and/or experience-focused. This type of question asks the applicant to describe as closely as possible the actual behavior that went on in a particular situation. The use of superlative adjectives such as most/least, best/worst, and toughest/easiest tends to stimulate specific events in

144

the mind of the interviewee and therefore makes it easier to respond. An example would be:

- On your resume you noted that you were the Director of Scheduling at XYZ Facility. Can you share with the committee a time where you had a double-booking scenario and how you dealt with the situation?

Another method for developing special questions is by using a problem solving/judgment type question that involves a scenario that might be common on the job. An example would be:

- You are the facility supervisor on a Friday night when you are called to the basketball court where a person is lying on the ground under the basket unconscious. You hear from the other individuals on the court that the player went up for a dunk, got undercut by another player, and came down back and head first on the floor. How would you handle this situation?

Once all candidates have been interviewed and evaluations collected from all members of the committee, usually candidates are rank ordered in preference of selection. At that point, the top candidate is pursued. The first step in this process is to conduct reference checks. It is important to remember that information received in an interview is biased and typically includes only what the applicant wants to share. A thorough reference check may produce additional information to help ensure that the most suitable candidate is hired. It is a way to clarify, verify, and add data to what has been learned in the interview and from other portions of the selection process. The best source of information on any candidate is a current or former employer, especially the direct supervisor if possible. On-the-job performance is the most useful predictor of future success. The supervisor can specify the quality and quantity of work, reliability, potential problem areas, and job behaviors. It is better to do phone reference checks rather than utilize written references provided by candidates – the validity of written references cannot often be verified. It is also important to contact multiple references (usually three minimum is a good standard) to verify that the information about the candidate is consistent.

Assuming all reference checks go well, it is time to offer the position. However, this is not the end of the recruiting and selection process. Many things can happen at this point …

- The person is offered the position and after negotiation they accept the position.
- The person is offered the position and after negotiation they decline the position.
- You offer the person the position, and they turn down your offer.

If they turn down your offer, you need to start the reference check process on your next choice, and depending on the results ...

- The individual(s) are offered the position and they either accept or decline the offer.
- The individual(s) are deemed not appropriate for the position.

Should the latter happen, the following process will take place:

- Re-review of applicants not offered interviews in the first round to determine if any of them are qualified for an interview.
- If so, the interview process starts again. If not, they either:
  - Re-post the position for new applicants.
  - Re-evaluate the need within the sport facility to see if current employees might be able to cover the responsibilities in-house, and hence adjust their positions.

If a person is selected for a position, they often need to come into the human resource office to complete paperwork. This may include:

- Contracts
- Personal demographic data
- Tax and work verification paperwork
- Payroll and benefits paperwork
- Verification of receipt of human resource and operations manuals.

They may also need to bring in updated or additional paperwork such as updated resumes, education transcripts, and medical clearance forms. In some cases, this paperwork process is conducted in coordination with orientation for the new employee ...

Orientation, training, and development of new personnel

Orientation involves introducing new employees to the organization; training is the education of the employee in their job tasks; and development is the further education of the employee to further their skills, and value to the sport facility. Each of these processes is integral to the proper management of human resources, and hence the effective and efficient operation of a sport facility.

New employee orientation is the first step in integrating personnel into the sport facility. Effectively orienting new employees to the sport facility and to their positions is critical to establishing successful, productive working relationships. The employee's first interactions with you should create a positive impression of the sport facility. The time you spent planning for the new person's first days and

146

weeks on the job will greatly increase the chance for a successful start. An effective orientation program will:

- foster an understanding of the organization culture;
- help the new employee make a successful adjustment to the new job;
- help the new employee understand their role and how they fit into the total sport facility operation;
- help the new employee achieve objectives and shorten the learning curve;
- help the new employee develop a positive working relationship by building a foundation of knowledge about facility philosophy, mission, objectives, policies and procedures, rules and regulations, organizational structure, and vision.

Depending on the education and experience of the new employee, training may be extensive or specialized. Extensive training may be for a new employee with little education or experience, or who has shifted into a new area of responsibility. Specialized training may be a new employee with many years of experience in the field, but is in need of specific knowledge individual to the sport facility. Training should be an ongoing process to help employees advance their knowledge and skills, and therefore advance the operation of the sport facility. Some of this training may be in the form of development and certification programs. These may include attending seminars, training, conferences, or even classes offered at a local educational service or college/university.

Performance management

Performance management is the process of evaluating the past and current performance of employees. This evaluation is usually conducted by the immediate supervisor of the employee, and is kept on file by the human resource coordinator. The process of performance management usually involves three ongoing stages. First is the planning of performance and development metrics, where goals are set and measurement parameters are agreed upon. Second is the managing of performance throughout the employment process, where the supervisor and the employee gauge the successful attainment of goals. The final stage is a performance review, where the supervisor (at a predetermined time – can be 90 days, six months, or annually) assesses progress and accomplishments to determine exceptional, acceptable, or non-acceptable performance. These performance reviews are governed by the appraisal system set forth by the individual sport facility.

Appraisal systems

Employee performance appraisal systems are crucial to the successful administration of a sport facility. They are an important tool for making decisions about employee advancement, retention, and termination; salary increases; and employee improvement. Appraisal systems usually include three basic steps – collecting data; evaluating performance based on the data; and documenting the evaluation in writing. In collecting the data, immediate supervisors should assess behaviors of the employee, and avoid personality issues and differences unless they impact performance. The evaluation is about the employee's performance and not their personality. Once the data is collected and evaluated, it can then be utilized to measure performance and appraise the employee's value to the sport facility.

A performance appraisal should be seen as a way to maximize performance for the employees and the overall organization in the future instead of focusing on what has happened in the past. The ultimate goal of performance appraisals is to enhance the career building of the employee and advance the operation of the sport facility. At times, this is not possible, which may result in the termination or voluntary separation of the employee from the organization. All performance appraisals should be done in writing and verbally reviewed with the employee. Employees should be given advanced warning when the evaluation meeting will occur. A good practice is to have the employee do a self-evaluation prior to the meeting so that discussion points can be created.

Appraisal processes can be both a very exciting yet stressful time for an employee, as there is always fear that the employee's belief of their performance is not the same as the supervisor's. However, if there has been regular discussion and evaluation throughout the year, rewards have been provided when attaining a certain level of performance, resources have been provided to the employee to succeed such as proper training and development to do their job, and clear organizational and personal goals have been articulated and agreed upon, then there should be no surprises during the appraisal process. Therefore, a well-prepared appraisal system explores the past, accurately examines the present, and creates a plan for the future – hence enhancing retention and personnel relations.

Reward systems

Reward systems are the policies and strategies of a sport facility that focus on compensating employees in a fair, equitable, consistent, and transparent manner. There are numerous reasons for rewarding employees, including:

- the added value they create for the sport facility;
- the exhibition of appropriate behaviors, or meeting the desired outcomes;
- the development of a performance-based organizational culture where accomplishment is rewarded;
- the motivation of people to be committed and engaged with the organization;
- the retention of high-quality employees;
- the development of positive employment relationships.

The total reward an individual receives could be either financial or non-financial in nature. The most basic of rewards is a raise in base salary or basic pay. Other monetary rewards may include bonuses/additional commissions, long-term incentives (such as pensions), shares in the organization, profit sharing, and other incentives such as company cars and use of company-owned property/equipment. Non-financial rewards may include flex time (partial days off), holidays, and memberships (such as country club or sport facility). One of the most significant non-financial rewards is earning a promotion, and is an element of succession management.

Promotions and succession management

Succession management is the process of making provisions for the development, replacement, and strategic application of key people over time. It is inevitable that people will retire, leave an organization, or be promoted to another position, hence a succession plan must be in place. In some cases, succession will come from within via a promotion. In other cases, it requires hiring a new employee. Regardless, succession management requires the identification of the organization's values, mission, and strategic plans in a proactive manner that ensures there is continuing leadership within the sport facility by cultivating talent, preferably from within the organization, through planned development activities.

Termination processes

While the overriding goal of sport facility managers is to hire, cultivate, and retain the best employees, it is probable that a sport facility manager will have to terminate an employee at some point in their career. The process starts by documenting all the reasons for terminating the employee, and then set up a meeting with that employee to discuss the following:

- Explain to the employee how and why they are no longer working at the company. It is important to tell the truth, including such facts as the employee's poor performance, regardless of how uncomfortable it is. It is also crucial that the discussion be based solely on the performance – do not make remarks about an employee's personal character.
- Let the employee know that the decision is final and when the termination will be effective.
  - If for poor performance – normally immediate.
  - If as a result of a layoff – the date in the near future.
- Inform the employee what benefits are available to them, if any. This may include unemployment, health insurance, and severance pay. Each municipality has laws that govern how and when final pay and vacation pay is handled.

149

- Provide the employee a written termination notice. If the employee does not show up for the meeting, or is being terminated because they failed to show up for work, send the termination notice via certified mail.
- Collect any keys, access cards, uniforms, equipment, and/or any other property that is owned by the sport facility.

With regard to the last bullet point, certain employees may have access to confidential material such as access codes and computer files, which need to have access denied prior to the termination meeting. In some cases, this confidential material may go with the employee and be used against the sport facility when they go and work for a competitor or another company where their knowledge may put the sport facility at a competitive disadvantage. To prevent such a problem, there are two courses of action: (1) have a company employee be with the employee after the termination meeting to observe them 'cleaning out their desk' and escort them off the premises; and (2) have an employee signed agreement when they were hired (usually found in the human resource manual) that seeks to ensure the preservation, protection, and continuity of the confidential business information, trade secrets, and goodwill of the sport facility.

CREATING HUMAN RESOURCE MANUALS FOR SPORT FACILITIES

The purpose for creating a human resource manual is to have a central document that articulates accurate and current information regarding the policies and procedures of the sport facility as they relate to employees/personnel/volunteers/other associated human resources. The information provided usually includes, but is not limited to, employment and employee relations, benefits and compensation, general information about the sport facility, and policies/procedures of the sport facility.

There are usually three sections to a human resources manual for a sport facility. The first section is the philosophy and expectations of human resources, which is a compilation of information to introduce the sport facility to the employee. This usually starts with a welcome to the employee and an articulation of the sport facility's philosophy, mission, and goals. This is followed by an explanation of the purpose of the manual – which usually focuses on the manual as an operational and reference guide for the employee. The rest of this section usually focuses on general statements deemed important by the ownership of the sport facility. These statements may include general information about ethics and conduct, pride of ownership, owner expectations, daily routines, attendance, scheduling, job descriptions, and contact information.

The policies and benefits section is the bulk of the human resource manual. This section itemizes each of the human resource policies that should be understood by an individual working with or in a sport facility. The following would be a sample of the inclusions within a human resource manual:

- A general statement about the human resource manual being a living document, that changes will be made as needed, and that notification will be provided within a reasonable amount of time.
- Policies whose offenses may result in sanction or termination – including equal employment opportunities, sexual harassment, and smoking/substance abuse.
- Employment policies including types of documentation needed, and confidentiality and privacy statements.
- Employee compensation and work information such as anniversary dates, evaluations, workday, pay information, overtime, and gratuity allowances.
- Benefits information related to payroll deductions, insurance, retirement plans, reimbursements, and leave allowances (holiday, vacation, illness, medical, funeral, jury duty and other legal obligations, personal time, and leave of absence).
- Performance-related policies including performance reviews, merit increases, performance improvements, separations, and severance.
- General sport facility policies as related to dress code, upkeep of facility and offices (including common areas, infrastructure, equipment, and appliances), and use of facility-issued utilities (electronic communication, keys, lockers, computers, phones).
- An employee agreement form that seeks to ensure the preservation, protection, and continuity of the confidential business information, trade secrets, and goodwill of the sport facility. Concepts included in this agreement may include employment issues, no solicitation obligations with respect to employees and customers, nondisclosure obligations, possession of company information and materials, absence of conflict agreement statements, remedies should there be a breach of the agreement, and any additional miscellaneous information deemed important to the sport facility.

The final section is the operations manual, which builds on the concepts embedded in the human resource manual to articulate how the sport facility is to be managed. This section will be covered in more detail later in the book (Chapter 10). A sample of the first two sections of a human resource manual as described above can be found in the online appendix to this book.

CHAPTER REVIEW

Human resource management is the function within a sport facility that is responsible for the recruitment, training, and retention of personnel, but goes much more in depth in an effort to strategically move the organization forward toward a vision. Typically in a sport facility, there are three types of human resources. First are professional staff, who are the employees of a sport organization who are hired to perform specific jobs/tasks in exchange for some form of remuneration. Within sport facilities, there are usually four levels of professional staff: executives have the most power and authority, are made up of senior or top managers within the sport facility, and are usually responsible for the majority of the overall sport facility; administrators are accountable for the day-to-day operations of specific departments or operations; supervisors are responsible for the day-to-day operations within a specific unit in a department; and specialists/general staff complete the tasks as assigned by the management structure within a sport facility. Second are volunteers, who are non-employees that willingly become involved with an organization or event for no compensation to assist with a need that could not otherwise be offered. Last are customers and clients, who are often participants and/or have some involvement with sport events that take place in sport facilities, hence provide both the inputs and outputs of the sport facility.

Regardless of the type of human resources, it is important to recognize the individual differences between people. Individual differences are usually affected by factors including personality, motivation, attitudes, and perceptions. Personality is defined as the unique and personal psychological characteristics of an individual which reflect how they respond to their social environment. Motivation is the influence that initiates the drive to satisfy wants and needs. For human resources in sport facilities, this may be achieved through motives such as accomplishment, fun, improvement of skill, health and fitness, or the desire for affiliation. Attitudes are states of mind or behavioral predisposition that is consistently favorable or unfavorable with respect to a product or situation. Perceptions involve gaining an understanding of the individual values, attitudes, needs, and expectations of the sport consumer by scanning, gathering, assessing, and interpreting those insights.

The most important function within human resource management in sport facilities, and most likely in any organization, is to understand the best way to manage people. Management is the process of planning, organizing, directing, and controlling tasks to accomplish goals, meet the mission of the organization, and work towards a vision. As such, human resource management focuses on planning, organizing, directing, and controlling people within the organization. However, there is more than just managing the people to maximize value and minimize costs to the sport facility operation. Effective human resource management also requires sport facility managers to understand human capital management – the concept that people are the most important asset to an organization and should be treated as such. This then results in the transformation of the management process more toward leadership – where employees are guided and influenced to the benefit of their individual growth and that of the sport facility.

To move a sport facility forward, the process of strategic human resource management must be implemented, which is an integrative approach to creating human resource strategies that seeks to accomplish goals based on the desired outcomes for the sport facility. This is most effectively implemented through the appropriate managing of knowledge, or the acquisition, sharing, and use of intelligence, understanding, and expertise within a sport facility to aid in the accomplishment of tasks, processes, and operations.

In order to guarantee the sport facility has the optimal level of knowledge, sport facility owners and managers must employ the best and brightest to effectively and efficiently run the operations of sport facilities, especially because of the intricate designs, skills, and knowledge necessary based on the wide variety of facilities. The stages involved with employing personnel starts with an analysis of the job to be filled by examining and evaluating the specific tasks to be completed within an organization and determining the best way to design a method for completing them in the most timely and relevant way. Then a job description is created to articulate the job responsibilities of the position opening and the expected competencies of candidates for the position. Next is the recruitment and selection of employees, accomplished through a process of submitting recruiting documents, engaging in the actual selection process, empowering a search committee, conducting interviews, carrying out reference checks, making the hiring decision, and completing contracts and other pertinent documentation. This is then followed by employee orientation (introducing the job and the sport facility to the new employees), training (the education of the employee in their job tasks), and development (furthering the education of the employee to improve their skills and value to the sport facility).

Performance management is the process of evaluating the past and current performance of employees. Performance is evaluated through appraisal systems to make decisions about employee advancement, retention, and termination; salary increases; and employee improvement. The ultimate goal of performance appraisals is to enhance the career building of the employee and advance the operation of the sport facility. Reward systems are often put into place to provide extra compensation (financial and non-financial) for employees who have been deemed worthy. A succession management process takes rewards a step further by making provisions for the development, replacement, and strategic application of key people over time. This process also helps to hire new employees when the termination process is implemented because of poor performance or layoffs.

All the information about human resources is usually documented in a human resource manual. Its purpose is to have a central document that articulates accurate and current information regarding the policies and procedures of the sport facility as they relate to employees, personnel, volunteers, and other associated human resources. The information provided usually includes, but is not limited to, employment and employee relations, benefits and compensation, general information about the sport facility, and policies/procedures of the sport facility. The manual usually has three sections: (1) the philosophy and expectations of human resources, which is a compilation of information to introduce the sport facility to the employee; (2) the policies and benefits section, which itemizes each of the human resource policies that should be understood by an individual working with or in a sport facility; and (3) the operation manual, which builds on the concepts embedded in the human resource manual to articulate how the sport facility is to be managed.

BIBLIOGRAPHY

Analoui, F. (2007). *Strategic human resource management.* London: Thomson Learning.

Armstrong, M. (2014). *Armstrong's handbook of human resource management practice* (13th ed.). London: Kogan Page.

Baron, A. and Armstrong, M. (2008). *Human capital management. Achieving added value through people.* London: Kogan Page.

Brook, S. (2005). What do sports teams produce? *Journal of Economic Issues, 39*(3), 792–797.

Budhwar, P., Schuler, R. S., and Sparrow, P. R. (2009). *International human resource management.* London: Sage Publications.

Case, R. and Branch, J. (2003). A study to examine the job competencies of sport facility managers. *International Sports Journal, 7*(2), 25.

Chelladurai, P. (2006). *Human resource management in sport and recreation* (2nd ed.). Champaign, IL: Human Kinetics.

Emery, P. R. (2002). Bidding to host a major sports event: The local organising committee perspective. *The International Journal of Public Sector Management, 15*(4/5), 316–335.

Erdener, E. (2003). Linking programming and design with facilities management. *Journal of Performance of Constructed Facilities, 17*(11), 4–8.

Hums, M. A. and MacLean, J. C. (2013). *Governance and policy in sport organizations* (3rd ed.). Scottsdale, AZ: Holcomb Hathaway Publishers.

Hums, M. A., Barr, C. A., and Guillion, L. (1999). The ethical issues confronting managers in the sport industry. *Journal of Business Ethics, 20*(1), 51–66

Jamrog, J. J., Vickers, M., Overholt, M. H., and Morrison, C. L. (2008). High-performance organizations: Finding the elements of excellence. *HR. Human Resource Planning, 31*(1), 29–38.

Kim, S. D. and Kim, I. G. (2014). The relationship between employees' knowledge management activities in sports center and organizational citizenship behavior: Focus on the mediating effect of organizational trust. *International Journal of Applied Engineering Research, 9*(21), 9549–9262.

Martinez-Tur, V., Peiro, J. M., and Ramos, J. (2001). Linking service structural complexity to customer satisfaction: The moderating role of type of ownership. *International Journal of Service Industry Management, 12*(3/4), 295–306.

McDonald, K., Stewart, B., and Dingle, G. (2014). Managing multi-purpose leisure facilities in a time of climate change. *Managing Leisure, 19*(3), 212–225.

Mello, J. A. (2014). *Strategic human resource management* (4th ed.). Independence, KY: Cengage Learning.

Meng, X. and Minogue, M. (2011). Performance measurement models in facility management: A comparative study. *Facilities, 29*(11/12), 472–484.

Miller, D. and Desmarais, S. (2007). Developing your talent to the next level: Five best practices for leadership. *Organization Development Journal, 25*(3), P37–P43

Misener, K. and Doherty, A. (2009). A case study of organizational capacity in nonprofit community sport. *Journal of Sport Management, 23*(4), 457–482.

154

Misener, K. and Doherty, A. (2013). Understanding capacity through the processes and outcomes of interorganizational relationships in nonprofit community sport organizations. *Sport Management Review, 16*(2), 135–147.

Nalbantian, H. R., Guzzo, R. A., Kieffer, D., and Dohery, J. (2003). *Play to your strengths. Managing your internal labor markets for lasting competitive advantage.* New York: McGraw-Hill Trade.

Pedersen, P. M. and Thibault, L. (2014). *Contemporary sport management* (5th ed.). Champaign, IL: Human Kinetics.

Petersen, J. C. and Piletic, C. K. (2006). Facility accessibility: Opening the doors to all. *Journal of Physical Education, Recreation and Dance, 77*(5), 38–44.

Vos, S., Breesch, D., Késenne, S., Lagae, W., Hoecke, J. V., Vanreusel, B., and Scheerder, J. (2012). The value of human resources in non–public sports providers: The importance of volunteers in non–profit sports clubs versus professionals in for–profit fitness and health clubs. *International Journal of Sport Management and Marketing, 11*(1), 3–25.

IN THE FIELD …

Interview with Kristin Houston, Director of Human Resources, Tampa Bay Buccaneers

Please explain to the reader about your current position and what your responsibilities are.

As Director of Human Resources, I report to the General Counsel for the Tampa Bay Buccaneers and am responsible for a multitude of functions. The role of human resources must be in alignment with the needs of the organization. When HR professionals are aligned with the business, they are thought of as a strategic contributor to business success in terms of diversity and inclusion, employee culture, change management, organization development, employee and labor relations, and employee benefits.

In my role, I manage the recruitment efforts for the organization including maintaining and monitoring all job vacancies, scheduling prospective candidate interviews, coordinating and implementing all aspects of the new hire process, conducting criminal background investigations, and auditing and verifying employee forms are completed. This includes overseeing the internship program, career fairs, recruiting efforts, and learning series.

I am also responsible for responding to and monitoring all unemployment notices and potential charges, including guiding management through the hearing process prior to attending hearing, and attending hearings as required. In addition, I monitor and maintain work eligibility for all employees, while ensuring federal compliance is maintained on a consistent basis for potential agency audits. Inclusive of these responsibilities is the maintenance of job

155

descriptions, including assisting management with updates and creating new descriptions when vacancies occur.

Another major responsibility involves acting as the primary contact for the health and welfare benefit plans for the employees, which includes addressing questions, resolving issues, providing resources, and handling benefit inquiries and complaints to ensure quick, courteous resolution. Furthermore, I coordinate with third-party benefit vendors to resolve insurance issues, conduct new hire orientation to ensure that employees complete mandatory new hire paperwork and are properly enrolled in benefit plans, coordinate COBRA activities including eligibility to vendors and communication with employees regarding COBRA events, complete and maintain life insurance and LTD underwriting applications and related status updates, maintain updated benefits related information on the Intranet, complete monthly invoicing and billing for health and life insurance plans, conduct annual benefits renewal process to include outside benefit comparisons, and administer the annual open enrollment period.

In addition, as Director of Human Resources, I am responsible for assisting employees with any personnel related issues, including coaching management and executives on best practice in adhering to local and federal employment laws. This also includes guiding management through employee termination process in compliance with local and federal laws, including conducting termination meetings, preparing, administering and monitoring severance packages, as well as coordinating payments through payroll.

Finally, as related to performance management, I work with outside auditors to complete annual plan audit, oversee and manage the annual tax filings for all benefit plans, ensure timely filing of extensions and submissions with the federal government, manage federally required reporting and submission, and maintain confidential record keeping and reporting within human resource information systems (HRIS). This also results in me assisting with annual employee handbook review and coordinating the production and distribution of revised policies and handbooks, and if needed the development of and revisions to the organizational chart.

Tell us a little about your track from your university years to get to the position you are in now.

I have been a human resources executive offering more than 25 years of experience driving organizations toward the established business goals and strategies. I have been recognized as a principal member of the senior management team who partners with and influences senior business leaders, effectively managing the human capital and protecting the company from

HR liability issues throughout all aspects of the organization. I have earned a Black Belt certification in Six Sigma, SPHR certification, and am also a certified Huthwaite sales trainer.

Prior to joining the Tampa Bay Buccaneers, I spent 25 years at the New York Times Regional Media Group in Sarasota, Florida and Santa Rosa, California. I held several key positions during my career at the newspapers including Human Resources Director, Innovation Director, Sales Manager, Operations Manager, and Human Resources Manager.

What advice would you give to someone wanting to get into the field of sport facility operations management specifically in the area of human resources?

The main piece of advice is to get involved with a professional association to expand your knowledge and network. For human resource professionals, the Society for Human Resource Management (SHRM) is one of the most well recognized (www.shrm.org).

Through SHRM you can earn your professional credentials as a PHR (Professional in Human Resources) or SPHR (Senior Professional in Human Resources) to help market yourself as a recognized expert in the human resource field. This distinction is globally recognized, and helps separate yourself as having a high level of expertise in the field and being a more valuable asset to an organization.

There are also many other specific certificate programs related to the various elements of human resource management that are available to further distinguish yourself as a HR expert.

TECHNOLOGY NOW!

Finding the right employee is always a challenge. Whether it be for an internship or a full time job, sport facility operations managers are on the lookout for the best employees to help their venue run smoothly and meet the needs of their guests.

One of the best tools online for posting positions and finding employees is TeamWork Online. Ranging from hundreds of individual facilities – to networks of facilities such as Arena Network and Delaware North Sportservice – to merchandising and food service companies such as Gameday Merchandising and Legends – to global facility management companies including SMG – all use TeamWork Online to find their employees and streamline their human resource process.

TeamWork Online is an online sports and live events job match-making engine that connects applicants with employers – and employers with the right candidates. The service provides an online job application process that networks the employment pages of their member employers. For over 15 years, TeamWork Online has provided employers with a talent management network, and the best pool of qualified candidates interested in all aspects of sports, including sport facility operations management. TeamWork Online goes beyond being a job posting service – it also provides face-to-face interactions through job and career fairs, and networking events.

Source: TeamWork Online (2014). Retrieved November 20, 2014 from www.teamworkonline.com

Implementation of management and operations

CHAPTER 8

FINANCIAL MANAGEMENT

CHAPTER OUTLINE

- ■ Introduction to sport facility financial management
- ■ Learning the language
  - ■ Financial accounting
  - ■ Management accounting
- ■ Finance fundamentals
- ■ Financial planning
  - ■ The budgeting process
    - ■ Define objectives
    - ■ Audit resources
    - ■ Operationalize strategies
    - ■ Allocate responsibility
    - ■ Prepare budgets
    - ■ Approve budgets
    - ■ Implement budgets
    - ■ Measure performance
    - ■ Act to control business
- ■ Chapter review

CHAPTER OBJECTIVES

This chapter is concerned with providing readers with an overview of why financial skills are an important part of the sport facility manager's overall portfolio of management skills. Finance has often been described as the 'language' of business. People who wish to progress their careers need to be fluent in this language both in terms of understanding it and being able to communicate in it. You will not become fluent in finance by reading one chapter of a book. However, having read this chapter we hope that you feel you have been pointed in the right direction and will have the enthusiasm to develop your financial skills further.

INTRODUCTION TO SPORT FACILITY FINANCIAL MANAGEMENT

For all sport facilities whether they be iconic stadia played in by professional teams, municipal facilities for public use, or a local recreational rugby club, it is essential that the overall governance of the organization is underpinned by sound financial management. Without needing to be an accountant and having a specific training in finance, there are two key questions to which all senior managers should be able to respond positively in the context of their business.

First, 'is the selling price higher than the cost?' In other words, is the organization making a profit? For non-profit organizations such as members' sport clubs and municipal facilities we can modify the first question to: 'is the organization operating within the resources allocated to it?' If sport facilities are not profitable or do not operate within their resources, then problems will follow. In the context of our own lives if we live beyond our means, then varying degrees of problems will occur. Initially, we may experience a cash flow problem such that there is a lot of the month left and we have exhausted the money available for the month. Next we might incur interest payments we are unable to meet; and finally we end up being declared 'bankrupt'. The same analysis is applicable to sport facilities and teams that do not operate within their resources.

HIGHMARK STADIUM AND THE PITTSBURGH RIVERHOUNDS

Built at a cost of over US$10m the Highmark Stadium opened in 2013 with what were described at the time as 'top notch' facilities and an excellent view of the field of play. The chief executive of the team went on record to say that in 10 years' time the Riverhounds would make it all the way to Major League Soccer. However, in March 2014 just days before the start of the soccer season, the companies behind the stadium and the team filed for what is known as Chapter 11 bankruptcy protection. Chapter 11 is a situation in which a failing business tries to work out a plan to return to profitability whilst paying back its creditors. If it cannot make a profit, then the business' assets will be sold off and the proceeds used to reimburse those to whom it owes money. Why would an enviable new facility and ambitious team find itself in such a position? The truth appears to be that the construction costs got out of control and were higher than expected. This in turn meant that even more revenue had to be generated from soccer matches and other events to service the additional loans and interest that built up. The actual revenue generated was insufficient to cover these costs and the club failed the first question 'is the selling price higher than the cost?' Regardless of the level of business, loans have to be paid back to the providers and when the point is reached where this is not possible, bankruptcy is the inevitable consequence. Operators will try to strike deals with banks to reschedule payments over a longer period to reduce immediate outgoings or to offer them a share of the business. In this regard, the case of the Highmark Stadium and the Pittsburgh Riverhounds is a classic example of what happens if businesses are not profitable.

Source: Adapted from http://pittsburgh.cbslocal.com/2014/03/27/highmark-stadium-riverhounds-owners-file-for-chapter-11-protection/

Suggested discussion questions

1   If you were asked to advise the owners of the Highmark Stadium on how they could get out of their financial problems, what would your advice be?
2   Revisit your answer when you have read this chapter and after reading Chapter 9 (Operational Decision Making). Reflect on your original answer. Would you change your recommendations and how do they relate to the basic theory covered in the two chapters?

How many 'one man band' gyms have you seen that have been opened by a body building enthusiast that are here today and gone tomorrow? Why do these businesses fail? The simple answer is that selling price is not higher than the cost; the business gets into financial difficulty and dies. By contrast, why do the iconic sport stadia survive? The simple answer is that they are profitable or the selling price is higher than the cost. When profits are made they can be reinvested in the business to improve it, to develop new products, and to keep ahead of the game.

The second question all businesses must answer is, 'is the business well set to continue trading?' In financial terms the second question is a reference to an organization's ability to pay its creditors as they fall due and having the freedom to pursue strategies of its own unfettered by external influences. Many business failures are not because there is limited demand for the product or that the selling price is too low. The principal cause of business failure is that despite buoyant demand for a product, the organization runs out of cash and is unable to meet its own obligations, as was the case with the Highmark Stadium and the Pittsburgh Riverhounds. In some cases, despite being profitable, a business may be 'highly geared', that is it has a high level of borrowing and therefore has to pay regular sums out to service interest and debt charges. When a business cannot service its loans the providers of debt finance become nervous and may call in their loans and a situation can arise whereby the providers of loans have more control over a business than those charged with the day-to-day running of the business. Under these conditions it is unlikely that a business would be well set to continue trading. In many respects success or failure in business generally, and sport facility management specifically, hinges crucially on the ability to be profitable, to be able to pay bills as they fall due, and to be able to service debts. Hopefully, having read the above you have thought to yourself 'this is little more than common sense really' and 'you don't need to be trained in finance to understand the significance of the two questions'. If you are with us so far, please carry on. If not please re-read the above and make sure you understand the two questions and why they are important for budding sport facility managers.

In the remainder of the chapter we will demonstrate how the two questions underpin an understanding of finance in a more formal way. First, we will examine operational finance issues such as financial reporting, budgeting, and breakeven analysis. Second, we will look at the issues involved in establishing new sport facilities. Every sport facility manager dreams of the day when he or she will be involved in a new build project. The challenge of opening a new venue, the kudos of brand new fixtures and fittings, and the smell of fresh paint and new carpet can all be career-defining moments. The extent to which you will get to enjoy such moments may well boil down to how good your financial skills are and the extent to which you can ensure your answers to the two questions discussed above are positive.

LEARNING THE LANGUAGE

In this section we cover two key points of terminology that help to illustrate how finance is the language of business. We start by looking at the definitions of 'financial accounting' and 'management accounting', which are the two types of accounting techniques used in all businesses.

Financial accounting

Financial accounting is defined as the classification and recording of monetary transactions of an entity in accordance with established concepts, principles, accounting standards, and legal requirements, and their presentation, by means of income and expenditure accounts, balance sheets, and cash-flow statements, during and at the end of an accounting period. There are three points of note concerning the above definition of financial accounting. First, financial accounting is concerned with the relatively passive activity of recording and classifying financial transactions. Second, financial accounting is governed by a series of prescribed procedures ranging from 'established concepts' through to 'legal requirements'. Third, the presentation of the results of financial accounting is in a specified form i.e. income and expenditure account, balance sheet, and cash-flow statement (known collectively as financial statements). It is a legal requirement for businesses to carry out financial accounting and in many countries companies are required to file their accounts with regulatory bodies. The significance of public filing of accounts is that often the published accounts of an entity will be the only financial information available in the public domain about the entity.

Management accounting

Management accounting is defined as the process of identification, measurement, accumulation, analysis, preparation, interpretation, and communication of information used by management to plan, evaluate, and control within an entity and to assure appropriate use of and accountability for its resources. There are three points of note concerning the above definition of management accounting. First, management accounting involves being proactive, that is, the information generated by management accounting is used for planning, decision making, and control, whereas financial accounting data is used for reporting what happened in the past. Second, management accounting is compiled and reported in a way that best suits the needs of an organization, rather than in the prescribed formats used in financial accounting. Third, management accounting is concerned with the efficient and effective use of resources. It therefore follows that assessment as to whether the management of a sport facility has been efficient and effective is most likely to be determined using management accounting techniques. There are no legal requirements to give external users access to management accounting data.

In reality, perceptive managers should acknowledge that financial accounting and management accounting are two sides of the same coin. We are required by law to record our financial transactions according to the rules of financial accounting. However, no professional manager will plan to record financial transactions and wait to see what happens after a year. In practice, good managers plan their operations so as to achieve desired outcomes. The only way to achieve desired outcomes is to plan and control your business. Planning and control disciplines are achieved by techniques such as budgeting, breakeven analysis, and capital investment appraisal. These techniques are some of the key disciplines found within management accounting and are demonstrated throughout this book.

In practice, there is a direct link between financial accounting and management accounting. The term 'financial management' could quite legitimately be defined as 'the application of financial accounting and management accounting techniques to the management of an organization'. It is in this sense that the term 'financial management' is used throughout this chapter.

FINANCE FUNDAMENTALS

Financial accounting uses a combination of concepts and rules to produce financial statements in a standardized form. These 'statements' are: the income and expenditure account; the balance sheet which is a statement of the assets, liabilities and a valuation of the net worth of a business (capital); and the cash flow statement which explains how much cash a business has generated and how it has used such cash. There are two common uses of financial accounting data that managers of sport facilities are likely to encounter. First, financial statements can be used to explain in-house financial performance. For example, the manager of a stadium could use his or her financial statements as evidence of the organization's overall financial performance in a meeting with shareholders or the providers of loans. Second, financial statements are often the only publicly available information from which to make a diagnosis of the financial health of other organizations, for example other businesses that you might consider trading with. Would you extend credit to a business which was not profitable and therefore might have problems paying your bills? The logic behind the practice of presenting and analyzing financial statements is that it is considered possible to make a diagnosis about an organization's financial health from its income and expenditure account, balance sheet, and cash-flow statement.

Typical questions might include:

▪ Can it afford to pay its bills?
▪ Does it have sufficient financial resources to be able to borrow funds to invest in new equipment?
▪ Is it worth investing in?

Careful use of financial accounting data can be used to report internal performance and to make diagnoses of external organizations. How a manager might set about answering these questions is best illustrated using a practical example as seen in Table 8.1.

The income and expenditure account is an analysis of how the capital or net worth of an organization has changed over a given period. If a concessionaire at a sport facility buys popcorn at 50 cents per portion and sells it for $5, then he has made a profit of $4.50, or in other words the concessionaire's net worth has increased by $4.50. This increase in net worth can then be used to pay towards the running costs of the concession such as rental, staff wages, and electricity as well as delivering some profit for the owner.

164

Table 8.1 Sample sports facility income and expenditure account

	Year 201Z	Year 201Y
Turnover	5,400,000	5,100,000
Cost of sales	3,900,000	3,828,000
Gross profit	1,500,000	1,272,000
Other expenses	1,140,000	1,110,000
Pretax profit for year	360,000	162,000
Taxation	108,000	48,600
Retained profit for year	252,000	113,400

The same thinking can be applied to a facility as a whole as shown in Table 8.1. In the year 201Z, the sport facility generated $5.40m worth of income (turnover) of which $3.90m was used on the direct costs of providing the service (cost of sales) leaving a gross profit of $1.50m. A further $1.14m worth of other expenses was off-set against the gross profit, leaving a pre-tax profit of $0.36m. The organization is required to pay tax on its profits of 30 percent or $0.108m and therefore the retained profit for the year was $0.252. To illustrate how the income and expenditure account is an analysis of how the organization's capital has changed, the bottom line of the income and expenditure account in Table 8.1 can be summarized as meaning: 'at the end of year 201Z the organization had $0.252m of extra resources available to it compared with the same time last year'.

The facility featured in Table 8.1 has clearly demonstrated a positive answer to our first key question 'is the selling price higher than the cost?' It is customary for financial statements to contain the data for two years' worth of trading activity, that is, the year in question and the comparative figures for the previous year. Therefore a follow up question might be, 'how does this year's performance compare with last year?' In Table 8.1, the current year 201Z shows a profit of $0.252m whereas in the previous year 201Y the profit was $0.113m. In simple terms it can be concluded that this year's performance has been an improvement on last year.

Another important question to ask is 'how does this year's actual performance compare with planned performance?' If the organization concerned had planned to make a profit of $0.20m then clearly a surplus of $0.252m demonstrates that not only has the organization been profitable, it has also been more effective than expected, because the actual surplus was $52,000 better than planned. Equally, had the profit target been $0.3m then despite making a profit, the organization would have been relatively ineffective because actual performance was $48,000 less than planned. Financial statements tend not to reveal planned performance to the outside world and therefore without management accounting data, financial statements should be used cautiously and with a realization of their limitations.

All businesses need to grow. It is a harsh fact of life that costs escalate every year and staff need pay rises to offset the effects of inflation. In this respect, it is necessary for businesses to grow simply to stand still. Thus if a business wishes to deliver on the first question 'is the selling price higher than the cost?' it has to grow to keep pace with its increased costs. On a positive note, businesses also need to grow in order to invest in product development, maintenance, marketing, and ensuring that the skills of key personnel are fit for purpose. Measuring growth is achieved by using 'horizontal' or 'year on year' analysis. Table 8.2 shows the data from Table 8.1 subjected to horizontal (year on year) analysis.

Table 8.2 Income and expenditure account horizontal analysis

	Year 201Z	Year 201Y	Change	% Change
Turnover	5,400,000	5,100,000	300,000	6%
Cost of sales	3,900,000	3,828,000	72,000	2%
Gross profit	1,500,000	1,272,000	228,000	18%
Other expenses	1,140,000	1,110,000	30,000	3%
Pretax profit for year	360,000	162,000	198,000	122%
Taxation	108,000	48,600	59,400	122%
Retained profit for year	252,000	113,400	138,600	122%

The growth calculation involves two parts: firstly, calculating the change in each component of the income and expenditure account (this year minus last year); and, secondly, expressing the change as a percentage of last year. Thus in Table 8.2, the absolute increase in turnover is $300,000 which in turn is a 6 percent increase on the previous year. Signs of successful growth are an increase in turnover and an increase in profit. In the case of Table 8.2, turnover increased by 6 percent and profits increased by 122 percent, which is clearly a sign of successful growth.

A second way of analyzing financial statements is using 'vertical' or 'common size' analysis, where a key variable (usually turnover on the income and expenditure account) is given a value of 100 percent and all other lines on the income and expenditure account are expressed as a percentage of this key variable. A fully worked example can be seen in Table 8.3.

In Table 8.3, in 201Z for every $1 of turnover, 28 cents was left over as gross profit whereas in 201Y for every $1 of turnover 25 cents was left over as gross profit. Efficiency can be defined as the relationship between inputs and outputs, in this case turnover and gross profit respectively. Thus in the case of Table 8.3 we can conclude that because there is more output for each unit of input, the facility has improved its efficiency. The same logic holds true for the bottom line, 'retained profit for the year'. For every $1 of turnover 5 cents is left over as retained profit, whereas in the previous year, 201Y, retained profit was only 2 cents per $1 of

166

Table 8.3 Income and expenditure account vertical analysis

	Year 201Z	Common size	Year 201Y	Common size
Turnover	5,400,000	100%	5,100,000	100%
Cost of sales	3,900,000	72%	3,828,000	75%
Gross profit	1,500,000	28%	1,272,000	25%
Other expenses	1,140,000	21%	1,110,000	22%
Pretax profit for year	360,000	7%	162,000	3%
Taxation	108,000	2%	48,600	1%
Retained profit for year	252,000	5%	113,400	2%

turnover. Thus at the retained profit level, the organization has also become more efficient. Bringing Tables 8.2 and 8.3 together it can be concluded that the organization has become more efficient because as turnover has increased (6 percent), costs (cost of sales and other expenses) have increased at a lower rate (2 percent and 3 percent respectively). Thus in simple, commonsense terms and in the absence of any other data such as an organization's business plan, it has proven possible to obtain useful information about an organization's financial performance from its published income and expenditure account.

The second question, 'is the business well set to continue trading', can in part be obtained from analysis of the balance sheet. Reading, interpreting, and explaining a balance sheet is not solely the domain of trained accountants. Any manager with a basic understanding of logic should be able to identify and articulate the meaning of a balance sheet. The purpose of a balance sheet is to put a value on the net worth of an organization. To do this requires a list of those things of value (assets) which the organization owns such as buildings and cash; and a list of those things the organization owes to others (liabilities or creditors). The difference between these two figures is the capital, net worth, or equity of the business. As an example, if you have a stadium worth $100m and your mortgage is $60m, then your capital (net worth) is $40m (i.e. $100m minus $60m). To illustrate the point, imagine that Table 8.4 is the balance sheet for the same sport facility whose income and expenditure account was featured in Tables 8.1, 8.2 and 8.3.

A balance sheet is no more than a listing of the assets and liabilities of a business and a valuation of its net worth. However, there is a little terminology that needs to be learnt to understand fully what a balance sheet represents. First, on a balance sheet 'fixed' means items of long-term value to an organization (i.e. two years or more), part of the business infrastructure, and not regularly traded on a day-to-day basis. Sport facilities hope to use gym equipment, as an example, for more than two years and the purchase and sale of gym equipment is not a regular part of the business' activities, therefore gym equipment is described as a fixed asset. By contrast businesses hope to convert stock of say food and drink for resale and debtors (people who owe the business money) into cash within a year and certain creditors need to be paid within a year. Anything which is planned to be converted into cash or paid within one year is said to be 'current'. Thus in Table 8.4 for the year ended 201Z, assets minus creditors equals $2.504m which in turn is the net worth of the business. Also in Table 8.4 the capital for 201Y was $2.252m, or in other words, the net worth of the business was $2.252m at the end of that financial year. The difference in capital between 201Z and 201Y is $2.504m minus $2.252m which equals $0.252m. This result is not a coincidence. The organization's income and expenditure account in Tables 8.1, 8.2, and 8.3 details a profit of $0.252m and the definition of the income and expenditure account is an analysis of how capital has changed over a period. Therefore, there is a direct link between the balance sheet and the income and expenditure account, i.e. the income and expenditure account 'explains' how the balance sheet or the value of the business has changed. If the selling price is higher than the cost, then the balance sheet will increase in value.

Table 8.4 Sport facility balance sheet

	201Z	201Y
FIXED ASSETS		
Buildings	2,000,000	1,980,000
Equipment	470,000	260,000
Total fixed assets	2,470,000	2,240,000
CURRENT ASSETS		
Stock	30,000	24,000
Debtors	15,000	9,000
Cash	217,000	123,000
Total current assets	262,000	156,000
CURRENT CREDITORS		
Creditors payable within 1 year	228,000	144,000
NET CURRENT ASSETS	34,000	12,000
NET ASSETS	2,504,000	2,252,000
CAPITAL		
Ordinary shares $1	500,000	500,000
Income and expenditure account	2,004,000	1,752,000
TOTAL CAPITAL	2,504,000	2,252,000

Implementation of management and operations

Two of the determinants of whether a business is well set to continue trading are the ability to pay its bills and the degree of control it has over its assets. The ability to read and articulate the meaning of a balance sheet is an important skill for the financial manager. One of the ways in which professionals read a balance sheet is to examine the relationship between its various components. For example, the ability to pay debts as they fall due is called 'liquidity' and is measured by liquidity ratios. Liquidity ratios compare the amount of current assets available to pay current creditors. The first of these is called the current ratio and simply compares total current assets with total current creditors (see Table 8.5).

Table 8.5 Current ratio calculation

	201Z	201Y
Current assets	262,000	156,000
Current creditors	228,000	144,000
Current ratio	1.15:1[1]	1.08:1
[1] (262,000/228,000):1		

The current ratio calculation shows that in 201Z, for every $1 of current creditors, the organization had $1.18 in current assets. This finding suggests that the organization can meet its bills. Furthermore, comparison with 201Y indicates that there has been a marginal improvement in liquidity from 1.08:1 to 1.18:1. It is sometimes the case that businesses are unable to sell their stock as quickly as they would like. As a result, a second liquidity ratio, the quick ratio, also known as the acid test, can be calculated. This is very similar to the current ratio but excludes stock from the calculation (see Table 8.6).

Table 8.6 Quick ratio (or acid test) calculation

	201Z	201Y
Current assets	262,000	156,000
Minus stock	(30,000)	(24,000)
Equals	232,000	132,000
Current creditors	228,000	144,000
Quick ratio[1]	1.02:1	0.92:1
[1](232,000/228,000): 1		

The acid test ratio reveals that in 201Z the organization still had sufficient resources to meet current creditors, whereas in 201Y, once stock is taken out of the equation there are only 92 cents available to meet every $1 of current creditors. As a basic principle, liquidity ratios of at least 1:1 would be regarded as being a prudent level of liquidity. Once a liquidity ratio falls below 1:1, further clarification might be necessary from an organization's management concerning their strategy for being able to settle debts as they fall due.

Liquidity tests are one of the ways in which managers can assess the credit worthiness of potential business contacts. For example, a sport facility manager might consider hiring out a venue for an exhibition or conference. Whether agreeing to hire out a venue proves to be a good or bad decision depends in part on whether or not full payment is received for the services offered. Credit terms might be offered to an organization with a strong balance sheet and acceptable liquidity levels, whereas a hirer without such credentials might be required to pay in advance or indeed be declined.

The extent to which a business is in control of its assets can be measured by the 'debt ratio', which is a measure of the extent to which an organization's assets are funded by creditors. The point can be illustrated using an everyday example of two home owners who both have houses worth $500,000. Owner A has a mortgage for $100,000 and Owner B has a mortgage for $250,000. Common sense tells us that Owner A is in a better position than Owner B, but how can the relationship be quantified to demonstrate the point?

	Owner A	Owner B
House (Asset)	500,000	500,000
Mortgage (Creditor)	100,000	250,000
Net worth (Equity)	400,000	250,000

The debt ratio measures the extent to which assets are funded by debts, so the debt ratio for each owner would be:

	Owner A	Owner B
House (Asset)	500,000	500,000
Mortgage (Creditor)	100,000	250,000
Debt ratio[1]	20%	50%

[1]Debt ratio = (creditors/assets) * 100

Applying the same logic to Table 8.4, the debt ratio for each year would be:

	201Z	201Y
Fixed assets	2,470,000	2,240,000
Current assets	262,000	156,000
Total assets	2,272,000	2,396,000
Total creditors	228,000	144,000
Debt ratio[1]	10%	6%

[1]Debt ratio = (creditors/assets) * 100

170

With debt ratios of 10 percent for 201Z and 6 percent for 201Y this reveals that the sports facility has very low levels of debt and therefore is in control of the vast majority of its assets. Organizations with high debt ratios can to all intents and purposes be controlled by their creditors. For example, if a balance sheet reveals very high levels of borrowings, it may well be that the banks and other loan providers are the real controllers of the business rather than the owners. In the case of a sport facility, this situation may manifest itself in the bank determining opening hours or influencing programming in return for continued financing or not calling in loans. Any business which struggles to pay its bills because of an adverse liquidity position, or which is not necessarily in control of assets, can reasonably be described as not being well set to continue trading. By contrast, if these indicators are positive it enables those with a business relationship with an organization to be confident that they are dealing with a financially sound enterprise.

The measures of financial performance we have examined thus far have been confined to data from the income and expenditure account in isolation (is the selling price higher than the cost?) and the balance sheet in isolation (is the business well set to continue trading?). It is however possible to combine measures from both the income and expenditure account and the balance sheet to gain further insights into business performance. An important relationship to consider in this regard is the trading performance of a business and the owners. In Table 8.4 it can be seen that the net worth or value of the sport facility is $2.5m. A sobering question for the owners to ponder is whether the $2.5m is best kept in the business or invested elsewhere. In economics this is known as the 'opportunity cost' or in other words what is the best option foregone as a result of having $2.5m tied up in a sport facility? To answer this question we can use the measure of retained profit for the year ($252,000) from the income and expenditure account and link it to the value of the business, or total capital, from the balance sheet ($2.5m). As with the other ratios illustrated above it is worth making the calculation for both years so that changes over time can be assessed.

	201Z	201Y
Retained profit	252,000	113,400
Total capital	2,504,000	2,252,000
Return on shareholders' funds	10%	5%

For the year 201Z the return on shareholders' funds is 10 percent and compares favorably with the return that might be achieved if you invested the same amount of money in a deposit account. This finding suggests that it is worthwhile running the business rather than settling for a lower return on investment from a 'safe' option such as having money on deposit. Furthermore, in the year 201Z the business has doubled its return on shareholders' funds from 5 percent in 201Y to 10 percent which indicates a very positive direction of travel. In short, the owners of the business can be satisfied with the business performance of the sport facility from an investment perspective.

In the commercial sector, people invest in businesses by purchasing shares in them. A share is a quantified stake in a business that gives the owner a right to a 'share' in the profits (or losses) made by that business. We can see in Table 8.4 that the balance sheet for our example sport facility states that there are 500,000 $1 shares. Linking this to the profit number from the income and expenditure account ($252,000) enables us to calculate that each share earned 50 cents in the year 201Z. Again, making the comparison with the year 201Y, in which earnings per share were 23 cents, we can confirm from yet another angle that the business has improved over the last year.

There are many more ratios and analysis techniques that can be used to assess the financial statements of business organizations. However, this section of the chapter has focused on the basic commonsense areas that sport facility managers should investigate. What you have seen thus far is a cursory overview. If you can understand the basics such as the two key questions and how you might provide answers, this will be a good start. Like any language, fluency comes with practice, experience, and immersion in the culture.

FINANCIAL PLANNING

For managers of sport facilities the most likely way they will experience the pressures of financial management is through the process of compiling and being held accountable to the budget. What you have seen so far has been an indication of the financial performance (income and expenditure account) and financial position (balance sheet) of a business. The income and expenditure statement you saw in Table 8.1 was the summary of a sport facility's performance for one year and the balance sheet in Table 8.4 was a snapshot of the business' financial position at a point in time. Businesses do not lurch from year to year and hope that their financial statements show a favorable outcome. Well-managed sport facilities are continually monitoring their performance on a daily, weekly, monthly, and quarterly basis. Questions we need answering include:

- How many admissions did we achieve today?
- How does this compare with target?
- How much did we sell to our customers when they were on site?
- How does this compare with target?
- How many staff hours did we use?
- How did this compare with target?

Financial performance needs to be managed so that you achieve what you set out to achieve. In this regard the budget can be said to be the objectives of an organization expressed in financial terms. The budgeting process helps us to address questions such as:

- Where are we now in financial terms?
- What are we trying to achieve in financial terms?
- How are we going to achieve it?

You will discover if you work in sport facility management that one of the key differences between a job and a career is that those people who have careers also have responsibility for budgets and are successful in achieving them. In the remainder of this section we will look at the budgeting process, the format for an operating budget, and how budgets can be used to monitor performance.

The budgeting process

The most frequently used budgeting process is 'continuation' budgeting, which refers to situations in which the business objectives of an organization continue from one financial period to the next. Under these conditions, it is sensible to continue with the same approach to budgeting. An example of a continuation budget might be a health and fitness club whose main aim is to make a profit for the owners of the business who will pursue the same approach to running their business as they have in the past. If the club's basic operations lead to a situation whereby the selling price is higher than the cost, then besides increasing the number of members of the club or how much they are charged for their memberships, there is no point wasting time and resources on a more complicated approach to the club's finances.

An important point about budgeting, when it is done well, is that it is an ongoing process rather than a one-off event. The actual mechanics of collating the numbers involved in a budget are a small part of the overall budgeting process. By bearing in mind that budgeting is designed to help an organization with planning, decision making and control, it is possible to appreciate that budgeting is a continuous part of business life. This point can be reinforced by viewing budgeting as steps in a logically sequenced planning process as shown in Figure 8.1, with each stage discussed in turn afterwards.

Define objectives

The first question to ask when involved with any financial business planning is 'in monetary terms, what are we trying to achieve?' This question should provide a clue that most sane business people would not answer by saying 'making a loss'. Losses are made in business but it is inconceivable to imagine that managers set out deliberately to make losses. Losses normally occur when there is a mismatch between what was planned and what happened in reality. Organizational objectives will vary according to the nature of the business. A community sport club

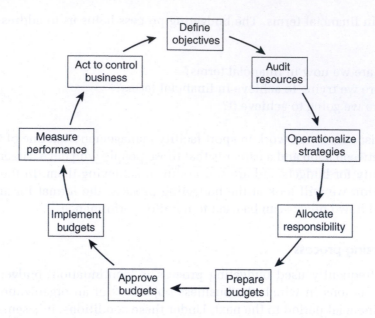

Figure 8.1 *Budgeting as steps in a logically sequenced planning process*

which exists for the benefit of the members may desire nothing more than to break even or to make a small surplus to maintain its existing facilities. A more complex organization such as the Barclay's Premier League franchise needs to balance the requirements of producing a successful team on the pitch (utility maximization) with the requirements of being a commercial franchise (profit maximization).

Audit resources

The audit of resources is a 'reality check' on the objectives. Its purpose is to ensure that the objectives and the resources required to achieve them are internally consistent. As an example Sheffield United Football Club needs around 15,000 spectators per home match to break even. With a stadium capacity of nearly 31,000, it is clear that 15,000 people can be accommodated at a home match so long as they can be attracted to the match in the first place. The term 'resources' should be used in the widest sense to include personnel and the skills required to ensure that those running the business are 'fit for purpose'.

Where there is a discrepancy between the objectives and the resources available to achieve them, two courses of action are possible. First the objectives can be changed so that they are compatible with the resources. Second, the gap between the resources available and the resources required can form the basis for prioritizing capital investment such as increasing the capacity of a stadium, or identifying training and development needs to ensure that staff have the skills to deliver what is required of them.

174

Operationalize strategies

Having defined objectives and confirmed that you have the resources to deliver them, the model proceeds to consider the day-to-day actions to be used to deliver the required performance. In a health and fitness club these might include the marketing plans, pricing policies, customer care protocols, and opening hours. If organizational objectives can be regarded as 'what' we wish to achieve, then operational strategies can be regarded as 'how' we plan to achieve the objectives. For example, a swimming pool manager aiming to achieve a turnover of $1m per annum from an annual throughput of 100,000 admissions needs to think carefully about how he or she can convert every click on the turnstile into an average of $10 in the cash till. This will probably be via a combination of parking fees, admission costs, secondary spend on food and drink, locker hire, use of drying machines, and the sale of items such as goggles and arm bands.

Allocate responsibility

The successful delivery of financial objectives does not happen by accident, or as the result of simply compiling a spreadsheet. Facility management in sport is primarily a service industry and the key people who determine the extent to which objectives are delivered are the facility's staff. So that people can see where their efforts and talents fit into a business' overall plan, it is good practice for staff to have agreed responsibility for their particular areas of work. Agreed responsibility is particularly important in situations where staff can be rewarded, or indeed punished, on the basis of their performance. For example, basic performance for a fitness consultant in a health club might be 20 new peak time members per month, with financial incentives on offer if the agreed target is exceeded. If it is known and clearly stated 'who is going to do what and by when?' then there is the basis for a meaningful comparison of actual performance compared with planned (or expected) performance.

Prepare budgets

It is worth noting that the actual preparation of budgets, that is the 'mechanics', does not occur until the mid-point of the budgeting model. This is important because it makes the point that budgeting is not some isolated or abstract process but is actually integral to the way an organization approaches business planning. When preparing a budget there are two important considerations to address, namely: 'how much' income or expenditure will there be; and 'when' will the expected income or expenditure occur? To illustrate the point, if a swimming pool is expecting 100,000 admissions per year at an average admission price of $7.50, then the answer to 'how much income will be generated?' is $750,000. However, it is unlikely that a pool will average nearly 2,000 admissions per week for 52 weeks of the year. There will be peak times such as during school holidays and off-peak times such as during the winter when it is cold. Hence, to make sure that the appropriate level of resources such as staff is in the right place and at the right time, it is necessary to plan the predicted level of activity on a week-by-week or month-by-month basis. Conducting such an exercise enables managers to plan ahead for situations where expenditure may be greater than income and there is insufficient cash to meet the shortfall. Having identified situations requiring management action, strategies can be put in place to deal with them such as negotiating an overdraft facility at the bank, rescheduling capital expenditure, or imposing an expenditure embargo on non-essential revenue items. The important point of note is that the process of budgeting identifies potential problems in advance so that appropriate action can be taken to avoid them or to mitigate their consequences.

It is more likely to be good fortune rather than good planning that the first draft of the budget will deliver the financial outcomes required. As a result managers may need to revise their budgets so that the desired outcomes are achieved. In practice there are five ways in which a budget can be revised:

1   Increase revenue whilst keeping costs constant, for example by increasing prices, increasing throughput, or a combination of the two methods. Note the assumptions that underpin the thinking here. In the case of deciding to increase prices to balance the budget, there is the assumption that the market will bear such an increase and that revenue will increase despite the likelihood that some people may either stop participating or take their business elsewhere.
2   Decrease expenditure whilst keeping income constant, for example by making savings on expenditure or reducing the amount of the service on offer (e.g. reducing opening hours).
3   Increasing income whilst decreasing costs, as 1 and 2 above are not mutually exclusive.
4   Alter the financial outcome required. It may be that it is not possible to bring the required outcomes and the budget into line by using 1, 2, and 3 above. Rather than altering income and expenditure, management may decide to alter the financial outcome required. This approach can work both positively and negatively. If staff provide managers with a budget that exceeds the required bottom line and the assumptions underpinning the budget are correct, then it would make sense to increase the overall budget target accordingly. Alternatively, imagine that the targeted outcome cannot be met by revisions to income and expenditure as a competitor has recently opened a new facility nearby and is poaching some of your customers. Under these conditions, managers might agree to settle for a reduced financial outcome, for example an annual profit of $0.45m rather than $0.50m, which in turn would require a reworking of the budget.
5   Alter the overall business objectives. It may be the case that it is impossible to arrive at an acceptable solution to a budget using steps 1–4 above. Under these conditions it may be that the required outcomes and the organization's capabilities

Implementation of management and operations

are not compatible. The only remaining alternative is to change the organization's objectives. As an example, it is often the case that municipal sport facilities are required to meet social as well as financial objectives. On occasion, pursuit of these differing aims may be incompatible in the sense that programming activities for target groups prevents revenue maximization. Every use of resource has an opportunity cost, that is the price of the best alternative foregone. In order to make the budget balance, it may be that some priorities which are no doubt desirable have to be sacrificed to protect more important business interests.

The relevance of preparing a budget, comparing it with business objectives and taking corrective action where appropriate, indicates the importance of achieving 'internal consistency'. Using the budgeting model shown in Table 8.5 helps to ensure that what an organization wishes to achieve in overall terms and the financial consequences of doing so are consistent. If potential problems can be identified at the planning stage, appropriate action can be taken by devising strategies to deal with adverse circumstances. This type of approach has a far greater chance of success and is more desirable than trying to deal with situations reactively as they occur without prior warning.

Approve budgets

When an acceptable balance has been achieved between an organization's business objectives and the subsequent financial consequences, then the preparation of budgets is complete. From this point the budget should be approved formally. It is recognized good practice for the approval of a budget to be formalized in the official records of a business such as the minutes of a board or committee meeting. In an ideal world, budgets should be approved in advance of the financial period to which they relate. This process ensures that those who have compiled the budget, and those whose performance will be judged by it, have a clear picture of their responsibilities. This clarity has two benefits. First, if you know what is expected of you, then evaluation of your performance can be based on hard facts rather than personal opinions. Second, expectation creates accountability, which provides managers with the focus to concentrate their efforts on those things that are important to meet the key business objectives.

Implement budgets

Once a budget has been approved, it can be implemented with effect from the date to which it applies. For example, if an organization's financial year operates from 1st April to 31st March, then it would be a reasonable expectation for the budget to be approved at least a month before the start of the new financial year. A less than ideal situation would be an organization entering a new financial year without an approved budget, as this would in effect be an admission that the business had no financial direction.

Measure performance

To reinforce the point that budgeting is integral to overall business planning, it is important to realize that the budgeting process does not end once the process of getting a budget to the implementation phase is complete. Once a budget is operational, it is good practice that periodically a check is made between how the business is actually performing compared with how it planned to perform. For operational issues such as admissions and staff hours used this might be a daily or weekly check, whereas for overall business performance monthly and quarterly checks are the conventional norms. Measurement of performance is not an end in itself and is only valuable if it is used to add value to the process of management in a business by being the basis for action where necessary.

Act to control business

Decision making should be made on the basis of the best information available to help those making the decisions. It is rare that there will be a perfect match between budget and actual comparisons, so the first decision to make is whether or not variances are within a tolerable range. If variances are tolerable, then major changes in policy are not necessary. By contrast, if variances are considered to be so large that pro-active management action is needed, then this is the time when good managers show their worth. Variances can of course be positive, for example when a business is considerably ahead of target. The only management action required here might be to continue with the same policies and to revise targets upwards. By contrast, if actual figures compared with budgeted figures reveal a significant shortfall in performance, then more pro-active corrective action may be needed. Such action might include: extra marketing effort to increase sales; reducing price to stimulate sales; or reducing costs in an attempt to maintain profit margins.

In concluding this section it is worth reiterating two key points about budgeting being a logically sequenced planning process:

1   Budgeting is a process designed to help managers make sensible decisions about running and controlling their businesses. The ability to contribute fully to the budgeting process and to be held accountable to it is one of the key differences between managers and the staff who they manage.
2   Compiling a budget is an iterative process. It is unlikely that the first draft of a budget will produce an acceptable result. Various scenarios will be modeled and differing assumptions will be tested until an acceptable solution is found. Table 8.5 is a simple model of an ideal process. The basic point is that each step of the model is a reality check on the previous step. The end game is to ensure that an organization's overall plans and the financial consequences of those plans are internally consistent.

178

CHAPTER REVIEW

The key point arising from this chapter is that sport facility managers require well-developed financial skills in order to be effective in their jobs and to develop their careers. Sadly a book chapter will not achieve this for you, but hopefully it will point you in the right direction in terms of the knowledge required to make a genuine career in this business. Finance does seem to have its own language and like all languages fluency comes with practice. Readers should not be intimidated by finance or finance professionals who seem to wield a disproportionate amount of power in some businesses. The vast majority of finance is little more than addition, subtraction, multiplication, and division plus the ability to use spreadsheets (which of course will do all of the 'number crunching' for you). Furthermore, finance is intuitively logical and once you understand the logic there will be no more smoke and mirrors to confuse you. However, you do not need to go to the other extreme and become an accountant so long as you can communicate confidently with accountants and other colleagues who are in charge of a business' finances. What this chapter has shown is that even for simple day-to-day operations, finance and financial skills are an important part of the knowledge base of a sport facility manager. If you wish to work at an even higher level such as managing the development and construction of new sport facilities, then you will require even more financial skills such as capital investment appraisal and negotiating leverage (or borrowings) to finance your ambitions. These are some of the more exciting aspects of sport facility management and it is well worth acquiring the skills and experience to be able to operate at this higher level. With a bit of luck, this chapter will have given you the confidence to realize that the first steps of acquiring skills in finance are not too difficult.

BIBLIOGRAPHY

Beech, J. and Chadwick, S. (Eds.) (2004). *The business of sport management.* Essex, UK: Prentice Hall Financial Times.

Chartered Institute of Management Accountants (1996). *Management accounting: Official terminology.* London: CIMA.

Naylor, D. J. (2001). *Managing your leisure service budget.* London: Ravenswood Publications Limited.

Robinson, L. (2004). *Managing public sport and leisure services.* London: Routledge.

Russell, D., Patel, A., and Wilkinson-Riddle, G. J. (2002). *Cost accounting: An essential guide.* London: Pearson Educational Ltd.

Shibli, S. (1994). *Leisure manager's guide to budgeting and budgetary control.* London: ILAM/Longman.

Tilley, C. and Whitehouse, J. (1992). *Finance and leisure.* London: ILAM/Longman.

Trendberth, L. and Hassan, D. (2012) *Managing sport business.* Oxford UK: Routledge.

Wilson, R. (2011) *Managing sport finance.* Oxford, UK: Routledge.

Wilson, R. and Joyce, J. (2008). *Finance for sport and leisure managers.* London: Routledge.

IN THE FIELD ...

Steve Bailey MBE, Chief Executive Officer, Sheffield International Venues Ltd (SIV)

Current position

The Sheffield City Trust (SCT) and its operating company SIV manages 18 sport, leisure, and entertainment venues including the English Institute of Sport Sheffield, Ponds Forge International Sports Centre, iceSheffield, Sheffield City Hall, Hillsborough and Concord Sports Centres, and four public golf courses. The company employs over 1200 staff (800 FTEs) and attracts over 5.5 million customers every year.

SIV is a business which provides sporting opportunities for participants at every level from beginner to World and Olympic champion. The ages of customers range from 6 months through to fitness members in their 90s. Over 60 sports are played in its venues and the company stages over 2,000 events every year. Events range from mass participation events to national, European, and World championships.

Steve's expertise in building positive relationships with a wide range of stakeholders and partners including Sheffield City Council, Sport England, UK Sport, Welcome to Yorkshire, Chamber of Commerce and Industry, universities, national governing bodies, hoteliers, and multinational suppliers has delivered outstanding results for the city and the region.

Steve leads a team which has enjoyed numerous awards for the excellence of its service. For example, the Motorpoint Arena has been voted nine times music venue of the year; SIV's sport facilities have attained some of the highest Quest management scores in the country; whilst its Fitness Unlimited gym membership is an unprecedented quadruple winner of the Fitness Industry Association's award, 'Centre of the Year'. Through strong leadership, innovation, and a forward thinking approach, Steve has been instrumental in transforming Sheffield's underused and closure-threatened sport facilities built for the 1991 World Student Games into highly sought after, modern, and developing venues for the whole community – creating a legacy for future generations. He attempts the impossible when everyone else around thinks there is no chance by drawing people into the dream.

Career progression

Steve has dedicated his career to leisure management and innovation. After leaving Sheffield Polytechnic (Sheffield Hallam University) he converted a floating barge into a public house in Grimsby and became the country's youngest licensee. He went onto manage squash clubs, seaside piers, theatres, amusement parks, and restaurants before moving to Blackpool in 1989 to manage the development of a three floor, ten-pin bowling center and the first 'Brannigans' theme pub, which led to the roll out of the concept throughout Great Britain. He moved to the world famous Blackpool Tower in 1989 to oversee a £17 million facelift and the centenary celebrations before becoming Chief Executive of the Sheffield City Trust group (SCT) and its principal operating company SIV in 1996. The SCT group has grown from 4 to 18 venues and increased turnover from £5m to nearly £30m per annum. In addition to its venues in Sheffield the group also manages venues in Scarborough and Whitby. In 2010 Steve was voted the Business Person of the Year in the region – and in the 2011 Queen's Birthday Honours list he was awarded an MBE (Member of the Order of the British Empire) for his contribution to the leisure industry.

Steve's advice for those who aspire to work in the industry ...

- Ensure you experience a wide variety of different roles in different organizations whilst in education and in the early stages of your career.
- Pay attention to leadership styles during your early career and note the good and bad points in different leaders. It is as important to learn what not to do, as it is to learn what you should do.
- Enjoy your work. You spend more time at work than anywhere else and life is too short for work to be a chore. Be able to laugh at yourself.
- Better to try and fail than not to try at all. Encourage your team to take some risks and try different ideas. Reward success but do not flog an employee for trying to improve your business.
- Be positive. Negative people do not get promoted.
- Encourage a 'can do' attitude amongst your employees.
- Demonstrate a consistent temperament. Staff do not respond well when their leader is moody and unpredictable.
- Treat people fairly and in the manner you would expect to be treated.
- Be honest with yourself and your colleagues. People respect honesty even if told difficult or disappointing news.
- Team building is critical. Construct a team with similar core values but with different skills and strengths. You do not need a team of people who mirror your own strengths.
- Commit to 'continuous improvement'. Always seek to develop your skills and experience. Do not stand still.
- Work hard. As the famous film producer Samuel Goldwyn once said: 'The harder I work the luckier I get.'

TECHNOLOGY NOW!

The city of Sheffield in England is home to the largest complex of sporting and theatre facilities outside of the capital, London. In an innovative partnership, Sheffield Theatres and Sheffield International Venues Ltd (SIV) have installed the Sheffield Ticketing Network (STN). This is an online system that integrates ticket sales data not only across different venues but also across different organizations. If you want to see Premier League Darts at the Motorpoint Arena, you can book online, or at any of the many locations around the city that has a STN terminal. The system has helped to reduce the costs of administrating ticket sales because with the option to print your ticket at home, there is no longer any need to print tickets or to send them out by mail. Tickets that are printed at home are scanned by barcode readers at the venues and provide access in the same way as conventional tickets.

For senior managers the system gives real-time access to how many tickets have been sold and how much revenue has been generated. Revenue is the most important financial measure in this context because the managers know what their costs are (as these are essentially all fixed) and therefore the key piece of missing information is how much revenue will be contributed towards these fixed costs. This knowledge enables managers to take timely action to control their business. For example, if a show is not selling as well as anticipated, it is possible to send emails or text messages to known ticket purchasers with a history of attending similar events making them a special offer. This type of business control is a practical example of the first key business question 'is the selling price higher than the cost?' Clearly it is unsustainable to put on sporting and theatrical events unless the cost of buying in and staging the shows is worthwhile. Where technology has helped in this goal is to reduce barriers to access tickets; stripping out costs in the booking process; and providing managers with real-time information that enables them to take corrective action where possible.

Sources: Sheffield International Venues (2014). Retrieved October 29, 2014 from http://sivtickets.sheffieldnetwork.com and www.sheffieldboxoffice.com

CHAPTER 9

OPERATIONAL DECISION MAKING

CHAPTER OUTLINE

- The nature of costs in sport facility management
- A costing matrix
- Practical applications of costing
- Chapter review

CHAPTER OBJECTIVES

In the previous chapter we examined the various finance functions that a sport facility manager needs to understand to be an effective professional in the field. In this chapter we develop the techniques used in management accounting to illustrate the nature of cost, cost behavior, and how knowledge of the underlying principles can support managers to make sensible decisions. By the time you have finished the chapter you will be able to explain: the three different types of cost that sport facility managers will encounter; how these costs behave in relation to changes in output; and how to use familiarity with cost behavior in planning, decision making, and control. In Chapter 8 we looked at the processes involved in putting together a budget. In real life, budgets rarely produce the desired outcome at the first attempt. In this chapter we will bring alive the budgeting process by looking at concepts such as breakeven analysis and the margin of safety. As you advance in your career you will find that the difference between those who progress and those who stagnate is the ability to take responsibility for courses of action such as increasing the number of people using your sport facility or the amount of money you are able to extract from customers via secondary spending. One of the best ways to be able to progress is to understand how your business works and to model the scenarios that will bring about desired outcomes. In addition to your knowledge of financial management you are also strongly advised to develop spreadsheet skills so that you can construct business models and carry out what is known as 'what if' scenarios. For example, 'what if' we put up prices by $5 per seat for games in our stadium and as a result we lost 5 percent of our paying spectators?' The techniques outlined in the chapter will help you to answer questions like this from an informed position rather than on the basis of random guesswork.

THE NATURE OF COSTS IN SPORT FACILITY MANAGEMENT

You should now be clear that the first and most important question to ask of any business is: 'is the selling price higher than the cost?' There is little point running say a 50,000 seat stadium if at the end of a game you have made a loss because the costs have been higher than the selling price. Given that it is costs which determine whether or not there is any profit left from the revenue, it is clearly important that we understand the nature of costs and how they behave in practice. How difficult would it be to manage a stadium effectively if you did not know what costs you incurred, how many seats you had available to sell, and what price you should sell them at? Without such information you cannot make sensible decisions about controlling costs, increasing revenue, and ultimately maximizing profitability. It is to address these sorts of issues that some simple cost accounting techniques can provides us with a framework through which we can plan, make decisions, and control our businesses.

Everything in business life has a cost, for example sport facilities need: staff, insurance, electricity, water, marketing, and maintenance expenditure. These costs will behave in different ways depending on the courses of action (or strategies) that are being implemented. It is therefore essential that we know about cost behavior and can model it accordingly. A new question to add your list is 'how much do I need to sell in order to break even?'

To begin to answer this question we need to know about the types of cost that exist and how they behave under certain business circumstances. The most basic type of cost is the 'fixed cost', which is a form of expenditure that does not vary in the short term relative to the level activity. There is a lot going on in this definition so we can unpack it by using an example. Consider the case of a stadium manager of a professional soccer club who earns $100,000 per year. At this stadium there might be 20 home games per season plus any number of extra events such as exhibition matches, private hires, and conferences – to name a few. Over the duration of a financial year (12 months) the salary of the manager will not change, nor will

184

it change if there are 25 home matches or 15 home matches, or any variation in the number of other events staged. So in the context of looking at the cost of the stadium manager, we can say that for over the next year his or her salary of $100,000 is a fixed cost relative to the level of activity taking place. We can model this situation as shown in Figure 9.1.

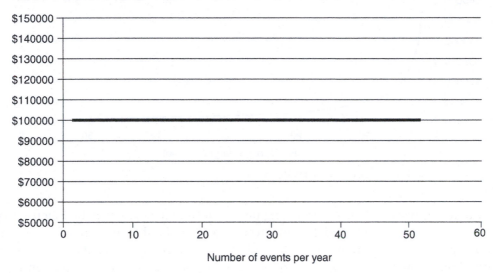

Figure 9.1 Fixed costs relative to activity

What Figure 9.1 shows clearly is that regardless of the number of events staged in the stadium, the salary of the manager does not alter. Salary is a great example of a fixed cost but others in sport facility management include expenses such as insurance, licenses, office equipment, and accountancy/audit fees. If we allocated fixed costs over the number of events staged, then we would see a very different picture on a per event basis. For example, if fixed salary costs of $100,000 were shared out over 10 events the cost per event would be $10,000, whereas if they were shared out over 50 events the cost per event would be $2,000. Again we can model this aspect of cost behavior as shown in Figure 9.2.

What we can see in Figure 9.2 is a curvilinear relationship between fixed costs and the level of activity if we allocate costs out on a per unit basis. An important learning point for sport facility managers is that in real life the majority of costs you encounter will be fixed and therefore there is a strong incentive to increase activity levels because this dilutes fixed costs over a greater level of activity and therefore creates more opportunities to generate revenue. This is a point that is reflected in the design of modern stadia. In England, Premier League football (soccer) clubs play in a league of 20 teams and each team in the league plays each other on a home and an away basis. Thus each team is guaranteed 38 matches of which 19 will be at their home stadium. If there are 19 match days there are 346

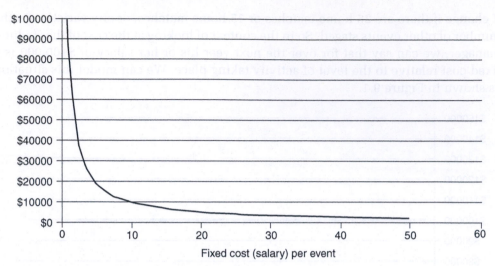

Figure 9.2 Fixed costs per unit of activity (event)

non-match days and this is a very long period of time for venues to be inactive. To overcome this problem, which is essentially a considerable amount of fixed cost being spread over relatively few days, clubs will stage other events such as concerts, boxing matches, and other sports to give themselves more opportunity to recover their fixed costs and to put the stadium facilities to good use. Accountants have been known to use the term 'sweating your assets' to describe the process of making the assets of a business work hard to generate income and profits – for a soccer stadium 19 days of work per year is hardly 'sweating'. Twickenham Stadium is the home of English rugby and stages around 12 matches per year in its 82,000 seat stadium. For the rest of the year the facility is put to good use for other events and boasts the following resources:

- 25 conference and event rooms;
- 150 corporate hospitality boxes for meetings or private dining;
- 5,000 square meters of conference and exhibition space;
- an auditorium with tiered seating for up to 400 delegates;
- banqueting suites accommodating from between 20 to 800 guests;
- four-star Marriott Hotel with 156 rooms and a health club;
- the World Rugby Museum; and
- car parking for more than 2,000 vehicles.

These resources enable Twickenham Stadium to run on an all-year-round basis and help to share out the fixed costs of the venue over a much wider array of events than just 12 rugby matches per year. As a contrast to fixed costs there are some costs that vary in line with variations in activity. Whilst most of the costs of operating a stadium might be fixed, we will find that in the catering and merchandising outlets within the stadium there are numerous examples of costs that vary in line with changes in levels of activity. For example, the more hot dogs or bottles of beer we sell, the more costs we incur; these are known as the cost of goods sold. Similarly, in the merchandise shops the more replica kits that are sold, the greater the cost of goods sold in buying those kits in the first place. If a case of 24 beer bottles costs $48 then if we sell one case the cost to us is $48 and if we sell 10 cases the cost will be $480. In the same way that we modeled the nature of fixed costs and fixed costs per unit in Figures 9.1 and 9.2 we can do the same with variable costs as shown in Figures 9.3 and 9.4.

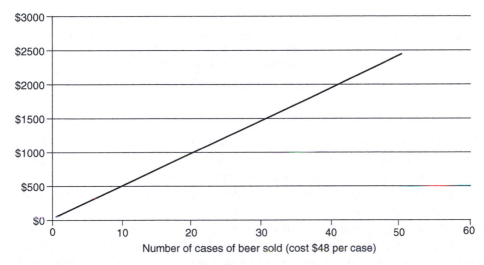

Figure 9.3 Variable costs relative to activity

Variable costs behave very differently to changes in the level of activity than fixed costs which can be appreciated fully by comparing Figure 9.3 with Figure 9.1. Understanding this point is fundamental to being able to use these principles to make operational decisions in facility management. If we look at how variable costs behave relative to the level of activity we will see a familiar picture. If we sell one case of beer our cost per unit is $48 and if we sell 20 or 50 cases the cost per unit will also be $48 as shown in Figure 9.4.

The variable costs per unit do not change in the short run with each case of beer sold in our example costing $48 regardless of the volume of cases sold. This is an identical image to Figure 9.1 where we see that fixed costs do not change in relation to the overall level of activity. In the case of Figure 9.4 we find that for each level of activity the cost per unit of goods sold is constant.

Life is not quite as simple as all costs being either totally fixed or totally variable and there are two types of costs that contain an element of fixed and variable costs

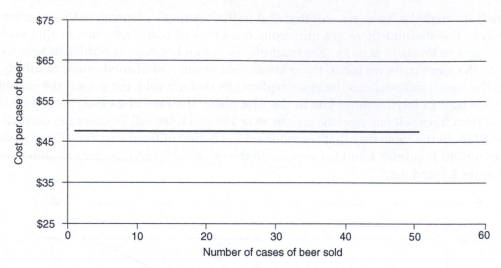

Figure 9.4 Variable costs per unit of activity (cases of beer sold)

to them. The two types of cost that contain this fixed and variable element to them are called 'semi-variable costs' and 'stepped costs'. These can be illustrated by continuing our sport stadium example. Utility supplies such as water, gas, electricity, and telephones often have elements of fixed cost and variable costs. For example, in order to have a water supply to a stadium the utility company will charge a standing charge which is fixed and then further costs dependent upon the volume of water used which is a variable charge. For a sport stadium the typical cost might be something like a standing or fixed charge of $25,000 per year with further costs of $5 per cubic meter of water used. Figure 9.5 models how this water supply would look in practice.

For the semi-variable costs shown in Figure 9.5 the important point of note is that the cost line on the graph does not start at the origin (0) because the stadium incurs an annual cost of $25,000 simply for having a water supply and before a single drop of water has been used. Added to the standing charge is the variable cost of $5 per cubic meter of water which does vary in direct proportion to the volume of water used (or activity) and which causes the line to have a steady slope upwards from $25,000.

The final category, 'stepped costs', is characterized by costs that do not vary steadily with changes in output but which step up (hence the name) once certain thresholds are reached. In the case of our stadium manager it may be the case that every time the stadium is opened up for an event there must a minimum of 100 stewards on duty for any level of activity from 0 admissions to 19,999 admissions. Between 20,000 and 29,999 admissions the licensing conditions might stipulate that another 50 stewards are required, and so on for every extra 10,000 admissions

188

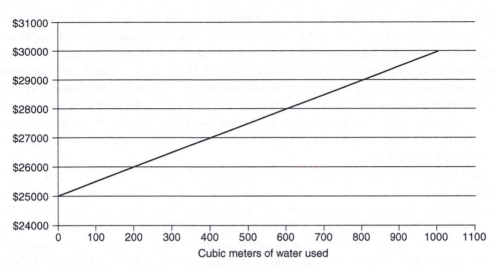

Figure 9.5 Semi-variable costs relative to activity

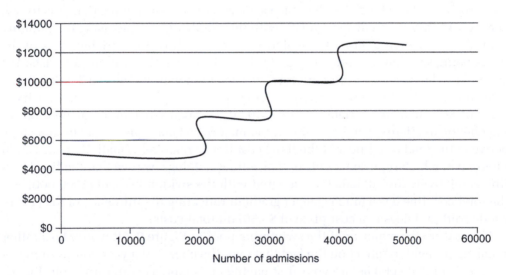

Figure 9.6 Stepped costs relative to activity

to the limit of 50,000. If each steward costs $50 per shift, then the cost model for running this aspect of the stadium would be as shown in Figure 9.6.

In this example, if the stadium is not open, then there are no costs incurred for stewards, which is why the line starts at the origin. However, once the decision is made to open the stadium, the license requires that 100 stewards are on duty which incurs a cost of $5,000 – a cost that holds good until 20,000 admissions are reached at which point we see a step up in cost for the extra 50 stewards required ($2,500) and then a plateau until the next break point at 30,000 admissions and further break points at 40,000 and 50,000. Managers need to plan in advance as to how many staff members they will need on duty to meet demand. It should be clear to see however that mistakes can cost serious amounts of money. If as stadium manager you gear up for 30,000 admissions and only 20,000 people turn up, then that is a bad decision which has a $2,500 price tag on it. Hopefully, the example serves to reinforce the notion that managers need to know their costs and how they behave in order to make sensible decisions.

As a logical consequence of identifying fixed and variable costs (including semi-variable and stepped costs), it follows that total costs are the sum of the two. In Figure 9.5 the cost line for the water bill of a sport stadium starts on the y axis at the level of fixed costs ($25,000) and increases in line with the volume of water used. This could also be the total cost for an entire business such as a stadium, swimming pool, fitness club, or indeed a catering or merchandising outlet within one of these facilities. What is interesting to note and important to know is that different types of businesses have different cost structures. For example, in a swimming pool, once opening hours have been decided, the vast majority of costs are fixed, that is to say, very few of the costs will vary in line with the number of people using the pool. By contrast, in a catering outlet the majority of costs will be the variable costs of the items being sold and the fixed costs will be staff time and any premises costs. We can model the nature of different cost structure as shown in Figure 9.7 and 9.8.

In the case of Figure 9.7, the swimming pool example, there are annual fixed costs of $500,000 and variable costs of $0.50 for say a wristband and pool cleaning chemicals. Here it can be seen that the majority of costs are fixed and the angle between the total cost line and the fixed cost line is relatively small. By contrast, in Figure 9.8, which represents the costs of selling hot dogs, we see that the fixed cost line is relatively low at $20,000 compared with the swimming pool ($500,000) and the total cost line has a much steeper gradient reflecting the influence of the cost of goods sold (hot dogs at a cost price of $1.50) on total costs.

If you were the manager of the swimming pool in Figure 9.7 it would be a rather sobering thought to reflect on the fact that over the course of a year you were incurring costs of $500,000 before your first paying customer. This in turn should focus your mind on the importance of generating revenue by achieving high levels of customer throughput at a price that will at least cover the costs and ideally generate a surplus. Armed with this type of information, it becomes possible to develop a plan based on evidence that gives you a chance of achieving your business objectives.

We started this section by saying that those people who advance in their careers as facility managers are the people who can use their knowledge of cost behavior to maximize profits. Now that we have acquired a good handle on the nature of cost and its relationship to activity, it is time to put it all into practice by looking at how such information is used in real life.

190

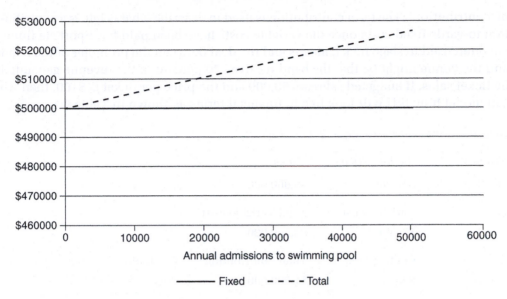

Figure 9.7 Total cost graph for a swimming pool – high fixed costs

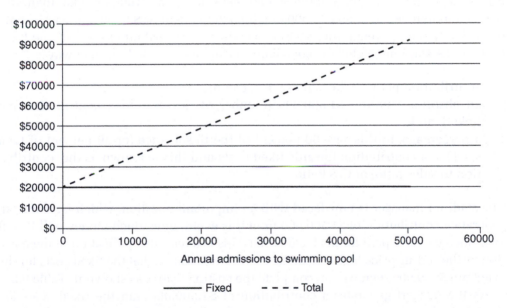

Figure 9.8 Total cost for hot dog sales – high variable costs

A COSTING MATRIX

In this section we use a series of different scenarios to model cost behavior which in turn can be used to evaluate business decisions. We start by introducing the notion of 'contribution'. The term contribution is used to describe what is left as a contribution towards fixed costs once the variable costs have been paid for. Sport stadiums are often used to stage rock concerts and the deal between the promoter of the band and the venue might be that the band receives 70 percent of the revenue generated by ticket sales. If budgeted sales are 50,000 and the price per ticket is $100, then we can model how this will look like in financial terms as shown in Table 9.1.

Table 9.1 Costing matrix to show contribution

Quantity	Selling Price	Sales	
50,000	$100.00	$5,000,000	
	Variable Cost	Total Variable Cost	
	$70.00	$3,500,000	
	Contribution	Total Contribution	C/S Ratio
	$30.00	$1,500,000	30%

Assuming the concert sells out the 50,000 seat stadium at $100 per ticket then, this will generate revenue of $5,000,000 of which 70 percent or $3,500,000 will be paid to the band and the remaining $1,500,000 will be a contribution towards the fixed costs of the stadium. Note how contribution can be expressed in three ways:

■ contribution per unit i.e. $30 per ticket sold;
■ an absolute amount, $1,500,000 (number of tickets sold x contribution per ticket); and
■ a percentage, in this case 30 percent of the ticket price (or 30 percent of total sales) is a contribution towards fixed costs and this is known as the 'contribution to sales ratio' or C/S Ratio.

The stadium manager is now faced with an important question, which is: if we can generate a contribution of $1,500,000 from this event, how much money will be left over once we have paid for the fixed costs? This is a real-life application of the question 'is the selling price higher than the cost?' If we assume that the fixed costs for the event are $900,000 then we can complete the costing matrix as shown in Table 9.2.

As the concert generates a contribution of $1,500,000 and the fixed costs are $900,000, then the event generates a net profit or surplus of $600,000 as shown in Table 9.2. This looks like good business at face value because if nothing else, the selling price or revenue of $5,000,000 is greater than the sum of the total costs of $4,400,000 (variable plus fixed costs). So assuming that all other operational issues fell into place and that the stadium was not missing out on a better opportunity, the wise decision here would be to accept the deal offered by the promoter and to stage the concert.

192

Table 9.2 Complete costing matrix

Quantity	Selling Price	Sales				
50,000	$100.00	$5,000,000				
	Variable Cost	Total Variable Cost				
	$70.00	$3,500,000				
	Contribution	Total Contribution	C/S Ratio			
	$30.00	$1,500,000	30%			
	Fixed Costs	$900,000	Breakeven Units	30,000	Breakeven Sales	$3,000,000
	Net Profit	$600,000	Margin of Safety Units	20,000	Margin of Safety	$2,000,000

At this point a good manager would realize that they had taken on a degree of risk and would ask themselves a couple of questions. First, 'how many sales do we need to make in order to break even?' Second, 'how many sales can we afford to lose from our planned level of sales to the point at which we start losing money?' The answer to the first question can be found in 'breakeven' analysis and the answer to the second in 'margin of safety' analysis. These concepts are shown to the right hand side of Table 9.2 and are worthy of further explanation.

If the fundamental question of business is if the selling price is higher than the cost, then breakeven analysis is concerned with the point at which the selling price equals the cost. That is we do not make any money but nor do we lose any. If we look at Table 9.2 and think about the breakeven point, it should become clear that the breakeven point is the point at which total contribution equals fixed costs. So in our concert example, at what level of sales would a contribution of $900,000 be achieved? We can now use some simple logic to tackle this question. If each ticket sold generates a contribution of $30 and to break even we need to generate $900,000, then the number of ticket sales required to achieve this is simply total fixed costs divided by the contribution per ticket.

Breakeven = Fixed Costs $900,000/contribution per unit $30 = 30,000 admissions

So at 30,000 admissions the event reaches the point at which all costs are covered but no profit is being made. However, as the event is budgeting for 50,000 admissions we have a margin of safety of 20,000 admissions. That is if we budget for 50,000 admissions we can afford to lose 20,000 of these before we would actually lose any money. The margin of safety is simply the difference between the planned

193

level of activity (50,000) and the breakeven point (30,000). However, we can also derive this logically as we did for the breakeven point.

Margin of safety = Net profit $600,000/contribution per unit $30 = 20,000 admissions

This analysis enables us to bring together the cost data with the income data to produce a chart that provides all of this in one place as shown in Figure 9.9.

In Figure 9.9 the total cost line begins on the y axis from the fixed costs of $900,000 and the total revenue line starts at the origin to reflect because no sales equals no revenue. The two lines have different gradients which means that they will collide and the place at which this collision occurs is the breakeven point. At all points before this, costs are higher than revenues and a loss is made. At all points after breakeven, revenue is higher than costs and a profit is made. The gap between planned for sales (50,000) and breakeven sales is the margin of safety. Note how for both breakeven sales and the margin of safety we can derive an answer in both units (x axis) and revenue (y axis). The ability to represent data in either the form of the costing matrix (Table 9.2) or in the form of a graph (Figure 9.9) is a useful skill for facility managers in sport. More important however is the ability to understand what it all means and to use it to support sensible decision making.

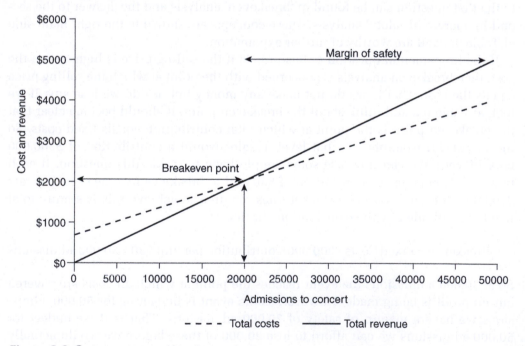

Figure 9.9 Cost, revenue and breakeven chart

Implementation of management and operations

PRACTICAL APPLICATIONS OF COSTING

Business is not predictable and often reality turns out differently from what was planned. The difference between the proactive manager and the reactive manager is the skill to use information wisely in the way in which you run your business. As a result of the difference between planned and actual outcomes, an important skill for managers is being able to model 'what if' scenarios. We know in our concert example that we can sell out a 50,000 seat stadium if the tickets are $100 each. What if we increased the prices to $120 and sacrificed 10,000 sales so that the attendance was 40,000? Would this be a good decision in financial terms? To answer the question we can adapt the costing matrix in Table 9.2 to show the outcome of the two different scenarios on our bottom line (net profit) in Table 9.3.

The idea of charging higher prices in return for a lower audience does not work in purely financial terms as shown by the reduction in net profit of $60,000 ($600,000 v $540,000). The first clue that this is not a good idea can be seen by the fact that it delivers a lower contribution than selling 50,000 tickets at the lower price of $100. Lower contribution equals lower profit because the fixed costs remain the same. The only positive is that it would reduce the number of sales required to break even from 30,000 to 25,000. There are also other considerations that need to be taken into account which require managerial judgment. By having 10,000 fewer admissions it might be possible to save a bit of money on staffing levels but at the same time there are negatives. First, 10,000 fewer spectators means 10,000 fewer people to sell car parking, food, drink, programs, and merchandise to, which may be a huge missed opportunity in terms of secondary spending at the event. Second, fewer people in the audience may mean less of an 'atmosphere' which has the effect of reducing the quality of the experience for those who are there, particularly the people near the empty seats. Third, empty seats do not look good especially if an event is being broadcast beyond the venue. Managers need to evaluate all of the influences that affect an event to implement a strategy that gives the optimum outcome. In this context an optimum outcome is achieving financial objectives, giving customers a good experience so they will come back again, and delivering an event that looks good. Using techniques like using the costing matrix and a 'what if' scenario therefore provide managers with the tools to be able to make decisions supported by information rather than relying solely on guesswork or intuition to deliver the optimum outcome.

A useful application of 'what if' analysis is called sensitivity analysis whereby managers model how sensitive their cost assumptions are to changes in some of the key variables in the costing matrix. For example, the promoter of the concert in our stadium example comes back to us and says that the finances will not work unless he was guaranteed $77 per seat instead of $70. This is an increase in the variable costs of 10 percent which will therefore lead to a reduction in contribution and a reduction in profit. The question that the good manager would ask here is 'how sensitive is my bottom line to an increase in variable costs of $7 per seat?' Using the costing matrix we can model this easily as shown in Table 9.4.

Table 9.3 What if scenario

Quantity	Selling Price	Sales
50,000	$100.00	$5,000,000
40,000	$120.00	$4,800,000

Variable Cost	Total Variable Cost
$70.00	$3,500,000
$84.00	$3,360,000

Contribution	Total Contribution	C/S Ratio
$30.00	$1,500,000	30%
$36.00	$1,440,000	30%

Fixed Costs	Breakeven Sales	Breakeven Units
$900,000	$3,000,000	30,000
$900,000	$3,000,000	25,000

Net Profit	Margin of Safety	Margin of Safety Units
$600,000	$2,000,000	20,000
$540,000	$1,800,000	15,000

Table 9.4 Sensitivity analysis

Quantity	Selling Price	Sales				
50,000	$100.00	$5,000,000				
50,000	$100.00	$5,000,000				
	Variable Cost	Total Variable Cost				
	$70.00	$3,500,000				
	$77.00	$3,850,000				
	Contribution	Total Contribution	C/S Ratio			
	$30.00	$1,500,000	30%			
	$23.00	$1,150,000	23%			
	Fixed Costs	$900,000		Breakeven Units	30,000	Breakeven Sales $3,000,000
		$900,000			39,130	$3,913,000
	Net Profit	$600,000		Margin of Safety Units	20,000	Margin of Safety $2,000,000
		$250,000			10,870	$1,087,000

The effect of a $7 or 10 percent increase in variable costs has a dramatic effect on the net profit of the concert, which as a result falls from $600,000 to $250,000 – a reduction of 58 percent. Aware of this sensitivity between increases in variable cost and reduced profit, the proactive manager now has the information at their fingertips to negotiate hard that this is not an attractive proposition and should be resisted strongly. In addition to delivering an inferior financial outcome relative to the original deal it also means that the venue bears an increased level of risk as demonstrated by the breakeven point rising from 30,000 to 39,130 sales and the margin of safety falling from 20,000 sales to 10,870 sales. These are much better arguments to counter the promoter with than simply saying 'no' or shouting and becoming aggressive.

Unfortunately not all events sell out and in the case of facilities such as swimming pools and gyms it is unlikely that operating at 100 percent capacity is feasible or realistic. This therefore means that once unsold capacity is lost, it is lost forever and cannot be recovered. To counter this problem of the perishable nature of services such as sport spectating and sport participation, managers can use their knowledge of costing to make some additional sales. If we continue the example of the 50,000 stadium, imagine that it is staging a football match and two days before kick-off there are several thousand seats unsold which normally sell for $80. As the venue manager you are faced with a choice. You can leave the seats and see if there are any walk ups on the day or you can show some initiative and try to recover some revenue from them. For example, assume that at the time of the match there was a conference in town with two thousand delegates. It would be a good strategy to contact the conference organizers and to offer to cut them a deal. We know that our cost base is fixed and will not change and we know that under these conditions any extra contribution equals extra profit. Assuming we cannot sell the tickets anywhere else we could say to the conference organizer as a special offer we can let you have 1,000 tickets at say $50 instead of $80. This would generate a further $50,000 in revenue; it would help with secondary sales; and it would reduce the number of empty seats visible. So faced with taking a risk on trying to get $80,000 for 1,000 seats and possibly getting nothing, or reducing your risk by going for $50,000, what would you do? Much would depend on your attitude to risk and the financial targets you had been set. But in a business like sport facility management where the majority of costs are fixed, then some contribution is better than no contribution and there is a place for special deals and discounts so long as they make a positive contribution to the bottom line. Steps such as these group discounts should however be used sparingly because there is the danger that you end up devaluing the product and your regular customers who were previously prepared to pay your original prices start to demand discounts as well. These are the techniques to be used in the push for full capacity and not the way you go about selling tickets from the outset.

Arguably one of the most important applications of knowing about costs and cost behavior is setting prices. This is one of the defining skills of a true manager compared with operational staff. If you are the manager of a swimming pool, how would you go about setting the price of an admission to the pool? In practice there are a variety of methods but the ones most likely to succeed are those which are at least in part based on knowledge of cost and cost behavior. There are in practice three main methods by which prices for activities can be set. First is cost-based pricing whereby the costs of providing a service are analyzed and managers work back from these to arrive at a desired outcome such as breakeven or a specified level of profit. Second is what is known as copycat pricing, whereby managers simply copy the prices that are being charged in comparable facilities. Third is market-based pricing, which takes into account what the market will bear for a service rather than basing prices on the costs of provision. All of these methods have their strengths and weaknesses; however, the confident manager will realize that the methods are not mutually exclusive and by using some or all of them simultaneously it is possible to make pricing decisions that are informed by a broad rather than narrow range of influences.

Table 9.5 represents the budgeted costs for a community swimming pool for which the financial objective is to break even. The facility will be open for 50 weeks of the year and will generate 1,000 admissions per week. Given the cost base what should the price per swim be?

Table 9.5 Swimming pool annual running costs

EXPENDITURE	
Staff Costs	$ 275,000
Premises	$ 125,000
Energy	$ 75,000
Water	$ 25,000
TOTAL EXPENDITURE	$ 500,000
REQUIRED PROFIT	–

If the throughput to the swimming pool is 50,000 admissions per year and the running costs are $500,000 it follows that in order to break even the cost per swim must be $500,000/50,000 which equals $10 per swim. This, if you like, is the 'cost of production' of one swim. However, there is no guarantee that people will be prepared to pay $10 to use a municipal swimming pool because it may be perceived as being a price which is too high to pay. As a test of reasonableness then, the manager might visit other pools either in person or via their websites to assess what comparable facilities are charging. If they are charging less it may well be because their cost base is lower and that to be competitive our manager needs to find some economies. It may also be the case that $10 is relatively cheap for the locality and there is room to increase prices. Hopefully it is at least implicit that simply copying the prices of another facility is not a good strategy for the proactive facility manager. The reasons for this view are as follows: first, we do not know the cost base of rival facilities; second, we do not know what the financial outcomes required from our rivals are; and, third, we ignore considerations such as what the market will bear. The third method of pricing, 'what the market will bear', is perhaps the most sophisticated and therefore reliable basis from which to work. We can find out in general terms what the market will bear by looking at rival facilities which might give us some ballpark figures that the price of most swims is somewhere between say $5 and $15. But what is the right price for a specific facility? This is often achieved via market research whereby the developers of a new sport facility will interview people and take the opportunity to explain the sport facility to them. An example of a question would be 'Would you use this sport facility?' If the response was yes, the follow-up questions would be 'How often would you use it?' and 'What price would you be willing to pay to use it?' If this type of market research is done properly and with sufficient sample it is possible to generalize that from a population of say 500,000 people we might be able to generate 50,000 swims per year at an average price of $10. If we achieve this, then we will break even and thereby achieve a situation whereby the selling price is at least equal to the cost.

It is important to realize that when we produce models of cost behavior and build up 'what if' scenarios we are using these tools as 'decision support systems' and not decision making systems. Take for example the case of a swimming pool, for which the costs are essentially fixed for a given level of output, namely opening hours. If the pool is open for 40 hours per week, what would be the cost of opening it for an extra hour so that a triathlon club could have exclusive use of the facility one evening? The premises, water, and energy costs would not change, but there would be an increase in staff costs to cover the extra hour. If we said that an extra hour of staff costs and any other variable costs were $20, what would we charge the triathlon club? We could charge $20 and in so doing would put the facility in a position whereby it incurred no additional cost or made any extra profit, that is, it broke even. Intuitively you should be able to realize that charging the marginal cost of an extra hour of swimming is missing a commercial opportunity. We know that the market will bear $10 per swim and if there were 20 members who used the exclusive club time, we could generate up to $200. This might be too much for the club, but it would certainly be possible to agree a price at around $100 to $150 for the extra hour which would show the club that they were getting the pool at a cheaper price than usual and also make more than the extra costs incurred for the swimming pool. It is this sort of thinking which forms the art of operational decision making to go alongside the science which underpins decision support systems. Art and science go hand in hand when managing sport facilities. We can acquire the science from books such as this, but the art comes from experience, gut reaction, and instinct. Used in tandem, art and science are more powerful than relying on art only or science only.

200

DYNAMIC TICKET PRICING IN MAJOR LEAGUE BASEBALL

Major League Baseball (MLB) franchises are faced with the task of playing 162 regular season games of which half (81) will be at home. Across the 30 MLB teams the average stadium capacity in round numbers is 40,000, which means that most will have approximately 3,240,000 tickets to sell during the season. Some games are more attractive than others. If a team is on a winning streak, the weather is good, or there will be a matchup between two rivals (such as the Boston Red Sox vs. New York Yankees), then it might be possible to sell the stadium out twice over. By contrast, if a team is on a losing streak, the weather is bad, or the game has nothing at stake, then it may prove very difficult to sell tickets. Poor crowds lead to a poor atmosphere in the stadium and large sections of empty seats can look embarrassing on television. To address these issues and to maximize revenues and crowds it has become almost standard practice within MLB to use a process known as dynamic ticket pricing. In essence dynamic ticket pricing alters the price of tickets in line with the demand for them. This ability to flex price in line with demand is made possible via online booking systems and complex algorithms that continually adjust prices in line with demand. Such an approach is much more proactive than fixed prices at the start of a season and sticking with these throughout regardless of the context surrounding a particular match. The evidence indicates that for games during poor weather, single game tickets will sell better at lower prices than higher prices. Similarly if a team is in with a chance of making the postseason, then demand will be high and it will be possible to raise prices accordingly. The San Francisco Giants were the pioneers of dynamic ticket pricing in 2009 and experimented with variable prices on 2,000 seats using variables that they believed affected demand such as the weather and star players on the opposition side. This experiment led to an increase in revenue of around $0.5m during the 2009 season. We have been subjected to dynamic pricing on airplanes and hotels since the 1980s and it has now found traction in professional sport.

Source: adapted from www.forbes.com/sites/sportsmoney/2012/06/08/is-dynamic-ticket-pricing-hurting-mlb-attendance/

Suggested discussion topics

1   What are your views on dynamic ticket pricing in sport? Do you prefer the price of tickets to be fixed and predictable throughout the season or are you happy for prices to vary on a game-by-game and day-by-day basis? Why do you hold these opinions?

2   Can you think of any other examples in the sport industry where dynamic pricing might have a role to play? If you were the manager of an open air swimming pool would you feel comfortable raising prices on hot days during the summer vacation when demand will be at its highest? Why do you hold these opinions?

CHAPTER REVIEW

In this chapter we have examined some of the skills that managers working at higher levels of responsibility within a sport facility are faced with as integral parts of their job. Lifeguards in a swimming pool ensure public safety but they do not set the prices of swims or venue hire. Staff who work in the concessions of a stadium sell hot dogs and beer but do not negotiate the price at which these are purchased and sold. This type of operational pricing decision is the domain of the manager and requires some specific skills. The first of these skills is to know about the nature of costs and the way in which costs behave in response to changes in levels of output. A feature of sport facilities is that whether we are providing a stadium, a swimming pool, or a gym the majority of costs will be fixed for any given level of output. This means that the only logical strategy to pursue is income generation to make sure that we are getting in enough money to contribute towards fixed costs. It is possible to reduce fixed costs by cutting back on staff, marketing, training, and maintenance. This however is generally a false economy because our staff, our business, and our facility slowly become neglected and unfit for purpose. In a predominantly fixed cost environment, the logical strategy is to generate more revenue. Generating more revenue is achieved by attracting more than the budgeted number of customers; knowing what the optimal price to charge is; and making sure that once customers are inside a venue we sell them as much as possible in secondary spend (food, drink, merchandise, etc.).

To help make sensible decisions managers should use decision support systems such as the costing matrix to quantify the cost behavior of their business. A very important skills set to have is the ability to use a spreadsheet to create costing models that are specific to a given set of circumstances. From here it then becomes possible to model 'what if?' scenarios and to conduct sensitivity analyses. These sorts of methods give managers an idea of what is important when certain assumptions are modeled. A further reason why the models we have demonstrated in this chapter are decision support systems and not decision making systems is because in order to drive the models we need data that is derived from other sources. The most notable amongst these is data from research. There is little point in saying 'given our cost base we need 50,000 admissions to achieve target' if market research

202

indicates that at best the market will only support 30,000 admissions. As an absolute minimum we need to be clear about what our breakeven position is and the extent (if any) of our margin of safety. Our models and spreadsheets are only as good as the data that drive them.

One skill or responsibility that clearly illustrates the difference between managers and staff is setting prices. This is often something of a juggling act which requires managers to balance the challenge of generating the required financial return; ensuring a high-quality customer experience; and in the case of broadcast events, making sure that an event looks good on television with no or minimal levels of empty seats. Each scenario you face as a manager will have its own particular challenges so there is no one-size-fits-all approach that is guaranteed to work. What you can do however is to learn from the more experienced as you progress through your career. If you treat your bosses as mentors, you can ask questions to them such as 'how many people did you think you would get in?', 'why did you choose that particular price?', and 'to what extent have we achieved what we set out to achieve?' Inevitably along the way we all make mistakes; this is all part of the learning process and can be forgiven so long as we do not make the same mistake twice. Using the tools and techniques outlined in this chapter will help to minimize the likelihood of error by underpinning the art of operational decision making with science.

BIBLIOGRAPHY

Beech, J. and Chadwick, S. (Eds.) (2004). *The business of sport management.* London, UK: Financial Times Prentice Hall.

Russell, D., Patel, A., and Wilkinson-Riddle, G. (2002). *Cost accounting: An essential guide.* London, UK: Financial Times Prentice Hall.

Shibli, S. (1994). *Leisure manager's guide to budgeting and budgetary control.* London, UK: Longman/ILAM.

Stewart, B. (2007). *Sport funding and finance.* Oxford, UK: Butterworth-Heinemann.

Trendberth, L. and Hassan, D. (2012). *Managing sport business.* Oxford, UK: Routledge.

Whitehouse, J. and Tilley, C. (1992). *Finance and leisure.* London, UK: Longman/ILAM.

Wilson, R. (2011). *Managing sport finance.* Oxford, UK: Routledge.

IN THE FIELD ...

Dan Porter, Head of Sport Services, Sheffield Hallam University

Current position

Dan is responsible for the strategic management and planning of sport opportunities for the University. His role involves developing sport at participation level, club level, and elite level. He also manages relationships with external partners such as local sport clubs and facilities which students use alongside the facilities on campus. There is also an important day-to-day operational role to ensure that the regular provision of sport on campus is delivered to the highest possible standard. In the last year Dan oversaw the delivery of a £6m investment which transformed the University's playing fields into a state of the art sport facility that serves the needs of students, the community, and local professional sports teams. He manages a team of 40 staff and is responsible for preparing and delivering revenue and capital budgets for the University's entire sport service.

Career progression

Studying for a degree in Sport Management and playing rugby for the University's 1st XV, Dan took up weight training in the gym. He was offered a part-time job in the gym and accepted it in order to earn some money to pay his way through university. After a year of doing various jobs Dan returned to Sheffield Hallam University to study for a Postgraduate Diploma in Human Resource Management. Again he took a part-time job in the gym and this was eventually converted into a full time permanent job. Since then Dan has worked his way up from gym instructor, to Senor Recreation Officer, to Operations Manager, to Sport Services Manager, and is now Head of Sport Services. As he has climbed each rung of the career ladder, the amount of hands on work has decreased such that his role now is one of managerial oversight and forward planning.

Dan's advice for those who aspire to work in the industry ...

- Get plenty of variety in your experience, particularly at the start of your career.
- Commit to a program of continuous learning throughout your career. It does not have to be formal activity such as going on a course but at all times you need to be fit for purpose.
- Keep up to date with what is happening in the industry – I love going to conferences and exhibitions to find out what is happening at the cutting edge of the industry.

- Have good social skills and be a good networker. I reckon that I know every University Director of Sport in the United Kingdom ...
- Work with people rather than against them. In particular when building a team recognise people's strengths and weaknesses and use this knowledge to get the best out of your colleagues.
- Work with good people, see the positives in them, and take them on the journey with you.

TECHNOLOGY NOW!

Hallam Active – Sheffield Hallam University's sport services

Providing sport services within a university environment poses particular managerial challenges that can be met by the effective use of technology. In the United Kingdom, a Bachelor's degree lasts for three years of which each year is made up of a nine month academic year and three months' summer vacation. Sheffield Hallam University has a student community of around 34,000 and many like to take part in a range of activities such as health and fitness, club sport, and elite sport. In the past there used to be huge queues at the start of the academic year as students attempted to enrol or re-enrol to use the sport facilities. This was off-putting for students and placed considerable strain on front office staff.

With the help of Gladstone MRM, a leading supplier of membership management software, innovative solutions have been devised which help to overcome problems and optimize revenue. The heart of the system is a database which can subsequently be used to deliver benefits to both gym members and staff. Students can now register to join the gym online, which eliminates queuing and enables front office staff to concentrate on value-adding activities. The software has the functionality to set up direct debits, which spreads the cost of membership over the year via monthly payments. Because of the nature of the academic year, it has been found that there is better retention of members if there is the option to freeze membership during the summer and then to reactivate it once the new academic year begins. What this means is that students do not have to make a decision at the start of each academic year as to whether or not to join the gym as continuity of membership is assumed.

Members can also derive further value from their membership using the online system. It is easy to book places on fitness classes using the online booking system which can be accessed via computers all over the campus or indeed via smartphones. To keep members motivated and inclined to use the gym more frequently, smartcards enable users to monitor their progress over time and to receive feedback on their performance from specific pieces of equipment. For the staff, online bookings provide a clear sense of the level of demand for classes which in turn helps to ensure the correct number of classes is put on and that best use is made of instructor time (and costs).

Using technology in this way is important because it helps managers to realise that financial success is best achieved by revenue generation and revenue protection. The vast majority of costs in the gym are fixed and do not vary in proportion to activity. Therefore, the good manager will set about putting in place a strategy that will maximise revenue within the fixed cost base. This means enabling easy access to membership via the online membership system; minimising the pain of payment via the direct debit system; giving good value for money via the 'freeze membership' option; and increasing personal motivation and frequency of usage by progress monitoring. The system in place at Sheffield Hallam University provides a personalised service for some 4,500 members, which would simply not be possible without the applied use of database technology.

Implementation of management and operations

CHAPTER 10

OPERATIONS MANAGEMENT

OPERATIONAL STRUCTURE

Chapter 2 on ownership structures covered the various legal business structures of a sport facility and the operational framework each allows is crucial to the operations and management of a sport facility from a legal and functional standpoint. In addition, there was an explanation that to appropriately govern a sport facility, a manager must have a clear understanding of the concept of organizational effectiveness, which is the concept of how efficient a business is in achieving the outcomes set forth in the planning processes. Chapter 6 introduced the concept of organizational behavior as the study of human behavior in the work environment, and how the concepts of leadership and organizational culture are crucial to the management of sport organizations. Chapter 7 on human resource management explored the recruitment, training, and retention of personnel, and their role of strategically moving sport facilities forward toward a vision. This includes how the organizational chart is utilized to integrate operations in the sport facility, and the job descriptions that articulate the responsibilities of personnel. The financial management chapter (Chapter 8) focused on why financial skills are an important part of the sport facility manager's overall portfolio of management of skills. Understanding each of these areas in detail serves as a framework for developing the operational structure of a sport facility. However, there are two additional concepts that must be understood before engaging in operations management – history and philosophy.

From a historical perspective, by knowing about what has happened in the past with regard to a sport facility, a manager can see why things are the way they are as of now, what potential there is in the future, and how the organization has functioned. It is important to know about history because you can then educate others who do not know as much. Without knowing what has happened in the past, a sport facility manager cannot truly understand the organization, and how the operation of the sport facility came to its current situation. In addition, by understanding what happened in the past and the current situation of today, the sport facility manager can better understand what can happen in the future because they can understand what should be avoided and what can be accomplished to move the sport facility forward toward a higher level of success.

From a philosophical standpoint, understanding the values and beliefs of the sport facility organizational structure provides a framework and reasoning for why operations are conducted. The philosophy also serves as a framework for the mission of the sport facility (the purpose of the organization), the vision (where the organization wants to be in the future), and the action plan (what the organization wants to accomplish – articulated through goals, objectives, and strategies; and within the parameters of policies and procedures).

The integration of all of these concepts serves as a framework for operations management. However, there is a need to have a complete and organized approach to operations management in order to succeed. This is where the principles of continuous improvement can be a significant asset to the sport facility manager.

Principles of continuous improvement

The concept of continuous improvement is crucial to the success of sport facility operations management. With the ever-changing environment ranging from customer needs to external factors such as the economy and social norms, sport facility operators must recognize quickly these changes and how they affect the operation of their sport facility. The foundations philosophy of continuous improvement comes from the Japanese concept of 'Kaizen', meaning good change. The goal of 'Kaizen' in terms of sport facilities involves engaging in business activities that continuously improve all functions of operations, and strives to involve all employees in the process. In sport facility operations management, three such principles of continuous improvement have been implemented most often – total quality management (TQM), ISO 9000 standards, and Six Sigma.

Total quality management (TQM)

TQM is a comprehensive, structured approach to operations management that was first prevalent in the 1980s and 1990s, but is still one of the most widely used continuous improvement principles in sport facility management. TQM seeks to improve the quality of facility services through constant refinements in response to feedback from users and staff. The main purpose for implementing a quality TQM program for a sport facility is for controlling operational and service quality with the end result being improvement of all aspects of activity implementation.

TQM processes are divided into four sequential categories: plan, do, check, and act (the PDCA cycle). The planning phase involves defining the problem to be addressed, collecting relevant data, and determining the main cause of the problem. The doing phase entails implementing a solution and choosing the best measurement to gauge its effectiveness. The checking phase is an evaluation of the results to confirm success or failure. The acting phase is the documentation of results, articulation of process changes to the entire organization, and making recommendations for the problem to be addressed in the next PDCA cycle.

There are four key reasons a sport facility manager implements a TQM process: (1) measure and analyze how tasks are being accomplished; (2) eliminate procedures that are not working; (3) allow for input from all employees within the sport facility based on their areas of expertise; and (4) eliminate stereotypical thinking and replace it with visionary thought processes. This measurement and analysis process is most often implemented through the process of benchmarking. Benchmarks are individual management tools used by a sport organization to plan for evaluation, measurement, and improvement. Benchmarking is an important concept for sport facility managers to implement for three key reasons. First, it helps sport facility managers to achieve better results by enabling them to understand the drivers of performance and how to influence them. This is achieved by both data benchmarking (comparing statistical performance with others) and process benchmarking (comparing the key decisions made to achieve good performance). Second, benchmarks provide much more authoritative reporting of performance than an organization's performance reported in isolation. Third, when benchmarking techniques become established as part of organizational culture, they provide the basis for a clear focus on the business essentials as well as the direction for continuous improvement. We will revisit this concept in the capstone chapter of this book (Chapter 16), where we will bring together various concepts from the entire book, and show how all aspects of sport facility management effectively interact with each other.

However, focusing specifically on operations management, the major goal is to ensure quality control through TQM. One of the most widely used models of quality control to measure business effectiveness prevalent in sport facility management is Deming's 14 Key Principles of Points for Management. In brief, the principles are:

1 Create constancy of purpose towards improvement of product and service.
2 Adopt the new philosophy.
3 Eliminate dependence on mass inspection and require statistical evidence that quality is built in.
4 Do not award business on the basis of price – quality is much more important.
5 Find problems and continually improve the quality control system.

6   Institute the most current methods of on-the-job training.
7   Implement the most current methods of supervision of employees to ensure maximum quality of operation and services provided.
8   Eliminate fear to increase level of employee effectiveness.
9   Break down barriers between departments/work areas.
10 Get rid of numerical goals and replace with quality goals.
11 Eliminate work standards and quotas.
12 Remove barriers that prevent part-time, hourly, and volunteer workers from having pride of ownership in the work produced for the sport facility.
13 Institute an efficient and effective program of education and retraining.
14 Create an operational structure in top management that forces implementation of the above principles on a regular basis.

Adapted from Juran (2002)

For a sport facility, there are four major areas of TQM that managers should be concerned with: (1) customer service; (2) empowering employees; (3) human resource management; and (4) media and public relations. Probably the most important is customer service, because without customers, there would be no purpose for the sport facility. There are five pillars of quality that are integral to customer service and the TQM process:

■   Quality services start with customer service, because only the customer can define whether the right service is being offered, and the quality of its offering.
■   There must be a commitment to continuous improvement.
■   There must be the ability and a willingness to be measured and evaluated.
■   Employee and staff must be empowered, be held responsible for their actions, and view themselves and their jobs as an integral part of a quality sport facility operation.
■   Quality service should be both recognized and marketed inside and outside the company.

Adapted from Friday and Cotts (1994)

As related to the empowerment of employees and overall human resource management, it is important to remember that the job of all within a sport facility is ultimately to sell its image. Therefore, employees must do their job in line with the guidelines of the human resource and operations manual, and other duties as assigned by supervisors and ownership. However, to most effectively sell the image, empowering employees with authority and power is integral to the process. Employees need to have an active role in the administration of the sport facility, because employees bring to the table a unique set of qualities that will allow any sport facility to operate at an optimal quality level. Management provides training, resources, and a safe work environment for employees; employees work together with management to control processes, identify problems, and be a part of the solution to improve performance with the ultimate goal of effectively and efficiently serving customers.

Media and public relations is one of the foremost means by which a sport facility seeks to control public opinion regarding its products and services. At times, information will need to be released to the customers, the media, and the general public regarding situations, problems, opportunities, and event results at a sport facility. The release of this information needs to be controlled, therefore unless specifically authorized by the operational structure of a sport facility, employees should never release information about the operations, policies, procedures, and actions associated with a sport facility to the public (customers, the press, or the general public). Quality control also involves the proper release of information by the proper authorities within a sport facility, and in a voice shared by all members of the organization. From a TQM standpoint, if unsure what to say, say nothing, 'no comment', or direct the individual to the person within the organization authorized to speak.

ISO 9000 standards

As TQM was being implemented in businesses across the United States, another set of international standards were developing and being utilized globally. The International Organization of Standards (ISO), an independent, non-government agency from Geneva, Switzerland, is the leading developer of voluntary international standards in the world. Of the nearly 20,000 standards they have developed over time, ISO 9000 has gained traction in the realm of business operations, and has spilled over into the area of sport facility operations.

ISO 9000 was first published in 1987, and designed to assist organizations in ensuring they were meeting the needs and wants of all stakeholders of a business within the legal and regulatory standards set within a specific industry. ISO 9000 focuses on the fundamentals of quality management, and the original version in 1987 focused on three main models. The first (ISO 9001) focused on quality assurance in design, development, production, installation, and servicing. This was developed for organizations that created new products, such as equipment and apparel companies. The second (ISO 9002) was dedicated to quality assurance in production, installation, and servicing for organizations that were not developing new products. Hence those with established businesses that were not developing new functions fell under this standard. The third (ISO 9003) was directed towards quality assurance in final inspection and testing, where the production process was not examined – only a look at the final product.

Over the years, ISO 9000 has evolved to address the evolution of industries. In 1994, an update of the standards was produced to include quality assurance via corrective and preventive actions (CAPA). However the most significant change came in 2000, where the three ISO 9000 standards were replaced with a new ISO 9001. In this iteration, the concepts of design and development procedures only were applied to those creating new products, and a significant change across other areas focused on the concept of process management. The aim of process management included (1) standards to monitoring and optimizing all activities of a business; (2) the oversight of standards must involve top management – where in the past it was acceptable to delegate to middle and lower management; (3) the incorporation of benchmarking and performance metrics as part of the quality management process; and (4) the need to strive for continuous improvement through the tracking of customer satisfaction. More about benchmarking and performance management will be discussed in Chapter 16 of this book.

After this modification, ISO 9001 was able to be more widely used across all aspects of the business industry, and was especially welcomed by sport facility operators across the globe. It provided them with standards of operation that examined processes; involved all levels of management and ownership; included analytics and metrics that provided feedback from customers; and created a continual process loop connecting development and implementation to evaluation and feedback. ISO reviewed their standards in 2008 with little change other than clarifications to requirements, and in December 2015 will publish a new version of the standards. The updated standards will embed the process approach more clearly within all requirements, and clarifications will be provided in the areas of structure, context, documentation, and terminology. However, the most significant and welcome change that will affect sport facility managers will be the elimination of preventive action and replacing it with a complete risk management process.

Six Sigma

Six Sigma is another continuous improvement process that is an evolution on TQM and Deming's Principles, and is gaining some traction in the sport facility operations industry. The goal of Six Sigma is to reduce variability in business processes and hence improve the quality of business operations by identifying and eliminating mistakes. This is usually accomplished through quality policies and procedures in place through an operations manual; using appropriate benchmarks, analytics, and metrics to evaluate and make positive changes; and creating committees or groups of employees to oversee and evaluate the operations process. The Six Sigma process is more of a statistical, analytics-based examination of operations processes, as the end result should effectively be a sigma rating for the process, where the effectiveness and efficiency levels of operations are at 99.99966 percent. As the evolution of analytics-based analysis continues to grow, the evolution of TQM towards Six Sigma will be inevitable.

GENERAL FACILITY OPERATING PROCEDURES

General sport facility operating procedures are put into place to provide a safe, efficient, and equitable functioning of a sport facility through a commitment to the provision and maintenance of appropriate physical facilities that contribute to a comfortable and conducive sporting and work environment. In sport facilities there are numerous general operating procedures – examples of some of the major operating procedures include:

- Hours of operation: the times that the facility will be open for business.
- User categories: individual and family members; daily users; guests; participants and spectators; licensees; employees and management.
- Fees and rates: the cost for use of the facility through various memberships, daily fees, admission fees, guest passes, and rentals.
- Reservation procedures and space allocation: methods for scheduling facility usage.
- Outsourced services: examples include camps, clinics, merchandise, food service, security, and parking.
- Procurement practices: procedures for securing needed inventory, supplies, and equipment.

Probably the most complex of these operating procedures is the reservation and space allocation process, which includes programming, scheduling, and prioritizations of both the use of the facility and maintenance of the facility. It is important to remember that when implementing a reservation and space allocation process to keep the following in mind:

- Strive to do what is best for the greatest number of users.
- Be consistent with all user groups.
- Continually evaluate the scheduling process and constantly improve the process.
- Take into account activities that are consistent with the mission of the sport facility.

Each sport facility will have a different scheduling and prioritization process based on the type of users, the programs that utilize the facility, the different facility spaces, and the day/time activities take place. Those last two are areas many forget about, as it is entirely feasible to have multiple prioritization schedules based on each part of the sport facility, and different days and times. For example, let us assume we are the assistant director of facility scheduling for a university sport complex. The programs that use the facility include physical education classes, university-sponsored sport teams, campus recreation/intramurals program, student-sponsored sport clubs, open recreation time (time for people to walk in and use facilities), and special events. A typical Monday-Friday 8am–3pm prioritization schedule for a gymnasium might look like the list, in order as above. However, from 3–8pm Monday–Friday, since many classes are completed by then, the prioritization schedule might change to the following:

1   University-sponsored sport teams
2   Campus recreation/intramurals program
3   Student-sponsored sport clubs
4   Open recreation time
5   Special events
6   Physical education classes.

From 8–12pm, it may change to:

1   Campus recreation/intramurals program
2   Student-sponsored sport clubs
3   Open recreation time
4   Physical education classes
5   University-sponsored sport teams
6   Special events.

On weekends, it may change again to:

1   Open recreation time
2   Special events
3   Campus recreation/intramurals program
4   Student-sponsored sport clubs
5   University-sponsored sport teams
6   Physical education classes.

With regard to the scheduling and organizing of maintenance, the general premise is to attempt to conduct as much of this work as possible during off-hours, especially overnight; between activities; or after major events. For sport facilities, off-hours are not always the typical overnight, because of the type of activities that take place and the late hour some go until. In general, the day shift usually handles the majority of the important work, while second and third shift take care of janitorial and painting tasks.

In addition to space allocation, scheduling, and prioritization, governmental guidelines and budget management play an integral role to the effective and efficient implementation of operating procedures. Governmental guidelines include those policies and procedures set by federal/parliamentary, state/provincial/regional, and local/municipality authorities. More detail about the legal responsibilities related to sport facilities will be provided in the next chapter (Chapter 11). Budget management (covered in Chapter 8, financial management) also plays a critical role in operating procedures, as annual and capital budgeting directly affect what sport facility managers can implement. Without money through the budgeting process and the planning that goes with that process, facility managers cannot hire staff, maintain facilities, implement change, purchase equipment and inventory, and keep the facility operating.

FACILITY OPERATIONS

Now that we have a basis overview of operating procedures, it would be important to recognize the various areas of operation within a sport facility. Sport facility operations can be divided in many different ways, based on the operational structure of the individual organization. For the purpose of this chapter, we will divide facility operating into the following categories: plant and field operations; maintenance and repair; alterations management; inventory management; energy management; waste management and recycling; and environmental management, greening, and sustainability.

Plant and field operations

Plant and field operations include managing the physical plant, including natural and artificial surfaces. Plant operations are the necessary infrastructure used in the support of facility operations and maintenance. While there are numerous types of specific plant infrastructure for specialized facilities – such as refrigeration and ice systems for ice arenas; filtration and chemical systems for swimming pool facilities; and watering systems for outdoor fields and artificial surfaces – generally the plant operations for a sport facility fall under five systems: (1) heating, ventilation, and air-conditioning (HVAC); (2) mechanical and electrical transportation (elevators); (3) major electrical systems; (4) plumbing; and (5) emergency power/generators.

Today, the expectation of facility managers in their role as plant operators is to be a technician with mechanical competence. This expectation is verified by the numerous examinations and certifications that test for technical knowledge and interpersonal skills that most sport facility plant operations require. The reason for this necessary competence is that the sport facility manager is responsible for expensive equipment, proper operating conditions, quality control and improvement, profits and losses, problem solving, community involvement, and the environment, among many other things. The sport facility cannot survive without quality management of plant operations, because lack of skills operating these functions will result in significant risk, damage, and costs to the sport facility. Therefore, sport facility managers must understand the unique plant within their sport facility, secure and keep up to date about the technical skills and knowledge related to the sport facility, operate in a safe manner with quality consciousness, and possess the effective communications skills required to ensure proper operations by all staff.

Maintenance and repair

All infrastructural problems and damages to facilities and equipment are detrimental to the continued operation of a sport facility. Shutting down facilities disrupts customer use and can be perceived as incompetence on the part of those running the sport facility. Hence proper coordination of maintenance and repair is crucial to operation success.

In general, all maintenance and repair needs that are discovered by staff should be communicated to the facility or operations manager responsible for this area, and be documented on a maintenance form. In addition to reported maintenance and repair, managing staff should, on a regular basis, conduct an evaluation of all infrastructure and equipment to determine the status of its condition, and organize and coordinate appropriate remedies. Based on the severity of the problem or damage, the remedy will take one of three ways:

- Maintenance: this refers to the work necessary to maintain the facilities and equipment. Maintenance includes periodic or occasional inspection, adjustment, lubrication, cleaning (non-janitorial), painting, replacement of parts, minor repairs, and other actions to prolong service and prevent unscheduled breakdown.
- Repair: this refers to restoring damaged or worn-out facilities and equipment to a normal operating condition. Repairs are curative, whereas maintenance is preventive. Repair can be classified as minor or major. Minor repairs are those associated with maintenance activities that do not exceed one to two workdays per task. Major repairs are those that exceed two workdays per task, or are beyond the capability of existing maintenance personnel.
- Replacement: this refers to facility and equipment components or systems needing to be replaced. It is the exchange or substitution of one fixed asset for another having the capacity to perform the same function. Replacement arises from an asset becoming obsolete, having excessive wear and tear, or being damaged beyond repair.

Alterations management

While all sport facilities are designed with space and needs in mind, it is inevitable that certain alterations need to take place. Many times these alterations are needed for three main reasons in a sport facility: (1) the need for additional storage; (2) the need for modified spaces for new programming; and (3) the need for additional office space for expanding staff. These alterations can be infrastructural (examples: building new spaces, splitting spaces by adding walls) and/or operational (examples include need for additional electrical outlets, plumbing, or communications). Many sport facilities are designed with the potential for alterations in the future, which in the long run reduces the costs of alterations. Alterations that are unplanned usually have a higher cost – as much as two to three times more than if they were planned for in the design of the sport facility. In some cases, alterations are temporary – usually as a result of a special event. In any case, to ensure that alterations are an appropriate outlay of money, sport facility managers should engage in a cost-benefit analysis to determine whether the benefit of the alteration is worth the money being spent.

Inventory management

Traditionally, we think of inventory management in terms of having available the products that customers desire, such as with merchandise, food service, and concessions. While these are each concerns of the sport facility manager, those individual tasks fall under the management of those ancillary areas, and will be discussed later in this chapter. Inventory management as related to facility operations involves two distinct areas. First is the inventory of available spaces in the facility, and how those spaces are reserved, scheduled, and allocated (as discussed earlier in this chapter). Second is the procurement process related to the inventory of equipment and supplies used in the various areas of the facility. Some of this inventory includes light bulbs for a gymnasium or arena, tools and supplies for conducting maintenance, cleaning supplies for custodial crews, and tables/chairs/and barricades for event set-up.

Energy management

Energy management is not a separate function but rather an activity that spans all aspects of a sport facility. Some of the traditional energy management measures include thermostat regulation and investing in energy-efficient capital equipment. However, electrical consumption control is the responsibility of all employees of a sport facility. Examples include lighting in offices being turned off when not in use; lighting in courts, spectator areas, and other activity areas being dimmed or turned off when not in use; thermostats being lowered during down times and closed times (turn down one hour before closing and turn up two hours before opening), and computers and other electronics being turned off when not in use. Energy costs are among the biggest expenses for a sport facility (usually second to staffing). Taking steps to reduce these costs can significantly improve the operation of a sport facility by increasing the financial resources available for other areas.

Waste management and recycling

One of the most overlooked costs of a sport facility is the result of the trash that it puts out. While a sport facility's main objective for reducing contribution to the local landfill is to cut costs, the social importance of environmentally friendly business

218

operations cannot be understated. Recycling mandates seem to be a trend that is starting to affect sport businesses everywhere. Some mandates are coming from city governments while others come from within the sport business itself. In addition to typical waste, sport facilities, as a result of general operations, often have a multitude of recyclables including paper (newspaper, white paper, all other); aluminum cans; glass bottles and jars (clear, green, brown); scrap metal; styrofoam; and cardboard. To deal with this, many sport facilities have segregated recycling bins at the rear of the complex.

The only way to reduce costs related to waste management is to reduce the amount of trash going to landfills, since landfill costs are determined by quantity. One of the biggest problems in trying to implement recycling as part of a waste management reduction program is getting customers to recycle. Having recyclables mixed in with the trash results in additional costs for the facility. Although the sport facility managers and staff are not in direct control, there are a number of things that a sport facility can do to influence visitors to recycle by raising their awareness. The first way to raise awareness of recycling is through video messages that are displayed during an event. Another important part of recycling awareness has to do with both the visual appeal and the prominence of the recycling bins that are located in the facility. Improving the ratio of bins to seats would make it much easier for people to recycle.

Environmental management, greening and sustainability

The concept of recycling and reducing the amount of waste goes directly into the concepts of environmental management. Environmental management is the process of managing the interaction between the human environment and the physical environment/habitats. Globally, ISO 14000 guidelines provide requirements for its relevance for organizations wishing to operate in an environmentally sustainable manner. In general, the purpose of the standard is to reduce the environmental footprint of a business and to decrease the pollution and waste a business produces. In sport facility management, this has become an important marketing function more than an operations function. Sport facilities that have the initiative to be more socially responsible are publicly being recognized for their efforts, and while a direct correlation may not be visible in any accounting documents, the cost of environmental awareness is at least partially justified in the positive affect it has on the image of the sport facility, which is a large component of public relations.

Two of the most relevant environmental management concepts crucial to sport facility operations management are greening and sustainability. Greening is the process of transforming a space into a more environmentally friendly area. Sustainability is the process of being renewable for an indefinite period without damaging the environment. In energy management, we discussed some of the ways to be more environmentally friendly (e.g. energy saving bulbs), as well as in waste management (e.g. recycling). However, one of the biggest issues is the disturbance and reduction of plant life, trees, grasses, and other natural environments due to the construction of sport stadiums and arenas (and associated ancillary areas), artificial surface fields, and sport environments in the natural environment (ski resorts, golf courses, etc.). In response, the list that follows is just a small example of what some organizations are doing to 'go green' and be more sustainable:

- According to research from a multitude of studies conducted across the United States, Canada, and Europe, both in cold weather and hot/humid weather environments, there are significant drainage and water storage possibilities from run-off on artificial turf fields. Storm water collection and collection and reuse of water from watering are gathered through the drain system under the fields, and then tied into large water retention pipes to allow the rainwater to return to aquifers underground.
- The National Ski Areas Association (NSAA) has implemented an 'environmental charter for ski areas' (www.nsaa.org/environment/sustainable-slopes) that provides voluntary environmental principles for ski area planning, operations, and outreach.
- The United States Green Building Council (USGBC) has developed LEED (leadership in energy and environmental design) standards for sporting arenas and stadiums (www.usgbc.org).

FACILITY SERVICES

All sport facilities are engaged in the service industry. As such, there is a need to provide a number of facility services over and above the general operating procedures of the sport facility. While the purpose of this section is not to delve into every aspect of facility services in detail, it is to provide information about the major facility services provided in sport facilities. Again, as with operations, there will be specialized services unique to specialized facilities, but the focus for this chapter will be on security, ticketing, parking, custodial/housekeeping, concessions, customer service, and event management.

Regardless of facility service, there are general rules and regulations followed by most, including standards of conduct, general guidelines, and appearance. Standards of conduct focus on providing users of the sport facility (members, guests, visitors, spectators) the best possible examples of conduct, decorum, and good citizenship. The behavior of employees sets the example for all to follow. The care, safety, and welfare of all are paramount, and it is important that any situations that may endanger the health, safety, or wellbeing of people be dealt with immediately.

220

An example of general guidelines within a sport facility may include some of the following:

- Treat members with respect and dignity. This is especially important when they are not treating you with respect.
- Be dependable, on time, and keep promises.
- Use positive guidance techniques including redirection, encouragement, and positive reinforcement. Set appropriate expectations and create program environments that minimize the need for discipline.
- Report any member's or guest's health issues, accidents, or other concerns which you feel need further attention to your immediate supervisor.
- Respect each member's and guest's right to not be touched in ways that make them feel uncomfortable. Respect their right to say no.
- Profanity, inappropriate jokes, sharing intimate details of one's personal life, and any kind of harassment in the presence of our members or guests is unacceptable.
- Information regarding organization members, guests, paid staff, and volunteers, both verbal and written, is often privileged and confidential. Personal information is not to be released without written consent of the individual involved.
- A specialized guideline regarding physical appearance of employees. A sport facility should expect all of its employees to represent the organization in a professional manner by being neat, clean, and dressed in professional attire that is consistent with their job responsibilities in the building.

Security

Security in a sport facility can range from in-house staff at a small recreational facility, to professional staff from global companies (Contemporary Services Corporation – www.csc-usa.com/home), local companies (Sentry Event Services in Florida – www. sentryeventservices.com), or league/event based (SAFE Management, the NFL's security company for the Super Bowl – www.safemanagement.net). Regardless of the level of security, there are some important features that all sport facility managers must recognize when working with security. While a more detailed look at security planning and management will be provided later in this book (Chapter 15), we will introduce some basic concepts important to facility operations and providing service here.

The director of security (or the authorized management member overseeing security) is the point person who is directly responsible for security procedures and systems. The head of security also provides liaison between the sport facility and the appropriate local law enforcement authorities. The head of security and other security personnel are not sworn peace officers or law enforcement officers and are not authorized to carry firearms in most cases, but are authorized by the ownership of the sport facility to fully enforce all rules and regulations.

While there are specific staff members hired to work as security, generally all employees of a sport facility act as members of the security team. Employees are the eyes and ears of a sport facility, and should report criminal activities or rule violations occurring as soon as possible to security, who then will respond as required. This response can range from internal disciplinary action to notification to the proper local law enforcement authorities.

Ticketing

The ticketing operation at a sport facility can range from a small box office of one person selling tickets for general admission to an event (such as a secondary school basketball tournament) to a full-service box office with a separate manager, paid staff, and relationships with secondary and tertiary ticketing services. Ultimately, whether it is the facility manager at a facility holding a small sporting event, or a full-time box office manager, both have the role of selling tickets and controlling admissions to events.

In order to effectively conduct a ticketing operation, the facility manager/box office manager must know their inventory – or the number of seats available to a specific event. Seating capacities vary based on the type of event. For example, certain shows may only require 180 degree seating, such as a concert; others 260 degree seating, such as a World Wrestling Entertainment event; while others need full facility seating (most sporting events). This information is then put into a manifest, which gives every seat in the facility a section/row/seat number and attaches the price of the ticket. This pricing can range from one price for all tickets (general admission or festival seating for all) to multiple pricing levels based on closeness to field of play, location in proximity to the center of the field of play, amenities offered in conjunction with the seat, among others.

With larger events, full-service ticket offices (such as for large stadiums and arenas) have additional responsibilities. Beyond overseeing general operations, hiring staff, training staff, and operating computer systems where manifests are stored for issuing tickets, the box office has to initiate on-sales events (first day tickets are on sale), and operate a will call window (a place when tickets purchased in advance can be picked up by attendees to events). In addition, box office managers need to coordinate operation with secondary and tertiary box offices. An example of a secondary box office would be individual teams who sell tickets in addition to the box office. The box office is the place that issues these tickets to the teams, usually through secure access to the manifest in the box office's computer system. Similar processes are utilized for tertiary box offices, which would include online ticketing companies such as Ticketmaster and StubHub.

Implementation of management and operations

Parking

A sport facility should offer enough parking for spectators, members, guests, employees, and management. The usual standard for a sport stadium or arena is one parking spot for every four seats if there is no mass transit to the facility; and smaller if there is mass transit available (dependent on quantity of transit and location). For a smaller facility, it really depends on projected usage. For example, a recreational facility with a fitness center and four basketball/volleyball courts may only need 30–40 spots, but if they plan on holding weekend tournaments, the need probably will blossom to 200 spots. Therefore, a parking plan integrated into the entire sport facility and event planning process is crucial for offering this service.

Sport facilities have a choice to keep parking services in-house, outsource to another company, or not offer parking at all. In-house ownership of parking services offers the opportunity for maximum financial benefit (if the facility charges for parking) as well as security and service. Especially for larger events, parking revenues can be significant. In addition, by owning the parking, the sport facility is providing a direct service to their customers. However, by retaining responsibility, the sport facility operator also incurs the responsibility for security. The cost associated with staffing and securing a parking area, along with the responsibility, sometimes outweighs the revenues that can be earned. In these cases, parking services are outsourced to parking management companies – where the sport facility receives a very small percentage of parking revenue but transfers all risks associated with security to the parking management company. Another type of outsourcing is related to offering limited or no parking services. This often takes place in larger cities where there is ample public parking. The sport facility receives no revenue from parking, but also does not have to worry about this service because the municipality covers it. For example, Quik Park manages all the city parking in New York for the new Yankee Stadium.

Custodial/housekeeping

Another important service in a sport facility is to ensure that it is clean and functional. This is where custodial and housekeeping services come in. Patrons do not want to come to a sport facility that is dirty or where simple items such as soap, paper towel, and toilet paper are not readily available. As with almost any other service, custodial and housekeeping can be outsourced or kept in-house. In-house offers more control over keeping the facility clean; however depending on the size of the facility and the scope of the events, outsourcing may be inevitable. Ultimately, the goal is to provide responsive service to meet the needs of the visitors to the sport facility, and to enhance the quality of the experience of sport facility users.

Concessions

Concessions are defined as a secondary business under contract or license from a primary business to exclusively operate and provide a specialized service. In sport facilities, the main two concessions areas are merchandising and food service. As with any other service, concessions can be outsourced or kept in-house. Most often, merchandising is an in-house function, while a majority of food service is outsourced – mainly because of the significant liability.

The major goals of both merchandising and food service is to create a market demand for the products and services offered, and increase the profitability and financial health of the entire sport facility. The major duties of a concessions manager are:

- inventory control including turnover, inventory management, shrinkage, and point-of-sales systems;
- creating effective displays and offering diverse product offerings;
- marketing and promotion of the merchandise (often in conjunction with the facility marketing manager);
- determine appropriate pricing points;
- manage inventory including variation of sizes, inventory on hand, variation of hard and soft goods, management of exclusive brands, and offering a variety of accessories;
- manage an effective website to promote merchandise and entice additional purchase online;
- in coordination with human resources hire and fire staff, as well as train the staff in the procedures of running the operation and offering high-quality customer service;
- secure the appropriate licenses and municipal approvals to operate a concessions operation;
- complete all associated accounting, billing, payments, bookkeeping, and payroll for the concessions operation;
- maintain all equipment including displays, kiosks, computer systems, and appliances.

Food and beverage services offer some additional challenges, which often involve implementing an additional planning process for safety. The purpose of this plan is to identify and prevent possible food safety problems in order to enhance food safety. The problems may relate to the purchase, receiving, storage, preparation, cooking, packaging, transport, or display of food. Especially important to ensuring food safety and management is the concept of cleanliness and sanitation. Food preparation areas, facilities, equipment, and all food contact surfaces should always be kept clean because food residues and dirt may contaminate food resulting in food poisoning. A cleaning program should be developed to ensure that cleaning and sanitizing be carried out in a systematic, regular, and effective manner. In addition, good personal hygiene is essential to ensure food safety. Food poisoning bacteria may be present on the skin and in the nose of healthy people. All food handlers

224

should therefore maintain a high standard of personal hygiene and cleanliness in order to avoid transferring food poisoning micro-organisms to food.

Customer service desk

The kiosk at the entrance to the sport facility. The customer service desk. The main office. These areas, and almost everything implemented at a sport facility, need to have customer service in mind at all times. However, the areas listed above are possibly the most important – as these are the first impressions members and guests have of the sport facility. The employees working in these areas have an important responsibility to project a positive image for the sport facility, to help maintain security of the sport facility by controlling ingress and egress, and truly set the tone for each person's visit to the sport facility.

Each individual facility will have their own policies and procedures for managing the customer service desk, however most will incorporate the following five policies:

- Every individual who comes in the door must have proof of admission. For larger events such as concerts and professional sport games, this is either in the form of a ticket or a credential. For a facility such as a recreational facility, it may be a card. If there is an allowance for non-members and guests, there should be a policy for signing in, completing appropriate paperwork, and/or paying a fee.
- Individuals restricted from entry to the sport facility should never be allowed to enter without the expressed permission of management or ownership.
- The front desk area (desk, office, and lobby) is kept clean at all times. There is no trash visible anywhere. Countertop is cleaned as needed.
- The only people behind the desk are paid and authorized employees. Members and guests are not allowed behind the desk.
- Customer service desk employees are readily accessible and willing to help members and guests.

Event management

While all of the previous services described are important to the operation of a sport facility, the single most important is event management. Without events, there would be no need for a sport facility. There are two categories of events in a sport facility – events that are offered through and by the sport facility, and those offered by outside entities that rent or lease the facility. In both cases, coordination between facility managers and event managers is crucial to success on both sides. However, there are usually issues between the managers, because the event manager is mainly concerned about a successful event, and the facility manager is concerned with operating the facility in a safe manner with no damage. These missions often clash, and compromise and teamwork often need to be implemented.

Chapter 13 of this text will discuss in some greater detail event planning and management from a facility end. It is important to recognize at this point that the role of facility operations is not to run an event; hence there will be little discussion about actual event management. From a facility operations standpoint, there are three major service roles:

■ coordination of event ingress and set-up;
■ support during the event;
■ coordination of event breakdown and egress.

RISK MANAGEMENT

Risk management is the process of attempting to prevent the possibility of loss from a hazard such as personal injury, property damage, or economic loss. Risk cannot be eliminated from the environment, but with careful planning it can be managed. Appropriate risk management practices are crucial to reduce legal exposure, prevent financial and human loss, protect facility assets, ensure business continuity, and minimize damage to the sport facility's reputation. All members of the sport facility management team – from ownership to hourly staff and volunteers – have a duty to act in a prudent manner and a duty of care to provide a reasonably safe environment for users of the sport facility.

While this topic will be covered in more detail in Chapter 14 (risk assessment and management), it is important to recognize that from an operational standpoint, the major areas of concern within risk management involve dealing with the following:

■ non-critical injury/illness;
■ critical injury/illness (requiring emergency medical personnel);
■ appropriate use of alarms and warning signals;
■ general emergency evacuation procedures;
■ evacuation of physically challenged persons;
■ dealing with:
    ■ electrical power failure;
    ■ elevator entrapment;
    ■ fire;
    ■ other natural disasters;
    ■ other facility disasters.

CREATING A FACILITY OPERATIONS MANUAL FOR SPORT FACILITIES

The purpose for creating a facility operations manual is to have a central document that articulates accurate and current information regarding the operational policies and procedures of the sport facility. The information provided usually includes the majority of the concepts provided in this chapter, and often more. The operations manual is often connected to the human resource manual (Chapter 7), because it builds on the concepts embedded in that manual, including how operations interact with employment and employee relations, and connects operations with the general information and policies/procedures of the sport facility. A sample of a sport facility operations manual as described above can be found in the appendix to this book available online.

STADIUM VICTORIA

You have just been hired as the facility manager for Stadium Victoria, a new 47,000 seat natural grass stadium that will be the new home for new professional soccer and rugby expansion clubs. The Chief Executive Officer (CEO) of Stadium Victoria wants you to create an operations manual that will help the building run efficiently while making your job easier to perform. The following is a list of priorities given to you by the CEO:

1   Operations management: the CEO wants you to describe and diagram the optimal organizational structure, and position descriptions with projected salaries.
2   Risk management: the CEO is very concerned with this area. Describe the overall function of risk management within the facility for soccer and rugby matches, as well as other potential events.
3   Marketing: the CEO wants a marketing plan developed for the facility that will attract clients and customers.
4   Event management: describe this process in your facility, including a chain of command for personnel (parking, security, ticket takers, ushers, etc.)
5   Concessions/food service: describe the function of concessions (food service and merchandising) in your facility. Give reasons why you would or would not own the concessions, have an agreement to get a percentage of concessions, or simply lease the space for concessions.

Suggested discussion topics

1   Where would you start with this operations plan? Identify the steps you will take to create a comprehensive, functional operational plan.
2   What special operational needs will be necessary as a result of the opening weekend for Stadium Victoria, where there will be a Friday night soccer match followed by a Saturday night rugby match? What special considerations need to be in place for environmental factors such as weather?

CHAPTER REVIEW

The role of sport facility operations is to consistently maintain quality visitor experiences without the depletion of resources. Good sport facility operations start with a functional organizational structure that allows for quality legal and financial management of the sport facility; understands the importance of operational effectiveness; recognizes the role of organizational behavior and culture as an operational function; and recruits, trains, and retains personnel that strive to strategically move a sport facility forward toward a vision. The implementation of these concepts in the operation of a sport facility can be best articulated through various principles of continuous improvement. One such principle is the process of total quality management (TQM) – a comprehensive, structured approach to operations management that seeks to improve the quality of facility services through constant refinements through the PDCA cycle (planning, doing, checking, and acting). The TQM process works well for sport facilities because it measures and analyzes how tasks are being accomplished; eliminates procedures that are not working; allows for input from all employees within the sport facility based on their areas of expertise; and eliminates stereotypical thinking and replaces it with visionary thought processes. Sport facility managers are most concerned with the TQM process as it relates to customer service, employee and human resource management, and media/public relations. Internationally, ISO 9000 standards are a set of principles for continuous improvement utilized to monitor and optimize business activities. This requires the involvement of top management in the improvement process, the incorporation of benchmarking and performance metrics as part of the quality management process, and the development of processess for continuous improvement through the tracking of customer satisfaction. A more recent application of performance improvement is the Six Sigma process – an evolution on TQM and Deming's Principles that focuses on reducing variability in business processes and improving the quality of business operations by identifying and eliminating mistakes through the use of appropriate benchmarks, analytics, and metrics to evaluate and make positive changes.

Operation management starts with the implementation of general sport facility operating procedures. These are put into place to provide a safe, efficient and equitable functioning of a sport facility through a commitment to the provision and maintenance of appropriate physical facilities that contribute to a comfortable and conducive sporting and work environment. While there are numerous categories of operating procedures, among the most important is how space is reserved and allocated, and what the user prioritization process is.

Operating procedures may differ based on the various operations and services provided within a sport facility. Major facility operations inherent in most sport facilities include plant operations, maintenance and repair, alterations management, inventory management, energy management, waste management and recycling,

228

and environmental management including greening and sustainability. Facility services, which may be outsourced or kept in-house, include security, ticketing, parking, custodial/housekeeping, concessions, customer service, communications/electronic management/information security, and event management. Each of these services will have their own general rules and regulations followed by most, including standards of conduct, general guidelines, and appearance.

One of the major concerns in facility operations is risk management, which is the process of attempting to prevent the possibility of loss from a hazard such as personal injury, property damage, or economic loss. Risk cannot be eliminated from the environment, but with careful planning it can be managed. The best way to reduce the amount of risk is to articulate all policies and procedures, rules and regulations, and philosophies and missions in one document. The facility operations manual is that central document that articulates accurate and current information regarding these areas. The operations manual is often connected to the human resource manual because it builds on the concepts embedded in the human resource manual, including how operations interact with employment and employee relations, and connects operations with the general information and policies/procedures of the sport facility.

BIBLIOGRAPHY

Abdi, S. A., Awan, H. M., and Bhatti, M. (2008). Is quality management a prime requisite for globalization? Some facts from the sports industry. *Quality and Quantity, 42*(6), 821–833.

Bridges, F. L. (2004). *Management for athletic/sport administration* (4th ed.). Decatur, GA: ESM Books.

Chen, H. H., Chen, K. K., Chang, T. T., and Hsu, C. C. (2010). An application of Six Sigma methodology to enhance leisure service quality. *Quality and Quantity, 44*(6), 1151–1164.

Cheng, K., Hsu, C., and Huang, C. (2012). A study on the application of 6-Sigma on the enhancement of service quality of fitness club. *Quality and Quantity, 46*(2), 705–713.

Friday, S. and Cotts, D. G. (1994). *Quality facility management: A marketing and customer service approach.* New York: Wiley.

Hon Yin Lee, H. and Scott, D. (2009). Strategic and operational factors' influence on the management of building maintenance operation processes in sports and leisure facilities, Hong Kong. *Journal of Retail and Leisure Property, 8*(1), 25–37.

International Organization for Standardization (2009). *ISO 14000 essentials.* Retrieved June 6, 2009 from: www.iso.org/iso/iso_14000_essentials

International Organization for Standardization (2014). *ISO 9000 – quality management.* Retrieved November 3, 2014 from: www.iso.org/iso/iso_9000

Juran, J. (2002). TQM: A snapshot of the experts. *Measuring Business Excellence, 6*(3), 54–57.

Liu, W. (2014). The optimized design and material saving of sports architecture. *Journal of Chemical and Pharmaceutical Research, 6*(5), 1586–1591.

McAdam, R. (2000). Three leafed clover? TQM, organisational excellence and business improvement. *The TQM Magazine, 12*(5), 314.

Moxham, C. and Wiseman, F. (2009). Examining the development, delivery and measurement of service quality in the fitness industry: A case study. *Total Quality Management & Business Excellence, 20*(5), 467–482.

National Ski Areas Association (2009). *Sustainable slopes.* Retrieved June 4, 2009 from: www.nsaa.org/environment/sustainable-slopes

Roper, K. O. and Payant, R. P. (2014). *The facility management handbook* (4th ed.). New York: AMACOM.

Sawyer, T. H. (2013). *Facility planning and design for health, physical activity, recreation, and sport* (13th ed.). Urbana, IL: Sagamore Publishing.

Shaw, L. L. and Rogers, C. (2013). Safety in the stadium. *Risk Management, 60*(3), 14.

Speegle, M. (2015). *Process technology plant operations* (2nd ed.). Independence, KY: Cengage Learning.

Uecker-Mercado, H. and Walker, M. (2012). The value of environmental social responsibility to facility managers: Revealing the perceptions and motives for adopting ESR. *Journal of Business Ethics, 110*(3), 269–284.

United States Green Building Council (2009). *LEED on.* Retrieved June 4, 2009 from: www.usgbc.org

IN THE FIELD …

Interview with Scott A Kelyman, Sr., Director of Building Operations Tropicana Field and the Tampa Bay Rays

Please explain to the reader about your current position and what your responsibilities are

Currently, I am, and have been since 2002, the Senior Director of Building Operations for Tropicana Field, home of the Tampa Bay Rays Baseball Club. I am employed by the team, not the City of St. Petersburg. My responsibilities include but are not limited to maintenance to the stadium (approximately 1.1 million square feet) and grounds (approximately 86 acres) with an operating budget of $3,500,000. My staff includes a conversion crew of four, two electricians, two plumbers, two management assistants and coordinators, one plant engineer, and three housekeepers. I also liaise with our cleaning partner and our heating, ventilation, and air conditioning (HVAC) provider who service our stadium respectively.

Tell us a little about your track from your university years to get to the position you are in now

I graduated Saint Leo College (now University) in 1993 with a BA in Sport Management, and was offered an entry level position with the New York Yankees upon graduation. In November of 1993, I was named the Business Manager of the minor league affiliate, the Tampa Yankees. At the conclusion of the 1994 season, I was named the General Manager of the Tampa Yankees, followed in 1996 with additional responsibilities as Florida State League Director. In 1998, I accepted a position with the Tampa Bay Devil Rays as Event Coordinator (within the Department of Stadium Operations) for their inaugural season. In 2002, I was promoted to Director of Building Operations, and in 2007 named Senior Director, which is the position I currently hold.

What advice would you give to someone wanting to get into the field of sport facility operations management?

Talk with everyone … you need to promote yourself … you never know who you may be speaking to and what they do, know, or may have a need.

Timing is everything and I can attest to that (right place – right time) and ALWAYS be willing to do whatever it takes or go the extra mile.

Separate yourself from others seeking the same position. As a single person out of college, you should have the philosophy of staying late, coming early, and volunteering with other departments to gain as much experience as you can.

TECHNOLOGY NOW!

Sport facility operations management involves many functions, but one of the most important is the scheduling of facilities and the related revenue management associated with facility use. Thousands of facilities around the globe including gyms, health clubs, fitness centers, personal training centers, university athletic/recreation facilities, parks/recreation departments, and multipurpose sport facilities of all types use EZFacility to manage their sport facilities.

EZFacility is an all-in-one web-based software that can help streamline the management of facility operations in a multitude of areas including facility scheduling, employee management, user and membership management, accounting administration, and front desk administration. From a facility scheduling standpoint, EZFacility allows the facility operations manager and their staff to manage space allocation, league scheduling and management, and event management support ranging from its online registration tool to staffing.

With regard to staffing, the software can not only manage the scheduling of employees, it has an embedded employee time clock to track work hours – and collaborates with the internal payroll function to manage employee compensation. Beyond payroll, the accounting and revenue functions range from a point-of-sales system including credit card processing ability to invoicing and payment tracking to multiple analytic reporting functions to track financial success of the sport facility.

Of course financial success cannot happen without users. EZFacility provides functions to enhance the experience of sport facility users including self-service functions for members to book space, lessons, or classes. The software can also track usage by users in general or even on specific equipment, and can also provide fitness assessments to members. The access system used by members also helps with the management of ingress to and egress from the facility. The front desk can manage the check-in process more efficiently, which also helps to track the number of people within the facility and to identify potential risk management situations. In addition to access control, the software can be used for locker and equipment tracking.

EZFacility also provides the sport facility operator with a quality customer relational management (CRM) system to keep client data, monitor communications, develop marketing strategies based on customer feedback, create client assessment reports to track fitness or design training programs, and manage payment and renewal processes. An all-in-one tool such as this is vital to the successful operation of a sport facility.

Source: EZFacility, Inc. (2014). Retrieved November 16, 2014 from www.ezfacility.com

CHAPTER 11

LEGAL CONCERNS FOR OWNERS AND MANAGERS

CHAPTER OUTLINE

- The relationship between legal concerns and sport facilities
- Effects of the legal environment on sport facility operations
- Legal principles and standards related to facility management
    - Negligence law and unintentional torts
    - Criminal law and intentional torts
    - Contract law
    - Marketing-based legislative issues
        - Intellectual properties
        - Ambush marketing
- How much legal expertise is enough?
- Chapter review

CHAPTER OBJECTIVES

The purpose of this chapter is to explore the relationship between legal issues and sport facility operations. This chapter is not intended to provide someone with in-depth legal expertise. It is also not intended to provide specific laws that are pertinent to sport facility management, as the global objective of the book would make much of that information useless to the reader based on their location. However, it is intended to articulate the effects of the legal environment on sport facilities. One of the major misconceptions in sport facilities is that risk management and sport law are the same. This is untrue, especially as related to the focus of this section of the text – the implementation of management and operations (risk management is an action item, and will be covered in depth in the next section of the book in Chapter 14). This chapter will provide an overview of the major legal principles and standards related to the management and operations of sport facilities including negligence/unintentional torts, criminal law/intentional torts, contract law, and marketing-based legislative issues including intellectual properties and ambush marketing. The chapter will conclude with a brief discussion about the level of legal expertise a sport facility owner and manager should have, and when they should defer to individuals with a higher level of proficiency in the law.

THE RELATIONSHIP BETWEEN LEGAL CONCERNS AND SPORT FACILITIES

Sport law and sport facility management have a significant relationship, including some of the issues already discussed in this book:

- laws of ownership structures and governance of sport facilities (Chapter 2);
- laws governing financing sport facilities (Chapter 3);
- laws related to allowable and appropriate capital investment appraisal (Chapter 4);
- legal issues related to design and construction of sport facilities (Chapter 5);
- lawsuit potentials as related to organizational management (Chapter 6);
- internal and external laws and regulations inherent to human resource management (Chapter 7);
- accounting, tax, and financial laws that are a part of financial management (Chapter 8);
- laws that have a direct effect on appropriate operation decision making (Chapter 9);
- legal aspects tied to risk management in operations (Chapter 10);
- legal issues will also be embedded in the upcoming chapters (Chapters 12–15) on marketing management, event planning, risk management, and security management.

As you can see, the law permeates all aspects of sport facility operations management. And while we cannot articulate all the laws and legal concerns that may affect a sport facility manager or owner (especially with the global differences in laws based on individual countries), we can communicate the effect the law has on the operation and management of a sport facility, and the major legal principles that are prevalent globally.

234

EFFECTS OF THE LEGAL ENVIRONMENT ON SPORT FACILITY OPERATIONS

Laws are a body of rules that govern individual or collective actions and conduct as defined by an authorized governing body and having binding legal force. Laws provide accountability and justice for citizens, and in the case of this text, the users and related constituencies of a sport facility. However, the challenge is that laws are constantly evolving through modifications and change, and that evolution has a direct effect on the daily conduct of the management and operation of a sport facility.

A great majority of laws are created by the governments of the world and their designees. These laws may be created at the highest level (usually federal or parliamentary); at regional levels (state and provinces); or at the local level by municipalities. In addition, there are laws that are administrative in nature, and are set by governing bodies such as the International Olympic Committee, and the various sport leagues and tournaments around the world. In an attempt to generalize the categories of law, we present the following four categories:

- Constitutional law: laws embedded in the constitution or charter of a country or region.
- Statutory law: those laws created and affirmed by sanctioned legislative bodies.
- Common law: laws that are created based on past legal decisions (precedence).
- Administrative law: rules and regulations created, implemented, and enforced by a specifically authorized agency.

While it would be impossible for a sport facility manager or owner to know every law that will have a direct effect on the management and operation of the sport facility, they do have a duty of care to their users and associated constituents to act in a legal manner. As such, sport facility managers and owners must have a basic understanding of the legal principles and standards that will directly affect them.

LEGAL PRINCIPLES AND STANDARDS RELATED TO FACILITY MANAGEMENT

Managers and owners should have a basic understanding of the legal principles and standards that are inherent to proper sport facility management and operations. Tort laws are the most significant set of laws that sport facilities encounter. Unintentional torts fall under the category of negligence, and intentional torts fall under the realm of criminal law. Managers and owners also deal with legal ramifications of their management and operations of a sport facility as related contract laws. In addition, two of the most prevalent legislative issues to impact sport facilities globally in the 21st century relate to intellectual properties and ambush marketing.

235

Negligence law and unintentional torts

An unintentional tort, more commonly known as negligence, is a failure to act in a manner equal to how a reasonable person would act under the same circumstances. As related to sport facilities, for there to be negligence, four elements must be proven: (1) duty; (2) the act itself; (3) proximate cause; and (4) damages. First is whether the designees of the sport facility had a duty of care or a duty to act. This duty can arise from an inherent relationship between the personnel or ownership of the sport facility and a user, or from duties that are required as a result of legal standing (employment laws, supervisory obligations, or administration of first aid are three examples). Second, the act almost always relates to foreseeing risks and preventing harm. Ultimately, all actions should meet a standard of care that limit inherent risks of activities in the sport facility, and prevents negligence behavior by those engaged in activities within the sport facility. Third is proximate cause, which means for a charge of negligence to be valid, the action of negligence causes a loss or injury. Fourth are damages, or that there was an actual injury, loss, or emotional harm.

Any party associated with a sport facility can be liable for negligence, ranging from individual employees to administrative staff to ownership. There are a variety of ways to protect against negligence – the most widely used in sport facilities are waivers, in which users contractually release the facility and their agents from liability. There are also assumption-of-risk statutes that protect the sport facility against negligence claims for injuries suffered from acts that are inherent and known to the part of an activity. Other ways to limit negligence liability is through the use of independent contractors for events – in essence transferring the risk of negligence to the contractor; and purchasing insurance to protect the entire operation in case a negligent act takes place.

Criminal law and intentional torts

An intentional tort is a civil wrong based on an intentional act. These types of torts fall under criminal law, and the purpose of these laws are to protect the general health, safety, and welfare of the public. As a result of the inherent activities in sport, there are times, both on the field/court and off, that disagreements and actions may go beyond the realm of what is acceptable in society and cross over to a criminal act. In addition, because of potential interactions between staff and uncooperative patrons, there must be an understanding of crossing the line from what is a duty of care or action, and a criminal act.

The major intentional torts that may take place in sport facilities are:

- Assault: when one individual tries to physically harm another in a way that makes the second person under attack feel immediately threatened; there does not need to be actual physical contact – threats, gestures, and other actions that would raise the suspicions of a reasonable person can constitute an assault.

- Battery: the unlawful and unwanted physical contact by one person to a second person with the intention to harm.
- Defamation: written (libel) or verbal (slander) communication of non-factual information with the intent to create a negative image.
- Invasion of privacy: interference with the right to be left alone – most often challenges in sport facilities are related to memberships and having a personal locker with a lock on it.

Contract law

Contracts are a major part of sport facility management. Other than employment contracts (see human resource management – Chapter 6), the largest and most significant contracts are those with events that wish to utilize the sport facility, and sponsorship contracts. No matter the type, there are five elements that are part of any contract: (1) the offer; (2) the acceptance; (3) consideration; (4) legality; and (5) capacity. The offer and acceptance is when one party tenders the contract, and a second party agrees to the terms. Consideration involves the exchange of value between the two parties, hence there must be a benefit of some type to both parties – in an event contract, it is usually a fee to the sport facility and the event acquire a place for it to take place. Legality is simply that the contract must not be against the law, and capacity is that both parties entering into the agreement have the authority and capability to do so. Within all contracts, there is additional language covering a multitude of issues. Some of the most common are terms and cancellation clauses with remedies, confidentiality statements, and damages should a breach of contract occur.

Event contracts are usually more detailed because there are a number of specialized elements that need to be included. First, the event itself is only a small part of the contract – there is also the pre-event set-up and post-event breakdown that must be detailed. In addition, any specialized lease agreements for facilities, equipment, and rentals must be spelled out and are often added as an addendum. There must also be an articulation of other ancillary benefits and options, including marketing and sponsorship efforts, concessions and merchandising offerings, and personnel inclusions (examples include set-up/breakdown staff, security, ushers, contractors, and site managers).

A sport facility sponsorship contract could be for naming rights on the entire complex, or for a specific part of the facility (a court, field, or room). Depending on the size of the sport facility and the location, these agreements can net up to $20 million per year over 40 years (example – the current deal between Citi and the New York Mets). In England, the Football Association (FA) offers advertising rights to Wembley Stadium (i.e. Wembley Stadium 'sponsored by' or 'in association with'), which brings in an additional £5 million per year. In addition to advertising and promotions specifications, the contracts may also include statements of exclusivity (prevents other sponsors in the same industry to enter into agreement with the facility) or non-exclusivity, options to renew, rights of first refusal for renewal, and any intellectual property rights concerns.

Marketing-based legislative issues

Upcoming in Chapter 12 will be an explanation of marketing management for sport facilities, including issues related to understanding the sport facility consumer from a marketing standpoint, marketing logistics in sport facility marketing, and the relationship of promotions and sport facilities. From a legislative point of view, there are two current issues that are significantly prevalent in sport facility management. The first was mentioned in the previous section – the relationship of intellectual property rights and sport facility management. The second is the effect of ambush marketing legislation on sport facilities.

Intellectual properties

With the continued growth of sponsorship and advertising agreements in sport facilities of all sizes, sport facility owners and managers are becoming more involved in the management of intellectual properties – both the facility's rights and the sponsors/advertisers' rights. Intellectual properties are creative intangible assets that have commercial value. There are three major categories of intellectual properties – patents, copyrights, and marks. A patent is any new and/or useful invention or improvement on a process, machine, or manufacturing method. While sport facilities rarely deal with this intellectual property, there are times when the personnel may be able to create a patented invention or improvement. At that point, the ownership or personnel should secure the services of a patent lawyer.

A copyright gives the owner of an artistic creation the exclusive right to copy, reproduce, distribute, publish, perform, or display the work. For copyright protection to be legal: (1) the work usually needs to be original and (2) it must be in a tangible form that can be reproduced. For sport facility managers and owners, any document, manual, or form may have the right to be copyrighted if it meets the above criteria. However, where the larger understanding of copyrights comes is as related to the operations or events in a facility. The use of music, public performances, and broadcasts are protected under copyright law. Any of these types of events that take place in your sport facility, should they be scheduled for re-broadcast, may be subject to copyright approval by the ownership for a fee.

The final area of intellectual property law that sport facilities will engage in are marks – specifically trademarks. A trademark is a word, phrase, symbol, or design, or a combination of words, phrases, symbols, or designs, that identifies and distinguishes the source of the goods of one party from those of others. Sport facilities have their own trademarks, and also need to manage the trademarks of those organizations associated with the sport facility. The purposes of a trademark include:

■ articulating the source and the standard of quality for the product or service offered by the sport facility, hence protecting the public from confusion and deception;

238

- distinguishing the products and services of the sport facility from their competition – often through the licensing process;
- serving as a major element of the advertising campaign for the sport facility.

One of the major challenges to intellectual property right protection for sport facilities is twofold. First, who is the true owner of the intellectual property – an event or the facility? This question should be answered in the contracting process. The second and bigger question today is the protecting of intellectual properties from ambush marketing efforts.

Ambush marketing

Ambush marketing is the attempt by a third party to create a direct or indirect association with a sport facility, the event it is hosting, or its participants without their approval, hence denying official sponsors, suppliers, and partners parts of the commercial value derived from the 'official' designation. This association is without the permission of the sport endeavor or its official partner(s), and the desire is to deceive the sport consumer into believing that there is an official association. Entities engage in ambush marketing because of their desire to be associated with a sport facility or the event being housed there. Reasons include not being able to pay the sponsorship fees, or being prevented from entering into an association with the sport event due to a contract of exclusivity or long-term association with a competitor.

AMBUSH MARKETING LAWS AROUND THE WORLD

For many municipalities around the globe, it has come to pass that governmental intervention is necessary to ensure sponsor protection during hallmark events. As a sport facility manager, you will need to be aware of these various legislations and work with local authorities and your sponsors to ensure ambush marketing is limited. We take a look at some of the laws around the globe.

United States

As of the print date of this book, there is no federal legislation, but municipalities hosting hallmark events have taken steps to ensure ambush marketing will not take place in their city when the country and potentially the world is watching. One example was in 2006 in Detroit, Michigan, where an anti-ambush marketing law created a no-ad zone around stadiums during the

Super Bowl and the World Series. Similar laws were enacted for future Super Bowls, and now The National Football League (NFL) has requirements for Super Bowl bids that require host cities to address ambush marketing. The league requires a one-mile anti-ambush marketing zone around the stadium where temporary signs, inflatables, and buildings wrapped with advertising banners are prohibited unless approved by the NFL – if this cannot be guaranteed, the host committee must provide $1 million to the NFL so they can establish it.

Australia

Australia has been at the forefront of controlling ambush marketing. With the 2000 Summer Olympics coming to Sydney, the Australian government passed the Sydney 2000 Games (Indicia and Images) Protection Act 1996, and the New South Wales government passed the Olympic Arrangements Act 2000. A significant part of both laws was Games-specific legislation enacted to prevent ambush marketing and provide for 'clean' Games venues to equip New South Wales and Australia for future sporting and large marketing programs. Since these Olympics, the Australian government has enacted similar laws for hallmark sport events, the most recent being the Melbourne 2006 Commonwealth Games Protection Act 2005.

South Africa

The South African Parliament has passed wide-ranging ambush marketing legislation to create boundaries for the sport marketing industry. The new restrictions tackle 'intrusion' marketing where a company seeks subtle exposure of its brand through the publicity generated by the event. The legislation, which amends the Merchandise Marks Act 1941, enables South Africa's government to designate certain events, such as the cricket World Cup and the FIFA World Cup, as being subject to new restrictions. Once an event is so designated, it will be a criminal offense to conduct ambush marketing in connection with the event and perpetrators could face jail. The laws prohibit use of any brand in relation to a designated event in such a manner which is calculated to achieve publicity for that trademark and thereby derive promotional benefit from the event without the prior authority of the organizer.

New Zealand

New Zealand has passed legislation to provide greater protection to sponsors of important events from ambush marketing: the Major Events Management

Act 2007. The purpose of the anti-ambush marketing part of the law is to prevent unauthorized commercial exploitation at the expense of either a major event organizer or a major event sponsor. Specifically, the law (1) prohibits representations that suggest persons, brands, goods, or services have an association with a major event when they do not; (2) prohibits advertising from intruding on a major event activity and the attention of the associated audience; and (3) prohibits the use of certain emblems and words relating to Olympic Games and Commonwealth Games (and other designated events) without appropriate authorization.

China

After being selected as the host of the 2008 Summer Olympic Games, the Chinese government passed the Protection of Olympic Symbols Relations 2002. This law protects Olympic symbols and names, but also includes an anti-ambush marketing clause. Ambush marketing is vaguely defined as activities that might be deemed by others as an existing sponsorship or other supportive relationship.

Brazil

The Brazilian government realized early on that their traditional intellectual property legal schemes did not specifically address most types of ambush marketing. There was some mention of ambush marketing protection addressed in the Brazilian Industrial Property Act of 1996, the Brazilian Copyright Act of 1998, the Brazilian Sports Act of 1998 (also known as the Pele Law), and even the Civil Code of Brazil – but none went far enough to protect against ambush marketing at the two most important sporting events in the world being hosted in Brazil – the 2014 FIFA World Cup and the 2016 Summer Olympics.

To start to address this shortfall, Brazil enacted the Olympic Act in 2009 to protect the use of Olympic symbols, mascots, and other trademarks to only authorized users – however this also did not address ambush marketing in an adequate manner. In 2012, the Brazilian World Cup General Law went significantly further to specifically address the issues of ambush marketing, including putting into law penalties for engaging in ambush marketing activities during the FIFA Confederations Cup Brazil 2013, the 2014 FIFA World Cup, and related events. Since then, the Brazilian government has tightened up the details within the Olympic Act of 2009 with additional legislation, protection, and penalties related to ambush marketing.

Sources

Downing, D. M., Bram, M. R., and Azevedo, R. (2014). *Ambush marketing: Coming to a stadium near you*. Retrieved November 3, 2014 from: www.acc.com/legalresources/quickcounsel/amcstasny.cfm

Schwarz, E. C. (2009). *The evolution of global anti-ambush marketing laws.* Paper presented at the 7th annual conference of the Sport Marketing Association, Cleveland, Ohio.

Suggested discussion topics

1   Research the current laws in place in Brazil for the 2016 Summer Olympics related to ambush marketing protection. Do you feel the Brazilian government has done enough to protect sponsors and the brand of the Olympics with their legislation? If so, what steps will the government need to take to ensure proper enforcement of the law? If not, what more do you think they need to do?

2   Take a look at the following countries that are hosting hallmark sporting events in the future. What preventative measures are each country's government enacting to combat ambush marketing while hosting the event?
    a   2018 FIFA World Cup in Russia
    b   2018 Winter Olympics in South Korea
    c   2019 Rugby World Cup and 2020 Summer Olympics in Japan
    d   2022 FIFA World Cup in Qatar.

HOW MUCH LEGAL EXPERTISE IS ENOUGH?

On a final note for this chapter, the question is raised 'how much legal expertise is enough for a sport facility manager or owner?' The reality is that with all the other responsibilities in management and operations of the sport facility, also dealing with keeping up-to-date on all the federal/parliamentary, state/regional, and local/municipality law changes and enactments is nearly impossible. In fact, it would be irrational for facility managers and owners to believe they can possess legal expertise in all of these areas as described in this chapter – as this is only a snapshot of the total breadth and depth of the law. Therefore, we cannot stress enough the importance of having access to legal expertise, and if possible, have legal council on retainer to stay on top of the legal concerns that affect sport facilities.

CHAPTER REVIEW

The law has a significant relationship to almost entirely all aspects of sport facility operations management. Laws are a body of rules that govern individual or collective actions and conduct as defined by an authorized governing body and having binding legal force. The challenge is that laws are constantly evolving through modifications and change, and that evolution has a direct effect on the daily conduct of the management and operation of a sport facility. The four major areas of law that sport facility managers and owners deal with include constitutional law, statutory law, common law, and administrative law. While it would be impossible for a sport facility manager or owner to know every law that will have a direct effect on the management and operation of the sport facility, they do have a duty of care to their users and associated constituents to act in a legal manner.

Sport facility managers and owners must have a basic understanding of the legal principles and standards that will directly affect them. Negligence law involves unintentional torts related to a failure to act in a manner equal to how a reasonable person would act under the same circumstances. Criminal law is an intentional tort, which is a civil wrong based on an intentional act that becomes a detriment to the general health, safety, and welfare of the general public. In sport facilities, the civil wrongs most often seen are assault, battery, defamation, and invasion of privacy. Contract law is a major part of facility management, especially as related to employment contracts, event contracts, and sponsorship contracts. Event contracts are usually more detailed because there are a number of specialized elements that need to be included such as pre-event set-up and post-event breakdown; specialized lease agreements for facilities, equipment, and rentals; and other ancillary benefits and options, including marketing and sponsorship efforts, concessions and merchandising offerings, and personnel inclusions. Sponsorship contracts could be for naming rights on the entire complex, or for a specific part of the sport facility (a court, field, or room). In addition to advertising and promotions specifications, the contracts may also include statements of exclusivity or non-exclusivity, options to renew, rights of first refusal for renewal, and any intellectual property rights concerns. In addition, marketing-based legislative issues related to intellectual properties (especially copyright and trademarks) and ambush marketing are significant legal issues that should be understood and addressed.

One of the biggest issues is determining how much legal expertise a sport facility manager or owner should have. In general, they cannot possess legal expertise in all of these areas as described in this chapter, and it is crucial to have access to legal expertise to stay ahead of the changes in laws affecting sport facilities.

BIBLIOGRAPHY

Chanavat, N. and Desbordes, M. (2014). Towards the regulation and restriction of ambush marketing? The first truly social and digital mega sports event: Olympic Games, London 2012. *International Journal of Sports Marketing and Sponsorship, 15*(3), 151–160.

Cotten, D. J. and Wolohan, J. T. (2013). *Law for recreation and sport managers* (6th ed.). Dubuque, IA: Kendall/Hunt Publishing Company.

Fletcher, G. P. and Sheppard, S. (2005). *American law in a global context: The basics.* Cary, NC: Oxford University Press.

Garner, B. A. (Ed.) (2014). *Black's law dictionary* (10th ed.). Eagan, MN: Thompson West.

Ironside, S. (2008). Major events management act 2007. *Managing Intellectual Property,* (184), 122. Retrieved June 5, 2014 from: www.managingip.com/Article/2041356/%20 Major-Events-Management-Act-2007.html

Khare, M. (2010). Foul ball! The need to alter current liability standards for spectator injuries at sporting events. *Texas Review of Entertainment and Sports Law, 12*(1), 91–107.

Kumar, S. and Agawane, V. (2013). The role of major-sport event cricket with respect to the consumer perception and attitude towards ambush marketing. *International Journal of Business and Management Invention, 2*(10), 76–81.

Maloy, B. P. (1993). Legal obligations related to facilities. *The Journal of Physical Education, Recreation & Dance, 64*(2), 28–30.

Maskus, K. (2000). *The global policy framework: Intellectual property rights and wrongs.* Retrieved February 17, 2014 from: www.iie.com/publications/chapters_preview/99/6iie2822.pdf

Schwarz, E. C. (2009). *The evolution of global anti-ambush marketing laws.* Paper presented at the 7th annual conference of the Sport Marketing Association, Cleveland, Ohio.

Schwarz, E. C. and Hunter, J. D. (2013). *Advanced theory and practice in sport marketing* (2nd ed.). Oxford, UK: Routledge.

Seguin, B. (2010). *Sponsorship and ambush marketing: Vancouver 2010.* Retrieved January 31, 2014 from: www.idrett.no/tema/internasjonalt/Documents/sponsorship.pdf

Seth, R. (2010). Ambush marketing – need for legislation in India. *Journal of Intellectual Property Rights, 15,* 455–463.

Thomaselli, R. (2005). Ambushing the super bowl: Ordinance to pare back sneak ad attacks in host city Detroit scaled down. *Advertising Age, 76*(26), 3.57.

Vassallo, E., Blemaster, K., and Werner, P. (2005). An international look at ambush marketing. *The Trademark Reporter, 95*(6), 1338–1356.

Wong, G. (2010). *Essentials of sports law* (4th ed.). Santa Barbara, CA: Praeger.

IN THE FIELD ...

Interview with Greg Riehle, Former Senior Vice President and General Counsel, Saddlebrook Holdings, Inc.

Please explain to the reader about your position and responsibilities specifically as related to your role as General Counsel for Saddlebrook Resort.

In the role of General Counsel, I provide consultation and advice regarding legal and insurance issues related to the business. This includes assessing the business implications of legal actions or inactions, analyzing contractual transactions, and identifying issues and risks that could cause harm to the company.

Tell us a little about your track from your university years to get to the position you are in now.

I received my undergraduate degree in American Studies from Notre Dame, and graduated from law school from the University of Southern California. I became an attorney, and am licensed in Florida, California, and Ohio. I practiced law privately (litigation) for about seven years. When my father-in-law purchased Saddlebrook Resorts, Inc., I came into the family business. I took the lead role in developing Saddlebrook Preparatory School, a fully accredited academic and boarding middle and high school for aspiring junior golfers and tennis players from around the world. A few years after it was founded, I assumed the role of President of our golf and tennis academies. Later, I took on the role of General Manager of Saddlebrook Resort. Following about 15 years managing the resort and our sports company/boarding school for athletes, I returned to the General Counsel role. I have worn so many hats because Saddlebrook is my family's business. My adaptability to a variety of positions has enabled me to adjust to the varying needs of our companies.

What advice would you give to someone wanting to get into the field of sport facility operations management?

Be as well educated, well read, and adaptable as you can. My advice is to learn to learn – as careers will continue to evolve. You must be ready to move into a different field when the challenge/opportunity presents itself.

TECHNOLOGY NOW!

The sport facility manager needs to stay on top of the most current information concerning legal changes in the field. The reality is that there are thousands of court cases that take place in local, state and federal courts that can have a direct effect on the management of sport facilities – ranging from changes in laws that directly affect the way a manager is required to run their facility, to situational cases that can serve as either a precedent or wake-up call on changes that should be made to the manner in which the facility is run.

It would be prudent for sport facility operations managers to stay on top of the latest court decisions that may affect them. One such tool is Westlaw, which provides over 40,000 database entries of case law, state and federal statutes, administrative codes, and publications. An important tool within Westlaw is KeyCite, which is a citation checking service that provides readers with information as to whether the case they are reading about is still valid, or if newer law is more current.

Another resource is LexisNexus, a computer-assisted legal research program to access legal documents and public records. LexisNexus also has divisions to provide consultation for business research and risk solutions, but the most relevant use is their academic research site that allows users to look up a legal case, get company information of over 80 million companies, and search the news for hot topics related to a specific industry.

If nothing else, packages of this type should help you to realize what your limits are and at what point you need to seek professional help with legal issues.

Sources

LexisNexus (2014). Retrieved November 17, 2014 from www.lexisnexis.com/hottopics/lnacademic/

Westlaw (2014). Retrieved November 17, 2014 from www.westlaw.com

PART III

ANCILLARY ISSUES IN MANAGEMENT AND OPERATIONS

CHAPTER 12

FACILITY MARKETING MANAGEMENT

CHAPTER OBJECTIVES

This chapter will cover the basic theories and principles of global sport marketing and communications related to sport facilities. The goal is for the reader to develop knowledge and skill in the marketing process as it relates to social responsibility and ethics, understanding the sport consumer, logistics, promotions, and public relations activities in sport facilities. Sport facility managers must understand their role as a sport facility marketer in terms of studying and understanding the consumer in terms of marketing a sport facility, developing marketing strategies for the sport facility, and clarifying a sport facility's needs and goals – through the marketing mix, market research and information systems, and consumer behavior. As part of these responsibilities, the sport facility manager must understand how to develop and implement a sport marketing plan through logistical functions including product management, supply chain management, and sales management, as well as through promotional efforts including advertising, sponsorship, and other communication management efforts.

INTRODUCTION TO SPORT FACILITY MARKETING MANAGEMENT

One of the biggest misconceptions in sport facility management is that the facility manager does not need to be involved with marketing – that their sole job is related to the operations and management of the actual sport facility. On the contrary, sport facility managers need to have a solid foundation in marketing and should be involved in all aspects of marketing that relate to the sport facility. The knowledge of the sport facility manager with relation to operations and management of the sport facility actually can serve as a significant asset in the development of marketing plans, helping with the understanding of the consumers who use the facility, efficient logistical administration of marketing efforts, and effective application of promotional activities though facility advertising, sponsorships, and atmospherics.

The purpose of this chapter is to provide an overview of how the association of sport marketing and sport facilities can interact to best provide products and services that satisfy the needs, wants, and desires of the consumer; aid in the planning, organizing, directing, controlling, budgeting, leading, and evaluation of a sport facility whose primary product and service is related to sport, recreation, leisure, and entertainment; and how the sport facility manager's understanding of the application of marketing can help with the transfer of goods and services from the producer (the sport facility, the events in the facility, and the organizations utilizing the facility) to the consumer (spectators and participants).

THE SPORT MARKETING MIX AND SPORT FACILITIES

The focal point of these marketing functions is in four specific areas known as the 4 Cs of marketing analysis: the consumer, the company itself, the competition, and the climate. The consumer is an individual or organization that purchases or

250

obtains goods and services for direct use or ownership. In the case of the sport facility, it is most often the purchase of a ticket to gain access for the purpose of experiencing an event. Sport marketers reach sport consumers through a series of processes – (1) segmentation is the concept of dividing a large, diverse group with multiple attributes into smaller groups with distinctive characteristics; (2) targeting seeks to find the best way to get a product's image into the minds of consumers, and hence entice the consumer to purchase the product ... accomplished by focusing on the Ps of sport marketing (product, price, place, promotion, publicity, and people); (3) positioning focuses on how a company seeks to influence the perceptions of potential and current customers about the image of the company and its products and services; and (4) delivery is the concept of producing or achieving what is desired or expected by the consumer. With regard to the company and competition, the framework is centered on the SWOT analysis. The managerial function of the company itself is most concerned with internal strengths and weaknesses. The leadership of the company tends to focus on the external opportunities and external threats posed by competition and the environment. The climate involves forecasting the factors that will have a direct effect on the internal and external functioning of the sport facility, including changes in societal values and beliefs, the economy, legal and political issues, the media, and changes in technology.

The sport facility manager is a crucial part of the marketing management team for the sport facility because of their experience within the climate, their understanding of the diverse consumers who come to the sport facility for various events, their knowledge of how similar sport facilities operate, and their direct involvement with the internal functions of the sport facility. However, there are significant challenges for the sport facility manager, because while the sport facility itself is a tangible building, the sport product is generally intangible, subjective, and variable. This makes the sport marketing efforts for a sport facility unique for numerous reasons, but most importantly because the primary sport product, and hence the market, is traditionally demand based, whereas most generic products are marketed based on need. The sport product takes many forms including a consumer good, a consumer service, a commercial good, or a commercial service; hence it has a wide and varied appeal. The sport facility manager has to have an equally wide and varied understanding of the multiple types and aspects of sport products and services that may take place in their sport facility, and how best to deliver what is promised to the consumers.

The sport facility manager must also recognize that the sport product is normally publicly consumed, and consumer satisfaction is directly affected by the environment – which is most often provided by the sport facility. As a result of the strong emotional connections elicited by involvement of the sport product, and the fact that since the sport product is a perishable commodity (when the game or event is over, it is the memory of the experience that remains), the sport facility manager must do everything possible to ensure that from the facility standpoint the customer is satisfied. This is most often accomplished by working with all sub-departments associated to the sport facility to ensure that the product extensions are adequate – including such things as quality concession stands, functional and clean lavatories, simple ingress/egress, good flow within the facility (including directions within the sport facility), top quality security, and overall cleanliness of the sport facility. Anything a sport facility manager can do to enhance the customer experience aids in marketing efforts.

UNDERSTANDING THE SPORT CONSUMER IN SPORT FACILITIES

The purpose of a sport facility is to provide a place for people to congregate and participate in sport and leisure-related activities. As such, it is the responsibility of the sport facility manager to understand who their customers are – ranging from participants to spectators. Sport facility managers are increasingly investing time and resources into understanding their sport consumers in two ways. First is through the creation of a sport management information system, which consists of all department, activities, and people within a sport facility being responsible for gathering, organizing, analyzing, evaluating, and distributing marketing information to ensure efficient and effective decision making regarding customer wants and needs. Second is understanding consumer behavior, which is the conduct that sport consumers display in seeking out, ordering, buying, using, and assessing products and services that the consumer expects will satisfy their needs and wants. Each is discussed in more detail in the pages that follow.

Marketing information systems

In order for the sport facility manager to understand consumers, they must be able to effectively and efficiently incorporate a marketing information system into their marketing efforts. The purpose of a marketing information system is to collect the various data available in one place for use in making sport marketing decisions through an intricate structure involving the interacting of people, infrastructure, and techniques to gather, sort, analyze, evaluate, and distribute relevant, well-timed, accurate information for use by sport facility directors so they can develop, implement, and manage marketing plans. The marketing information system is made up of four elements – the marketing research system, the internal reports system, the marketing intelligence system, and the marketing decision support system.

Market research

The marketing research system is the process of designing, gathering, analyzing, and reporting information that is utilized to solve a specified sport marketing issue or problem. The sport facility manager must engage in a process to determine where there is a lack of information available about a need – ranging from the available

250

target market to a need within the sport facility. As a result of a problem being defined, the sport facility manager comes up with a list of potential solutions articulated in terms of goals and objectives, and then engages in the research process. This process includes collecting primary and secondary data through various methods (surveys, focus groups, case study analysis, market tracking studies, industry standard reports, etc.); tabulating and evaluating the data collected; and utilizing the information to develop programs to meet the needs of the consumer, or modify policies and procedures as necessary.

Internal reports system

The internal reports system serves as a framework for the marketing information system by allowing the sport facility director the ability to examine the internal operations of the sport organization to enhance the marketing efforts of the sport facility and associated events. Utilizing the information collected from various departments through inputs from the order-to-payment cycle, the point-of-sale system, and data mining, the sport facility manager is better able to understand the sport organization they are working with, and hence its relationship to prospective and current customers.

Intelligence system

The marketing intelligence system is a crucial element of the marketing information system because it opens the door to understanding the external environment that affects the sport facility and the organizations it serves. By using the primary and secondary intelligence collected through the various methods of scanning, and evaluating that data through the scanning dissemination process, the sport facility manager can gain a better understanding of the opportunities, threats, and trends that can affect the sport facility. In addition, this intelligence is utilized to enhance the internal reports of the sport facility, and can serve as a framework for future sport marketing research.

Decision support system

The marketing decision support system (DSS) assists sport facility managers and other decision makers both within the sport facility and the organizations it serves by taking advantage of information that is available from the various sources and using that information to make strategic decisions, control decisions, operational decisions, and marketing decisions. This system looks at both the decision process and decision outcomes, with the goal of making changes in selected sport marketing that lead to higher profits, a stronger and more positive image for the sport facility, and to increase sport consumer satisfaction. Therefore, the results from the decision support system are utilized to make strategic, control, operational, and marketing decisions that interact with all parts of the sport facility and the associated organizations.

Consumer behavior

While it is important to have knowledge about the marketing information system, this is only the functional part of understanding the sport consumer. The sport facility manager, to effectively engage in marketing management, must also comprehend and apply the principles of consumer behavior. Consumer behavior is the conduct that consumers display in seeking out, ordering, buying, using, and assessing products and services that the consumers expect will satisfy their needs and wants.

The sport facility manager must understand the internal and external factors that affect sport consumers. The internal factors include the personality of the sport consumer, the learning process of sport consumers, the process of motivating sport consumers, the attitudes of the sport consumer, and the perceptions developed by sport consumers about a sport product. External factors resulting from environmental influences include culture, subculture, international and global interaction, social setting, and social class.

In order to effectively understand consumer behavior, sport facility managers must understand the marketing concept, which is a consumer-oriented philosophy that suggests that satisfaction of consumer needs provides the focus for product development and marketing strategy to enable the firm to meet its own organizational goals. In terms of sport facility management, the marketing concept focuses on the socialization, involvement, and commitment of spectators and participants through the sport product itself, the production of sport (through the experience of the 'event'), and the sale of sport (including the product extensions).

The sport facility manager will be an active member of the problem solving and decision making processes to ensure that the needs and wants of the consumer are being met. In problem solving, the sport facility manager will engage in brainstorming, formulating various solutions, analyzing all solutions to determine a course of action, implementing the course of action, and evaluating the success of the course of action chosen to ensure that optimal success is attained from a sport facility operations standpoint. The decision making process that works hand-in-hand with problem solving focuses on the economic, passive, cognitive, and emotional needs of customers before they enter the sport facility, while they are in the sport facility, and after they have left the sport facility. Ultimately, sport facility managers look at three key determinants of success as related to marketing management: (1) did the marketing program influence sport consumers to come to the sport facility; (2) did the advertisements and other collateral materials stimulate sport consumer purchasers to come to the facility; and (3) was the spread of information about the sport facility via word of mouth in an effective, controlled, and positive manner?

The overriding goal is to market the facility utilizing the various processes in consumer behavior to influence the sport consumer into coming to the sport facility for an event. Once in the sport facility, the goal is to have the sport consumer believe that the sport facility is delivering a sport product and experience that meets

254

and satisfies their needs, which in turn results in the sport consumer purchasing another sport product in the future, and hence using the sport facility.

SO WHO IS THE SPORT CONSUMER?

There has been much discussion as to the true identity of the consumer for a sport facility. Traditionally, they were grouped into two categories – participants (individuals who are involved or play a part in a spectacle – such as a sport event or concert), and spectators (individuals who are present and observe a spectacle such as a sport event or concert). While these definitions are generic in nature and encompass a wide range of individuals, there is a need to take a closer look into who the sport consumer is and understand that the sport facility manager looks at the sport consumer in smaller, more detailed categories.

From the participant point of view, the sport facility manager must understand the needs of the players, the coaches, the trainers, and management. Sport facility managers market their facility to these constituents every day, ranging from the quality of the field/court of play to the amenities of the offices and locker rooms. The participants are the direct internal clients of the sport facility, and it is the goal of the sport facility manager to meet the needs and wants of these clients in order to assure continued use of the facility by those clients.

From the spectator point of view, the sport facility manager must understand the various external consumers of the sport facility. A.T. Kearney, an innovative, corporate-focused management consulting firm that provides management advice concerning issues on CEO agenda, conducted a study to classify the sport consumer into different segments. They defined the sport consumer as either traditional or new. Traditional sport consumers included sport fanatics and club/team loyalists, and new sports consumers were segmented into social viewers, opportunistic viewers, star-struck spectators, and sport indifferent consumers.

Traditional sport consumers

There are two categories of traditional sport consumers – sport fanatics and club/team loyalists. Sport fanatics are individuals who share a persistent interest in the sport and tend to be the most loyal to their team and the associated facilities. Demographically, sport fanatics are predominantly young, male, and either actively participate in or attend sporting events. They diligently follow news and scores and have significant knowledge of sports, team, and facility statistics, and use multiple media and new technologies during their attendance at sporting events to enhance their experience. The majority of the money they spend on sport is related to merchandise and associated peripherals. Club/team loyalists do not take fanaticism to the extreme level, but they tend to be very loyal to a particular club or team – and hence a sport facility. After sport fanatics they are the most likely group to attend sporting events and spend significant money on team-related products and services both at the venue and in associated stores.

New sport consumers

With the implementation of new technologies and expanded television/media coverage, a new crop of sport consumers have evolved. These individuals are not necessarily the fanatics and loyalists of yesteryear – but they have become integral consumers for a sport facility and the associated events.

Social viewers use sport as a tool for social interaction – mainly as a place to be seen by those who matter, and for meetings by corporate consumers who use sport events to meet with clients or business friends. These consumers are not necessarily loyal to any club or team, but they are happy to spend significant money – for corporate suites and related facility services (food/beverage, technology) – on behalf of their company.

Opportunistic viewers are individuals that typically consume sport through traditional channels such as television or the Internet, and will attend a sport event when asked by friends. To these consumers, sport is simply one form of entertainment, and there are many others that carry equal weight. Sports facility managers want to entice these individuals into thinking that their money is best spent on the opportunity to see a sport event in the facility.

Star-struck spectators are consumers that tend to follow a superstar rather than a team or sport. Many believe this has been created by the significant influence of fantasy sports. The goal is to capture the hearts of these consumers and transfer it to a team or a sport before the star retires (or moves on to another team), hence getting them into the facility as soon as possible to be a part of the experience.

Sport indifferent consumers are individuals who are not very interested in sport teams, sporting events, or sport programming and only attend or read about major events that everyone seems to be interested in. Sport facility managers seek to market the experience in the sport facility to these consumers so they might return for other events of interest in the future.

Source: adapted from A T. Kearney (2003). *The new sports consumer.* Chicago, IL: AT Kearney, Inc.

SPORT MARKETING LOGISTICS IN SPORT FACILITIES

After the sport facility manager understands the intricacies of the sport consumer,
they then need to understand the major logistical functions in sport marketing that
affect how they position their sport facility, and deliver the sport product through
the sport facility. The major logistical functions a sport facility manager must
understand in terms of sport marketing are product and service management, and
sales management.

Product and service management

Sport product and service management usually starts as a function of the sport
marketing planning process. This process involves the development of the sport
organization's products and services marketing strategies, including the tactics and
programs to be implemented during the lifespan of the plan. It starts by defining
the competitive set, which is the process of determining the direct competitors to
a sport organization in the specific product or service area. Then the sport organization engages in category attractiveness analysis, in which aggregate marketing
factors, segment factors, and environmental factors are considered. This is followed
up with competitor and consumer analyses.

For the sport facility manager, they have products and services that they have
total control over (internal), and products and services that they have limited control over (external). Internal products include the facility itself – the playing surface
and related equipment, seating, scoreboard/message boards, bathrooms, concession areas, and the general infrastructure. Internal services include maintenance,
housekeeping, security, customer service, and first aid. External products include
all aspects of the event taking place in the sport facility. External services are the
added benefits provided by the event and other external entities to enhance the
experience of the customer.

Marketing of the internal products and services is an important job that the sport
facility manager must undertake. Just as with any other product or service, increasing

awareness and image is crucial to not only attracting events to the facility, but attracting customers to attend the events in the sport facility. Hence, the sport facility manager must be acutely aware of the sport product and service life cycle, and how each stage is directly affected by the realities of competition, saturation, and change.

The internal development stage begins with the idea of a new product or service (in the case of a new facility) or a new twist on an existing product or service (in the case of a modified facility). Introduction to market is the time when the sport organization puts its plan into action and starts capturing market share by introducing products and services to the market. In this stage, the benefits of holding events in the sport facility to event coordinators, and building brand awareness and equity within the community, is vital. The growth stage is when the sport facility that offers the best product and/or service (both in the types of events and the experience within the facility) rises to the top and separates itself from the competition. Maturity refers to the time at which the sport facility has maximized profits and is seeking to maintain a stable place in the market through regular events and a standard schedule. The goal is to maintain a regular place in the market as long as possible. However, as with any product, there will come a time when the saturation point is reached. This is when the sport facility must come to the realization that it needs to reevaluate the sport product or service life cycle because they are no longer increasing their market share. Often this means that events and people are not coming to the venue because it is viewed as deteriorating or moving towards obsolescence. The decline stage is the last stage before obsolescence, and either the sport facility should have introduced new services or a next generation of the product (such as a renovation or refurbishment), or the sport facility needs to exit the market (usually through demolition and replacement).

Marketing of the external products and services works in a similar manner. The sport facility manager keeps their eye out for new products or services that can be presented through the sport facility, such as a new event in the marketplace that is of interest to the general public. At the same time, regular events such as local teams and annual events need to be on the radar of the sport facility manager, and plans made to attract them to the sport facility. When the event is introduced to the market, the goal is to attract these new events to the sport facility – hence capturing market share. The growth stage is when the reputation of the sport facility grows and the best events will want to appear there. As that calendar of events grows, there will be a time of maturity, where the image and awareness of the sport facility is at its highest, and the job of the sport facility manager is to balance the schedule and not extend beyond the capability of the sport facility. A sport facility manager also needs to realize at this time of maturity that as events grow in scope (and hence their needs expand), and more modern facilities open, it is possible that events may move on to other venues. The goal, as with the internal plan, is to maintain a regular place in the market as long as possible through positioning and differentiation.

Sales management

Sales are the backbone of any sport organization, and this is equally true of sport facilities. While the sport facility manager may not necessarily have direct involvement in the sales process, they need to have an acute awareness of the entire process, and be prepared to offer advice, consultation, and opinions about sales efforts related to facility inventories. In addition, the sport facility manager, through their staff, build and nurture personal relationships with customers – since many of the staff become the face of the sport facility because of their direct contact with the guests.

Sport facility managers are involved with the sales process on numerous sport facility inventories including leasing/rental of the facility for events; ticketing and box office management; premium access (suites, club seating, public seating licenses/debentures); product branding through pouring rights; and various promotional sales efforts including advertising (signage and promotions) and sponsorships (naming rights and endorsements).

Sport facility managers are often in charge of selling their sport facility to potential clients for a variety of events, including sports, concerts, corporate rentals, hospitality events, graduation, fundraisers, and a number of other types of events. The sport facility manager is often involved in the negotiation of these rental contracts – covering everything from costs of the spaces to be used to various costs including set-up/break-down, security, housekeeping, electrical/technology, special equipment usage, permits, fire/police clearance, storage, and insurance.

Another major area sport facility managers must oversee is ticketing and box office management. From a ticketing standpoint, the sport facility manager needs to coordinate with teams and events to understand the various ticketing structures, inform ticket taking staff of those structures, employing enough staff to service the guests, and ensure that ushers and security understand the level of access that tickets (and in many cases credentials) allow. As far as the box office, many do not realize that the facility owns the box office – not teams or events. There are times when some of the box office operations are outsourced (example – via team/event ticketing or outside vendors such as Ticketmaster and RazorGator), but all ticketing for events at some point must go through the box office. Usually there is a box office staff that reports to and works with the sport facility manager to determine ticketing based on space available, facility configuration for a specific event, and changes that may occur after the event has been set up. The box office is also responsible for creating a manifest, which is a listing of every seat available in a sport facility that is used to coordinate with teams, customers, promoters/booking agents, and outsourcing vendors to track pricing and availability of seating in the venue. This master list serves as the main source of information for every event. In addition to manifesting and ticketing, the sport facility manager – through the box office – is also responsible for coordinating relationships with the tenants of the sport facility, on-sales for new events coming to the venue (both marketing of the on-site and the management of the on-sale day), security of the box office (since a lot of money does go through the box office daily), and event day ingress/egress.

Premium access is a financially lucrative part of running a sport facility, and sport facility managers need to pay special attention to ensure that users of these inventories are receiving value for the money they have paid. There are four main types of premium access seating – premium seating, club seating, luxury boxes/suites, and personal (or sometimes permanent) seat licenses (PSLs). Premium seating is the best seats in the sport facility – front row at the basketball game, behind the plate or dugout at a baseball game, or midfield at a soccer or rugby game. Club seating is specialized seating in the sport facility with special access and amenities that usually include food and beverage with the price of admission. Luxury boxes/suites are private rooms with seating for those with access to the box/suite, a lounge area, private bathroom, and food/beverage service either catered or available through wait staff. PSLs, which are also known as debentures, are where customers pay a one-time fee to gain ownership of a specific seat, then must pay a yearly season ticket fee to maintain the license.

The food and beverage industry is an integral part of the sport facility. While the operations may be kept in-house or outsourced to another company, product branding through pouring rights is one area in which the sport facility manager must be closely involved. As a result of exclusive agreements where beverage companies such as Coca Cola and Pepsi, or alcohol companies such as Anheuser Busch, Miller, or Coors have the pouring rights in a sport facility, the sport facility manager is often the individual who is involved with these negotiations. Usually their involvement involves leveraging the contract to include dedicated funds for sport facility upgrades and improvements, and specific guidelines on how the branding of the sport facility by the vendor can be implemented.

Sport facility managers are also involved with numerous promotional sales efforts, including advertising and sponsorship sales. The final section of this chapter will cover the promotional aspects of the sport, and how the sport facility manager involvement in promotional mix elements includes and goes beyond just the sale of advertising and sponsorship.

PROMOTIONAL ASPECTS OF SPORT MARKETING FOR SPORT FACILITIES

Promotions are a very involved communications process that aids in providing information about the sport facility to consumers through the promotional mix. The elements of the sport promotional mix that sport facility managers work with include advertising, sponsorship, public relations, and atmospherics. To coordinate the interaction between the elements of the sport promotional mix, a strategy must be developed that focuses on building brand loyalty and product credibility, developing image, and positioning the brand. The strategic process involves promotional integration, which is the actual creation and delivery of the promotional message that involves defining how the message is to reach the consumer, ensuring that the promotional message will be received and understood, and that the promotional message will lead to the purchase of a product or service – in the case of a sport facility, attending an event. The ultimate goal is to build brand awareness for the sport facility through a series of integrations (image, functional, coordinated, consumer-based, stakeholder-based, and relationship management) that will lead to the overall strategic promotional implementation.

There are a number of generalizations that can be made about promotions. Promotions temporarily increase sales substantially; promotion in one product category affects sales of brands in complementary and competitive categories; and promotions can result in increased traffic to the sport facility. Most of the generalizations are true, however it is important to understand how to utilize these elements in order to ensure that the results are longer lasting, and lead to maintaining current customers and attracting new customers to the sport facility.

Advertising

Advertising is the process of attracting public attention to a sport product or sport business through paid announcements in the print, broadcast, or electronic media. As a primary element of the sport promotions mix, it is the communication process utilized most often in sport marketing for sport facilities. Through advertisements, advertising campaigns, and integrated brand promotion, advertising helps establish and maintain relationships with the sport consumer by providing a conduit for listening and reacting to the sport consumer through their attendance at an event hosted by a sport facility.

Advertising in sport facilities is an integral tool of marketing as related to brand development and management, segmentation, differentiation, and positioning. As a result, advertising efforts need to be in congruence with the sport facility's brand strategy and the branding process. The brand strategy has a direct impact on the sport facility's value in terms of market capitalization and corporate value. The branding process provides the sport consumer with a clear understanding of the attributes and values of the sport facility. Sport facility advertising efforts will be unique to each facility and on the events and services being offered, however, the ultimate goal is to utilize the advertising efforts to enhance sport facility loyalty through brand association, and build image through the association with the brands being advertised.

The sport facility manager is involved with the marketing, sales, and implementation of advertising in a sport facility. The goal of sport facility advertising is to maximize the visibility of the brand's image and build brand association and loyalty with customers to the sport facility – while enhancing the image and awareness of the sport facility. Sport facility managers are involved with developing the partnerships since they are the individual that will ultimately be involved with implementing and managing the advertisement efforts within the sport facility. The majority of this implementation usually involves signage in the sport facility. The most common types of signage include banners, infrastructure (embedded onto the framework), field/court surfaces, and scoreboard/computerized. However, in recent years, sport facility managers have become very creative with the inventories available for advertising signage. These include step signage, wall wraps, turnstiles, garbage cans, bathrooms, and in-game equipment (such as silhouetted advertisements on nets above the glass in ice hockey arenas or field goal nets behind football uprights).

Sponsorship

Sport sponsorship involves acquiring the rights to be affiliated with a sport product or business in order to obtain benefits from that association. Sport sponsorships play a significant role in the sport promotional mix, and take place at multiple levels of the sport business landscape. Especially in the United States, the most lucrative sponsorship agreements are naming rights with sport facilities. As such, sport facility managers are involved with the management of these sponsorships to ensure that these terms of the sponsorship are being upheld in terms of exclusivity, signage within the sport facility, implementation of promotional activities, and accuracy in the delivery of the corporate image and likeness.

Sport sponsorship agreements between corporations and sport facilities are documented within a sponsorship proposal. These packages are designed to articulate the benefits derived from the agreement for all parties involved. The reason for entering into a sport sponsorship agreement varies from organization to organization. Corporations have numerous goals as a result of sport sponsorship, including increasing public awareness, enhancing their company image, building business and trade relationships with other sponsoring organizations, changing or improving public perception of their company, increasing community involvement in the target area, and enhancing personnel relations by offering opportunities for employees to attend sponsored events, including attendance at hospitality areas. The goals of a sport facility as a result of sponsorship include taking in additional revenue from the agreement, and increasing target market awareness, image, sales, and market share.

Sport facility sponsorships are naming rights agreements for stadiums, arenas, and other sport facilities. Since 2000, this is the fastest growing area of sport sponsorship, as many sport facilities around the world have sold their naming rights to sport corporations. These deals are usually long term and significant in value. Also, the value of the sponsorship will vary with the size of the market, the level of competition playing, and the assortment of events scheduled by the facility. In Table 12.1 there are some examples of major sport facility naming rights deals that are currently in place around the world. You will note that the deals in the United States are significantly longer in term and have a higher cost per year than other parts of the world.

262

Table 12.1 Global sport facility naming right deals

Location	Name of facility	Location	Terms (in millions)
United States (in USD)	Citi Field	New York	$400m for 20 yrs.
	MetLife Stadium	East Rutherford, NJ	$400m for 25 yrs.
	Reliant Stadium	Houston, TX	$310m for 31 yrs.
	Levi's Stadium	San Francisco, CA	$220m for 20 yrs.
	American Airlines Center	Dallas, TX	$195m for 30 yrs.
	Mercedes Benz Superdome	New Orleans, LA	$100m for 10 yrs.
Canada (in CND)	Rogers Arena	Vancouver, BC	$70m for 10 yrs.
	Bell Centre	Montreal, QC	$64m for 20 yrs.
	Air Canada Centre	Toronto, ON	$40m for 20 yrs.
	BMO Field	Toronto, ON	$23.7m for 10 yrs.
	Scotiabank Saddledome	Calgary, AB	$20m for 20 yrs.
Europe (local currency)	Etihad Stadium	Manchester, England	£100m for 10 yrs.
	Allianz Arena	Munich, Germany	€60m for 15 yrs.
	Aviva Stadium	Dublin, Ireland	€50m for 10 yrs.
Asia (local currency)	Nissan Stadium	Yokohama, Japan	¥470m for 5 yrs.
	Mercedes-Benz Arena	Shanghai, China	CNY397m for 10 yrs.
Africa (local currency)	Bidvest Stadium	South Africa	ZAR450m for 5 yrs.
Australia (in AUD)	ANZ Stadium	Sydney, NSW	AU$31m for 7 yrs.
	Suncorp Stadium	Brisbane, QLD	AU$6.6m for 5 yrs.
	Etihad Stadium	Melbourne, VIC	AU$5m for 5 yrs.
South America (local currency)	Allianz Parque	Sao Paulo, Brazil	BRL$300m for 20 yrs.

Enhancement of other promotional mix elements

Sport facility managers also are involved in enhancing other aspects of the promotional mix – especially public relations and atmospherics. Public relations is the collection of activities, communications, and media coverage that convey what the sport organization is and what they have to offer, all in the effort to enhance their image and prestige. Through public relations, the sport facility director focuses on getting information out to the public through various methods to enhance the image and awareness of the sport facility and the events to be hosted. In order to get the best value, sport facility managers focus on the use of unpaid, non-personal promotion of the facility through a third party (usually the media) that publishes print media or presents information through radio, television, or the Internet. The goal of any good publicity is that it is viewed as coming from an unbiased, neutral source. A sport facility manager understands that utilizing public relations is critical to success, as it is the management function that helps to evaluate public attitudes, articulate policies and procedures of an organization that may be of public interest, and execute programs of action to acquire public understanding and approval.

The most important relationship is with the media. Media relations are the activities that involve working directly with individuals responsible for the production of mass media including news, features, public service announcements, and sponsored programming. Effective media relations maximize coverage and placement of messages and information in the mass media without paying for it directly through advertising. Most media relations activities are designed to get free media coverage for programs and issues. As such, the sport facility manager engages in a number of efforts to give the media more access than the general customer. This includes a press box/press row exclusively for the media; credentials for sideline/on-field access/locker room, and behind-the-scenes access; areas for holding exclusive and group press conferences/interviews; and access to communications (phones/faxes/Internet technology) to file stories efficiently. Since the media will also be at the events in the sport facility for longer than the general public, the sport facility manager works with catering to ensure that food and beverage services are provided either in the press box or in a press-only dining area. The goal of providing a significant amount of access and service to the media is for the purpose of getting free media coverage that shows the sport facility in a positive light among the significant competition that is vying for limited amount of air time or print space.

Another aspect of promotions which is under the major control of the sport facility director is atmospherics. Atmospherics utilizes the design of visual communications in an environment to entice the sport consumer's perceptual and emotional responses to purchase the sport product or service. As a result of the operational function, the sport facility manager is able to control the environment based on the needs and wants of the consumer. Examples include:

- Temperature: control the HVAC systems, or in the case of a retractable roof facility – opening and closing the roof.
- Lighting: control the type of bulbs, the angle of lighting, and the control of natural lighting.
- Sound: ensure the speakers and public address systems are maintained to allow for maximum clarity.
- Color: since the sport facility manager is in charge of the in-house maintenance staff, the sport facility areas can be painted in colors that create an aesthetically pleasing appearance.
- Traffic flow: by alleviating the clutter throughout the sport facility – especially in concourses and entryways – the movement/ingress/egress of guests will be more efficient.

CHAPTER REVIEW

Sport facility managers need to have a solid foundation in marketing and should be involved in all aspects of marketing that relate to the sport facility. The association of sport marketing and sport facilities interact to best provide products and services that satisfy the needs, wants, and desires of the consumer; and aid in the planning, organizing, directing, controlling, budgeting, leading, and evaluation of a facility whose primary product and service is related to sport, recreation, leisure, and entertainment.

The focal point of these marketing functions is in four specific areas known as the 4 Cs of marketing analysis: the consumer, the company itself, the competition, and the climate. Sport marketers reach sport consumers through segmenting the population, targeting specific groups, positioning the sport facility to influence potential customers to attend an event at the sport facility, and then deliver on what is promised. With regard to the company and competition, the framework is centered on the SWOT analysis – internal strengths and weakness of the company, and external opportunities and threats posed by competition and the environment. The climate involves forecasting the factors that will have a direct effect on the internal and external functioning of the sport facility.

The sport consumer can be broken down into numerous categories. From a simple breakdown – it is participants and spectators. In reality, there are multiple levels of spectators, including sport fanatics, club/team loyalists, social viewers, opportunistic viewers, star-struck spectators, and sport indifferent consumers. In order to understand these various consumers, sport facility managers must be able to effectively and efficiently incorporate a marketing information system into their marketing efforts. The purpose of a marketing information system is to collect the various data available in one place for use in making sport marketing decisions through an intricate structure involving the interacting of people, infrastructure, and techniques to gather, sort, analyze, evaluate, and distribute relevant, well-timed, accurate information for use by sport facility directors so they can develop, implement, and manage marketing plans. The marketing information system is made up of four elements – the marketing research system, the internal reports system, the marketing intelligence system, and the marketing decision support system. In addition, the sport facility manager must also comprehend and apply the principles of consumer behavior – the conduct that consumers display in seeking out, ordering, buying, using, and assessing products and services that the consumers expect will satisfy their needs and wants. The various factors of consumer behavior that a sport facility manager must understand include internal factors (personality, learning processes, motivation, attitude, and perceptions) and external factors (culture, subculture, international/global interaction, social class, and social setting).

The sport facility manager must also understand the major logistical functions in sport marketing that affect how they position their sport facility, and deliver the sport product through the sport facility. The major logistical functions a sport facility manager must understand in terms of sport marketing are product and service management, and sales management. Product and service management includes the products and services they have total control of (internal), and products and services they have limited control over (external). Internal products include the facility itself – the playing surface and related equipment, seating, scoreboard/message boards, bathrooms, concession areas, and the general infrastructure. Internal services include maintenance, housekeeping, security, customer service, and first aid. External products include all aspects of the event taking place in the facility. External services are the added benefits provided by the event and other external entities to enhance the experience of the customer. The sales management function is the backbone of sport facilities, because without customers the facility would have no purpose for existence. Sport facility managers are involved with the sales process on numerous inventories including leasing/rental of the sport facility for events; ticketing and box office management; premium access (suites, club seating, public seating licenses/debentures); product branding through pouring rights, and various promotional sales efforts including advertising (signage and promotions) and sponsorships (naming rights and endorsements).

Hand in hand with logistics are the promotional aspects involved with marketing sport facilities. Promotions are a very involved communications process that aids in providing information about the sport facility to consumers through the promotional mix. The elements of the sport promotional mix that sport facility managers work with include advertising, sponsorship, public relations, and atmospherics. Advertising in sport facilities is an integral tool of marketing as related to brand development and management, segmentation, differentiation, and positioning. As a result, advertising efforts needs to be in congruence with the sport facility's brand strategy and the branding process. Sport facility managers are involved with the management of sponsorships to ensure that these terms of the sponsorship are being upheld in terms of exclusivity, signage within the sport facility, implementation of promotional activities, and accuracy in the delivery of the corporate image and likeness. Through public relations, the sport facility director focuses on getting information out to the public through various methods to enhance the image and awareness of the sport facility and the events to be hosted. The most important relationship is with the media, and therefore the sport facility manager engages in a number of efforts to give the media more access than the general customer – including press box/press row exclusively for the media; credentials for sideline/on field access/locker room, and behind-the-scenes access; areas for holding exclusive and group press conferences/interviews; and access to communications (phones/faxes/Internet technology) to file stories efficiently. As far as atmospherics, the sport facility manager is able to control the environment based on the needs and wants of the consumer – including temperature, lighting, sound, color, and traffic flow.

Ancillary issues in management and operations

BIBLIOGRAPHY

Bhattacharjee, S. and Rao, G. (2006). Tackling ambush marketing: The need for regulation and analysing the present legislative and contractual efforts. *Sport in Society, 9*(1), 128–149.

Chadwick, S. (2005). Sport marketing: A discipline for the mainstream. *International Journal of Sports Marketing and Sponsorship, 7*(1), 7.

Coderre, F., St-Laurent, N., and Mathieu, A. (2004). Comparison of the quality of qualitative data obtained through telephone, postal and email surveys. *International Journal of Market Research, 46*(3), 347–357.

Funk, D. C. and James, J. D. (2004a). Exploring origins of involvement: Understanding the relationship between consumer motives and involvement with professional sport teams. *Leisure Sciences, 26*(1), 35–61.

Funk, D. C. and James, J. D. (2004b). The fan attitude network (FAN) model: Exploring attitude formation and change among sport consumers. *Sport Management Review, 7*(1), 1–26.

Hassanien, A. and Dale, C. (2012). Drivers and barriers of new product development and innovation in event venues. A multiple case study. *Journal of Facilities Management, 10*(1), 75–92.

Henry, P. C. (2005). Social class, market situation and consumers' metaphors of (dis) empowerment. *Journal of Consumer Research, 31*(4), 766–778.

Hess, R. L., Rubin, R. S., and West Jr., L. A. (2004). Geographic information systems as a marketing information system technology. *Decision Support Systems, 38*(2), 197–212.

Hock, C., Ringle, C. M., and Sarstedt, M. (2010). Management of multi-purpose stadiums: Importance and performance measurements of service interfaces. *International Journal of Services Technology and Management, 14*(2/3), 188–207.

Hopwood, M. K. (2005). Applying the public relations function to the business of sport. *International Journal of Sports Marketing and Sponsorship, 6*(3), 174–188.

James, J. D. and Ross, S. D. (2004). Comparing sport consumer motivations across multiple sports. *Sport Marketing Quarterly, 13*(1), 17–25.

Kwok, S. and Uncles, M. (2005). Sales promotion effectiveness: The impact of consumer differences at an ethnic-group level. *Journal of Product and Brand Management, 14*(3), 170–186.

Lilien, G. L., Rangaswamy, A., Van Bruggen, G. H., and Starke, K. (2004). DSS effectiveness in marketing resource allocation decisions: Reality vs. perception. *Information Systems Research, 15*(3), 216–235.

Marber, A., Wellen, P., and Posluszny, S. (2005). The merging of marketing and sports: A case study. *Marketing Management Journal, 15*(1), 162–171.

Schwarz, E. C., Hunter, J. D., and LaFleur, A. (2013). *Advanced theory and practice in sport marketing* (2nd ed.). London: Routledge.

Smolianov, P. and Shilbury, D. (2005). Examining integrated advertising and sponsorship in corporate marketing through televised sport. *Sport Marketing Quarterly, 14*(4), 239–250.

Trail, G. T., Anderson, D. F., and Fink, J. S. (2005). Consumer satisfaction and identity theory: A model of sport spectator conative loyalty. *Sport Marketing Quarterly, 14*(2), 98–111.

Wang, J. (2013). Research on market development and management mode of stadiums of colleges and universities in Hunan Province. *Journal of Applied Sciences, 13*(21), 4744–4748.

Yoon, S-J. and Choi, Y-G. (2005). Determinant of successful sports advertisements: The effects of advertisement type, product type and sports model. *Journal of Brand Management, 12*(3), 191–205.

Yoshida, M. and James, J. D. (2010). Customer satisfaction with game and service experiences: Antecedents and consequences. *Journal of Sport Management, 24*(3), 338–361.

IN THE FIELD ...

Interview with Daniel E. Ballou, PhD, Director of Sports Sales and Marketing, Albuquerque Convention & Visitors Bureau

Please explain to the reader about your current position and what your responsibilities are.

As the Director of Sports Sales and Marketing for the Albuquerque Convention and Visitors Bureau, my role is to present Albuquerque to sport planners and National Governing Bodies, and sell them on bringing an event here. The 'presentation' process starts typically with a prospecting call, followed up by identification of an event that may work well in the city, collecting the planner's Request for Proposal (RFP), completing that RFP in a professional manner, and then follow up calls or meetings to discuss or clarify information or points of contention. Often times these conversations are related to the venue, and how the operation of that event is expected to function. This is a consideration for both the planner of the event and the Local Organizing Committee (LOC) as well.

Albuquerque has hosted many top-tier sport events including many rounds of the NCAA Men's and Women's Division I Basketball Tournament, the NCAA Men's and Women's Division I Indoor Track & Field Championships, the USA Track & Field Indoor National Championships, the Gildan New Mexico Bowl, and many others that bring national/international media and attention to the city, as well as the consumption of hotel room nights. Ultimately my job lies in bringing out-of-town sport competitors, family members, and fans to Albuquerque to spend nights in our hotels, rent our cars, eat at our restaurants, and visit our attractions. This is done to drive economic benefit in the form of new, direct spending dollars.

Tell us a little about your track from your university years to get to the position you are in now.

My career goals were always to work in the athletics industry and I have been fortunate enough to have done so. I spent seven years working in collegiate athletics at Kansas State University prior to my current position. While employed in this job I earned my doctorate in Sport Administration at the University of New Mexico and the next step on my career path is to teach in a Sport Administration Department at the university level.

What advice would you give to someone wanting to get into the field of sport facility operations management?

The advice I recommend to aspiring sport event managers, or athletics industry professionals as a whole, is to volunteer for events wherever, and whenever you can. Students on campus have a built-in advantage because you can get involved with the athletic teams at your school. I would not limit yourselves to just football and men's basketball either. You can gain a tremendous amount of hands-on experience by working the non-revenue generating sports because you get exposed to so many different varieties of functions that must occur prior to hosting a sport event.

Those students in a city with professional sports, or other sports outside your college teams, should also volunteer and seek internships whenever possible, whether paid or not. The competition for jobs in athletics is getting tougher each and every day and separating yourself with a do-anything attitude will go a long way in setting up the first step in your professional journey.

TECHNOLOGY NOW!

Within the realm of marketing for sport facilities, one of the most important departments is sales. The sales function for a sport facility may range from selling tickets to events through the box office to selling advertisement and sponsorship within the facility. As the new millennial generation enters the workplace, the challenge of training them in the areas of sales and service is often a challenge. One of the reasons for this challenge is in the way the new millennial employee prefers to learn new skills.

According to the Sales Huddle Group, 'By 2020, 50% of millennials will have logged over 10,000 hours on some type of gaming platform before the age of 21'. In addition, 'currently 91% of college graduates say they are unprepared entering the workforce, and 72% of companies do little or no training, resulting in 42% of college graduates being either unemployed or underemployed'. The combination of these concepts has helped sport industry professionals to realize that today's generation may actually not lack the skills necessary to succeed in the workforce, but rather lacks the experiences needed to develop the skills and habits that are critical to succeeding at their job. Since this new generation has grown up with the Internet and gaming platforms, why not use gaming mechanics that place employees in situations that enhance the likelihood of developing the necessary skills for the workforce?

The Sales Huddle Group has developed multiple platforms that can be used by sport facility operations managers to help prepare this new generation to succeed in sales and marketing, as well as facility and event service management. The Training Game is an innovative simulation platform customized to a specific sport facility or organization using existing sales, service, and training processes, and 'gamifies' them to not only meet the needs of this new generation of employees, but provide an opportunity for repeated, 24/7, in real-time, personalized training in perpetuity both in theoretical content and real-world role playing scenarios.

The Sales Game version of the game focuses on skills needed in the area of revenue generation, while the Service game focuses on the non-revenue generating team members whose job is to ensure that the experiences of the guests/customers are positive. Each game provided the opportunity to custom build scenarios, personalize the design and branding of the sport facility, and individualize the training process to ensure optimal implementation of the game. It is a functional tool that can be used in multiple environments because of its online capabilities. There are multiple styles of play from individualized training to team exercises, which allows the sport facility manager to create multiple training scenarios. The tools can also be used in a range of time formats from short refresher training to longer retreat or formal training sessions. Through the gaming platform, the training becomes fun, engaging, competitive, and provides opportunities to use real analytics to create rewards systems and incentive programs for employees. Ultimately, the goal of the tool is create a culture of 'winning', resulting in a higher level of success when applying these skills in real-world situations on the job.

Source: Sales Huddle Group (2014). Retrieved November 12, 2014 from www. saleshuddlegroup.com

CHAPTER 13

EVENT PLANNING IN FACILITY MANAGEMENT

CHAPTER OBJECTIVES

Without events, there would be no purpose for a sport facility. Events can range from free open recreation time to a full-scale hallmark event such as the Olympic Games or the FIFA World Cup. The purpose of this chapter is to explore the relationship between sport facility operations management and event planning. This chapter is not intended to provide an in-depth analysis or explanation of event management; it is intended to articulate the role sport facility operations management plays in supporting event management. This first important factor to understanding is the entire sport facility event planning process, as well as the various event relationships that a sport facility manager may engage with. This will lead to examining the sport facility's role in pre-event, during-event, and

> post-event operations including the activation of a sport facility event marketing plan, event implementation, level of involvement in managing events, preparation for the unexpected, and evaluation after the event has taken place.

SPORT FACILITY EVENT PLANNING PROCESS

The sport facility event planning process involves the development of the event from conceptualization through activation to implementation and eventual evaluation by event managers. However, a part of the process that is often not described is that sport facility management and ownership go through a similar process in preparation for events coming to the sport facility. Hence the sport facility event planning process will mirror the sport event planning process, but with some intricate differences. This first section of the chapter will discuss the planning process from setting objectives and developing conceptualizations to contract signing and moving forward towards implementation of the event.

The first step in the event planning process is setting objectives. All sport facility managers and owners need to make some decision as to what type of events they want their facility to host. Often, these decisions go back to the philosophy, mission, and vision (PMV) of the sport facility. For instance, if this is a community-based recreation facility, the types of events to be hosted would need to be focused on community building and the needs of that local municipality. In contrast, a large, commercial-focused stadium or arena is seeking to maximize revenues through high attendance rates at high profile events. However, there will always be questions at this stage, especially for commercially focused sport facilities – but not immune to community-based sport facilities – about events that may be beneficial socially or financially, but are contrary to the mission of the sport facility. These may include events that may be politically (ranging from a local politician speaking engagement to a political convention), culturally (religious ceremonies), or socially (events such as an arts and crafts show) motivated, and may cause questions in the community. In addition, certain sporting events, depending on the jurisdiction, may not be considered appropriate – the most common sport this occurs with today is mixed martial arts (MMA). In general, when setting objectives for determining what events will be held in a sport facility, there will be a general list of accepted events, but there also needs to be flexibility to consider other options that may be financially and socially viable. Some of the questions that should be answered to set these objectives include:

- What does the sport facility management ownership want to achieve by hosting the event?
- Who are your target audiences and participants?

272

- Is there an understanding of the history of the potential event?
- Does the event have a track record of success or failure?
- Does the sport facility have access to partnerships that can aid in the success of the event?
- Is there support from key stakeholders and partners for hosting the event in the sport facility?

After objectives are understood, the sport facility management needs to develop concepts of how it views these potential events in their facility. In conjunction with all pertinent personnel from the facility, the ownership and management will lay out what the general framework of these various events would look like. This includes the functions of ingress/egress, seating, timing, scale, facilities and equipment needed, marketing plans, set-up, during-event responsibilities, breakdown, and evaluation processes. As a part of this process, the sport facility will develop a series of strategies for success for the event. These strategies should be: (1) realistic; (2) result in having a positive influence on the sport facility, the event, and the community; (3) able to be accomplished within the available infrastructure; (4) and able to be realized within the available budget. In conjunction to effectively creating these strategies, three main questions need to be answered:

- What is the importance of the event to the sport facility and the community?
- What are the benefits of hosting the event to the sport facility and the community?
- Who are the parties within the sport facility (and potentially the community) that should have input into creating the strategies?

Once these functions are analyzed, the sport facility ownership and management must determine whether it is feasible to host each type of event being analyzed. Feasibility is determined by first conducting a situation analysis (SWOT) to see what strengths the sport facility brings to the table for this type of event, where the weaknesses that can prevent success are, and what opportunities and threats this event brings to the sport facility. In addition, a competitor analysis will be conducted for two reasons: (1) if there is a bid process for a larger event, to try to gain information that will aid in the success of the securing of the bid; and more importantly (2) to see if those competitors have run similar events, and try to acquire information that will help in managing that type of event.

When all of this research and analysis is completed, the information is evaluated and a determination needs to be made whether to proceed with this type of event being hosted in the sport facility. If the evaluation is no, then either reconceptualization of the event needs to take place to determine whether through modification the event would be appropriate for the sport facility, or the event is deemed not appropriate – and negotiation for those types of events will not be conducted. If it is determined that the event would be a good fit for the sport facility, it is time to seek out those events (just as events are seeking out facilities) and get the parties together to negotiate contracts.

Prior to negotiating contracts, the sport facility managers and owners will develop a pro forma budget to anticipate what the general costs of hosting an event will be for the sport facility. This budget will become more detailed once contracts are negotiated and signed, but this advanced budget creates a general financial framework place for the specific type of events and a starting place for negotiations. If similar events have been held at the sport facility in the past, those final budgets can be used to support the developing budget for the new event. It is also important that the developers of the budget keep in mind political, economic, and infrastructural issues that may skew or change costs. In general, when creating the budget, the following questions should be considered:

- Do you have information from previous event budgets that can help create the current event budget?
- Have all pertinent costs been included in the budget?
- Have all internal and external factors related to the sport facility been taken into account in the budget?
- Have errors and omissions been built into the budget for unforeseen expenses, unexpected costs, or miscalculation of budget number that causes going over budget?
- Who from the sport facility is ultimately in charge of managing the budget and controlling cash flow?
- Who will be the secondary level of budget management in charge of auditing and monitoring the budget?

When the parties responsible for negotiating on behalf of the sport facility and the event get together, there are two end goals: (1) signing a contract agreeing to the use of the sport facility to host the event; and (2) discussion about the implementation of pre-event processes. Usually representing the sport facility are the facility manager and their designee (depending on the scope of the facility and/or the event), as they are usually the persons responsible for scheduling and booking the sport facility, and have been actively involved with marketing the venue to event managers and promoters. From the event side, usually a promoter will negotiate on behalf of an event, however again depending on the scope of the event, the actual event manager or owner may be involved. The biggest challenge in this process is that the event (ranging from team owners to concert promoters to hallmark event managers) is only concerned about the event itself and maximizing profits through the event, whereas the sport facility is mostly concerned about how the event is presented and produced, as the appearance is a reflection on the sport facility in the community. These clashing philosophies often lead to some contentious discussions, and hence it is strongly recommended that all discussions and agreements are documented and clearly stated in all contracts. This includes the implementation of pre-event planning, such as determining:

274

- Who is responsible for marketing what aspects of the event where?
- What event staff is going to be provided through the sport facility, and what staff will the event be providing?
- How long before the event can ingress for set-up begin?
- How long before the event must set-up be completed so proper authorizations (as needed) can be given by the facility manager, police department, fire marshal, etc.
- What time will doors open?
- Who is responsible for what from the time doors open through the event and until doors close?
- How long does the event have to break down and egress from the sport facility?
- How will any financial issues be settled at the end of the event?

The list above is only an example of the numerous questions that should be answered during the pre-event planning process. This time of negotiating contracts and responsibilities not only serves to set parameters for the event's use of the sport facility, it provides an opportunity for the sport facility manager (and in some cases the ownership) to understand the relationships that are being forged. The most significant of these relationships is between the sport facility manager (and the appropriate staff) and the event manager (and their designated staff) as discussed above. However, depending on the scope of the event, there may be additional relationships forged as a result.

One such relationship is with the media. The scope of the event will gauge the interest from the media – the relationship with media for local, small events will be limited, whereas for larger events media involvement will grow. For instance, a local secondary school football tournament at a municipal facility will certainly have less media coverage than a professional football match at the new Cowboys Stadium or the new London Olympic Stadium, and obviously that media coverage will pale in comparison to the media coverage when the Olympic Stadium in Rio de Janeiro hosts the opening ceremonies of the 2016 Summer Olympics.

CONFLICT BETWEEN FACILITY SPONSORSHIP AND SPONSORED HALLMARK EVENTS

Another relationship is with potential sponsors. Depending on the scope of the event, this relationship could be minimal or on a grand scale. The biggest issue regarding this relationship is ensuring that sport facility sponsors do not clash with event sponsors. When this happens, significant problems can occur.

An example of this can be found in two separate incidents at the Pepsi Center in Denver, Colorado. In 1999, the Colorado Avalanche of the National

Hockey League (NHL) submitted a bid for the 2001 All-Star Weekend in the arena they played in at that time – McNichols Arena. During this same time in Denver, a new arena was being built to house the Denver Nuggets of the National Basketball Association (NBA) and the Colorado Avalanche (NHL). Naming rights were sold later that year (1999) to PepsiCo for $3.4 million per year for 20 years. The major dilemma came because Coca-Cola is the official non-alcoholic drink sponsor of the NHL. So the NHL All-Star Game, with the NHL's sponsor Coca-Cola in tow, would be held at the Pepsi Center.

At the same time, the Denver Nuggets of the NBA were keeping a close eye on this situation. They were looking for ways to host the 2003 NBA All-Star Game at the Pepsi Center, but the NBA contract with Coca-Cola is even stronger than that of with the NHL. The contract between the NBA and the Sprite brand-name is a 100-year global marketing alliance estimated to be worth well in excess of $1 billion.

How could the clashing naming rights of the facility and the sponsorship of the hallmark event be solved so Denver could reap the rewards of hosting these two All-Star events? Let's take a closer look ...

NHL All-Star Weekend – Coca-Cola wins this battle

During the 1980s and 1990s, in an effort to become the #1 soft drink company in the United States, Coca-Cola and Pepsi engaged in mutually targeted advertisements on all media fronts and marketing campaigns. Now in 2000 and 2001, the fight was over whose name would be allowed to appear in conjunction with the NHL All-Star Weekend: Pepsi as the facility sponsor, or Coca-Cola as the event sponsor. The main issues were: (1) previous partnerships are considered in negotiations, but it is one item to consider among many; and (2) despite venue exclusivity, there are permitted exceptions for certain events, including those deemed as 'jewel events' such as all-star games. After months of negotiations and threatened litigation, it was determined that Coca-Cola would have precedent over Pepsi for this one-time event because the contract was signed for the All-Star event to be played in the old arena, and the move to the new arena and subsequent naming rights by Pepsi did not hold precedence over the Coca-Cola event sponsorship. As a result:

- Coca-Cola forced the Colorado Avalanche and the NHL to erase the formal name of the arena (Pepsi Center) from all all-star tickets.
- The NHL required the broadcaster of the game (ABC) not to refer to the venue as the Pepsi Center. The only approved references for the arena were 'Home of the Colorado Avalanche'; 'Welcome back to Denver'; 'Coming to

you from Denver'; and 'Back in Denver'. In addition, any blimp or other aerial shots had to be from the side of the facility so the title of the arena could not be seen.

- Since Pepsi, as the facility sponsor, had pouring rights, it was still served – but in generic, NHL cups.
- Coca-Cola, still not totally satisfied, withdrew some of its financial support for the event – and the Pepsi Center had to cut the NHL an undisclosed six-figure check to host the all-star game to make up for the deficit created by Coca-Cola's reduction in support.

NBA All-Star Weekend: Pepsi scores a victory

The Denver Nuggets had lobbied for years to host the event, but feared it would not be for at least 100 years because they did not believe the NBA would want to alienate a top sponsor by bringing All-Star Weekend to an arena named after its competitor. Fortunately, the NBA decided in 2003 that the All-Star Game would come to Denver and be played in the Pepsi Center. Coca-Cola was of course not happy about it because the reverse was happening – the Pepsi Center facility sponsorship came before the event contract with the NBA. However, Coca-Cola did put some pressure on the NBA, and insisted that some mutual agreements with Pepsi had to occur. They included:

- All Pepsi signage in the arena could remain visible, but the floor where the game would be played could not say Pepsi Center.
- Sprite (a Coca-Cola product) would be the prominent presenting sponsor of the Slam Dunk competition across all media and branded on scorer's tables, judge's tables and scorecards, and in the staging area for athletes.
- In the hospitality areas, all vending machines would be Coca-Cola products, however if any product was brought out of hospitality in to the arena, either the drinks needed to be poured in cups (for cans), or labels taken off plastic bottles. For those who did not – an usher would approach the patron or media member and ask them to comply.
- During media coverage by TNT (Turner Network Television), the Pepsi Center could only be named once verbally and once via on-screen graphic during the broadcast on All-Star Saturday – the rest of the time, the event was referred to as being in Denver. For the All-Star Game on Sunday, TNT was asked to limit their use of the arena title – according to Front Row Marketing, the Pepsi Center received 12 seconds of on-screen graphics, 5 verbal mentions, and 40 seconds of visible in-arena signage (no blimp or aerial coverage of the front of the arena – only the side).

277

Suggested discussion topics

1   There has always been a contentious relationship between Coca-Cola and Pepsi – but that is not the only industry segment where corporations have had issues with their sponsors. Review the issues with the original United States Olympic Basketball Dream Team in 1992, and explain the issues between Nike and Reebok that led to some athletes covering the Reebok logo with the American flag during the medals ceremony.

2   Explain how the individual player sponsorship and endorsement deals of independent contractor athletes such as professional golfers and tennis players are handled when their sponsor is a direct competitor of an event sponsor (such as a golfer playing in the Honda Classic, but being sponsored by Toyota and wearing Toyota's logo on their shirt).

ACTIVATING THE FACILITY EVENT MARKETING PLAN

Just as an event would engage in marketing, a sport facility also will engage in marketing of events they host. Some of these marketing efforts will be in partnership with events, while others will be independent of each other. Ultimately, it is important to remember that partnered marketing efforts will focus on the event's desire to maximize attendance and profits, and the independent facility marketing will focus on the presentation and production of the event desired by the community, and the appearance of the sport facility as a significantly positive reflection of that community.

The facility event marketing plan is a comprehensive framework for identifying and achieving a sport facility's marketing goals and objectives through the event. A marketing plan is developed by the sport facility managers and personnel for each individual event, and includes the following steps:

- Identify the purpose of the plan in terms of the event, including developing mission and vision statements; creating goals and objectives; and ensuring involvement and communication with all pertinent sport facility personnel.
- Analyze the event in terms of tangible goods, intangible support services, and the event itself.
- Conduct a SWOT analysis to forecast the market climate/environment in terms of the event.
- Position the sport facility in terms of the event to your primary and secondary markets.
- Segment and target the market based on pertinent market research concepts related to the event – i.e. demographics, psychographics, and geographics.

278

- Package the event so it becomes attractive to the consumer. This may include special packages with hospitality opportunities, or advanced on-sales of tickets.
- Work with the event management and the box office to price the event appropriately.
- Promote the sport facility first, and the event as an add-on, through advertising, the media, community relations, word-of-mouth, promotional efforts, public relations, and sponsorship partnerships.
- Set up a plan for effective distribution of tickets or other admissions efforts for the event. This includes coordination with the box office, and working with the box office to meet the needs of secondary and tertiary box offices such as teams, events themselves, and online ticket agencies (Ticketmaster, StubHub).
- Once marketing efforts have started, and throughout the process of marketing the sport facility and the event, conduct constant evaluation and collect feedback to maximize marketing efforts.

There are two main issues to remember here. It is important to make sure that although some marketing efforts by sport facilities and sport events may be conducted independent of each other, both parties must be aware of what the other is doing to avoid conflicting information being publicized. Second, if there is conflicting information being publicized, the two parties must get together and ensure that the problem is rectified immediately. Ultimately, both parties want a full facility for the event, and confusion among customers will only lead to problems – and in most cases the sport facility personnel will be the individuals to deal with the problem as they are the local entity the customer will expect to get answers from, and the sport facility wants to ensure their image is not tarnished in the mind of the community.

EVENT IMPLEMENTATION AND ACTIVATION FROM THE FACILITY VIEWPOINT

Event implementation planning from the sport facility viewpoint starts the day a contract is signed with an event. From that point, management will determine the scope of the work necessary to have the event staged in the sport facility; tasks that need to be completed will be analyzed and itemized; schedules and timelines will be established; and personnel given responsibilities to complete. The scope of the work to be completed will vary based on the size of the event, the contract stipulations, and the amount of work that can be conducted prior to the day of the event.

The busiest time for a sport facility is the 24-hour period that encompasses the ingress, set-up, implementation, activation, breakdown, and egress of the event. This usually includes the 12–16 hours or so before the doors open, the entire duration of the event, and usually the four hours after the doors close. During this time, the level of involvement of sport facility personnel with the event significantly increases. There are also special relationships that need to be addressed, including those with unions and outsourced vendors. In addition, throughout this process, there is a constant need to prepare for unexpected situations that may cause chaos during the event.

Level of involvement of facility personnel in managing events

Again, the level of involvement in the activation will be strictly stipulated in the contract between the sport facility and the event. The sport facility manager will often have a checklist of responsibilities that need to be accomplished prior to opening the doors. These checklists usually encompass three parts: (1) work break-down structures, which are itemized by task, personnel, and operational area; (2) an inventory of assignments sequenced in a priority listing to ensure which tasks are accomplished first, and how long it should take to complete the tasks; and (3) an event life cycle, or schedule/timeline of events scripted to the minute. Probably the biggest challenge for the sport facility manager is when there are two events that are back-to-back, and an even greater challenge when there are multiple events in a single day. This means that while one event is breaking down, another is trying to set up. Keeping this phase of event activation organized is crucial to success.

Working with unions

However, in many sport facilities, these processes of set-up and breakdown are not totally controlled by the management of the sport facility. Many sport facility managers and event promoters have the additional challenge of coordinating operations within a unionized facility. As such, many of the functions that need to be accomplished as related to daily operations, event set-up, event activation and implementation, and event breakdown are controlled by the union guidelines. This may include number of hours a person can work and required breaks, minimum number of union employees for certain tasks, weight limitations on lifting and moving, specialists required for certain tasks (examples include forklift drivers, electricians, plumbing, construction, and sound/lighting), and overtime stipulations.

Working with outsourced service vendors and facility services

In addition, as most events come in from the outside, the management of the sport facility also has a responsibility to act as a liaison between the event and ancillary services. These ancillary services may be managed in-house to the sport facility, or may be outsourced to vendors. One of the biggest challenges for a sport facility manager is maintaining the quality expected of the sport facility, and dealing with the multitude of expectations of an event. Coordination of event needs has to be communicated to various constituencies including concessionaires (especially food service and catering), parking, security, and housekeeping/custodial. In some cases, the sport facility will provide these services for a fee within the event contract. The bigger challenge is when the event has its own ancillary services (such as their own concessionaires and security personnel). The need to communicate and coordinate with the sport facility services to ensure everyone is on the same page and understands the parameters of their responsibilities is vital to the success of both the event and the proper management of the sport facility.

Preparing for the unexpected

As with any event within a sport facility, problems are bound to occur. The sport facility manager's reaction to these unexpected issues is crucial to event success, and to keeping the reputation of the sport facility at its highest level. There will be some issues that are beyond the control of the facility manager such as acts of God and power outages. Others are fully within the grasp of the sport facility manager and their personnel to deal with. The best piece of advice to provide here is twofold. First, always remember Murphy's Law, which states that 'anything that can go wrong will go wrong with little advanced notice'. Sport facility managers and personnel that can, on a moment's notice, dissect a problem and solve it without customers knowing anything happened are high-quality sport facility personnel. The second item to always remember is the six Ps of facility and event management: 'prior proper planning prevents poor performance', which is also stated as 'if you fail to plan, then you plan to fail'. Therefore, if you engage in quality and complete planning as far in advance as possible, the likelihood of a problem or poor performance is reduced exponentially.

EVALUATION OF EVENTS BY FACILITY OWNERSHIP AND MANAGEMENT

Once you have supported an event and the event has left the building, it is time to sit back and reflect on the successes and failures of the event. This is usually accomplished through an outcomes assessment process. When the sport facility event management plan was put together, there should have been goals and objectives created. Those goals and objectives need to be measureable in order to effectively measure them. This will include measurements of the event as a whole, specific task analyses, and performance evaluations of both the sport facility personnel and of the outside event. These evaluations will result in one of four decisions: (1) have the type of event at the sport facility again in the future with no modifications (which 99.9 percent of the time does not happen); (2) have the type of event at the sport facility again with enhancements or modifications; (3) have that type of event again, but significant changes need to occur before the event is repeated; or (4) no longer hosting that type of event in the future.

The National Center for Spectator Sports Safety and Security (NCS[4]), at The University of Southern Mississippi, offers a security planning process designed to promote a standardized methodology for security planning at sporting venues and events throughout the United States. This planning process, known as Sport Event Security Aware (SESA), defines a minimum threshold for security policies, procedures, and operational plans. SESA was designed and developed by NCS[4] personnel (Dr. Walter Cooper, Dr. Stacey Hall, Dr. Lou Marciani, Jim McGee, and Frederick Gardy), funded by grants from Mississippi Homeland Security and the U.S. Department of Homeland Security (DHS), and receives continuous support from sport safety and security subject matter experts, DHS, and NCS[4] National Advisory Board. SESA assessments are available to all professional, collegiate, high school, and event organizations that own or operate sports facilities. The assessment is designed to be a repeated cycle implemented by venue or event managers to enhance preparedness, prevention, response, and recovery efforts.

Key components of the SESA assessment cycle

As shown in Figure 13.1, there are four components that make up the Sport Event Security Aware (SESA) Model. The first component is risk assessment. During this process, a list of recommended self-assessments is provided for use by the individual sport facility to conduct a self-assessment of risks to the venue or event. The goal is to identify gaps in existing security and response plans, identify areas in which targeted investment in security enhancements would reduce risk, and revise plans for a long-term security strategy.

The second component is training. Appropriate training can come from a collection of currently available local, state, and federal catalogues – recommended training courses typically include leadership, supervisory, and line staff training.

Figure 13.1 SESA assessment cycle

Third is exercise planning and performance. Venues or event organizations implementing the SESA process participate in planned and directed discussions as well as table-top exercise. Personnel from organizations that own/operate venues or events supporting those venues during events are expected to participate in this exercise. Exercise scenarios are determined for the venue or event based on the results of risk assessments and venue feedback at prior events with an emphasis on evaluation of plans, procedures, and operational utility.

The final component is recommendations. After assessing plans, procedures, training, exercise outcomes, and event operations, a written report of the assessment is provided to the sport facility. The assessment will provide a determination of whether the individual venue or event implements best practices in the industry for the safety and security of venues or events. It also recommends measures for improving general security, anti-terrorism security, and emergency preparedness.

CHAPTER REVIEW

No matter the size or type, facilities need events – and events need facilities. Sport facilities engage in their own independent sport event planning process as a part of their operations and management. The sport event planning process from the standpoint of the sport facility involves the development of the event from conceptualization through activation to implementation and eventual evaluation as related to the infrastructure and support services offered. This planning process involves setting objectives; developing a conceptualization of how the event will be implemented; creating realistic strategies that can be accomplished within the infrastructure, at a cost that is affordable, and brings a positive image to all constituencies; and finalizing feasibility studies and SWOT analyses. Once accomplished and a decision is made to move forward with an event, the sport facility manager and ownership will enter into negotiations to host an event. This may be accomplished through a series of bid processes or through direct contact with an event promoter. As a part of negotiating contracts, a pro forma budget would be created in advance to anticipate what the general costs of hosting an event will be for the sport facility. Once all terms are agreed upon, contracts are signed and pre-event preparation begins immediately.

A major responsibility of the sport facility manager at this point is ensuring that the event is presented and produced in a professional manner, as the appearance is a reflection on the sport facility in the community, and that the sport facility is not damaged. This is a challenge at times because event promoters are often only concerned about the event itself and maximizing profits. In addition, as a result of the event, the sport facility manager must often also forge additional relationships with the media and sponsors to ensure there are no conflicts.

Some of the responsibilities of the sport facility manager at this point include activating the sport facility's event marketing plan, implementing and activating the event plan (set-up, pre-event, during the event, post-event, and breakdown), determining the level of involvement of sport facility personnel, coordinating tasks with unions and facility services (both in-house and outsourced), and preparing for any unexpected problems that may occur. Once the event has left the sport facility, an evaluation process must take place to determine whether to have the event at the sport facility again in the future with no modifications, have the event at the sport facility again with enhancements or modifications; have the event again, but with significant changes; or choose to no longer host the event in the future.

BIBLIOGRAPHY

Buratto, A. and Grosett, L. (2006). A communication mix for an event planning: a linear quadratic approach. *Journal of Operations Research, 14*(3), 247–259.

Castellano, J., Perea, A., Alday, L., and Hernández-Mendo, A. (2008). The measuring and observation tool in sports. *Behavior Research Methods, 40*(3), 898–905.

Covell, D. and Walker, S. (2013). *Managing sport organizations: Responsibility for performance* (3rd ed.). London: Routledge.

Florek, M. and Insch, A. (2011). When fit matters: Leveraging destination and event image congruence. *Journal of Hospitality Marketing & Management, 20*(3/4), 265–286.

Masterman, G. (2014). *Strategic sports event management* (3rd ed.). London: Routledge.

Pereira, G., Ganser, R., Wood, G., and De Conto, S. (2014). Environmental impact assessment and the planning process of major sports events in Brazil: A case study of the Rio 2007 Pan American Games. *Impact Assessment and Project Appraisal, 32*(1), 55–65.

Schwarz, E. C., Hunter, J. D., and LaFleur, A. (2013). *Advanced theory and practice in sport marketing* (2nd ed.). London: Routledge.

Supovitz, F. and Goldblatt, J. (2005). *The sports event management and marketing playbook.* Hoboken, NJ: Wiley.

Taylor, P. (2010). *Torkildsen's sport and leisure management* (6th ed.). London: Routledge.

UK Sport (2005). *Major sport events – the guide.* London: UK Sport. Retrieved July 16, 2014 from: www.uksport.gov.uk/docLib/Publications/Major-Sports-Events-Guide-2005/major-sports-events-the-guide-april-2005.pdf

Waters, K. (2006–2007). A practical step-by-step guide to organising successful events. *The British Journal of Administrative Management, 56.* 17.

IN THE FIELD …

Leah MacPherson, Hospitality and Sales Coordinator, Western Massachusetts Sports Commission (a division of the Greater Springfield Convention and Visitors Bureau)

Please explain to the reader about your current position and what your responsibilities are.

I am the Hospitality and Sales Coordinator at the Western MA Sports Commission (WMSC), a division of the Greater Springfield Convention and Visitors Bureau. Our job in the sales department at the Commission is to be that one-stop-shop for meeting and event planners who are looking to bring their convention/sports/group meetings to Western Massachusetts. We work to sell our destination as a whole to the planners by working with our convention center, venues, area hotels, and attractions. Along with that, once those are events are booked, it is my job to make sure all the attendees have a memorable experience and get to enjoy the many unique and great attractions that are located here! Through our hospitality program I am able to provide these groups with welcome signage, visitor information, and welcome tables staffed by our knowledgeable Ambassadors, plus much more!

Tell us a little about your track from during your college years to get to the position you are in now.

I attended Saint Leo University where I pursued a double major in Sport Business and International Hospitality & Tourism Management. While in school I made it a point to get involved and immerse myself in as many opportunities I could, that would help build my resume. While in school I worked under the supervision of the department of Sport Business where I learned an immense amount about the industry from my educators. I completed an apprenticeship with the Saint Leo University Athletics Department with a focus on event management and an internship in the sales department at the Embassy Suites Tampa – Airport/Westshore. After walking across the stage at Saint Leo University in April 2013, I moved back to Massachusetts where I am originally from, to complete my final sport business internship at the WMSC. During my internship I learned the ins and outs of this part of the industry, what everyone's role is, and the importance of creating and fostering relationships with people in the industry. Two weeks prior to the completion of my internship, I was given the opportunity to join the Bureau team permanently as the Hospitality and Sales Coordinator.

What advice would you give to someone wanting to get into the field of sport facility operations management on the event planning side with a company like the Sports Commission?

The most important advice I could give to someone who wants to get into the field of sport facility operations management on the event planning side is you have to be extremely organized, have the ability to multitask, and most importantly be willing to stick your hand out, when given the opportunity, to forge relationships with people you could do business with.

TECHNOLOGY NOW!

SportsSignup, an all-in-one sport event management, is one of Inc. 5000 Fastest Growing Private Companies in America in 2014 (#131). It provides an easy-to-use online sport management service for online registrations, fee payment processing, coach and volunteer background checks, tournament/team registrations, database management, communications, online shopping, and website development. The history of SportsSignup started as a family concept to simplify the soccer registration process for a league in upstate New York which has evolved with the acquisition of Canadian sports software company LeagueToolbox to become one of the fastest growing companies of this kind to help manage sport events taking place in facilities of all sizes.

SportsSignup utilizes the latest Customer Relationship Management (CRM) tools and automated systems to securely manage customer information. All of their services are online, database-focused, and fully customizable by the authorized sport operations manager. This provides the opportunity of full control and customization of the event management process.

The integrated sport management services section of the website provides the ability to do registrations, background checks, and website design for leagues and teams – as well as a 'store' to manage fundraising efforts and philanthropic events. The organizational communication tools available include text messaging alerts, email blasts, team chats, and schedule publishing. The software can also provide reporting and analytics, manage financial transactions, and much more.

Source: SportsSignup (2014). Retrieved November 12, 2014 from www.sportssignup.com/

CHAPTER 14

RISK ASSESSMENT IN FACILITY MANAGEMENT

CHAPTER OUTLINE

- Risk management
- Risk assessment
  - Sport venue risk assessment model
    - Step 1.0: Identify sport event security action team (SESAT)
    - Step 2.0: Characterization of assets
    - Step 3.0: Threat assessment
      - Terrorism
      - Hooliganism
      - Crowd disorder
      - Vandalism
      - Personal assault
      - Theft
      - Fraud
      - Logistical failure
      - Inclement weather
    - Step 4.0: Vulnerability assessment
    - Step 5.0: Consequence evaluation
    - Step 6.0: Risk assessment
    - Step 7.0: Consequence reduction proposals
- Risk evaluation, control, and response
  - Risk probability, consequence severity, and financial loss
  - Risk control and response strategies
    - Risk avoidance
    - Risk reduction
    - Risk transfer
    - Risk retention
- Chapter review

287

RISK MANAGEMENT

Risk is the possibility of loss from a hazard such as personal injury, property damage, or economic loss. Risk cannot be eliminated from the environment, but with careful planning it can be managed. Risk is best understood as the product of the consequence (severity) of an event and the probability (frequency) of the event occurring, also represented as:

Risk = Probability x Consequence Severity

Risk increases as the consequences and probability of occurrence increases (see Figure 14.1). When risk probability is low and consequence severity is low, the risk level is depicted in Figure 14.1 as RP1, CS1. As the level of risk probability and level of consequence severity increases, the risk level increases to RP2, CS2. The three main types of risk are mission (function) risks, asset risks, and security risks. Mission risks prevent an organization from accomplishing its mission. Asset risks may harm an organization's physical assets, and security risks have the potential to harm actual data and people.

Quality risk management practices are imperative to reduce legal exposure, prevent financial and human loss, protect sport facility assets, ensure business continuity, and minimize damage to the sport organization's reputation. First and foremost, a sport facility owner or operator must act in a prudent manner. He or she has a duty of care to provide a reasonably safe environment for patrons. In the event of an incident, organizational plans and policies will be reviewed to assess the standard of care provided. Sport facility managers tend to understand the need and value of risk management but fail to do the necessary planning thereby exposing their programs to risk and eventual financial loss. Sport facility managers tend

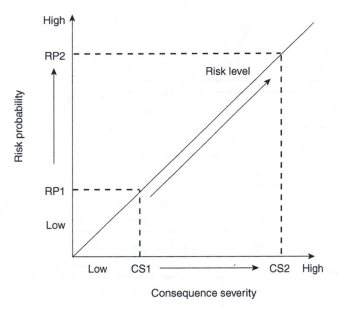

Figure 14.1 Risk probability and consequence severity

to react to events and circumstances rather than taking a proactive approach and implementing effective plans and policies to prevent catastrophic losses. Sport facility managers must develop an effective risk management program to reduce risks and mitigate consequences of incidents.

RISK ASSESSMENT

The United States Department of Homeland Security identified major sport stadiums and arenas as key assets. Key assets are individual targets whose destruction could create local disaster or damage to the nation's morale or confidence. Sport facility managers face a significant challenge in determining potential threats and must prepare for a wide range of possible incidents. In order to identify potential threats, sport facility managers should conduct a risk assessment of their sport facility. Risk assessment is the process of evaluating security-related risks from threats to an organization, its assets, or personnel. The assessment process gathers critical information to aid the sport facility manager in the decision making process.

Sport venue risk assessment model

The NCS[4] developed a sport venue risk assessment model based on US Department of Homeland Security risk assessment principles (see Figure 14.2).

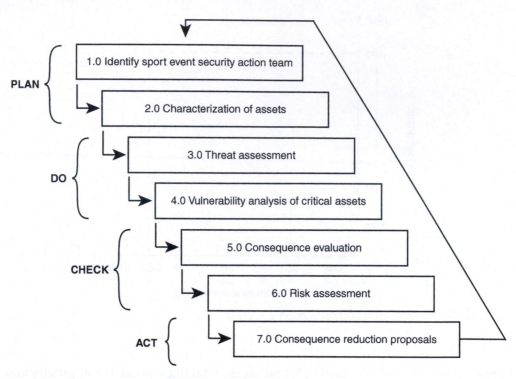

Figure 14.2 Sport event security assessment model (SESAM)

Step 1.0: Identify the sport event security action team (SESAT)

Step 1.0 involves identifying the sport event security action team (SESAT) or 'Working Group'. These individuals are key players in the security operations and planning at facility sport events. The team is responsible for providing information about the sport facility and surrounding area. SESAT members may include: sport facility manager, local police chief, local emergency management director, emergency medical services, fire/HAZMAT, public health, and public relations. A combination of representatives from all agencies ensures multi-discipline cooperation and the ability to gather knowledge and information from different perspectives.

Step 2.0: Characterization of assets

Step 2.0 allows managers to characterize assets. An asset is a person, place, or thing and can be assigned a monetary value. Assets to be assessed include both sport facility assets and surrounding area (community) assets. Assets to be protected may include people (i.e. athletes), physical assets (i.e. stadium), information (i.e. electronic data), and processes (i.e. supply chains and procedures). Table 14.1 provides examples of assets under each category.

Ancillary issues in management and operations

Table 14.1 Sports venue assets

Human assets	Physical assets	Information and processes
Athletes	Facility buildings	Electronic data
Spectators	Stadium and contents	Non-electronic data
Staff	Command post	Supply chains
Contractors	Police department	
Visitors	Fire department	
Community residents	Hospitals	
	Public works	

Step 3.0: Threat assessment

Step 3.0 identifies potential threats. A threat is a product of intention and capability of an adversary to take action which would be detrimental to an asset. Sport facility mangers must decide what their main threats are at an early stage and determine how vulnerable the organization is to an incident. Terrorism is one of the most common cited risks associated with the security of sports venues. Sporting events are at high risk due to the common elements of large crowds, national/international participants, national/international audience, and the known date, time, and location of events.

The most relevant threats to sport facilities that need to be assessed include terrorism, hooliganism, crowd disorder, vandalism, personal assault, theft, fraud, logistical failure, and inclement weather.

Terrorism

The US Federal Bureau of Investigation (FBI) defines terrorism as the unlawful use of force or violence against persons or property to intimidate or coerce a government, the civilian population or any segment thereof, in furtherance of political or social objectives. A sport stadium or arena is considered a high-value terrorist target because of the potentially high casualty rate. There are two primary categories of terrorism: domestic terrorism and international terrorism. Domestic terrorism is the unlawful use, or threatened use, of force or violence by a group or individual based and operating entirely within the home country. International terrorism is the unlawful use of force or violence against persons or property committed by a group or individual who has some connection to a foreign power or whose activities transcend national boundaries (FBI, 2014).

Hooliganism

Hooliganism involves disorderly fans and criminal activity that occurs before and after events. Incidents may be organized (pre-planned) or spontaneous. Spontaneous hooliganism is a low level disorder in or around stadiums and is not as violent. Organized hooliganism is the more serious form of hooliganism where violence is the norm and people get injured or killed. The primary purpose is to fight with rival supporters and police officials, and cause disruption at the event and destroy property. Hooliganism has been known as the 'English disease' because of its origination in Britain, but it is also prevalent elsewhere around the world.

Crowd disorder

Crowd disorder may involve demonstrations or protests inside and outside the venue, or spectator intrusions onto the playing field. Fan celebrations are sometimes over-exuberant, resulting in 'rushing the field'. Crowd congestion has been the cause of many horrific incidents in the sporting world. This problem has primarily been the result of the number of fans exceeding venue capacity. Other reasons may include excess alcohol consumption, inadequate access control, or inadequate design of sport facility structure.

Vandalism

Webster's dictionary defines vandalism as the willful or malicious destruction or defacement of public or private property. Individuals or groups may cause damage to the stadium or arena building or equipment installed at the venue. Acts of vandalism normally occur during non-event days when security is lenient and can range from graffiti to arson.

Personal assault

Sport facility managers must plan for all types of assault, including player and fan violence. Assault cases on and off the playing field have become a major problem in recent years, especially at youth sports events. In many previous cases, parents have assaulted one another or an officiating referee.

Theft

Sport organizations and associations need to plan for financial loss caused by the illegal disappearance of money or inventory. Management, employees, and visitors are all susceptible to theft and/or embezzlement. Many organizations experience 'shrinkage' of inventory that may be attributed to an outsider or staff member. This reinforces the need for employee background checks or similar policies to prevent hiring dishonest staff.

Fraud

Ticket scalping and fraudulent tickets are a problem in the sport industry. Entities selling tickets are sometimes selling above face value which is illegal in some parts of the world. Furthermore, fraudulent tickets infiltrating the ticket market has caused serious problems in the past, especially the sale of these tickets through online Internet sites. An example of this problem transpired at the 2007 Liverpool–Milan UEFA Champions League Final in Athens, Greece. Many fans with valid

292

tickets were locked out of the Athens Olympic stadium for the final match because fans with counterfeit tickets purchased on the black market had successfully gained entry to the venue.

Logistical failure

Sport facility event operations may be disrupted due to logistical failure (i.e. loss of power and/or resources). Plans need to be developed to address unplanned events and ensure continuity of operations through back-up systems or event relocation agreements. Mutual aid agreements with a neighboring facility may provide relief in case the unexpected happens and the sport facility is unable to host an event.

Inclement weather

Natural disasters or inclement weather can cause chaos to sporting organizations and their events. In fall 2005, Hurricane Katrina, known as the worst natural disaster in US history, caused massive devastation to the Gulf South region and New Orleans area. Many professional and collegiate sport programs in the affected areas suffered major destruction and financial loss. Some programs were eliminated or relocated to another part of the US. The New Orleans Saints Football team relocated to Baton Rouge, Louisiana for the 2005 season. The team returned to their home venue in September 2006. It cost an estimated $180 million to renovate the Superdome facility. The sudden onset of storms, tornadoes, or lightning can pose real problems for sport facility operators ranging from mass evacuations of stadiums and arenas to becoming emergency shelters during such conditions.

Table 14.2 provides examples of sport event incidents from around the world. Besides major threats to sport facilities previously discussed, the sport facility manager must also identify specific risks associated with the venue and its activities. These may include employee accidents, breach of contract, negligence, product defects, discrimination, environmental hazards (i.e. slippery surfaces), infrastructure hazards (i.e. design defects), programmatic hazards (i.e. supervision and training), emergency care hazards (i.e. appropriate treatment), and transportation hazards (i.e. properly maintained vehicles).

Step 4.0: Vulnerability assessment

Step 4.0 assesses current vulnerabilities. Vulnerability is defined as an exploitable security weakness or deficiency at a sport facility. Vulnerabilities expose the sport facility to a threat and eventual loss. A vulnerability assessment identifies weaknesses in physical structures, personnel systems, and processes that may be exploited and is a key component of the risk assessment process. Common vulnerabilities at major sport venues include the lack of emergency preparedness, perimeter control, physical protection systems, access control, credentialing, training, and communication capabilities.

Table 14.2 Global sport event incidents

1972: At the Munich Olympic Games a group known as Black September took several Israeli athletes hostage.

1984: Violence erupted outside the Tiger Stadium after the Detroit Tigers defeated the San Diego Padres in the World Series.

1985: European Cup soccer match between English and Italian teams at Heysel Stadium, Brussels, Belgium, where 41 persons died when a crowd barrier collapsed under the weight of people trying to escape from the rioting between rival fans.

1988: Nepalese Hailstorm – a violent hailstorm resulted in 93 fatalities and over 100 casualties during a soccer match at the national stadium in Nepal. Hundreds of spectators attempted to exit the open stands when the storm broke, although the gates were locked and many fans were trampled to death.

1989: San Francisco earthquake during Game 3 of the Major League Baseball (MLB) World Series between San Francisco Giants and Oakland A's at Candlestick park. Stadium remained intact and no fans received serious injuries.

1989: Sheffield, England, Hillsborough Stadium disaster, which killed 95. Crushing took place in a standing area of the stadium. Fans entering the stadium through a vomitory were unaware that the pushing was crushing people at the fence line of the terrace, and officials were slow to detect the crush and relieve the pressure.

1993: Monica Seles stabbing – during the second set of a quarter-final match in Hamburg, Seles was stabbed between the shoulder blades with a 25 cm knife by a fan. Seles was unable to return to playing tennis for 28 months because of the psychological harm.

1993: 12,000 fans rush the field in Madison at college football game between Michigan and Wisconsin at Camp Randall Stadium. Fans were hurt when chain-link and rail fences collapsed under a wave of jubilant Wisconsin fans who pushed toward the field after the game.

1996: At the Atlanta Olympic Games two people died and 110 were injured from a pipe bomb blast at Centennial Olympic Park during an open-air concert.

1996: 100 died in a crowd crush at a tunnel leading to soccer stadium seating in Guatemala City at a World Cup qualifying match. Too many tickets had been sold.

2000: 13 people were trampled to death in a riot at a 2002 FIFA World Cup qualifying match in Zimbabwe between South Africa and Zimbabwe.

2002: An FBI alert warned that Al-Qaeda's Manual of Afghan Jihad proposed US football stadiums as a possible terrorist target. People with links to terrorist groups were downloading stadium images.

2002: A father and son attacked Major League Baseball (MLB) Kansas City Royals first base coach Tom Gamboa at Comiskey Park.

2004: Mayhem broke out at a National Basketball Association (NBA) Indiana-Pacers game when fans and players exchanged punches in the stands.

2004: A street reveler was killed at a Boston Red Sox celebration when she was hit in the eye by a projectile filled with pepper spray.

2005: UEFA Champions League quarterfinal match between AC Milan and Inter Milan was abandoned after Inter fans threw missiles and flares onto the pitch. One of the flares hit the AC Milan goalkeeper.

2005: Hurricane Katrina caused the displacement of many professional and collegiate sports programs in New Orleans and the Gulf Coast region of the United States.

2005: An Oklahoma University student killed himself by prematurely detonating a bomb strapped to his body outside an 84,000 seated stadium.

2006: The National Football League (NFL) received a radiological dirty bomb threat that indicated several stadiums were subject to attack.

2006: A major on-field altercation between Florida International and Miami University collegiate football players led to the suspension of 31 players. It took two dozen police officers to control the situation.

2006: Ten players were ejected following the NBA New York Knicks-Denver Nuggets brawl.

2007: A police officer was killed in Sicily, Italy, when fans rioted at a Serie A soccer match between Catania and Palermo, leading to the suspension of all league matches and a safety assessment on all stadiums.

2007: UEFA Champions League lock-out – many fans with valid tickets were locked out of the Athens Olympic stadium for the final match between Milan and Liverpool. It is alleged that fans with counterfeit tickets purchased on the black market had successfully gained entry to the venue.

2008: At the Summer Olympics in China, Cuban Taekwondo champion Angel Matos kicked a Swedish referee in the head, pushed a judge, and spat on the floor after being disqualified in the Bronze Medal match due to his Kye-shi time-out elapsed.

2009: Philadelphia Phillies fan David Sale (22) was beaten to death outside the Philadelphia Citizens Bank Park after an argument over a spilled beer.

2009: A 60-year-old female spectator at the Tour De France cycling event was killed after being hit by a police motorcycle that accompanied the cyclists.

2010: Near the end of an international cricket match between Australia and Pakistan, a drunken Australian fan ran onto the field and tackled Pakistan's Khalid Latif before being detained by security.

2011: Texas Rangers baseball fan Shannon Stone (39) died after falling from the stands at Arlington Stadium while trying to catch a ball tossed toward him by Rangers outfielder Josh Hamilton.

2011: Bryan Stow was nearly beaten to death in a parking lot after the 2011 opener in Los Angeles between the Dodgers and Giants. He suffered brain damage and is permanently disabled, requiring constant physical therapy.

2012: A soccer match ended in riots and eventual civil unrest in Port Said, Egypt, after Port Said's Al-Masry beat Cairo's Al Ahly 3–1. This incident resulted in 73 deaths.

2013: During the 117th Boston Marathon on April 15, 2013, two pressure cooker bombs exploded near the finish line killing three people and injuring an estimated 264 others.

2014: During a UEFA Euro 2016 qualifying match between Serbia and Albania in Belgrade, Serbia, a small remote controlled drone with Albania's flag suspended from it hovered over the stadium. An Albania player removed the flag which led to a large brawl involving players, staff, and spectators from both teams. The game was suspended at 0–0 in the 41st minute.

Step 5.0: Consequence evaluation

Step 5.0 evaluates potential consequences of an incident. This includes analyzing the potential number of people requiring hospitalization, potential loss of life and infrastructure, economic impact, and level of social trauma. There will be consequences to all types of incidents, for example, a slip and fall accident may result in one personal injury and a single lawsuit. Alternatively, a major crowd crushing incident could cause hundreds of casualties, huge financial loss, and a social stigma to the sport team, league, or governing body. Consequence is also referred to as the 'criticality' impact of loss which differs at each sport facility, the greater the potential for loss or damage to human and physical assets, the higher the impact of loss. Consequence evaluation can be classified as essential (catastrophic loss), critical (serious loss), important (moderate loss), or not important (minor loss). Consequence classifications are discussed later in the chapter.

Step 6.0: Risk assessment

Step 6.0 involves determining the overall risk level for the sport facility. After analyzing the threat, vulnerability, and consequence levels of each potential incident, a total risk level for the sport facility is determined. The level of risk may be categorized as high, moderate, or low. The sport facility manager must decide whether the determined risk level is acceptable or not, and make necessary adjustments to safety and security policies and procedures.

Step 7.0: Consequence reduction proposals

Step 7.0 is the final stage in the process which offers the opportunity to provide consequence reduction proposals (countermeasure improvements). They are provided to management to enhance decision making abilities. Possible security measures to reduce risk may include physical security, good personnel practices, and information security. Sport facility managers should conduct regular reviews of security measures and exercise plans to ensure they remain accurate and workable. Furthermore, all staff should understand the importance of security and assume responsibility to raise concerns and report observations. Other consequence reduction thoughts include: policy review, evacuation routes, traffic rerouting, vendor/usher/volunteer training, stadium lockdown, lighting upgrades, parking restrictions, and emergency lights and signs.

The sport venue risk assessment model is a cyclical model. Assessments must be continuously completed on facilities to ensure adequate plans and security measures are in place and updated over a period of time. A sport facility's threat and vulnerability level may change depending upon circumstances in the country or local community. Evaluations of potential threats and existing vulnerabilities are used to determine what dangers to prepare for, how to address them, and how to prioritize preparedness efforts. Determining which threats are the most dangerous

296

allows managers to decide where they should invest their time and effort in preparedness methods.

CASE STUDY: SPORTSPLEX THREAT ASSESSMENT

The XYZ Sportsplex is a multipurpose outdoor facility, hosting soccer, rugby, and athletic events. The facility management team has decided to conduct a threat assessment in order to identify potential risks and gaps in their security operational system.

The XYZ facility management team appointed a sport event security action team (SESAT), representative of police, fire, emergency medical services, public relations, and public health officials. A pre-planning meeting occurred to inform agencies of the situation and their role in the assessment process. Facility and surrounding assets were characterized, and potential facility threats were discussed.

Stadium location and features:
- Built in 1994
- 60,000 club seats, plus 1000 box seats
- Located in a major metropolitan city
- Access to major public transportation systems
- Residential and business area surrounding facility
- 16 main entrances with turnstiles
- Parking immediately adjacent to facility
- Press box with CCTV capabilities
- Command Post in Press box area
- Concession deliveries scheduled once a week
- Event security is outsourced to local security provider
- Local police, fire, and emergency medical services available on event day.

Assets:
- Stadium infrastructure
- Human asset (i.e. spectators, athletes, officials)
- Equipment storage area
- Residential and business assets
- Public transportation infrastructure
- Local response agencies.

Threats:
- Active political activists in city area
- Biological agent release in facility

- Active shooter incident
- Suicide bomber
- Fan/player violence
- Tornado warning
- Vehicle Borne Improvised Explosive Device (VBIED).

The sport event security action team discussed the following issues:

1 The facility was built in 1994 with little focus on security features.
2 The multipurpose facility hosts soccer, rugby, and athletic events.
3 Fan demographics are different per sport.
4 Previous incidents of fan violence.
5 Screening of spectators entering facility.
6 Alcohol consumption.
7 Evacuation procedures (full, partial, or shelter-in-place) have not been established.
8 Concern over training requirements for security staff and volunteers.
9 Facility break-ins have occurred in the past year resulting in theft of property.
10 Restricted areas of facility are unsecured during event time.
11 There is inadequate facility lighting at entry gates and in parking areas.
12 Credentialing of athletes, officials, and security staff.
13 Control and monitoring of concession deliveries.
14 Facility equipment and maintenance storage is unsecured and stores chemicals that may be used for terrorist purposes.
15 If an incident were to occur, the possible hospital surge of casualties would overwhelm current emergency medical resources in the city.

After further discussion, the team decided to implement the following countermeasure improvements:

1 Conduct a structural assessment of the sport facility and reevaluate/redesign security features within facility.
2 Evaluate threats and risks for each event as they may differ.
3 Utilize security technologies, i.e. text messaging system, to identify trouble-makers.
4 Develop emergency response and evacuation plans.
5 Practice evacuation drills to test operations.
6 Require all staff to complete security training, i.e. terrorism awareness training.

7 Ensure proper and consistent screening procedures.
8 Schedule concession deliveries when security officials are present.
9 Ensure all restricted areas (e.g. press room, storage space) are secured at all times.
10 Establish mutual aid agreements with response agencies and ensure alternative playing sites for continuity of operations.

Discussion questions

1 Discuss the risk assessment process. Are there any other potential threats or vulnerabilities to the XYZ Sportsplex? What additional countermeasure improvements would you recommend?
2 Identify potential threats and vulnerabilities at a local sport venue.
3 Research the 2013 Boston Marathon bombing incident. Discuss the event operations and response strategies.

RISK EVALUATION, CONTROL, AND RESPONSE

Risk probability, consequence severity, and financial loss

Risk probability refers to how frequently a risk may occur. How frequently a risk may occur is dependent on the current vulnerability levels. If existing countermeasures are effectively protecting the sport facility from all threats, the vulnerability will be low and in essence the risk probability will be low. However, the reverse is also true. If current vulnerabilities are not protected, the sport facility is exposed to a high potential for loss. Sport organizations can classify the probability (frequency) of risks into four categories – extremely high, high, medium, and low.

The consequence severity of a threat and eventual loss must also be evaluated. The manager must consider both the severity and financial impact on the sport program. Each threat must be evaluated individually and the impact it will have on the sport facility or organization to perform its mission. Consequence severity (impact of loss) can be classified into four categories – essential, critical, important, and not important. Subsequently, the resulting financial loss is equated as catastrophic, serious, moderate, or minor:

- ■ Essential: a successful threat would cause complete loss of sport facility operations, resulting in a *catastrophic* loss.
- ■ Critical: a successful threat would cause severe impairment to sport facility operations, resulting in a *serious* loss.

- Important: a successful threat would cause noticeable impact on sport facility operations, resulting in a *moderate* loss.
- Not important: a successful threat would not cause a noticeable impact on sport facility operations, resulting in a *minor* loss.

A catastrophic loss is one that requires major tax or fee increases; or in private industry it may result in bankruptcy. Critical loss would require major service cut-backs, program cancellations, and/or closings. Moderate loss indicates temporary service reductions, or minor fee increases. Minor losses can be absorbed by the organization with current operating revenues and no program reductions. In order to aid sport facility managers in risk management decisions, consequence and probability data is presented in a risk logic matrix (see Figure 14.3).

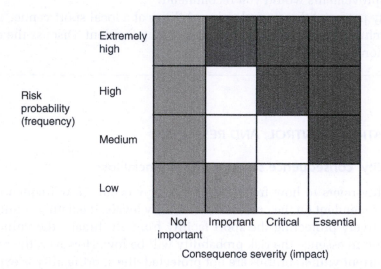

Risk management guideline

These risks are very high and measures should be taken to eliminate them or transfer liability to a third party.

These risks are moderate and management may determine to address them to reduce the level of risk.

These risks are low and management may decide to retain and reduce the level of risk.

Figure 14.3 Risk logic matrix

Risk control and response strategies

Evaluating risk and potential loss assists the facility manager's decision making process to reduce, re-assign, transfer, or accept identified risks. An acceptable level of risk is usually determined by the sport facility manager or owner.

Risk avoidance

Severe risks with the potential for a high degree of loss and which may occur frequently should be avoided. These risks need to be identified prior to an incident and avoided completely. Risks that are categorized in the darkest zone in Figure 14.3 should be avoided, or significant safety and security upgrades implemented to reduce risk to the greatest degree possible. For example, if a sport activity or event has a history of potentially fatal accidents or crowd management problems, the facility manager may wish to eliminate the activity or cancel the event.

Risk reduction

Sport facility managers can reduce risk through staff training, preventative maintenance, and development of a risk management plan. Risks that are categorized in the grey or white zones in Figure 14.3 may be reduced. For example, if a sport facility manager has experienced acts of hooliganism at a venue, it would be prudent for the manager to identify the culprits and ban them from future events to prevent future incidents. Alternatively, the manager may wish to implement buffer zones between rival fans to prevent confrontational issues. Sport facility managers can also reduce likelihood of threats by improving physical protection systems such as implementing access controls, closed-circuit television (CCTV) security cameras, venue lighting, personnel background checks, credentialing measures, interoperable communication networks, and developing emergency response and evacuation plans. Further safety and security measures to reduce threats and risks are presented in Chapter 15.

Risk transfer

Average frequency and moderate severity risks can be transferred to someone who's willing to assume the risk. Risks categorized in the darkest zone in Figure 14.3 may be transferred to a third party. Commonly used transfer methods are insurance, independent contractors, liability waivers, and indemnification clauses. The two main types of insurance available to a sport facility manager are personal injury liability insurance and property insurance.

Personal injury liability coverage is protective insurance in case a spectator, participant, or employee is physically injured by something a sport facility manager did or did not do. For example, a spectator is injured by a stray baseball that traveled through an undiscovered hole in the protective barrier around the field. This incident may result in a lawsuit in order for the victim to recover damages for direct injuries, and pain and suffering. Property insurance is important when considering protecting the facility and its contents from damage or destruction. There are two types of property insurance – (1) named perils, and (2) all-risk insurance policy. Named perils insurance will cover only what is stated in the policy. Most common named perils are natural occurrences such as fire, hail, explosion, lightning, malicious mischief, tornadoes, vandalism, and smoke.

Other methods of risk transfer include waivers, independent contractors, indemnification clauses, and leasing or rental agreements. A waiver transfers risk from the sport facility management team or owner to the person signing the document. There are several principles to be followed for a waiver to be valid. The waiver must be voluntarily signed by an adult. The waiver must be explicit and in clear language, stating that the waiver is for the negligence of the provider and acknowledgement of inherent risks of an activity. The participant must be aware that they are signing a waiver; however, the waiver cannot release the sport facility management team from intentional, or willful and wanton acts, or gross negligence.

Some sport programs may wish to use independent contractors to conduct an activity or provide a service. Independent contractors can be individuals or organizations. Employees such as event staff and security officials can be utilized to transfer risk. These individuals are responsible for the liability of their services and for their own insurance coverage. The sport program may contract with private organizations to provide a program or service. For example, an organization may wish to contract with firms for concessions, facility maintenance, or security. It is important to note that when selecting an independent contractor, facility management must take reasonable care to select a competent person or organization that possesses the necessary credentials. Sometimes facility management will lease or rent the facility for other events such as concerts. In this case, facility management should include an indemnification clause (sometimes referred to as hold harmless agreements) to allow the facility to be compensated by entities leasing or renting the facility, if damage occurs during the event.

Risk retention

Sport facility managers may decide to retain the risk and assume responsibility. Risks categorized in the light grey zone in Figure 14.3 may be retained. Facilities choosing to retain the risks become financially responsible for any injuries or financial risks associated with an incident. Risk financing strategies for retention may include current expensing, unfunded reserves, funded reserves, borrowing, self-insurance, and joint pooling. In a current expensing (or 'pay-as-you-go') system the organization pays for losses as they arise out of their budget. An unfunded reserve is an accounting technique by noting the likelihood of future loss payments that reminds management of future expenses for financial losses. A funded reserve is money set aside in the organization's budget to pay for future losses. Borrowing is an option for the organization when it does not have sufficient resources to pay for losses. The organization can borrow from internal or external sources, although it is often difficult to borrow from external sources to pay for a loss. Table 14.3 illustrates examples of sport facility risks, probability of occurrence, consequence severity, risk control response, and possible financing options.

Table 14.3 Risk control and response matrix

	Threat/risk identification	Risk probability	Consequence severity	Risk control	Financing option
1	Vandalism	Medium	Not important (minor loss)	Reduce	Retention (current expensing)
2	Terrorist attack	Low	Essential (catastrophic loss)	Avoid/ Transfer	Transfer (insurance)
3	Theft/ embezzlement	Medium	Critical/important (serious/moderate loss)	Reduce	Retention (current expensing)
4	Spectator or participant injury	Medium	*Either (dependent upon extent)	Reduce/ Transfer	Transfer (insurance, waiver)

2014 LONDON MARATHON RISK CONTROL AND RESPONSE ASSESSMENT

The safety and security planning for the 2014 London Marathon involved three key agencies: the Metropolitan Police Service assumed the lead role, and the City of London Police and British Transport Police served in supporting roles. There had been no history of political violence or terrorism linked to this large-scale event, although, the UK is aware of its own risks from home-grown terrorists given previous incidents, such as the 2007 subway bombings.

Pre-event safety concerns included:

- General public disorder and petty crime – incidents of drunk and disorderly behavior, as well as number of burglaries during marathon time, had increased after the 2013 event.
- Anticipated acts of political violence and terrorism – the national terrorism level in the UK at the time was substantial, however, the event itself was considered low-risk. Nonetheless, much attention was directed to the finish area and subject to enhanced screening procedures. These measures included access control and requirement of official ticketing and accreditation. Public service announcements were utilized, as well as explosive teams which were deployed to focus on vehicles and suspicious packages.
- Dangerous and disruptive individuals – attention seekers/troublemakers can be disruptive, therefore, it is good practice to identify these individuals beforehand.

Policing strategies

The London Metropolitan Police has a long history with major sport events, such as Wimbledon, English Premier League/international soccer matches, and the 2012 Olympics. The security concept adopted was to be unobtrusive ensuring an enjoyable experience for the public and athletes, but minimizing the potential for disruptions.

- A significant number of law enforcement was deployed along key routes to manage, and be responsive to, real-time intelligence communications.
- On-the-ground management and implementation of traffic control, route searches, crowd management, protest management, policing of transport networks, and validation of vehicle and people accreditations.
- Resources were deployed to safeguard certain areas of concern such as drinking water stations, emergency service vehicle access, and authorized cross-route access for vehicles and pedestrian crossings along the marathon route.

The 2014 London Marathon was classified as a low-risk event. The philosophy and approach to the security operations was one that understood that not every threat can be anticipated; therefore, it is critical to have the necessary manpower and resources on hand to respond efficiently and effectively to incidents as they arise.

Source: S. McCarthy and M. Tarbitt (2014). The 2014 London and Boston Marathons: An assessment of security protocols. *The International Centre of Sport Security, 2*(2), 33–39.

CHAPTER REVIEW

Risk is the possibility of loss from a threat. Risk increases as the consequences and probability of occurrence increases. Risk management is important to sport facility managers in order to meet legal obligations, prevent financial loss, and ensure business continuity. An all-hazards approach must be employed when assessing potential threats and risks (including man-made and natural events, i.e. terrorism, crowd management, natural disasters, theft, and fraud). Risk assessment involves the following key steps: identify SESAT, characterize assets, assess threats, assess vulnerabilities, evaluate consequences, analyze risk levels, and provide countermeasure improvements. Countermeasures are used to reduce the probability and consequence severity of a threat/risk. The sport facility manager can control risk through several strategies. They can avoid, transfer, reduce, or retain identified risks.

304

BIBLIOGRAPHY

Ammon, R., Southall, R., and Nagel, M. (2010). *Sport facility management: Organizing events and mitigating risks* (2nd ed.). Morgantown, WV: Fitness Information Technology, Inc.

Appenzeller, H. (2000). Chapter 24: Risk assessment and reduction. In H. Appenzeller and G. Lewis, *Successful sport management: A guide to legal issues.* Durham, NC: Carolina Academic Press.

ASIS Commission on Standards and Guidelines (2013). *General security risk assessment guideline.* Alexandria, VA: ASIS International.

CRS Report for Congress (2004). *Critical infrastructure and key assets: Definition and identification.* Retrieved October 31, 2014 from: www.fas.org/sgp/crs/RL32631.pdf

Decker, R. J. (2001). *Key elements of a risk management approach.* United States General Accounting Office. Retrieved November 4, 2014 from: www.gao.gov/new.items/d02150t.pdf

Durling, R. L., Price, D. E., and Spero, K. K. (2005). *Vulnerability and risk assessment using the Homeland-Defense operational planning system (HOPS).* Retrieved November 4, 2014 from: www.llnl.gov/tid/lof/documents/pdf/315115.pdf

Federal Bureau of investigation (2014). *Terrorism.* Retrieved November 7, 2014 from www.fbi.gov/about-us/investigate/terrorism/terrorism-definition

Fried, G. (2010). *Managing sports facilities* (2nd ed.). Champaign, IL: Human Kinetics.

Hall, S. (2006). Effective security management of university sport venues. *The Sport Journal, 9*(4), 1–10.

Hall, S., Marciani, L., and Cooper, W. E. (2008). Sport venue security: Planning and preparedness for terrorist-related incidents. *Sport Management and Related Topics Journal, 4*(2), 6–15.

Hall, S., Marciani, L., Cooper, W. E., and Rolen, R. (2007a). Introducing a risk assessment model for sport venues. *The Sport Journal, 10*(2), 1–6.

Hall, S., Marciani, L., Cooper, W. E., and Rolen, R. (2007b). Securing sport stadiums in the 21st century: Think security, enhance safety. Anser Homeland Security Institute: *Journal of Homeland Security,* 1–7.

Hurst, R., Zoubek, P., and Pratsinakis, C. (2003). *American sports as a target of terrorism: The duty of care after September 11th.* Retrieved October 29, 2014 from: www.martindale.com/legal-library/Article_Abstract.aspx?an=entertainment-sportsandid=2342

Kaiser, R. and Robinson, K. (2005). Risk management. In *Management of Park and Recreation Services.* Washington D.C: National Recreation and Park Association.

Long, L. E. and Renfrow, N. A. (1999). *A new automation tool for risk assessment.* 15th Annual NDIA Security Technology Symposium. Session: Risk and Threat Assessment Techniques.

National Counterterrorism Security Office (2011). *Counter Terrorism Protective Security Advice for Stadia and Arenas.* Association of Chief Police Officers in Scotland. Retrieved November 5, 2014 from: http://nactso-dev.co.uk/system/cms/files/121/files/original/Stadia___Arenas_2011.pdf

Sauter, M. A. and Carafano, J. J. (2012). *Homeland Security: A complete guide to understanding, preventing, and surviving terrorism* (2nd ed.). New York: McGraw Hill.

Stevens, A. (2007). *Sports security and safety: Evolving strategies for a changing world.* London: Sport Business Group.

Steinbach, P. (2006, September). Storm: A year removed from the dark days of hurricane Katrina, college athletic departments are now being viewed in a new light – as disaster response specialists. *Athletic Business,* 38–46.

Taylor, J. (2006). *A survival guide for project managers.* New York: AMACOM Division, American Management Association.

Texas Engineering Extension Service (TEEX) (2005, January). *Threat and risk assessment (local jurisdiction)* (3rd ed.). Texas: College Station.

United States Department of Homeland Security (DHS) (2014). *DHS Organization*. Retrieved November 4, 2014 from: www.dhs.gov/organization

United States Department of Homeland Security (DHS) (2003, July). *Vulnerability assessment report*. Retrieved November 4, 2014 from http://www3.cutr.usf.edu/security/documents/DHS_OPD/Vulnerability%20Assessment.pdf

UK Sport (2005). Security and policing. In *Staging major sports events: The guide.* Retrieved September 30, 2014 from: www.uksport.gov.uk/docLib/Publications/Major-Sports-Events-Guide-2005/major-sports-events-the-guide-april-2005.pdf

IN THE FIELD WITH SPORT SECURITY PROFESSIONALS

Excerpt from D. Ritchey (2011, July). Game on! How the pros secure facilities, manage risk and protect the brand. Full article available at: www.securitymagazine.com/articles/print/82162-82162-game-on-how-the-pros-secure-facilities-manage-risk-and-protect-the-brand

Security Magazine assembled a panel of professionals in sport security from Major League Soccer, the NFL, NASCAR, professional tennis, the NBA, and professional golf. This included: Evan Dabby, former Senior Director, Operations for Major League Soccer; Mike Lentz, Director, Security, NASCAR; Mike Rodriguez, Director of Security for the U.S. Open and USTA Billie Jean King National Tennis Center; Jim Cawley, Senior Vice President, Security, NBA; Jeff Miller, Chief Security Officer, NFL; and Joe Funk, President, US Safety & Security for the LPGA.

Security magazine: what is your biggest security challenge inside and outside of your facility?

Evan Dabby: Inside and outside the stadium, the supporter groups are our biggest opportunity. They add life to the entire event, inspire the players and create an unmatched atmosphere in domestic sports. The supporters are our most avid fans who are located in a designated section, who sing and cheer throughout the 90 minutes of action.

At the same time, the supporters are our biggest challenge. Their passion sometimes translates into misconduct, and approximately 90 percent of our violations come from these sections. We constantly work to elevate the enthusiasm while ensuring behavior does not conflict with our Fan Code of Conduct.

Mike Lentz: The size, scope and length of events require an incredible amount of coordination with track and law enforcement agencies. At some venues, because of our strong fan following, we become the second or third largest city in the state and the competitors and fans are on site for multiple days. Coordination with tracks is the key to hosting a safe event and that's an ongoing process. Each year, NASCAR hosts an annual summit, where hundreds of representatives from tracks and law enforcement agencies gather to discuss the latest technology, best practices and current trends. Information sharing is an important part of this conference as is the networking among the tracks.

Mike Rodriguez: The biggest challenge inside the stadiums is player security on-court and monitoring the crowd for issues. In this 'YouTube' world we live in we have more individuals that just want their 15 minutes of fame. Outside the stadiums, crowd management is of concern. We need to constantly be aware of the crowd movements throughout the complex so that we do not get surprised by overcrowding issues at any of the field courts and grounds.

Additionally, because the event takes place in late August and the temperatures are high we need to pay attention to dehydration issues with our patrons. We use announcements through the PA system to remind patrons to drink water and hydrate themselves. We have numerous first aid facilities throughout the site, in addition to roving paramedics.

Jim Cawley: We strive, every game, to establish and maintain a unique atmosphere and dynamic between fans, media and our players. Basketball is an exceptional fan experience that features equally complex security challenges that are carefully managed at each venue. We work diligently to establish the appropriate levels (and methods) of access screening, sweeps and other security related checks, while maintaining schedules that are critical for the business to run with minimal impact to the game and fan experience.

Joe Funk: The LPGA has events that are less attended than the PGA, yet have a much more dynamic footprint. The success of the LPGA is based on a fan friendly atmosphere, and that is my biggest challenge. At a PGA event you rarely see the players interacting with the crowds. With us, the players walk through the crowds and interact with them at all times throughout the course. So the challenge is managing the fan friendly and accessibility atmosphere.

Jeff Miller: Inside the stadium we are really engaged with fan conduct. The Fan Code of Conduct that we instituted in 2008 has been successful in helping us raise the level of quality behavior inside of the stadium and create more value for the fans. From a security perspective it keeps our fans safe and creates an environment where you can bring your children to NFL games. We do not want to see people act out in ways that offend others. Outside the stadiums our concerns are related to not only securing our facilities, but also with parking. Our fans like to tailgate, so we not only have camera technology outside of the stadiums, but also have roving alcohol management teams, in addition to security in the tailgate areas.

TECHNOLOGY NOW!

Sport security professionals use a wide variety of technology to mitigate risks to fans, players, and personnel at sporting events; including social media, simulation software, phone apps, security cameras, digital two-way radios, and license plate recognition software.

Social media

Monitoring Facebook and Twitter posts can yield information on potential security threats. Monitoring social media before, during, and after an event can help identify any plans or ideas for illegal activity.

Simulation software

The NCS[4], in conjunction with INCONTROL, has developed simulation software called SportEvac to help with emergency response training and planning. This software allows venues to exercise scenarios specific to their site, such as ingress and egress under normal circumstances, or an evacuation during an emergency incident.

Phone apps and text messaging

Today's sports venues have phone apps for sport facility maps, seat upgrades, food service, and security assistance. Some venues have an anonymous text messaging system to report problems and to request security assistance. The information is monitored in the command center and relayed to security staff on the ground in order to resolve a problem efficiently, and before it escalates.

Security cameras

Camera capabilities and their associated systems have been one of the most innovative improvements in recent years, for example, cameras that have analytics allow you the ability to discern certain behaviors. Computerized searching has also made it possible to find things almost instantaneously in hours of recording.

Ancillary issues in management and operations

Digital two-way radios

According to *RCR Wireless News*, digital two-way radios are cost-effective, have excellent sound audio and high level of security, and offer the ability to look up necessary information instantly. They also have the ability to contact certain groups of people, such as those near an incident. The radio has a GPS locator so users can identify the closet person to the scene and dispatch immediately to handle the problem.

License plate recognition software/automatic number plate recognition (ANPR)

Casinos were the first to use license plate recognition. Sport facilities such as racetracks also use ANPR technology as quite a number of people are banned for various integrity reasons.

Source: Ludwig, S. E. (2014). Using technology to mitigate risk at sporting events. *Security: Solutions for Enterprise Security Leaders, 51*(10), 44–46.

CHAPTER 15

SECURITY PLANNING FOR FACILITY MANAGEMENT

CHAPTER OUTLINE

- ■ Security management
  - ■ Lessons learned from the United Kingdom
- ■ Protective measures
- ■ Venue design and safety
  - ■ Physical protection systems
  - ■ Perimeter control
  - ■ Access control and credentialing
  - ■ Communications
  - ■ Security Personnel
  - ■ Training and exercise
  - ■ Crowd management
  - ■ Emergency management
  - ■ Business continuity
- ■ Chapter review

CHAPTER OBJECTIVES

This chapter will address global security issues involved in protecting sport facilities from threats and risks identified in Chapter 12. Security best practices, systems, and planning options are provided to equip the 21st century sport manager with an all-hazard's approach to facility security planning. Security management and planning involves the development of plans, policies, and protective measures. Protective security measures addressed in this chapter include: venue design and safety, physical protection systems, perimeter control, access control and credentialing, communications, security personnel, training and exercise, crowd management, emergency management, and business continuity.

310

SECURITY MANAGEMENT

Security management systems are employed to reduce risk and exposure to sport facility vulnerabilities. A sport facility manager is expected to act in a reasonably prudent manner regarding the safety and security of their sport facility; this includes: (1) keeping the venue in safe repair, (2) inspecting the venue to discover hazards, (3) removing hazards or warning of their presence, (4) protecting patrons from foreseeable dangers, and (5) conducting facility operations with reasonable care for the safety of all. Sport facility managers reduce liability exposure by successfully managing risks and foreseeable actions that lead to injuries. Several legal issues related to event security management include inadequate security, negligent employment practices, and handling disturbances, ejections, and arrests.

Security management requires the coordination and collaboration of many individuals, government agencies, and private contractors. Figure 15.1 illustrates the multiple stakeholders involved in providing a safe and secure sporting environment. Sport organizations should designate a security director to oversee security operations and coordinate security efforts with stakeholders. The security director forms a leadership (planning) team with representatives from the stakeholder groups, known as a sport event security action team (SESAT). The sport facility manager, owner, or operator is normally responsible for the safety and security management of events. However, they may rely upon other agencies, locally and regionally, in the case of a major incident. Regardless of the type and criticality of an incident, the sport organization should have established a working relationship with external agencies as noted in Figure 15.1. Multi-agency collaboration ensures effective planning, response, and recovery efforts.

Planning is a critical component to the overall security management system. In order to effectively plan, the sport facility manager must first identify facility risks, threats, and vulnerabilities. Addressing specific threats ensures appropriate planning measures are implemented, such as relevant policies, procedures, and security measures. To reduce risk, the sport facility manager should develop a list of essential venue safety and security policies, i.e. alcohol policy, fan conduct policy, search policy. A sport facility emergency response plan should be developed with annexes for game day operations, evacuation procedures, incident response, and business continuity and recovery. A game day operations plan provides the general administrative, operational, and security strategies for game day. A game day operations plan may include the following items:

- Ticketing policies
- Ticket samples
- Seating policies
- Radio communications
- TV broadcast information

- Stadium staff directory
- Gate designations
- Parking information
- Parking maps
- Parking pass samples
- Traffic flow information
- Credential samples
- Tailgating policies
- Severe weather plans
- General information policies, i.e. admission, prohibited behavior/items, alcohol, camera, first aid, disability accommodations, guest services, lost and found.

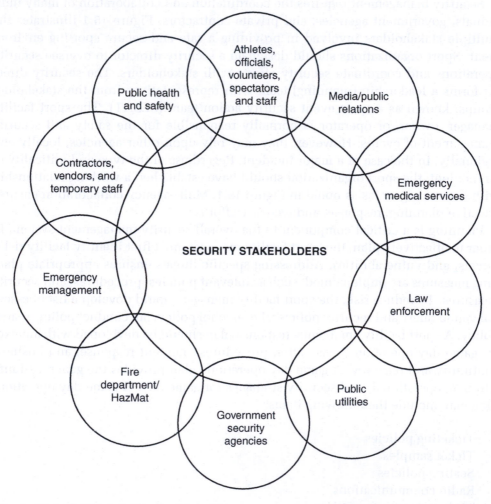

Figure 15.1 Sport event security stakeholders

Ancillary issues in management and operations

To successfully implement security plans, sport facility managers, event staff, security personnel, and emergency response personnel require adequate training in their respective roles and responsibilities. Crowd control methods, spectator safety, and terrorism awareness training is essential for security staff to detect suspicious behavior or criminal activity. Training should be conducted on a continuous basis and refresher courses utilized to emphasis individual tasks. Beyond basic training, security stakeholders should conduct some type of exercise to test security plans for effectiveness and to identify resource gaps.

Post 9/11, US professional sport organizations have enhanced security efforts. The National Football League (NFL), National Basketball Association (NBA), and National Hockey League (NHL) developed a best practices guide of recommended protective security measures to assist league members. Security management was also upgraded at the collegiate level. The National Collegiate Athletic Association (NCAA) issued a Security-Planning Options guide for American college athletic programs. The NCAA is a voluntary organization that governs American college and university athletic programs. The NCAA national office staff consulted with stadium managers and law-enforcement representatives from across the USA to compile the list of options to assist NCAA members with security planning. Planning options included items related to deliveries, personnel, coordination with public safety agencies, lockdown, metal detectors, parking and perimeter, prohibited items, and publicity. A 30-item game day security operations checklist of pre-event, game time, and post-event considerations are presented in Table 15.1.

Lessons learned from the United Kingdom

Britain is a pioneer in the implementation of security standards through government regulation. Hooliganism in British football (soccer) has been well documented for many years and legislative and administrative changes introduced by the English Football Association (FA) and British government have helped control the problem.

Since the Hillsborough Stadium disaster in 1989, and the 1990 Taylor Report on football stadium safety, new legislation and safety and security measures have been imposed on football teams. The Football Disorder Act (1989); Football Spectators Act (1989); Football Offences Act (1991); Football Act (1999); Football Disorder Act (2000); and Football Disorder Bill (2001) were enacted by government. These pieces of legislation prohibited hooliganism; categorized the different offenses that a person would be charged with; covered both domestic and international terrorist threats to sport stadiums; and assured that individuals who were banned would be prevented from attending matches inside and outside of Britain. Additionally, the Football Intelligence Unit was created to collect and disseminate information and intelligence about domestic and international issues that occur at or near sport stadiums. Football Intelligence Officers are assigned to each football team to gather

Table 15.1 Game day security operations checklist

Pre-event considerations

- Write a formal risk management plan
- Implement a pre-event training program for all event staff
- Be aware of nearby dangerous/explosive sites
- Be aware of the quantities of antidotes within the region
- Coordinate your plans with the local and state police
- Conduct background checks on all employees including students and seasonal employees
- Verify that first responders have a small stockpile of drugs and medications for rapid response use should a biological weapon be released
- Utilize 24 hour live security teams in concert with a sophisticated surveillance system
- Lockdown the venue prior to the event
- Prohibit all concessions deliveries 90 minutes prior to the event
- Utilize bomb-sniffing dogs
- Test air quality prior to the event
- Issue holographic personal identification cards for all media
- Purchase and install clear refuse bags and receptacles
- Escort all cleaning crews

Game time considerations

- Secure no-fly zones over the venue
- Patrol air space above the venue, parking lots, and adjacent access roads
- Secure the services of a mobile emergency room to be on site
- Utilize portable biological detection equipment
- Use undercover surveillance teams/individuals
- Utilize 1 crowd observer for every 250 spectators
- Utilize radio equipped security personnel in parking lots and key access points
- Have key personnel wear inexpensive hazmat smart strips that detect the presence of nerve agents, cyanide, and other chemicals
- Invoke periodic broadcasts detailing security practices and restricted areas within the facility
- Implement electronic scanning of all tickets and match these records with detailed records of all your season ticket holders
- Frisk/wand every spectator
- Ban all carry-ins and backpacks
- Prohibit re-entry by spectators

Post-event and general considerations

- Implement a formal post-event debriefing of all personnel
- Vary your security practices so as not to create a pattern in your system

Adapted from Pantera, M.J. et al. (2003).

intelligence and identify potential trouble-makers or prevent banned offenders from entering the stadium.

Most significant, under new safety legislation each football club is required to hold a stadium 'safety certificate'. The government produced and published a set of safety requirements in the *Guide to Safety at Sports Grounds* (2008) for every club playing in the top four divisions in England. The local government authority

Ancillary issues in management and operations

(municipality) is responsible for issuing the safety certificate and ensuring the stadium complies with the requirements issued in the safety guide. In addition, each football club is designated a safety officer to assist the sport facility manager with safety strategies on match day. Safety officers are responsible for the recruitment and training of all stewards. The safety officers formed the Football Safety Officers Association to share best practices (www.fsoa.org.uk). Specific safety and security measures utilized in the English football system are outlined below.

- Football clubs ban any person who is arrested or ejected from a stadium.
- Football clubs operate travel clubs for away matches and only issues tickets to supporters who are members.
- Each club in the top two divisions (English Premier League and Championship) are required to restrict admission of spectators to seated accommodation only.
- National legislation introduced by government outlaws: (1) the possession of alcohol on trains and/or coaches when traveling to a match, (2) entering a stadium drunk or in possession of alcohol, (3) throwing objects towards pitch or spectators, (4) entering the pitch, (5) indecent or racist chanting, and (6) ticket touting.
- Any person convicted of a football-related offense receives a banning order preventing the offender from attending matches at home or abroad for three years. Failure to obey this ban is a criminal offense.

PROTECTIVE MEASURES

Sport facility managers must have adequate security measures in place to protect spectators, athletes, officials, and staff. Protective security measures reduce vulnerabilities and enhance preparedness among supporting agencies to respond and resolve potential incidents. Protective measures are designed to meet one or more of the objectives listed below.

- *Devalue:* lower the value of a sport facility to terrorists, criminal activity, or crowd management issues; thereby making the sport facility less attractive as a target for illegal or unruly behavior.
- *Detect:* spot the presence of suspicious people, unruly fan behavior, and/or dangerous materials, and provide responders with information needed to execute an effective response.
- *Deter:* make the sport facility difficult to attack or less vulnerable to fan/player violence and criminal activity.
- *Defend:* respond to an attack, protect the sport facility, and mitigate any effects of an incident.

Some protective measures are designed to be implemented on a permanent basis to serve as routine protection for a sport facility and are sometimes referred to as 'baseline' security measures. Other measures may be enforced as security threats arise. To establish a sport facility's baseline security measures, the sport facility manager must assess threats and vulnerabilities (as discussed in Chapter 14). Specific threats, vulnerabilities, and organizational policies provide a foundation for development of baseline protective security measures. Sport organizations should consider protective security measures in the following key areas:

- Venue design and safety;
- Physical protection systems;
- Perimeter control;
- Access control and credentialing;
- Communications;
- Security personnel;
- Training and exercise;
- Crowd management;
- Emergency management; and
- Business continuity.

FIFA WORLD CUP 2002 JAPAN/KOREA SECURITY MEASURES

1 South Korean Armed Forces positioned mobile surface-to-air missiles at stadia to prevent terrorist attacks.
2 South Korea Air Force jets patrolled the skies over world cup stadia and no-fly zones over venues were established for other aircraft.
3 Japan's airliner, All Nippon Airlines (ANA), stationed sky marshals on flights into Japan to guard against possible terrorist/hooligan attacks.
4 Japanese riot police conducted disaster drills – 200 police in riot gear and biohazard suits removed a car bomb and hazardous materials from a soccer stadium in central Japan.
5 800–1,000 security personnel were assigned at every event.
6 Security checks at gates included 17 banned items, including alcohol, umbrellas, helmets, and frozen substances.
7 Fans used different entrances/exits.
8 Fans were separated in different sections.
9 FIFA banned the showing of replays on giant TV screens in stadiums during matches to prevent the replaying of controversial incidents or goals.
10 'Spotters' were utilized – European security personnel working under cover, seated among fans.

316

11 A hooligan register (database) was sent to Japanese police prior to the event.
12 Korea's anti-hooligan task force was equipped with water cannons, police trained in martial arts like taekwondo and judo were deployed, and they used trained police dogs.
13 Match tickets featured holograms to enhance security. Security production and distribution of tickets was paramount: 3.2 million tickets for 64 matches spread over 20 venues in 2 different countries, with 32 nations taking part. To tighten security and minimize black market activity: (1) tickets were personalized to an individual or sponsor, (2) no more than four members of a household could purchase tickets, (3) tickets were non-transferable to prevent block booking, and (4) all tickets for second round matches and beyond were issued smart cards which could be read at special kiosks at each venue.

Source: Korean Security Measures (2002). Holograms provide security for FIFA World Cup 2002. *Holography News*, *16*(6), 3.

VENUE DESIGN AND SAFETY

Venue design and safety features are pre-determined to an extent by occupational safety and health administration regulations, environmental regulations, fire codes, seismic safety codes, life safety codes, transportation regulations, and zoning regulations. However, security trends in the 21st century are guiding the work of sport architects and engineers developing the next generation of sport facilities. Designers are now working in collaboration with security professionals and first responders during the design process.

Designers can control stadium accessibility by restricting the size of grounds surrounding the stadium to provide limited space for loitering, less space for event staff to patrol, and limited vehicle access to the stadium. Securing the sport facility perimeter can be established by installing vertical posts (sometimes called bollards) around the stadium to create a physical separation. Parking garages should not be attached to a sport facility and separated with as much distance as possible so terrorists cannot park a vehicle loaded with explosives. The planning committee for Liverpool Football Club's new proposed stadium at Stanley Park insisted planners design the stadium to minimize openness to terrorist attacks, specifically suicide bombers. Design standards set forth by the Association of Chief Police Officers (ACPO) set parameters for construction and design of grounds to reduce crowd management issues and likelihood of attacks. The planning scheme includes a high level CCTV system, fully equipped control room, and its own on-site mini-prison (or custody suite).

Most stadiums built today include a modern command center (also known as a command post) with communication capabilities for security forces to monitor events inside and outside of the stadium. The command center controls the security functions of the sport event. The center is normally staffed with the security director, facility management (operations and security), fire, police, emergency medical services, private security, and media representatives. Copies of security plans, phone directories, and backup technology systems are normally located at this facility in case of an incident. The center has reliable communications and the capability to access the sport facility public announcement system, fire alarm system, voice activation system, turnstile system, and door access control system.

SCOTTISH FOOTBALL ASSOCIATION STADIUM ARCHITECTURE AND DESIGN SAFETY FEATURES

- All seated grounds in respect of Safety Certificate requirements under the Safety at Sports Grounds Act 1975.
- Adequate provision of turnstiles and exit gates.
- Professional stewarding.
- Spacious internal and external concourses.
- Provision of dedicated parking areas for both 'home' and 'away' fans.
- Provision of parking areas for Emergency Service vehicles.
- Internal and external CCTV systems linked to modern police control room.
- High-quality public address systems and fire alarm systems.
- Modern public address, steward's control, and medical control rooms in close proximity to each other.
- Good internal and external lighting.
- No smoking policies in vulnerable areas.
- Electronic turnstile counting mechanisms.
- Provision of retractable tunnel to protect players and officials from injury by thrown objects.
- Wide, hard surface tracks around the perimeter of playing surfaces onto which fans can be evacuated in emergency situations.
- Easily opened emergency gates giving access from stands and terraces towards the playing areas.
- An absence of fencing between stands/terraces and the playing areas.
- Provision of sand buckets to quickly douse any flares or fireworks that are thrown.
- Provision of electronic scoreboards and jumbotron screens that are capable of displaying written text messages.

318

- Tried and tested police and stewarding operations.
- Passageway patrols by stewards.
- Substantial season ticket holdings, which means fans sit beside each other at every match and therefore settle into patterns of behavior that are acceptable to each other and the authorities.
- Policies that ensure matches are all-ticket, minimizing queues and crushing.
- The employment of Safety Officers who are empowered to take action against fans whose behavior is unacceptable.
- The employment of Ticket Center Managers and Stadium Managers who ensure that ticketing and maintenance matters are properly supervised.
- The employment of Health and Safety Managers to ensure all procedures adopted by clubs are safety based.
- Policies of full cooperation with the police, fire, and building control authorities whom regularly undertake 'spot' checks within grounds.
- Pre-match inspections 24 hours before matches.
- Pre-match meetings 48 hours before matches.
- Provision of external bins to encourage the disposal of bottles, cans, etc.
- Provision of doctors, paramedics, and first aid personnel at matches.
- Provision of first aid stations within grounds.
- Provision of televisions on internal concourses, which broadcast games 'live' and therefore encourage an even distribution of fans to fast food outlets throughout matches.
- Application of plastic seals to exit gates which, without impeding emergency opening, deter unauthorized openings.
- Adoption of Ground Regulations, Safety Policies and Emergency Action Plans.
- The attendance at matches on standby of Scottish Power personnel and Lift Engineers in the event of system failures.

Source: Football Safety Officers Association Scotland. *Football safety design.* Retrieved Febraury 20, 2014 from: www.footballsafety.com/design.cfm

Physical protection systems

Physical security is imperative in preventing a multitude of threats and vulnerabilities. An annual structural inspection of the sport facility will determine current structural damage or future problems. Alarm and card access entry points can restrict parts of the building to unauthorized persons. Stadiums design restricted areas to protect food sources, communication centers, and public media outlets. Sport facility managers can protect restricted areas by requiring a magnetic–striped key for entrance to ensure access to the appropriate keyholder. The stadium and press box should be equipped with an Integrated Security Management System (ISMS) consisting of CCTV. Cameras may be utilized to monitor the sport facility including perimeter, concourses, playing field, and concession areas. Sport facility managers should monitor: (1) stadium entrances and exits, (2) spectators and employees for suspicious behavior, and (3) individuals standing in prohibited areas, taking pictures of the stadium without consent, drawing maps, or appearing in large groups outside the stadium during the event.

Sufficient lighting at gate areas is needed for adequate searching of bags and persons. Ventilation systems should be secured and capable of blocking hazardous agents such as anthrax. Air quality monitors can detect changes in air quality and identify biohazards and radioactive materials. Additionally, a mobile command center may be utilized. In England, a mobile command center known as the 'Hoolivan' is located at high profile football matches. The Hoolivan is a vehicle equipped with CCTV for surveillance operations and maintains radio contact with officers inside and outside the stadium.

Perimeter control

Establishing perimeter control measures helps prevent illegal entry onto premises, or into the sport facility. A secure outer perimeter of at least 100 feet should be established around the sport facility. This normally encompasses the property boundary, including parking areas. Roads and streets adjacent to the sport facility should be blocked off when feasible. Security forces may utilize barricades, such as jersey barriers, concrete planters, or bollards. Clear ingress and egress routes are established for emergency medical services, fire, and police in case of emergencies. An inner perimeter should be established around the stadium with limited and controlled pedestrian access points twelve hours prior to an event. The stadium should be locked down 24 hours prior to an event and allow only controlled access during this period. During events, security personnel are assigned to guard vulnerable systems. All buildings located within 100 feet of the stadium should be inspected prior to the event and secured by lock or security guard. Vehicles should be requested to park more than 100 feet away from the stadium. If a vehicle needs to be parked close to the stadium, permission must be granted ahead of time from stadium officials.

Access control and credentialing

Access control and credentialing measures are enforced to prevent unwanted persons or vehicles from entering the sport facility premises or restricted areas. Access control considerations include prohibiting coolers, bags, large backpacks, containers, weapons, and outside food or beverages, except as required for medical or family needs. Some stadiums implement a no re-entry policy, except for medical emergencies. Event staff can divide spectators into two groups for stadium entry: one with bags and other items, and those with no items. This allows for better traffic flow into the stadium. The use of portable metal detectors and standard pat-down procedures at stadium entry gates has been employed at many major sport stadia.

Technology-based security solutions include electronic scanning of tickets or contact cards capable of capturing season ticket holder information. Several UK football teams (i.e. Manchester City, Wigan Athletic, Fulham, and Rangers FC) use a 'SmartCard' system for fans. Instead of paper-based tickets, fans are issued a plastic card containing a microchip stored with ticket and gate access information. Fans scan their card at turnstile locations at their designated gate entrances. This method of entry provides reliable information to the sport facility manager as spectator data is collected and analyzed in real-time. For security purposes, it minimizes queues and reveals exactly who is sitting where. The SmartCard technology is also used for marketing and customer relation purposes. These cards provide consumer profiles and insight into consumer buying habits; this enables the football club to target specific audiences for matches. The SmartCard can be charged with electronic credit allowing fans to buy match tickets, refreshments, and merchandise.

Additional technology-based security tools, such as FaceTrac and Biometric systems, are used to identify fans, run database searches, and send images to security personnel on the ground. Facial recognition technology was used by the NFL in 2001 for Super Bowl XXXV in Tampa, Florida, and at each Super Bowl subsequent. This technology locates faces, constructs facial print templates, and matches facial images with those previously stored in a database allowing law enforcement to identify suspicious facial photos. Biometric systems are suitable for use in protecting sport facilities with a high risk rating (i.e. government) or high risk areas within a sport facility, such as a command center. During the 2006 FIFA World Cup in Germany, organizers recorded the biometric facial data of known hooligans and suspected trouble-makers.

Credentialing considerations include conducting background checks on all vendors, employees, contractors, and volunteers. Credential systems can be simplified by indicating zone access and color code by game function. Management should issue photo credentials to all regular game day employees, staff, media, vendors, and subcontractors and require those designated to pick up their credentials to do so in person, using government issued photo ID. Management should schedule limited daily or weekly delivery times for vendors, and ensure food dispensing and handling procedures are secure to prevent contamination. Credentials need to be worn at all times and clearly displayed. Credentials will include name, photograph, personal identify number, and areas of authorized access. Additionally, a record of persons issued credentials should be maintained for control purposes.

3. Entry to the Stadium and Stadium Conduct

3.1 Entry into a stadium, which includes specifically indicated areas of the stadium being under the control of the FIFA Confederations Cup Authorities (as defined in clause 3.3 below) on a Match day ('*Stadium*'), will be authorised on a Match day during the official opening hours as determined by FIFA and only upon the presentation of a valid Ticket by each person seeking to gain entrance, regardless of his/her age. The Ticket Holder must retain his/her Ticket during the Match for verification purposes.

3.2 Each Ticket is official evidence authorized by FIFA to indicate a personal, revocable license to enter and stay in the Stadium on a Match day during the opening hours of the Stadium as determined by FIFA subject to the terms and conditions set forth under these GTCs and applicable laws. This means that a Ticket shows permission from FIFA to enter and remain in the Stadium subject to the conditions identified in these GTCs, in particular in this Clause 3. FIFA remains the owner of the Ticket. All Ticket Holders must comply with:

(a) the GTCs,

(b) the sales regulations applicable to the Ticket Applicant outlined in the Ticket Application Form, which is available through the sources identified in Clause 11.2 below (the '*Ticket Sales Regulations*'),

(c) the Stadium Code of Conduct, and/or

(d) any other relevant laws, by-laws, regulations, ordinances or instructions given by FIFA, the local organizing committee for the 2014 FIFA World Cup™ (Copa do Mundo da FIFA 2014 – Comitê Organizador Brasileiro Ltda.) ('*LOC*'), the FIFA Ticketing Centre ('*FTC*'), the FIFA Ticketing Office ('*FTO*'), the Stadium management and/or the Brazilian public authority(ies) responsible for safety and security in connection with the Match, and their respective employees, volunteers, agents, representatives, officers and directors (together the '*FIFA Confederations Cup Authorities*')

3.3

(a) A Ticket, and consequently the license to enter and stay in a Stadium, will be automatically revoked in case of a violation of any terms of the GTCs, the Stadium Code of Conduct, the Ticket Sales Regulations and/or any of the relevant laws, by-laws, regulations, ordinances of, or instructions given by, the FIFA Confederations Cup Authorities. Examples of prohibited conduct include: to be noticeably under the influence of alcohol, narcotics or any behaviour-modifying substance; to express any offensive messages, of racist nature, xenophobic nature, or which stimulate other forms of discrimination; to promote any political, ideological messages or any charitable cause; to hinder or harass other individuals, including players and Match officials; to behave, or to show a tendency to behave violently, harmfully or in a manner likely to disrupt public order.

(b) Examples of items prohibited in the Stadium include: weapons of any kind or anything that could be used as a weapon, fireworks, flares or other pyrotechnics, commercial materials or similar items which could infringe any rights of FIFA for the Competition, and other objects which could compromise public safety and/or harm the reputation of the Competition.

(c) Examples of instructions that may be given by the FIFA Confederations Cup Authorities include: an instruction by which a Ticket Holder is requested to leave the stadium, move to a different seat for safety and security reasons, due to technical requirements or to ensure the orderly and smooth implementation of the Competition, and to cover or to remove any materials displaying commercial or otherwise prohibited content.

3.4 The FIFA Confederations Cup Authorities may give instructions on the basis of these GTCs, the Sales Regulations and the Stadium Code of Conduct. The FIFA Confederations Cup Authorities will be entitled to carry out checks on any Ticket Holder. Each Ticket Holder is required to cooperate with the FIFA Confederations Cup Authorities. The Ticket Holder must provide proof of his/her identity, including photographic identification, upon request, and must consent to the confiscation of items prohibited in the Stadium that may be in his/her possession.

3.5 Individuals who have been banned from attending football matches by competent authorities or sports governing bodies in any country, or who are considered as a security risk, are prohibited from receiving Tickets and from entering or remaining in the Stadium.

3.6 Ticket Holders leaving the Stadium will not be re-admitted unless otherwise approved by the FIFA Confederations Cup Authorities. The FIFA Confederations Cup Authorities will not replace any lost Tickets.

3.7 Each Ticket is personalised with the identification of the Ticket Applicant and numbered to identify a specific seat. Each Ticket Holder must sit in the seat allocated to the respective Ticket. However, the FIFA Confederations Cup Authorities reserve the right to substitute the seat identified on the Ticket with another seat, if appropriate for security or technical reasons, even if the seat is in a different block but at least of the equivalent category. The ticket holder acknowledges that such substitution does not change the value of the seat and the services which a ticket holder is entitled to receive with the ticket and does not entitle the ticket holder for any refund or further compensation.

3.8 The FIFA Confederations Cup Authorities cannot guarantee:

(a) that a specific player or team will participate in the Match;

(b) the duration of the Match;

(c) that the ticket holder will have entirely uninterrupted and/or uninhibited view of the match from the seat provided; The ticket holder acknowledges that any of the above does not change the value of the seat and/or the services which a ticket holder is entitled to receive with the ticket and does not entitle the ticket holder for any refund or further compensation.

3.9 Due to applicable laws in Brazil, the purchase or use of certain tickets by residents of Brazil is subject to a personal condition defined by law (including but not limited to age or residence) (the 'personal condition'). These personal conditions do not apply to individuals not being a resident of Brazil. If the purchase or use of a ticket is subject to a personal condition, in addition to proof of his/her identity, the ticket holder must carry and present at any time, upon request of the FIFA Confederations Cup authorities, the required official Brazilian documents which evidence his/her fulfilment of the personal condition required for the purchase or use of the ticket. This means that, regardless of the provision in item 3.2, a ticket which is subject to a personal condition does not grant by itself (without the presentation of the required official Brazilian documents), permission from FIFA to enter and remain in the stadium.

Source: FIFA. *Ticketing: General terms and conditions*. FIFA Confederations Cup Brazil 2013. Retrieved February 20, 2014 from: www.fifa.com/confederationscup/organisation/ticketing/legal/terms-conditions/index.html

Communications

The sport organization should have an interoperable communication system in place with access to the stadium's command center. An efficient interoperable communication system may require hand-held portable multi-channeled radios, cell phones, pagers, or a combination thereof (Department of Homeland Security, 2008). All responding agencies must be able to communicate with each other on the same network to coordinate security management, response, and recovery efforts. Security personnel on the ground must have the capability to report problems to authorities at the center and receive relevant intelligence on disruptive behavior or suspicious activity. The NFL implemented a new text-messaging system that allows fans to report drunk or disorderly fans without confronting them. Fans send a quick text message to the stadiums command center for security to respond. Teams are able to compile databases of complaints and how they were resolved, as well as track areas in a stadium where complaints are frequent. By 2009, all NFL stadiums had to have a text message line or telephone hotline installed.

In addition to possessing adequate communication equipment and systems, the sport organization should have a risk communication system in place that is operational and ready to be activated. Successful risk communication reduces the length, strength, and frequencies of controversies resulting from an incident. Sport organizations should develop contingencies for a press conference post incident with key representatives including emergency services. Risk communication needs to take into consideration the target audience, including cultural background, shared interests, concerns and fears, and social attitudes.

Security personnel

The sport organization should appoint an experienced employee as the security director to deal with daily security matters and emergency incidents. A successful security staff plan has properly screened, trained, and educated staff. An employee background screening program for all sport facility personnel and contracted staff should be established. All personnel and contracted staff working events should be trained in appropriate standard operating procedures (SOPs) for emergency response, security awareness (i.e. suspicious persons and packages), and notification protocols. Recommended training for security personnel includes first aid, CPR, crowd management, drug awareness, emergency response, and defensive techniques. The sport organization may utilize outsourced personnel in the form of contractors, vendors, or security forces.

There should be adequate supervision and oversight of sport facility employees. The number of security personnel needed to staff an event or facility may vary according to the type of event, stadium capacity, or relevant intelligence. The National Fire Protection Association (NFPA) industry standards for fire prevention and safety apply to crowd management principles. There should be one trained crowd management professional for every 250 spectators in any facility with a capacity over 250 people. It is important security personnel are visible during the event. Visible security forces may deter illegal activity or unruly fan behavior; additionally, personnel are easily accessible to spectators in case of an emergency. Major sports events, such as the Olympics and FIFA World Cup, require a very large workforce. The FIFA 2006 World Cup in Germany employed 52,000 staff to oversee the security program, including 30,000 federal police officers, 15,000 private sector security professionals, and 7,000 armed forces personnel.

Training and exercise

Staff training is a key component in protecting critical infrastructures such as sport stadia and arenas. The three main levels of staff training are: (1) multi-agency team training, (2) supervisory training, and (3) event staff training. Multi-agency team training is conducted with the sport event security action team (SESAT) (leadership/planning team). Supervisory training is conducted with main supervisors in charge of event staff and security personnel. Event staff training is conducted for all other venue staff (full-time, part-time, or volunteer). These may include parking attendants, contracted security personnel, gate security, ticket takers, ushers, concessionaires, vendors, and maintenance. Training should be conducted at routine times, for example, pre-season, during season, and post-season. Written responsibilities and duties for each position, and how each position's job function is linked to the overall sport facility safety and security program, should be provided.

Sport organizations should conduct exercises to test plans and promote awareness of staff roles and responsibilities during an incident scenario. There are seven types of exercises defined by the US Department of Homeland Security Exercise and Evaluation Program (HSEEP), and are considered either discussion-based or operations-based. Discussion-based exercises familiarize participants with current plans and policies, or may be used to develop new plans and policies. Types of discussion-based exercises include: seminars, workshops, table-top exercises, or game simulations. Operations-based exercises validate plans and policies, clarify roles, and identify resource gaps in security operations. Types of operations-based exercises include: drills, functional exercises, and full-scale exercises.

Crowd management

Crowds need to be managed for several reasons. Large gatherings of people increase the odds of something happening and make changes in action slower and more complex. Furthermore, communications tend to be slower and more complicated than normal. Most importantly, in the event of an incident at a mass gathering, the possible number of injuries increases. People have been injured or killed at sport venues around the world from crowd crushes, fires, bombs, heat exhaustion, structural collapses, overcrowding, and rioting. The Australian Open has been fast gaining a reputation for fan violence. In 2007, more than 150 Serbian and Croatian fans attacked each other with flagpoles and bottles. In 2008 the tournament was overshadowed when police had to use pepper spray on unruly Greek fans. Again, in 2009, fans from the Serbian and Croatian communities clashed, hurling chairs and missiles at each other during Serbian Novak Djokovic's win over Bosnian born Amer Delic who now represents the US.

Critical components of a crowd management plan include:

1   Trained staff in crowd control methods: staff training has been emphasized in several areas of this chapter. It is evident that human capital is critical to the effective coordination and response efforts of all security and safety related programs. Employees should have an understanding of the sport facility, including the location of emergency medical services to assist fans.
2   Established policies and procedures for possible incidents: specific policies and procedures are needed to address incidents such as disruptive and unruly fans, or public drunkenness and disorder. Parking and traffic control is critical in the management of crowds entering or exiting the sport facility. Poor traffic and parking control can result in stalled crowd ingress, delaying the event's start, or fuel aggressive behavior by fans because of frustration.
3   Effective communication systems: an effective communication network integrated with the stadium command center allows for efficient reporting of incidents and response and recovery efforts.
4   Appropriate signage: adequate signage is the final component of the crowd management plan. There should be prominent signage providing guidance on responding to and reporting suspicious behavior.

A crowd management plan should include an alcohol policy. Protective measures concerning alcohol include staff training in alcohol management, identification checks to prevent underage drinking, limiting the number of alcohol drinks sold to one individual, and ending alcohol sales at a certain point during the event. The NFL requires stadiums to stop selling beer at the end of the third quarter and is considering more drastic measures to prevent unruly fan behavior. In fall 2008, the NFL and all 32 NFL clubs issued a fan code of conduct to promote a positive fan environment and address behavior that detracts from the fan experience.

NFL FAN CODE OF CONDUCT

The National Football League and its teams are committed to creating a safe, comfortable, and enjoyable experience for all fans, both in the stadium and in the parking lot. We want all fans attending our games to enjoy the experience in a responsible fashion. When attending a game, you are required to refrain from the following behaviors:

- Behavior that is unruly, disruptive, or illegal in nature.
- Intoxication or other signs of alcohol impairment that results in irresponsible behavior.
- Foul or abusive language or obscene gestures.

- Interference with the progress of the game (including throwing objects onto the field).
- Failing to follow instructions of stadium personnel.
- Verbal or physical harassment of opposing team fans.

Event patrons are responsible for their conduct as well as the conduct of their guests and/or persons occupying their seats. Stadium staff will promptly intervene to support an environment where event patrons, their guests, and other fans can enjoy the event free from the above behavior. Event patrons and guests who violate these provisions will be subject to ejection without refund and loss of ticket privileges for future games.

Source: M. McCarthy (2008). NFL unveils new code of conduct for its fans. USA TODAY, Retrieved February 1, 2014 from: http://usatoday30.usatoday.com/sports/football/nfl/2008-08-05-fan-code-of-conduct_N.htm

Controlling fan violence must be a priority for sport organizations. To manage crowd behavior and effectively design fan violence prevention efforts, one must understand the basic principles that underlie individual decision making. It can be argued that humans are a product of their environment and make decisions based on what is happening around them, as well as a personal cost-benefit analysis. According to the Situational Crime Prevention (SCP) model developed by crime scientist, Ronald V. Clarke, people choose a course of action by using physical and social cues in their environment by answering the following questions:

1 How much effort is needed – is this the easiest course of action?
2 What are the risks involved – will I be detected or harmed?
3 What are the rewards – are the benefits worth the risk?
4 Do I feel provoked – will this satisfy an immediate/pressing need?
5 Can I excuse my behavior – will I be able to justify it to others?

This model insinuates that people are more likely to engage in behavior that requires little effort or risk, while offering high rewards, and will likely act if they feel provoked and can rationalize their actions.

According to Dr. Tamara Madensen, Director of the Crowd Management Research Council at the University of Nevada-Las Vegas, crowds provoke violence due to unwanted physical contact between strangers, increased wait times increased frustration and stress, movement is more difficult, and mass-panic emergency situations can lead to crowd crushes. Furthermore, large crowds also make engaging in violence easier, less risky, more rewarding, and excusable. With that being said, Dr. Madensen believes that it is possible to manipulate environmental cues in sport facilities to make violence a less-attractive option. Sport facility managers may do so by using the SCP model, which presents 25 different prevention techniques – five techniques for each perceptual dimension:

- Increase the Effort: harden targets, control facility access, screen exits, deflect offenders, and control weapons.
- Increase the Risk: extend guardianship, assist natural surveillance, reduce anonymity, utilize place managers, and strengthen formal surveillance.
- Reduce the Rewards: conceal targets, remove targets, identify property, disrupt markets, and deny benefits.
- Reduce Provocations: reduce frustrations and stress, avoid disputes, reduce emotional arousal, neutralize peer pressure, and discourage imitation.
- Remove Excuses: set rules, post instructions, alert conscience, assist compliance, and control drugs and alcohol.

Emergency management

The four primary components to all-hazards emergency management are mitigation, preparedness, response, and recovery. Mitigation activities try to prevent emergencies or lessen the damage of unavoidable disasters. Preparedness activities such as training and exercise drills enhance the ability of agencies to respond quickly in the aftermath of an incident. Response activities focus on damage assessment or assisting the affected population. Recovery actions, such as providing economic aid, ensure the successful recovery of the affected location. Figure 15.2 depicts the interrelated components and offers potential considerations under each area.

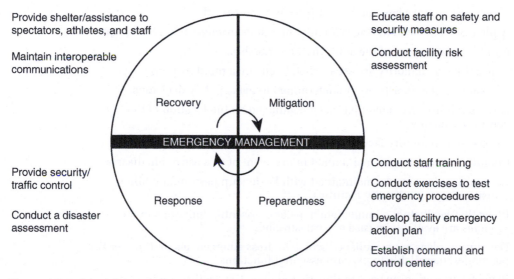

Figure 15.2 Principles and components of sport event emergency management

Business continuity

Business continuity involves developing measures and safeguards allowing an organization to continue to operate under adverse conditions. The development of a business continuity program includes the formation of a sound contingency plan. A contingency plan includes the steps taken before, during, and after an incident. Contingency plans include the sport facility's emergency management policy, personnel responsibilities, emergency scenarios that could occur, and where response operations will be managed. The plan highlights how core elements of the emergency management system will be organized, such as: communications, community outreach, recovery and restoration of systems, operations, administration, and logistics. Supporting documentation to the plan may include: building and site maps, floor plans, escape routes, emergency equipment inventories, emergency procedures, and personnel call lists. The London 2012 Olympic Games Organizing Committee had a contingency budget of £2.7 billion. Additionally, contracts should be in place for immediate restoration and secondary locations identified to hold event bookings in case of an incident. For example, in 2006, the English FA provisionally booked Cardiff's Millennium Stadium in case Wembley Stadium in London was not completed in time to host the 2007 FA Cup Final. The ultimate goal is to return the facility and its stakeholders' quality of life to the same level it was before the incident. Sport facility managers may use the continuity capability checklist in Table 15.2 as a resource tool for planning purposes.

Table 15.2 Continuity capability checklist

Continuity capabilities	Yes	No
Essential functions have been identified and prioritized.		
A plan is available to manage essential functions throughout an emergency.		
Employees are aware of the authority of leadership.		
Delegations of authority are established to ensure a rapid response.		
Delegations of authority are predetermined to make policy decisions.		
A vulnerability assessment has been conducted on the location of the continuity facility.		
Access to a continuity facility can be achieved within 12 hours.		
Communications can be maintained in the event of a catastrophic disaster.		
Communications can be maintained with leadership personnel while transitioning to continuity facilities.		
Plans that facilitate the immediate transfer of essential functions to other agencies are available in case of a catastrophe.		
Devolution plans are established which address emergencies that render key personnel unavailable to perform essential functions.		
Plans for transitioning back to the original operating facility are in place.		

Continuity capabilities	Yes	No

Procedures for phasing down alternate facility operations and returning operations, personnel, records, and equipment to the primary facility are in place.

Vital records are kept to ensure confidentiality of records during a disruption of normal operations.

Vital records are protected either by use of duplicate hardcopy or electronic files.

Procedures are in place that address the needs of personnel during a continuity event (i.e. pay, communication, hiring).

An action plan is in place for hiring of new personnel due to the unavailability of personnel during an emergency.

A written document has been developed for conducting training and exercise programs regarding the continuity plan.

Exercises are conducted regularly using the components of the continuity plan.

The likelihood of potential threats or hazards has been identified and assessed.

Strategies have been created to minimize the likelihood of high-risk scenarios.

Budgetary procedures that allow for the availability of resources before, during, and after a continuity event are in place.

Procedures to acquire resources necessary for continuity operations are available on an emergency basis.

Procedures are in place that review the best course of action based on the organization's readiness posture.

The organization is prepared to implement executive decisions based upon a review of emergencies.

CASE STUDY: 2013 BOSTON MARATHON BOMBING

During the 117th Boston Marathon on April 15, 2013, two pressure cooker bombs exploded near the finish line, killing three people and injuring an estimated 264 others. The bombs exploded about 13 seconds and 210 yards (190 m) apart with more than 5,700 runners yet to finish the race. At least 14 people required amputations, with some suffering traumatic amputations as a direct result of the blasts. As the attack occurred at the finishing line, emergency medical technicians (EMTs) and triage stations were available to respond quickly to the immediate aftermath of the explosions. Casualties were treated in 27 different local hospitals.

Officials had swept the area for bombs twice before the explosions; with the second sweep occurring one hour before the bombs detonated. The blasts blew out windows on nearby buildings but did not cause any structural damage. The marathon was halted abruptly. Police, following emergency plans, diverted the remaining runners away from the finish line and evacuated nearby buildings. Many people dropped backpacks and other bags as they fled, requiring each to be treated as a potential bomb. Police closed down a 15-block area around the blast site. As a precaution, the Federal Aviation Administration restricted airspace over Boston and issued a temporary ground stop for Boston's Logan International Airport.

The Massachusetts Emergency Management Agency suggested people trying to contact those in the vicinity used text messaging, instead of voice calls, because of crowded cell phone lines. The American Red Cross helped concerned family and friends receive information about runners and casualties. The Boston Police Department also set up a helpline for people concerned about relatives or acquaintances to contact, and a line for people to provide information. Google Person Finder activated their disaster service under *Boston Marathon Explosions* to log known information about missing persons as a publicly viewable file.

The Federal Bureau of Investigation led the investigation, assisted by the Bureau of Alcohol, Tobacco, Firearms and Explosives, the Central Intelligence Agency, the National Counterterrorism Center, and the Drug Enforcement Administration. United States government officials stated that there had been no intelligence reports that indicated such a bombing would take place. House Intelligence Committee Representative Peter King stated that he received two top secret briefings on the current threat levels in the United States the previous week to the event and there was no evidence of an imminent attack.

Police identified two suspects after the immediate investigation and review of video surveillance, photographs, and social media materials. Russian-born brothers Dzhokhar and Tamerlan Tsarnaev (26 and 19 years old respectively), who subsequently became US citizens, had planned and implemented the bombing attacks. After an extensive manhunt, on April 19, one brother was captured and the other died in an exchange of fire between the suspects and police forces.

Key factors

First responders

Qualified emergency medical teams (EMTs) and associated resources in close proximity to the bombings ensured that injuries were treated quickly and

Ancillary issues in management and operations

effectively. The success of the immediate response efforts was also a function of where the bombings took place. If the bombs had detonated at less notable points on the marathon route, the death toll may have been higher due to the lack of EMTs, first responders, and hospital facilities within a short distance. The start and finish lines are the two most secure and prepared locations on a marathon route.

Surveillance

Law enforcement officials were able to process huge amounts of video, photography, and social media offered by the public in response to a request for the public's help in the identification of potential suspects. The role of the community in providing data, videos, and photographs of the bombing scenes and suspects was crucial in the evidence collection process.

Crowd management

Security officials along the marathon route were primarily facing the athletes because in the past the primary concern was security breaches that would interrupt the runners. Police would observe the crowd for disruptive activity that could impact athletes on the course; they were not looking for individuals with intention to injure spectators.

Lessons learned

Critical role of first responders

When dealing with an open access event, locations where spectators and athletes are the most vulnerable, and where officials are most prepared for dealing with a crisis, must be identified. Enhancing the security of an event may include an increased EMT presence and actively recruiting volunteers who have backgrounds in emergency response.

Evolving role of surveillance

Officials are able to observe assets, athletes, and the crowd during an event and are able to return to the time of a security breach and collect evidence. Video technology can be an important asset in emergency response, recovery, and crisis management throughout a post-event investigation. Following the Boston Marathon bombings, there may be a greater need and demand for additional surveillance at open-access sporting events.

Crowd management personnel training

Open-access sporting event officials may decide to distribute their focus and attention equally between the athletes, the event, and the crowd/spectators.

Community education programs

Empowering communities and providing them the tools, education, and awareness knowledge to identify suspicious behaviors and anomalies is critical in a constantly evolving threat environment. Cooperation between the community and law enforcement is fundamental in identifying and preventing potential terrorist threats.

Source: Todt (2013).

Discussion questions

1   What were the key strengths of the response effort and what areas needed improvement?
2   What suggestions would you recommend for securing open-access events?
3   What additional training would you suggest for crowd management personnel?
4   Do you think surveillance efforts should be increased at all open-access events? Why?

CHAPTER REVIEW

Security management systems are employed to reduce risk and exposure to sport facility vulnerabilities. Sport facility managers are responsible for keeping a venue in safe repair, discovering potential hazards, and protecting patrons from foreseeable dangers. Security management requires the coordination and collaboration of many stakeholders including individuals, government agencies, and private contractors. The sport facility manager should develop an emergency response plan with annexes for game day operations, evacuation procedures, and incident response for various emergency scenarios.

Industry best practices, planning options, and guidelines are available to the facility manager for assistance in security planning. Britain has successfully implemented national legislation and standard stadium requirements and protocols to combat hooliganism. Protective security measures are designed to devalue, detect, deter, and defend the sport facility from attack or illegal activity. Baseline protective security measures should be implemented on a permanent basis as routine

334

inspection for a sport facility. Protective security measures should be considered in the following key areas: venue site design, safety and sustainability, physical protection systems, perimeter control, access control, communications, security personnel, training and exercise, crowd management, emergency management, and business continuity and recovery.

BIBLIOGRAPHY

Ammon, R., Southall, R., and Nagel, M. (2010). *Sport facility management: Organizing events and mitigating risks* (2nd ed.). Morgantown, WV: Fitness Information Technology, Inc.

ASIS International (2014). *About ASIS.* Retrieved November 12, 2014 from www.asisonline. org/About-ASIS/Pages/default.aspx

Connolly, E. (2009). Balkan fans riot at Australian Open tennis. *The Guardian.* Retrieved December 2, 2013 from: www.guardian.co.uk/world/2009/jan/24/australian-open-riot

Covello, V. T. and Allen, F. A. (1988). *Seven cardinal rules of risk communication.* Washington, DC: US Environmental Protection Agency.

Doukas, S. G. (2006). Crowd management: Past and contemporary issues. *The Sport Journal, (9),* 2.

Fried, G. (2010). *Managing sports facilities* (2nd ed.). Champaign, IL: Human Kinetics.

Department for Culture, Media and Sport (2008). Guide to safety at sports grounds (5th ed.). London: The Stationary Office.

Goss, B., Jubenville, C., and MacBeth, J. L. (2003). *Primary principles of post-9/11 stadium security in the United States: Transatlantic implications from British practices.* Retrieved February 19, 2009 from: www.iaam.org

Hall, S. (2006). Effective security management of university sport venues. *The Sport Journal, (9)* 4.

Hall, S., Marciani, L., and Cooper, W. E. (2008). Emergency management and planning at major sports events. *Journal of Emergency Management, 6*(1), 43–47.

Henricks, M. (2007). A blueprint for building success. IAAM Facility Manager. Retrieved February 19, 2009 from: www.iaam.org/Facility_manager/Pages/2007_Oct_Nov/ Feature_3.htm

Homeland Security Exercise and Evaluation Program (HSEEP) (2013). Volume I: *HSEEP overview and exercise program management.* Retrieved November 14, 2014 from: www. llis.dhs.gov/hseep

Hurst, R., Zoubek, P., and Pratsinakis, C. (2003). *American sports as a target of terrorism: The duty of care after September 11th.* Retrieved February 20, 2009 from: www.martindale. com/legal-library/Article_Abstract.aspx?an=entertainment-sports&id=2342

Kinney, J. A. (2003). Securing stadiums: Keeping them safe for successful special events. *Stadium Visions, 2*(1), 10.

Leonard, H. B., Cole, C. M., Howitt, A. M., and Heymann, P. B. (2014). Making Boston stronger. *International Centre for Sport Security Journal, 2*(2), 15–23.

Madensen, T. (2014). *Understanding crowds key to controlling fan violence.* Athletic Business. Retrieved November 14, 2014 from: www.athleticbusiness.com/event-security/ understanding-crowd-dynamics-key-to-controlling-fan-violence.html

Marsden, A. W. (1998). Training railway operating staff to understand and manage passenger and crowd behaviour. *Disaster Prevention and Management, 7*(5), 401–405.

McCarthy, M. (2008). NFL unveils new code of conduct for its fans. *USA Today*, August 8. Retrieved Februayr 1, 2009 from: http://usatoday30.usatoday.com/sports/football/nfl/2008-08-05-fan-code-of-conduct_N.htm

Muret, D. (2006). Staying on guard. *Street & Smith's SportsBusiness Journal*, (8), 43.

Muret, D. (2008). NFL, stadiums rethinking alcohol policies. *Street & Smith's SportsBusiness Journal*, (10), 41.

National Counterterrorism Security Office (2006). *Counter terrorism protective security advice for stadia and arenas.* Association of Chief Police Officers in Scotland. Retrieved September 13, 2014 from: www.footballsafety.com/design.cfm

Pantera, M. J. (2003). Architectural design and game day considerations for new or retrofitted sport facilities. *The Sport Supplement*, *11*(4).

Pantera, M.J. III, Accorsi, R., Winter, C., Gobeille, R., Griveas, S., Queen, D., Insalaco, J., and Domanoski, B. (2003). Best practices for game day security at athletic & sport venues. *The Sport Journal*, *6*(4).

Sauter, M. A. and Carafano, J. J. (2005). *Homeland Security: A complete guide to understanding, preventing, and surviving terrorism.* New York: McGraw Hill.

Stevens, A. (2007). *Sports security and safety: Evolving strategies for a changing world.* London: Sport Business Group.

Tackling Football Violence (1996). *Football violence in Europe: tackling the problem.* Social Issues Research Center. Retrieved November 12, 2014 from: www.sirc.org/publik/fvtackle.html

Todt, K. E. (2013). Lessons in response and resilience from the Boston Marathon bombing. *International Center for Sport Security Journal, 1*(2). Retrieved April 1, 2014 from: http://icss-journal.newsdeskmedia.com/lessons-in-response-and-resilience-from-the-Boston-Marathon-bombing

U.S. Department of Homeland Security (2004). *Department of Homeland Security hosts security forum for sports executives.* Office of the Press Secretary, July 23. Retrieved October 23, 2014 from: http://dhs.gov/dhspublic/display?content=3863

U.S. Department of Homeland Security (2008). *Protective measures for US sports leagues.* Retrieved October 23, 2014 from http://www.southeasttourism.org/upload_images/file/DHSProtectiveMeasuresGuideforSportsLeagues.pdf

UK Sport (2005). Security and policing. In *Staging major sports events: The guide.* Retrieved June 17, 2009 from: www.uksport.gov.uk/docLib/Publications/Major-Sports-Events-Guide-2005/major-sports-events-the-guide-april-2005.pdf

IN THE FIELD …

Commissioner William Evans, Boston PD

When the two bombs exploded at the Boston Marathon finish line in April 2013, there was chaos. Hundreds were seriously injured. Participants and spectators were panicked, not knowing where to turn for safety. Were there more explosive devices set to go off in a few seconds?

Within 22 minutes, chaos was quelled, and the area was secured.

How?

"Through planning and training," Boston Police Department Superintendent William Evans told *Security Director News.*

Three people died at the Boylston Street scene and 264 more were injured. And while the deaths were horrible, Evans said, he takes solace in the fact that none of the hundreds of injured taken to area hospitals, many with traumatic injuries, died. "Our officers were putting out people on fire, they were putting tourniquets on people's legs. The teamwork by everyone was amazing. That is why we did not have more deaths," he said.

Evans spoke at the recent 2013 National Sports Security and Safety Conference & Exhibition held in Orlando, Florida. A 32-year BPD veteran who heads the department's Bureau of Field Services, Evans led the response to the bombings.

Interestingly, Evans, 54, had just completed the marathon that Patriots' Day Monday—his 18th—with a time of 3:34. After reuniting with his wife and son at the finish line, he drove them home, and then headed to the Boston Athletic Club to connect with other marathoners from the BPD, a tradition. He was in a hot tub, he said, when he got the news about the bombings, which occurred about 2:45 p.m.

He rushed back to the finish line. And while it was a tragic sight, he was proud of the response.

"A lot of what we had already done paid off that day," he said.

"We conduct a lot of tabletop exercises every year leading up to the marathon, especially since 9/11," he said.

Over the past two years, the department also has conducted large-scale Urban Shield exercises, funded by the Department of Homeland Security. "We simulate [scenarios like] a Mumbai attack and other scenarios. Partners from all over the community participate.

"All these agencies come together and conduct scenarios of 'what if?' What if there is a water main leak, how will we divert the traffic? What if there is an explosion? All our partners [the fire department, hospitals, EMTs, the Boston Athletic Association, which sponsors the marathon and others] participate and we get familiar with each other's capabilities, familiar with what each party can bring to the table," he said.

Still, the training did not anticipate an attack four hours and 10 minutes into the race. In trying to think like a terrorist, he said, "we were thinking, 'where can I make the most impact?' We were geared up for [an attack] at the 2:05 finish, when most of the elite runners finish, but not at 4:10."

He has looked at video of the bombing "quite a bit," he said. "When everyone else was running away, the responders were running toward it, even without knowing if there was another device," he said. "We trained for days for this, and it showed the benefit of being prepared. It shows the benefits of that training, because a day like this can happen to anyone."

As most know by now, the private sectors' video surveillance footage was vital in identifying the two bombing suspects. That is another relationship that paid off, Evans said. "We work very closely with commercial businesses on Boylston Street, and the video from them was tremendous. It was a very orderly process."

Many businesses in that area are part of the Back Bay Neighborhood Association and the Back Bay Security Network. BPD representatives meet monthly with the BBSN. "We know all the cameras in that area," Evans said.

In fact, in another high-profile case, private surveillance cameras helped BPD catch the so-called "Craig's List Killer" in 2009, Evans said. Private-public partnerships are important.

Boston has a number of municipally owned surveillance cameras throughout the city, mostly in "violent hotspots" and at busy intersections, he said. Massachusetts Bay Transportation Authority cameras were used in the bombing investigation as well, and those cameras are in the process of being integrated with the city's cameras, Evans said.

Four days after the bombings, Tamerlan Tsarnaev, the first suspect, was killed in a police shootout, an MIT security officer had been killed, allegedly by the suspects, and an MBTA security officer was seriously injured with a gunshot wound.

Evans, having been up for hours on end, was the incident commander in Watertown, where a resident reported seeing someone hiding in a boat in his yard. That someone turned out to be Dzhokhar Tsarnaev, the second suspect. Evans and two other officers, the first on the scene, alerted the FBI and other authorities. A helicopter armed with FLIR Systems infrared cameras showed there was a person hiding in the boat, and Dzhokhar Tsarnaev was eventually taken into custody.

Things might have turned out differently without the proper training in place, Evans emphasized. "When it actually happened, to see it work was great," he said. "Do your training, do tabletops, simulate worst-case scenarios with all of your partners. You cannot do enough role-playing."

And, he added, "Get as much video out there as you possibly can."

Source: A. Canfield (2013). An interview with William Evans, Lead Boston Marathon bombings investigator. *Security Director News*. Available at: http://securitydirectornews.com/public-sector/interview-william-evans-lead-boston-marathon-bombings-investigator

TECHNOLOGY NOW!

Technology-driven safety and security measures have been designed to help secure sporting events. Based on scientific knowledge, they must also be practically applicable to secure and protect people, assets, and information during sporting events. Key characteristics that define security technology are:

- risk and impact based (relevant to perceived or real threat);
- flexible (scalable and unobtrusive);
- proven (tried and tested technology); and
- affordable (including the ability to integrate seamlessly with other technology and systems).

Embedding all technology is not always possible at the facility design stage as technology can become obsolete; however, the safety and security by design principle should be followed and continual innovation and upgrades/retro-fit will be required when new technologies are introduced.

Most prevalent sport stadia security technologies can be categorized as access control and technical security systems. Access control systems include doors, locks, turnstiles, fences, as well as electronic access controls and mechanical counting systems providing real-time data analysis of crowd flow and attendance. Technical security systems consist of access control systems, intruder detection, surveillance, people and goods screening systems (including chemical, biological, radiological, nuclear, and explosives detection). Emerging technologies include but are not confined to the following five examples.

- *Millimeter-wave technology:* emergence of mass non-intrusive 'stand-off' screening allows for the screening of large groups of people rather than one-by-one fan at a time.
- *Facial recognition*: CCTV systems with digital enhancement and facial recognition capabilities can help control access to events and identify known dangerous/disruptive individuals and deny them stadia entry.
- *Smartphone biometrics*: biometric data available on smartphones can be cross-referenced with the data uploaded at time of ticket purchase, and with the ticket holder present that can prevent ticket fraud, expedite ticket checking process, and with personal identification.
- *Smartphone access control*: fans can use their smartcard or mobile phone-based ticket to access the stadium for cashless payments. In time, the combination of mobile phone and radio-frequency identification (RFID) technology can be used to guide spectators to their seats and shortly prior to kick-off (after stadia operators assess unused premium seats) offer fans by way of text message the opportunity to upgrade their seats at a discount.
- *Unmanned aerial drones*: the unmanned craft can be fitted with surveillance cameras, high resolution streaming video, explosive-detection devices, and chemical-detection sensors.

Source: McCarthy (2014).

PART IV

EFFECTIVENESS OF MANAGEMENT AND OPERATIONS

CHAPTER 16

PERFORMANCE MANAGEMENT AND BENCHMARKING

CHAPTER OBJECTIVES

Performance management and benchmarking are important techniques for sport facility managers, for three key reasons. First, they help sport facility managers to achieve better results by enabling them to understand the drivers of performance and how to influence them. This is achieved by both data benchmarking, comparing statistical performance with others; and process benchmarking, comparing the key decisions made to achieve good performance. Second, benchmarks provide much more authoritative reporting of performance than an organization's performance reported in isolation. Third, when benchmarking/performance management techniques become established as part of organizational culture, they provide the basis for a clear focus on the business essentials as well as the direction for continuous improvement. This capstone chapter will ensure that the book concludes on a high note by bringing together various concepts that out of necessity have been treated separately earlier in the book such as: strategic management; financial management; the four 'e's of economy, efficiency, effectiveness, and equity; customer satisfaction; and service quality. It will draw on the principal benchmarking systems internationally, including the Sport England National Benchmarking Service, and the Centre for Environmental and Recreational Management Performance Indicators (CERM PIs) system from Australia.

This chapter will draw together various strands of performance management referred to throughout the book, for example: staff turnover ratios (human resources), extraction ratios (e.g. dollars per head of secondary spend); return on investment in marketing (e.g. coupons returned as a function of promotion cost); and so on. The basic point is that which gets measured gets managed so therefore managers need to be clear about what their priorities are and what measures they need to monitor in order to demonstrate personal, team, facility, and corporate effectiveness.

INTRODUCTION TO PERFORMANCE MANAGEMENT AND BENCHMARKING

It might be tempting to suggest that good managers are intuitive, with natural skills for dealing with people and making decisions, using inspiration and flair. This romantic vision of management probably fits a few inspirational entrepreneurs. However, it is totally inappropriate for the large majority of good managers. All the principles of good management suggest that as well as personal skills, it is important to have, among other things, evidence to guide decisions. At the heart of this chapter, therefore, is the concept of good performance evidence. It is this evidence that will:

- demonstrate whether or not strategies and objectives are being realized;
- identify key financial changes and guide financial decision making;
- demonstrate how customers are feeling about products or services and guide marketing decisions;
- identify the quality of service provision and guide human resource decisions.

344

Furthermore, it is not advisable to just examine evidence for one's own organization in isolation. Comparisons are also important in order to judge how the organization is doing in relation to other providers of similar products or services, whether or not they are competitors; and also in relation to previous periods. Comparison is the essence of benchmarking, which is another key element to this chapter.

Utilizing appropriate evidence about organizational performance in order to improve decision making and comparing this evidence with similar providers and past achievements are the essentials of performance management and benchmarking. This chapter first provides examples of performance management frameworks, the organizational processes which stimulate the right evidence and the right use of it. Second, concepts of performance are examined, demonstrating that it is a multi-faceted phenomenon. Third, appropriate performance indicators are discussed (i.e. the pieces of data which are selected to represent organizational performance). Finally, benchmarking is considered, with the help of a case study of a benchmarking service used for sports facilities in the UK.

The term 'performance management' is often used interchangeably with 'quality management' because they cover very similar principles.

- Performance management is defined by IDeA, the improvement and development agency for local government in the UK, as 'taking action in response to actual performances to make outcomes for users and the public better than they would otherwise be' (IDeA, 2006). It is a process of improving organizational performance by informing management decisions with appropriate planning, objectives, targets, performance measurement, and review.
- Quality management is defined by The Chartered Institute of Quality as 'an organization-wide approach to understanding precisely what customers need and consistently delivering accurate solutions within budget, on time and with the minimum loss to society' (Chartered Quality Institute, 2009). Typically broader in concept than performance management, quality management also includes measuring and analyzing performance using a process designed to achieve continual improvement in products, services, and the methods that deliver them to the customer.

PERFORMANCE MANAGEMENT FRAMEWORKS

A number of frameworks have been devised to facilitate performance management. They are used interchangeably as performance management frameworks or quality management frameworks. We examine two – one a general model for any organization (EFQM) and the other a framework specifically designed for public sector cultural services in the UK (TAES).

The European Foundation for Quality Management (EFQM) Excellence Model

EFQM was established on the premise that to be successful, an organization needs to establish an appropriate management system. The EFQM Excellence Model is a practical tool to help organizations do this. It does so by measuring where they are on the path to excellence, helping managers to understand the weaknesses in performance, and then stimulating solutions through actions.

Introduced in 1992, the EFQM Excellence Model, also known as the Business Excellence Model, is a management framework that can be used to provide continuous improvement to any organization, in any area of activity. It works by self-assessment by an organization's managers, rather than external assessment. An organization is assessed by its managers against the relevant criteria which constitute quality performance and a score is allocated.

By matching the organization against the model's criteria, strengths and weaknesses can be identified. Within this non-prescriptive approach, there are some fundamental concepts which underpin the model:

- Results orientation: satisfying the needs of all stakeholders.
- Customer focus: the essence of service quality is to identify the needs of customers and satisfying these needs.
- Leadership and constancy of purpose: without effective leadership in seeking continuous improvement, it is unlikely to be achieved.
- Management by processes and facts: i.e. systematic management based on reliable evidence.
- People development and involvement: realizing the potential of staff through a culture of trust and empowerment.
- Continuous learning, innovation and improvement: requiring sharing and an organizational culture which embraces change and development.
- Partnership development: mutually beneficial relationships based on trust.
- Corporate social responsibility: an ethical approach to service delivery which demonstrates responsibility to the wider community.

The EFQM Business Excellence Model is based on nine criteria, and is reproduced in Figure 16.1. Five of these criteria are 'Enablers', covering what an organization does. Four are 'Results' covering what an organization achieves. Feedback from Results helps to improve the Enablers.

The EFQM is the most widely used organizational framework in Europe and has become the basis for many national and regional Quality Awards, including a quality accreditation system in the UK designed specifically for sport and leisure services – Quest (see www.questnbs.info)

346

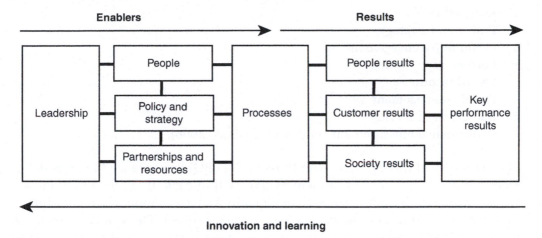

Enablers

Results

Leadership	People		
Policy and strategy		Processes
Partnerships and resources		

People results	
Customer results	Key performance results
Society results	

Innovation and learning

Figure 16.1 Business Excellence Model: EFQM

Towards An Excellent Service (TAES)

TAES was introduced in 2006 by IDeA, the improvement and development agency for local government in the UK. It is a national framework for performance management in cultural services. It was developed in consultation with a number of other agencies, including the relevant government department (Department of Culture, Media and Sport), the government watchdog for public services (Audit Commission), and major professional institutes in sport and leisure (Institute for Sport, Parks and Leisure, Institute of Sport and Sport Management, and the National Association for Sports Development).

TAES is a self-assessment and improvement planning toolkit, which is designed to complement and embrace other quality frameworks and awards such as EFQM. It is described by IDeA as a 'journey' rather than a scheme, because it is a continuous process of improvement. Continuous improvement is necessary because of continuous changes in both community needs and customer expectations. Continuous improvement requires an organization to:

- Clearly establish what it is trying to achieve (i.e. objectives).
- Establish what causes success.
- Identify current performance.
- Take actions to improve on a continuous basis.
- Go back to step one and carry on (IDeA, 2006).

TAES identifies eight key 'themes' that influence the quality of cultural services, with 'equality' and 'service access' integrated into every theme:

1 Leadership
2 Policy and strategy
3 Community engagement
4 Partnership working
5 Use of resources
6 People management
7 Standards of service
8 Performance measurement and learning (IDeA, 2006).

The similarity of these criteria with those of the EFQM Excellence Model is deliberate – it is designed to complement EFQM. Within each of the themes, there are criteria which define key aspects of high-quality service. A number of 'descriptors' for the criteria allow performance in them to be measured. The system is evidence based; evidence schedules identify the sorts of evidence required to demonstrate that a particular criterion has been met or not – 'the evidence schedules are vital to the integrity of the framework' (IDeA, 2006, p. 12). From the evidence emerging from self-assessment, an organization can identify its position in relation to four levels of performance: poor, fair, good, excellent. A lack of evidence automatically leads to a rating of 'poor' under the TAES self-assessment and reinforces the point made throughout this book that sensible decision making is best done on the basis of high-quality supporting information.

IDeA focuses on the improvement plan as the most important part of the TAES process – 'it is the very reason for carrying out the self-assessment in the first place' (IDeA, 2006, p. 12). Key attributes of an improvement plan are:

■ Improvements are prioritized, focusing first on those which will make the biggest impact.
■ The plan must be such that specific tasks are identified which are realistic, resourced, with clear accountability and deadlines set for delivery.
■ The improvements are themselves measurable and you can monitor if the actions planned are having the desired effect (IDeA, 2006, p. 12).

PERFORMANCE MANAGEMENT PRINCIPLES

A well-designed performance management system must be based on:

■ a systematic analysis of the relationships between the objectives of the organization;
■ the performance indicators employed in representing these objectives;
■ the management targets set for the performance of the organization; and
■ the actions taken to realize these targets.

348

To some sport managers, as indicated by the Audit Commission in Britain, the differences between these concepts have been vague. However, since that seminal report, a range of performance management systems has been devised to help managers achieve continuous improvement. But why measure performance? As noted in Figure 16.2, it is likely that without the right evidence it is not easy to see where you are, let alone what is right or wrong with an organization.

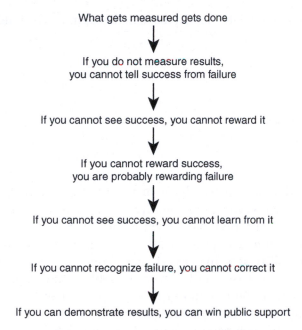

What gets measured gets done

↓

If you do not measure results,
you cannot tell success from failure

↓

If you cannot see success, you cannot reward it

↓

If you cannot reward success,
you are probably rewarding failure

↓

If you cannot see success, you cannot learn from it

↓

If you cannot recognize failure, you cannot correct it

↓

If you can demonstrate results, you can win public support

Figure 16.2 Why measure performance?

Objectives

An essential first stage in performance management is setting appropriate organizational objectives. An objective is a desired future position. Taylor (1996) identifies a number of desirable attributes for organizational objectives:

- Objectives should be specified so that, at the end of an appropriate period, it is clear whether or not they have been achieved or not. This means that objectives need to be quantifiable. Each objective requires appropriate performance indicators, by which measurement of performance is possible.
- Objectives are concerned with ends not means. For example it is not an objective to 'set low prices for disadvantaged groups in the community'; the objective here is 'to increase visits to the service by people from such disadvantaged groups' and this objective can be served by a number of means, of which pricing is just one.

- The prioritization of objectives is important. Sometimes objectives may conflict, for example 'increase revenue' might conflict with 'increase usage of a sport facility by the lowest socio-economic groups in the community'. Where trade-offs between conflicting objectives are apparent, priorities need to be identified. Failure to specify such priorities means that targets and management actions become compromised.

The attributes of appropriate objectives can be summarized in the mnemonic MASTER:

M = measurable
A = actionable
S = specific
T = time-specified
E = ends not means
R = ranked

It has often been the case, particularly in the public sector, that organizational objectives are expressed vaguely or generally, so that it is difficult if not impossible to identify whether or not they have been achieved. Such inaccurately specified objectives include 'achieving sport for all', 'serving the community's needs', and 'providing a high-quality sporting experience'. These are 'aims' rather than objectives – they are broadly based and non-measurable. They require more specific, measurable objectives to be monitored through performance indicators which in turn are used for management decision making.

Objectives for public sector sport organizations are likely to be more complicated than those of private, commercial firms – the reason being that social, non-profit objectives such as usage by disadvantaged groups are of importance to public sector organizations, as well as financial and customer satisfaction objectives. Social objectives extend to the impacts of public services, such as improved health and citizenship, and reduced crime and vandalism. Impacts are typically less easily expressed in a measurable form than operational objectives.

Performance

Performance for a sport organization can mean any number of things, depending on what objectives are specified. It is possible, however, to generalize about the nature of performance, and do so in the context of any type of organization. Before discussing specific performance indicators it is important to identify the different aspects of performance that sports managers will be interested in.

The most common type of performance found in the private sector is financial performance (see Chapter 7). This is often simplified to mean profits, but in fact financial performance means much more than this. It can include income,

350

growth, margins, debts, liquidity, and risk. But for both operational and strategic appraisal purposes it is necessary to examine the different strands of performance, as accountancy does.

Related to financial performance is the concept of economy. This is solely concerned with the input side of the production process, and with costs. It is not concerned with outputs. Economy is achieved if inputs are acquired at minimum cost. Over-emphasis on economy is not wise unless it is seen as the main reason for weak performance. In the public sector it has often been the case that performance has been 'measured' by expenditure on inputs, i.e. increased spending is taken to automatically mean an increase in service output. But of course this is no measure of performance at all. It says nothing of the actual outputs of the service, which could be highly ineffective, inefficient, and wasteful of resources despite the rising expenditure.

Efficiency is concerned with achieving objectives and targets at minimum cost. So efficiency considers the best possible relationships between inputs and outputs. It is sometimes given the terms 'cost effectiveness' or 'cost efficiency', and is also what is meant by the terms 'productivity' and 'value for money'.

Effectiveness is concerned solely with the achievement of output targets. It does not, therefore, consider the costs of achieving the output targets. A basic measure of effectiveness is throughput volume, such as the number of visits in a given time period, an example being the number of bathers at a swimming pool. However, this is a rather basic indicator because it contains no indication of the types of visitors that have been attracted, nor the extent to which the service has met the needs of the visitors.

Effectiveness is an important performance aspect in public sector leisure services, since they are concerned with social objectives that are largely non-financial in nature. These objectives include education, notably with services such as swimming and other activity classes. They also include increasing visits by particular, disadvantaged target groups such as people from minority ethnic groups.

In the public sector, organizations are also interested in the effectiveness of services in terms of achieving impacts in society. Therefore, whilst throughput is concerned with the volume of visitors, and outputs are concerned with direct effects such as the type of visitors, or the revenue they provide, impacts are concerned with broader effects on society, such as improvements in health, citizenship, or quality of life.

In addition to economy, efficiency, and effectiveness, sometimes another 'e' is added to the list of important performance dimensions, particularly in public sector organizations. This is equity, which is concerned with fairness in the treatment of all customers. This has a variety of interpretations, such as equality of opportunity to visit; prioritizing visits by the poorest members of society; or alternatively service benefits distributed according to how much tax people have paid to support the service.

Another performance dimension which is increasingly common is customer satisfaction, which can be measured directly by such methods as questionnaire surveys, comments slips, or complaints. A wider view of customer satisfaction which is common in the public sector is satisfaction with services by local citizens, regardless of whether or not they have actually used the service. This may seem contradictory – if a person has not actually used a service, how can they possibly comment? However, it is often the case that the community has a collective interest in the performance of a service. An example is sport for young people at risk. A wide range of people will have a view on whether or not such a service is satisfactory, from parents and neighbors to anyone with a fear of nuisance or worse from bored young people.

Performance indicators

Ideally, indicators of performance should have certain qualities to make them suitable for management purposes. A set of performance indicators should:

- reflect all the objectives of the leisure service accurately;
- cover different dimensions of performance, such as effectiveness and efficiency;
- be capable of being measured for separate parts of the service, since it is likely that different objectives and different targets are applicable to different parts of the service, even within the same facility;
- be administratively manageable and easily understood; and
- be consistent over time and between service elements and different organizations – this is particularly important for benchmarking.

In the UK public sector the Audit Commission has provided two forms of advice in relation to performance measurement. Although designed for the public sector, much of this general advice is transferable to other sectors. First, it is necessary to consider the general characteristics of indicators that can help to ensure that proposed indicators will be useful and effective. Second, it is important that the data collected is reliable. Good quality data is the essential ingredient for reliable performance information.

The Audit Commission identified thirteen criteria for assessing the robustness of a performance indicator – see Table 16.1. Devising a performance indicator that fulfills all of the criteria in this table is challenging. Inevitably a performance indicator will score less well against some criteria. For national indicators, the Audit Commission advises that a performance indicator should be clearly defined, comparable, verifiable, unambiguous, and statistically valid. Indicators that are published for the benefit of the local community should first and foremost be relevant and easy to understand.

Effectiveness of management and operations

Table 16.1 Criteria for good performance indicators

Criteria	Explanation
Relevant	Indicators should be relevant to the organization's strategic goals and objectives. They should also be relevant to the people providing the data.
Clear definition	The performance indicators should have a clear and intelligible definition in order to ensure consistent collection and fair comparison.
Easy to understand and use	Performance indicators should be described in terms that the user of the information will understand.
Comparable	Indicators should be comparable on a consistent basis between organizations and this relies on there being agreement about definitions. They should also be comparable on a consistent basis over time. Comparability of performance indicators should include consideration of the context within which the comparison is taking place because external or internal circumstances can differ to such a degree that comparison is invalid. For example inter-authority comparisons could be misleading if there is considerable variation in the characteristics of the areas being compared.
Verifiable	The indicator also needs to be collected and calculated in a way that enables the information and data to be verified. It should therefore be based on robust data collection systems, and it should be possible for managers to verify the accuracy of the information and the consistency of the methods used.
Cost effective	There is a need to balance the cost of collecting information with its usefulness. Where possible, an indicator should be based on information already available and linked to existing data collection activities.
Unambiguous	A change in an indicator should be capable of unambiguous interpretation so that it is clear whether an increase in an indicator value represents an improvement or deterioration in service.
Attributable	Service managers should be able to influence the performance measured by the indicator.
Responsive	A performance indicator should be responsive to change. An indicator where changes in performance are likely to be too small to register will be of limited use.
Avoid perverse incentives	A performance indicator should not be easily manipulated because this might encourage counter-productive activity.
Allow innovation	Indicators that focus on outcome and user satisfaction are more likely to encourage such innovation to take place than indicators that are tied into existing processes.
Statistically valid	Indicators should be statistically valid and this will in large part depend on the sample size.
Timely	Data for the performance indicator should be available within a reasonable time-scale.

Source: Audit Commission (2000b).

The Audit Commission defined six key characteristics that can be used to assess the quality of data used to construct performance indicator scores – see Table 16.2. Most of these criteria directly echo those stipulated for performance indicators in Table 16.1, i.e. not only relevance, validity, and timeliness but also reliable (= comparable) and accurate (= verifiable). The one additional consideration in Table 16.2 is completeness – an important reminder that validity and reliability are as much dependent on what is missing as on what is collected.

Having stated these requirements, however, it is necessary to stress that any set of indicators is unlikely to fulfill all of these properties. This is simply because these qualities are difficult to achieve – all indicators have their good points and their bad points. However, using the basic principles outlined in Tables 16.1 and 16.2 provides the basis for a robust framework around which to construct a set of context-specific performance measures.

Private, commercial sector

For a private, commercial organization, performance is, in the main, specified in financial terms, although there are other important considerations. Business accounting ratios are designed principally for planning purposes (strategic appraisal) and control purposes (operational appraisal). The ratios are concerned not just with profit, but also with liquidity, asset utilization, capital structure, and investment potential. A sample of such ratios is given in Table 16.3 and can be seen to mirror closely the principles and measures outlined in Chapter 7.

These financial ratios, and many more, are detailed for individual companies and industry sectors by commercial sources which facilitate a rudimentary form of external benchmarking.

A major advantage of ratios is that they put performance into a consistent perspective. For instance it is one thing to declare $100,000 profit, but this figure takes on more meaning if it is put in the context of turnover, or capital, as 'rate of return' figures do. Ratios commonly involve two monetary sums, such as the ratio of a firm's profit to its income, so they enable financial comparisons to be made over time, without having to worry about adjusting for inflation. They also hide potentially sensitive or confidential information by expressing data as a ratio rather than disclosing the absolute value – e.g. labor costs expressed as a percentage of total operating costs reveals neither the actual labor costs nor the actual operating costs.

Ratios have to be interpreted very carefully. Many are more appropriate for comparing a single firm's performance over time than comparing different firms, particularly if the firms are from a different industry or sector. You would not ordinarily seek to compare the financial performance of a sports stadium with that of a swimming pool in any meaningful way. Some ratios involve estimates which can be done in various ways, so comparing like with like can be problematic – for example valuing inventories and intangible assets.

Table 16.2 Criteria for suitable performance indicators' data

Dimension	Description
Accuracy	Data should be sufficiently accurate for its intended purposes, representing clearly and in sufficient detail the interaction provided at the point of activity. Data should be captured once only, although it may have multiple uses. Accuracy is most likely to be secured if data is captured as close to the point of activity as possible. Reported information that is based on accurate data provides a fair picture of performance and should enable informed decision making at all levels. The need for accuracy must be balanced with the importance of the uses for the data, and the costs and effort of collection. For example, it may be appropriate to accept some degree of inaccuracy where timeliness is important. Where compromises have to be made on accuracy, the resulting limitations of the data should be clear to its users.
Validity	Data should be recorded and used in compliance with relevant requirements, including the correct application of any rules or definitions. This will ensure consistency between periods and with similar organizations. Where proxy data is used to compensate for an absence of actual data, organizations must consider how well this data is able to satisfy the intended purpose.
Reliability	Data should reflect stable and consistent data collection processes across collection points and over time, whether using manual or computer-based systems, or a combination. Managers and stakeholders should be confident that progress toward performance targets reflects real changes rather than variations in data collection approaches or methods.
Timeliness	Data should be captured as quickly as possible after the event or activity and must be available for the intended use within a reasonable time period. Data must be available quickly and frequently enough to support information needs and to influence the appropriate level of service or management decisions.
Relevance	Data captured should be relevant to the purposes for which it is used. This entails periodic review of requirements to reflect changing needs. It may be necessary to capture data at the point of activity which is relevant only for other purposes, rather than for the current intervention. Quality assurance and feedback processes are needed to ensure the quality of such data.
Completeness	Data requirements should be clearly specified based on the information needs of the organization and data collection processes matched to these requirements. Monitoring missing, incomplete, or invalid records can provide an indication of data quality and can also point to problems in the recording of certain data items.

Source: Audit Commission (2007).

Table 16.3 Performance ratios for commercial organizations

Profitability

$\dfrac{\text{Either gross or net profit}}{\text{Sales}}$	No rules of thumb. It varies widely between industries and firms. (See vertical analysis in Chapter 7)
$\dfrac{\text{Net profit after tax}}{\text{Total assets}}$	'Return on Capital Employed'. No standard definitions, so care is needed in making comparisons between firms and industries.

Liquidity

$\dfrac{\text{Assets}}{\text{Current liabilities}}$	'Current Ratio'. Rule of thumb = 2:1
$\dfrac{\text{Current liabilities} - \text{inventories}}{\text{Current liabilities}}$	'Acid Test', 'Quick' or 'Liquidity' Ratio. A more discriminating test of ability to pay debts. (See liquidity tests in Chapter 7)
$\dfrac{\text{Balance sheet trade debtors} \times 365}{\text{Total credit sales}}$	Average collection period of trade debts, i.e. average number of days before an account is paid.

Asset Utilization

$\dfrac{\text{Sales}}{\text{Fixed assets}}$	Indicates the effectiveness in using fixed plant to generate sales.
$\dfrac{\text{Cost of goods sold}}{\text{Inventories}}$	'Stock Turnover'. Varies a lot between industries.
$\dfrac{\text{Sales}}{\text{Number of employees}}$	Indicates revenue productivity of labor.

Capital Structure

$\dfrac{\text{Net worth}}{\text{Total assets}}$	Indicates shareholders' interest in the business. (Net Worth is ordinary shares + preference shares + reserves)
$\dfrac{\text{Borrowing}}{\text{Net worth}}$	'Gearing'. An indication of the riskiness of the capital structure.

Investment

$\dfrac{\text{Dividend per share}}{\text{Market price per share}}$	'Dividend Yield'. Indicates rate of return on investment in shares.
$\dfrac{\text{Net profit} - \text{preference share dividend}}{\text{Number of ordinary shares}}$	Earnings per ordinary share.
$\dfrac{\text{Market price per share}}{\text{Earnings per share}}$	'Price/Earnings Ratio'. Indicates the market's evaluation of a share.

Private firms are also interested in other aspects of performance apart from financial ratios. Market share is an important objective that is normally measurable, even at the local or regional level. Market share is one indicator that is highly important for measuring organizational performance – the demand for the product. It is vital for any organization, from whatever sector, to be informed about changes in demand for the service they are providing. Market research is a typical means of generating this evidence.

Most large private leisure organizations have marketing departments, with market research functions. As well as continual monitoring of demand for their goods and services by this means, they regularly employ outside market research agencies or consultancies to conduct specialist market research. This point reinforces the importance for organizations to be outward looking in addition to inward looking. It might be great news to find out that your business has grown by 10 percent compared with its performance last year, but if the sector as a whole has grown by 20 percent, then you have actually lost ground to your rivals who have in turn reduced your market share.

Public sector

Public sector sport providers have had to become accustomed to performance measurement in the UK, with the advent of fundamental reviews of the way in which public services are provided. Local authorities no longer have a divine right to be providers of services and their role has shifted towards being enablers, particularly when more cost effective alternatives exist. The management of sport facilities and leisure centers is increasingly being undertaken by private sector organizations and trusts which can provide better services at lower cost than the local authorities themselves. New government requirements have obliged local authorities to publish performance information for a set of national performance indicators. Table 16.4, however, shows that the indicators relevant to public sector cultural services are rather narrow in number and scope. Local authorities can choose which indicators to report, and the final column in Table 16.4 shows that this take-up is variable for cultural indicators.

Table 16.4 Public sector national indicators for culture in the UK
Performance indicators for local authorities in the UK

National Indicator name	Local area agreements including NI/152	
	Number	Rank/152
Participation in regular volunteering	42	43
Adult participation in sport and active recreation	82	16
Use of public libraries	10	95
Visits to museums and galleries	2	142
Engagement in the arts	24	65=
Children and young people's participation in high-quality PE and sport	24	65=
Young people's participation in positive activities	75	75

Source: IDeA, www.idea.gov.uk/idk/core/page.do?pageId=8399555

At the local level and in specific consultancy services, however, a much more comprehensive list of performance indicators can be found. For example, Sport England's National Benchmarking Service for sport and leisure centers (NBS) compiles data for 47 performance indicators across four dimensions of performance. These are listed in Table 16.5.

This NBS list illustrates the compromise that is often necessary between what indicators are desirable and what indicators can be measured reliably and at reasonable cost. The NBS does not attempt to measure wider impacts of sports provision, such as improvements in health, improved quality of life, reduced crime and vandalism, or education benefits – these are considered too difficult to measure regularly in the specific context of sports provision. However, the NBS does provide indicators relevant to another impact objective – social inclusion – via the access indicators. The NBS also does not measure non-users' attitudes and barriers – this would require research in local communities which is expensive; nor the views, behavior, etc. of young people under 11 years old, who are not considered suitable for the questionnaire survey employed.

Table 16.5 Performance indicators for Sport England's national benchmarking service

a) Access: usage by specific groups or market segments

Key
% visits 11–19 years ÷ % catchment population 11–19 years
% visits from NS-SEC classes 6&7 ÷ % catchment population in NS-SEC classes 6&7 [1]
% visits 60+ years ÷ % catchment population 60+ years
% visits from black, Asian & other ethnic groups ÷ % catchment population in same groups
% visits disabled, <60 years ÷ % catchment population disabled, <60 years

Other
% visits 20–59 years ÷ % catchment population in same group
% of visits which were first visits
% visits with discount card
% visits with discount cards for 'disadvantage' [2]
% visits female
% visits disabled, 60+ years ÷ % catchment population disabled, 60+ years
% visits unemployed

Notes
1 NS-SEC classes 6 & 7 are the two lowest socioeconomic classes in the official classification used in the UK.
2 Disadvantage eligibility for discount cards includes over 50s, students, unemployed, disabled, single parents, government support, government funded trainees, widows, exercise referrals, and elite performers

Effectiveness of management and operations

b) Utilization

Key
annual visits per sq. m. (of usable space)

Other
annual visits per sq. m. (of total indoor space)
% of visits casual, instead of organized
weekly number of people visiting the center as % of catchment population

c) Financial

Key
subsidy per visit

Other
% cost recovery
subsidy per resident
subsidy per sq. m.
total operating cost per visit
total operating cost per sq. m.
maintenance and repair costs per sq. m.
energy costs per sq. m.
total income per visit
total income per sq. m.
direct income per visit
secondary income per visit

d) Service attributes for customer satisfaction and importance scoring

Accessibility
Activity available at convenient times
Ease of booking
The activity charge/fee
The range of activities available

Quality of facilities/services
Quality of flooring in the sports hall
Quality of lighting in the sports hall
Quality of equipment
Water quality in the swimming pool

Water temperature of swimming pool

Number of people in the pool

Quality of car parking on site

Quality of food and drink

Cleanliness

Cleanliness of changing areas

Cleanliness of activity spaces

Staff

Helpfulness of reception staff

Helpfulness of other staff

Standard of coaching/instruction

Value for money

Value for money of activities

Value for money of food/drink

Overall – satisfaction only

Overall satisfaction with visit

It is really up to each organization to choose a manageable array of indicators to reflect its objectives and performance priorities. For a public sector provider, this may include throughput indicators for particular groups of clients, such as women, the elderly, lower socioeconomic groups, and the disabled, since this would monitor the effectiveness of the organization in reaching important target groups. It may also include very conventional indicators of financial performance such as those relevant to the private supplier in Table 16.3, particularly for parts of the service which have no particular 'social service' function, such as the bar, cafe, vending machines, and other merchandise sales.

How often should performance indicators' evidence be produced? It is very common for performance indicators to be calculated on an annual basis. However, there are good reasons for wanting operational performance indicators to be available on a far more regular basis. Decisions about promotion, programming, and staffing arrangements may be modified at any time, so a regular flow of up-to-date information assists such decisions.

Targets

Targets are precise statements of what is to be achieved by when. They are an obvious implication of measuring performance indicators which reflect management objectives. A target provides a concrete and unambiguous reference point against which to ask 'is this objective being achieved?' A target typically takes the form of a numerical target, such as we need to achieve 1,000 admissions per week. Targets can also be applied to non-financial data, so, for example, given the objective of increasing usage by the disabled, and using as an indicator the ratio of percentage of visits by the disabled to percentage of local population who are disabled, a target figure of 1 would mean trying to increase usage by the disabled to a level which is representative of their numbers in the local population. This is a good example of the way in which a target can provide specificity to an objective.

Evidence of previous performance or evidence of the performance of similar organizations elsewhere provides a quantitative basis for setting targets. Such evidence enables the target setter to reach the difficult balance between ambition and realism. Targets need to be challenging but they also need to be achievable. If they are too easily reached, or if they are impossible to reach, they quickly fall into disrepute. Targets can and do change in the course of time. They need to remain under continuing scrutiny for their relevance to the operating circumstances of the organization.

Balanced Scorecard

One of the best known models for performance measurement is the Balanced Scorecard, a system devised by Robert Kaplan and David Norton in 1992 (Kaplan and Norton, 2005). A motivation for the Balanced Scorecard was to add strategic non-financial performance measures to the traditional financial measures, to give a more 'balanced' view. The structure of the Balanced Scorecard is represented in Figure 16.3.

The figure demonstrates not just the development of performance measurement beyond the financial, but also a consistent process of specifying objectives, devising measures for these, setting targets, and devising initiatives to achieve the targets. It is the last of these processes that turns the Balanced Scorecard into a performance management system, not just a performance measurement tool.

BENCHMARKING

So far we have been discussing evidence that is appropriate for an organization to collect in order for its managers to know how the organization is performing and whether changes are occurring as a result of their decisions (or in spite of them!). However, it is also likely that the organization will want comparisons to be made with other similar organizations. Benchmarking is a process which facilitates this.

- Data benchmarking involves comparison with numerical standards (e.g. averages) calculated for performance indicators in a particular service. They are typically organized into relevant categories or 'families' of similar organizations.
- Process benchmarking involves comparison of different procedures adopted in different organizations. Used in conjunction with performance data, process benchmarking facilitates an understanding of the procedures which improve performance.

External benchmarks for performance are important because they enable a judgment to be made on the relative performance of an organization, which in turn gives a competitive impetus to the organization. They also enable other bodies to assess the relative performance of each organization. This is particularly important in the public sector where the central government is very interested in monitoring the relative performance of individual local government services, if only because it directly funds around half the costs of these local services in the UK.

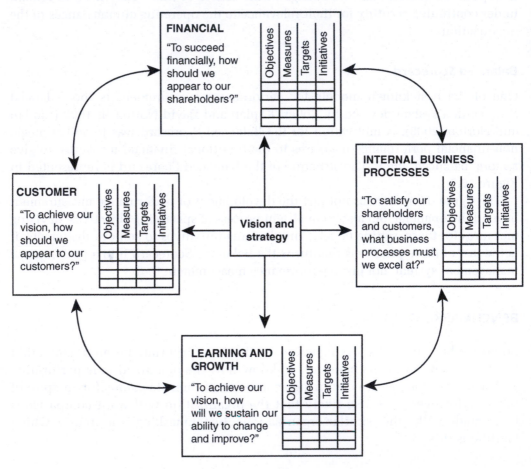

Figure 16.3 Balanced Scorecard structure

Comparative performance information is available in both the private sector and the public sector. In the public sector in the UK, benchmarks are provided for sport in two publications by the Chartered Institute of Public Finance and Accountancy (CIPFA). These are *Culture, Sport and Recreation Statistics* and *Charges for Leisure Services*. The former in the main contains financial statistics, and they are estimates rather than outturns. Furthermore, CIPFA does not group the data for comparative purposes, so care needs to be taken in selecting authorities to compare with.

Three other explicit benchmarking services can be identified for sport. First, in Australia and New Zealand, the CERM Performance Indicators Project is operated by the University of South Australia. Designed for public aquatic centers and leisure centers, it now extends to a range of sport and leisure services, including golf courses, caravan and tourist parks, campgrounds, skate parks, and outdoor centers. CERM PIs provides benchmarks for 26 performance indicators, including services (e.g. program opportunities per week), marketing (e.g. promotion cost as a proportion of total cost), organization (e.g. cleaning and maintenance cost per visit), and finance (e.g. surplus/subsidy per visit).

In the UK there are two benchmarking services relevant to sport – APSE Performance Networks and Sport England's National Benchmarking Service for sport and leisure centers (NBS). APSE's service, operating since 1998, covers all local authority services, with separate reporting for each – sport and leisure facility management being one. It provides data on management and finance with customer satisfaction as an optional extra. APSE compares an individual local authority's performance with other local authorities of a similar type in terms of local policy, demography, and size and type of operation. Sport England's NBS is featured in the case study below.

SPORT ENGLAND'S NATIONAL BENCHMARKING SERVICE (NBS)

The NBS measures performance standards for indoor sport and leisure centers with one or both of the following core facilities: a sports hall of four badminton courts or more; and/or a swimming pool of at least 20 meters length. This helps to ensure that the service is focused on similar types of facilities. The performance indicators measured in this service are identified in Table 16.5. They are designed to cover as many dimensions of performance as are practical for a reasonable cost. However, as noted earlier, they do not cover many of the broader impacts of sport in the community, such as improvements in health and education.

To generate the data the NBS requires clients to conduct a survey of customers and submit a form with management and financial information. In addition, population data for the local catchment area is derived from the

363

National Census by the University of Edinburgh. Data from clients is checked carefully – there can be considerable discrepancies and inaccuracies in quite basic pieces of management information, such as throughput counts and cost estimates. Similarly the administration of the user survey has to ensure valid and reliable results. An NBS guidance document is designed to give advice to try to ensure as much consistency in data as possible between clients.

The NBS results for access, finance, and utilization performance are compared with benchmarks for four families which have been empirically tested and proven to have structural effects on performance:

■ Type of center – wet; dry (with/without outdoor sport facilities); and mixed (with/without outdoor sport facilities).
■ The socioeconomics of a center's location – high deprivation; medium deprivation; low deprivation – measured by the percentage of the catchment population in the bottom two socioeconomic classes.
■ Size of the center – large; medium; and small.
■ Management type at the center – in-house local authority; trust; commercial contractor.

Three benchmarks are employed. The 25 percent, 50 percent, and 75 percent benchmarks are the quarter, half, and three-quarters points in the distribution of scores for a PI, if all the centers' scores were organized from the lowest score at the bottom end of the distribution to the highest score at the top end.

For the importance and satisfaction attributes (see Table 16.5), the NBS reports on the satisfaction scores in comparison with industry averages for wet, dry or mixed centers; the gaps between importance and satisfaction mean scores from customers; and the percentage of customers dissatisfied with each attribute. These methods of reporting satisfaction are preferred by customers to the comparison with benchmarks employed for the other performance indicators.

Another important feature of the NBS output is the information on sport facility users from the user survey. Frequency distributions of responses to all the user survey questions include visit characteristics (e.g. activities done, frequency of visit) and the profile of visitors (e.g. travel distance and time, travel mode, home postcodes).

NBS clients have emphasized a number of benefits from the service. These include:

■ Awareness of the state of the service, often confirming preconceived ideas but objectively.

- Challenges to preconceived ideas held by managers and politicians, causing a reassessment of priorities and delivery methods.
- Real data to help set targets for objectives.
- Experience of research data develops an awareness of further information needs, helping to develop an evidence-based management culture.
- Benchmarking data enables selection of process benchmarking partners with whom to discuss how to generate better performance for specific performance indicators.

In addition, NBS clients have demonstrated a number of commendable responses to the processes of performance management:

- generating the right information;
- interpreting the results meaningfully;
- utilizing the results in performance planning – i.e. immediate action plans, and longer-term contract specification and strategy development.

As a 'killer fact', it has been shown that the difference in financial performance between centers in the top quartile and the bottom quartile can be as much as £400,000 per year. This is a considerable wake up call to the poor performing centers in the UK and has stimulated considerable interest in process benchmarking i.e. asking the questions of peers 'what are you doing better than us and how can we learn from you?'

Suggested discussion topics

1   Take one of the NBS indicators from each of the categories of access, utilization, and financial identified in Table 16.5, and consider its merits against the Audit Commission criteria in Table 16.1.
2   As a sport facility manager, why would you want to compare the performance of your facility with benchmarks for other facilities?

The scope of benchmarking is almost unlimited and can be applied to almost any facet of sport facility management. In human resource management one of the most disruptive issues managers encounter can be turnover of staff. If you are the manager of a stadium and you need 300 stewards on duty for every match or concert you do not want to be spending all of your time recruiting staff who will be with you for one event and then gone forever. Thus if staff retention is important to you, then you measure it. The employee turnover ratio can be derived by calculating the proportion of employees who leave an organization over a set period (usually a year), expressed as a percentage of total staff numbers. If we have good staff we like to retain them and if we have a good working environment then staff are more likely to stay. Under these conditions, a staff turnover ratio of 10 percent is much more preferable than 50 percent particularly when large numbers of staff are involved.

Benchmarking is not the sole confine of managers and it can be used for operational purposes to help motivate staff and to focus their attention on what is important. So for example, if you manage a stadium and have a target to sell an average of $10 per head on food and drink this needs to be communicated to staff and their individual performance needs to be monitored against the target. Those who achieve above target should be rewarded accordingly and those who do not should be trained so that they meet the required standard or alternatively be replaced.

In day-to-day operations such as marketing we can also use benchmarking. For certain events the marketing department might take out an advertisement with a special offer such as a coupon giving free admission to one child for every full paying adult. How would we know if this promotion had been successful? One method might be to have a target for how many get returned. Often vouchers used in mass media have a redemption rate of around 1 percent. If this were in a newspaper with a circulation of 200,000, it would mean 2,000 admissions. This would then need to be considered alongside other factors such as the original cost of the advertisement and whether or not the people using the vouchers were over and above 'business as usual' or simply people who were planning to attend any way and who received unnecessary discount.

The point which unites the three examples above is that they are all courses of action which are important to managers and who in turn require feedback as to whether the decisions they have made have been effective decisions. The saying 'that which gets measured gets done' could not be more appropriate.

CONCLUSIONS ABOUT PERFORMANCE MANAGEMENT AND BENCHMARKING

Performance management and benchmarking are essential tools in the quest for continuous improvement. At the heart of these systems is appropriate evidence of performance. However, acquiring appropriate evidence is not an easy matter. Performance indicators have to be selected which fully represent an organization's objectives. One of the problems encountered with the NBS is that feasible performance measurement falls short of desired performance measurement in public sector sports facilities. Much of the modern emphasis in justifying taxpayers' subsidies to such facilities rests on social impacts, particularly in improving users' health. However, measuring improvements in health and relating them specifically

Effectiveness of management and operations

to visiting sport facilities is a difficult task, and one beyond the cost of a reasonable performance measurement system.

Another threat to the promise of performance management is the difficulty of assembling accurate and consistent measurement data. Financial data may be subject to accounting regulations but even so there is considerable variation in the way in which some standard ratios are calculated and 'creative accounting' can be used to disguise problems if the wrong organizational culture has set in. Another increasingly essential component of management evidence is market research of customers, but there are enough precedents at national and local level to warn that market research can all too easily be conducted in an inappropriate manner, which can bias samples, or lead respondents into answering questions in certain ways.

Nevertheless, if these constraints can be overcome, the promised land of performance management beckons, where the right evidence enables weaknesses to be identified, plans to be made, actions to be taken, and outcomes to be improved. The last two decades in particular have seen an accelerated take-up of performance management and measurement systems. Benchmarking is increasingly the norm. This can only help to secure continuously improving performance in sports facilities and management practice.

CHAPTER REVIEW

This chapter started by showing the similarity between two concepts – performance management and quality management. Two examples of performance management frameworks are described – EFQM and TAES. EFQM is one of the oldest generic systems and it is possible to see similarities between this and many other systems which have been subsequently developed. TAES is a system devised specifically for cultural services in the UK public sector.

Objectives are a cornerstone of good performance management and they need to be specified much more specifically than organizational aims. Criteria for good objectives are given.

The meaning of 'performance' is discussed and whilst it is driven in an organization by its objectives, there are many different facets to performance. The major elements relevant to sport facility management are detailed.

Performance indicators have to be devised to represent the performance that is relevant to objectives. Indicators are the way in which performance is measured and the chapter discusses the criteria for good performance indicators, and the requirements for good data from which to calculate performance indicator values. Differences between performance indicators in the commercial sector and public sectors are demonstrated.

As well as measuring performance indicators, it is important for organizational improvement to set targets for them. These targets will be determined by the objectives of the sport facility.

The Balanced Scorecard is an example of a performance measurement system, designed for the commercial sector, to reflect more than simply financial performance. The Balanced Scorecard reinforces the essential principles of performance management – objectives, targets, measurement, action, and review.

Finally the concept of benchmarking is explained – i.e. comparing performance with either other sport facilities, or with previous performance. Examples of benchmarking systems for sport facilities are identified and one in particular, the NBS, is featured in a case study.

BIBLIOGRAPHY

Audit Commission (1989). *Sport for whom? Clarifying the local authority role in sport and recreation.* London: HMSO.

Audit Commission (2000a). *Aiming to improve: The principles of performance measurement.* London: Audit Commission.

Audit Commission (2000b). *On target: The practice of performance indicators.* London: Audit Commission.

Audit Commission (2007). *Improving information to support decision making: Standards for better quality data.* London: Audit Commission.

Balanced Scorecard Institute (2014). *What is the balanced scorecard?* Retrieved September 8, 2014 from: www.balancedscorecard.org/BSCResources/AbouttheBalancedScorecard/tabid/55/Default.aspx

The Chartered Institute of Public Finance and Accountancy, Statistical Information Service. (2007/08). *Charges for leisure services.* London: The Chartered Institute of Public Finance and Accountancy, Statistical Information Service.

The Chartered Institute of Public Finance and Accountancy, Statistical Information Service. (2013/14). *Culture, sport and recreation actuals.* London: The Chartered Institute of Public Finance and Accountancy, Statistical Information Service.

Chartered Quality Institute (2014). *What is quality?* Retrieved November 3, 2014 from www.thecqi.org/The-CQI/What-is-quality/

EFQM (2014). The *EFQM excellence model.* Retrieved September 8, 2014 from: www.efqm.org/the-efqm-excellence-model

IDeA (2006). *Towards an excellent service: A performance management framework for cultural services.* London: IDeA.

Kaplan, R. S. and Norton, D. P. (2005). The balanced scorecard – measures that drive performance. *Harvard Business Review, 83*(7), 172–180.

Taylor, P. D. (1996). The role of management information systems in the provision of recreation. In G. Ashworth and A. Dietvorst (Eds.), *Tourism and special transformation.* Wallingford, UK: CAB International.

IN THE FIELD …

Mike Hill, Joint Director of Leisure-net Solutions Limited

Current position

Mike Hill is a Joint Director of Leisure-net Solutions, a company he founded after a successful career in sport facility management in which he gained experience of working in both private and public sectors covering health and fitness, ice rinks, pools, and food and beverage. Mike set up Leisure-net Solutions in 1999 having seen the need for the industry to improve its knowledge base and understanding of the needs of its customers. Leisure-net Solutions is now seen as the 'go to' organization for customer insight in the sport and leisure industry in the UK.

Career progression

I studied at Loughborough University, the United Kingdom's leading sport university, and achieved my bachelor's degree in Physical Education, Sport Science and Recreation Management. After graduation, I went on to work in various facility management roles for 14 years before setting up my company. In addition to Leisure-net Solutions, I have other business interests including a restaurant which helps to keep my skills sharp.

Mike's advice for those who aspire to work in the industry …

My advice would be do not specialize too early in your career, but when you do make sure you are one of the best. I think it is really useful to have a good wide grounding in the sector that you wish to build your career in, there really is not anything like experience of 'having done it myself', when you are consulting/advising people on how to improve their business or drive forward customer service developments. Secondly find a unique selling point (USP) for yourself/your services, concentrate on something that emphasizes that difference. For me it was putting myself through a Net Promoter Score Partner course. At the time in the leisure sector very few people knew about or were using the Net Promoter Score to benchmark their customer experience. Finally try and embed yourself in the sector you want to work in. If you want to work in the area of data collection and benchmarking, try to work hand in hand with the industry organizations that will have a stake in using these benchmarks.

TECHNOLOGY NOW!

A new and improved National Benchmarking Service

The National Benchmarking Service (NBS) has existed as a resource for sport and leisure facilities in England since 2000. During this time it has evolved from being a manual data entry and analysis system to one which is fully automated. In the latest generation of the NBS, data will be entered and processed using a web-based platform that will provide three key service improvements for users:

1 *Improved data presentation:* data will only be used to inform current practice if it is easily understood such that managers have confidence in it. The new NBS makes use of the latest data visualization technology to produce dashboards, dials, and other graphics that are much more user friendly and inviting than the output that can be produced in packages such as Excel. Road testing the product with potential users revealed considerable enthusiasm from existing users of the service.
2 *Bespoke analysis:* subscribers to the NBS are now able to conduct their own secondary analysis of the data. Each client has their own password protected log in which provides access to the NBS data. If a particular indicator is a cause for concern, it is possible for managers to drill down deeper into the data to gain further insight into the problem as a first step in identifying solutions.
3 *A benchmarking community:* the NBS online tool enables managers to interact with each other to share good practice. Whilst it is useful to know how your center performs on a particular indicator, it is even more useful to take action to improve facility management and service delivery. Subscribers to the NBS can now communicate directly with top performing managers, which in turn facilitates the more important technique of process benchmarking.

The rationale for the NBS is to help drive up standards and performance in public sport and leisure facilities. The NBS online platform improves the efficiency of data entry and processing, enabling managers to focus on striving to achieve continuous improvement in service delivery and efficient use of resources.

Source: National Benchmarking Service (2014). Retrieved October 28, 2014 from www.questnbs.org/the-national-benchmarking-service

INDEX

374

mobile command centers 320
mobile phones *see* smartphones
moderate financial losses 300
most economically advantageous tender (MEAT) 65–6
motivation 109–11, *110*, 137
motivator factors 110
multi-agency collaboration 311, *312*
multi-agency team training 326
multiparty arrangements **50**
Munich Olympic Games 3, 293
municipal bonds 46
municipalities *see* local authorities, UK; public sector

Nafe, Rick 10–11
named perils insurance 301
naming rights **49**, 52, 237, 262, **263**
National Basketball Association (NBA) 5, 52, 128; fan violence **294**; security 313; sponsorship conflicts 276, 277
National Benchmarking Service (NBS), Sport England 357, **358–60**, 363–5, 370
National Center for Spectator Sports Safety and Security (NCS) 282, 289
National Collegiate Athletic Association (NCAA) 313
National Council for Voluntary Organisations (NCVO), UK 135
National Fire Protection Association (NFPA) 325
National Football League (NFL): alcohol policies 327; ambush marketing laws 240; bomb threats **295**; facial recognition technology 321; fan code of conduct 327–8; security 313; text messaging systems 325
National Hockey League (NHL) 52; security 313; sponsorship conflicts 275–7
National Lottery, UK 39
National Ski Areas Association (NSAA) 220
natural disasters 293, **294**
natural environments 220
NBA *see* National Basketball Association (NBA)
NBS *see* National Benchmarking Service (NBS), Sport England
NCAA *see* National Collegiate Athletic Association (NCAA)
NCS *see* National Center for Spectator Sports Safety and Security (NCS)
NCVO *see* National Council for Voluntary Organisations (NCVO), UK
negligence law 236
negotiation, contract 259, 274–5

Nepal 4, **294**
net present value (NPV) 73–5, **73**, **75**, *75*, 76–7, **76**, **77**
New Orleans Saints Football Team 293
New York Giants 62–3
New York Islanders 52
New York Jets 62–3
New York Yankees 62–3
New Zealand 240–1, 363
NFL *see* National Football League (NFL)
NFPA *see* National Fire Protection Association (NFPA)
NHL *see* National Hockey League (NHL)
non-directive interview questions 144
non-guaranteed bonds 46
non-profit corporations 21
non-profit governance 24–5
nonprogrammed decisions 120, 121
Norton, David 361
NPV *see* net present value (NPV)
NSAA *see* National Ski Areas Association (NSAA)

objectives, organizational 86; and budgeting 173–4, 176–7; and event planning 272–3, 281; and performance management 349–50
OECD *see* Organization for Economic Cooperation and Development (OECD)
Ohio State University 112–13
Olympic Games: Atlanta **294**; Beijing 241, **295**; London 42, 330; Munich 3, 293; Rio de Janeiro 241; Sydney 240
online systems: benchmarking 370; booking 205–6; event management 286; membership 205–6; recruitment 157–8; ticketing 182, 222, 279
operational strategies 175
operations-based exercises 326
operations management 207–32; alterations management 217–18; associations 2–3; concessions **49**, 223–5, 280–1; continuous improvement 209–13, 347; custodial and housekeeping services 223; customer service desk 225; definitions 2; employee standards of conduct 220–1; energy management 218; environmental management 219–20; and event management 225–6; general operating procedures 213–16; inventory management 218, 224; maintenance and repair 217; manuals 151, 226–7; parking **49**, 223, 317, 327; plant and field operations 216; software 11–12, 232; waste management and recycling 218–19; *see also* risk